CLASSIC ROSES

R. canina

PETER BEALES

CLASSIC ROSES

An illustrated encyclopaedia
and grower's manual of old roses,
shrub roses and climbers

HENRY HOLT AND COMPANY
NEW YORK

Published in the United States by
Henry Holt and Company, Inc.,
115 West 18th Street,
New York, New York 10011.

Library of Congress Cataloging-in-Publication Data
Beales, Peter.
Classic roses.
Bibliography: p.
Includes index.
1. Roses. 2. Rose culture. 3. Roses—Dictionaries.
SB411.B38 1985 635.9′3372 85–14159
ISBN 0-8050-1002-5

Reprinted 1987, 1988
Many of the illustrations in this book, and both
the jacket illustrations, are by Peter Beales.
Others are acknowledged on page 10, and all are credited
with the photographer's initials against each picture
Designed by Vera Brice
Maps by Leslie Robinson
Illustrations by Norman Bancroft-Hunt
Phototypeset in Monophoto Baskerville and Photina
by Ace Filmsetting Ltd, Frome, and SX Filmsetting, Rayleigh
Colour origination by Gilchrist Bros Ltd, Leeds
Made and printed in Great Britain by
William Collins Sons & Co. Ltd, Glasgow

10 9 8 7 6 5 4 3

ISBN 0-8050-1002-5

I dedicate this book to all those around me
who have so often accepted second place to a rose,
but without whom I could not have grown even a briar.

R. pomifera duplex, photographed $1\frac{1}{2}$ times actual size

Contents

Acknowledgements

This book, and indeed the building of my collection of old roses, would not have been possible without the generous help of the many friends I am privileged to have made during my years as a rose grower: in the case of my collection, friends who have willingly shared their roses with me; where the book is concerned, friends who have generously given their knowledge and expertise. In particular I wish to thank those who have opened their gardens to me and given me, with no preconditions, facilities to take photographs without which this book would be very dull indeed:

James Russell, Castle Howard, North Yorkshire.

Len Turner (now retired) and the present day secretary of The Royal National Rose Society, Colonel Ken Grapes, and their staff at Bone Hill, Hertfordshire.

The Royal Horticultural Society, Wisley

Keith Money, Carbrooke, Norfolk

Humphrey Brooke, Lime Kiln, Claydon, Suffolk

Robin and Laurel Walpole, Mannington Hall, Norfolk

David and Shirley Cargill, Alby Hall, Norfolk

Lord and Lady Tollemache, Helmingham Hall, Suffolk

William and Meredyth Proby, Elton Hall, Peterborough

Maurice and Margaret Mason, Larch Wood, Beachamwell, Norfolk

Henry and Julie Cecil, Warren Place, Newmarket

Ted and Tess Allen, Copdock, Suffolk

The National Trust

To John Beales, my thanks for his photographs and his patience.

To Vincent Page, for both his many photographs and valuable expertise in helping to select from thousands of others.

To Richard Balfour, special thanks for trusting me with his complete collection of slides and for permitting me to use, in his own words, 'as many as are needed'.

Thanks to Michael Gardner, Romford, Essex, for his assistance in compiling the section on *R. moschata* and *R. brunonii*.

Other photographs were kindly loaned by Michael O'Dell of Universal Rose Selection UK, Hazel le Rougetel, Trevor White, Ian Limmer and Keith Money.

To Vera Brice of Collins Harvill, the designer, my thanks for her artistry and understanding in transplanting my work into this book.

To Joan, my wife, Amanda and Richard, my children, Bob Reeve, our nursery manager, and his staff: infinite gratitude for more help even than they knew of.

Foreword

A garden filled with the beautiful roses Peter Beales tells us about in this book is not an unattainable ideal. No matter where we live, no matter what our gardening situation, as long as we are blessed with some sunshine and the soil, of whatever composition, has good drainage, there are roses for us, as this book will show and describe to us.

Classic Roses made its appearance in this country shortly after the rose had been declared our National Flower. If many people had, at that time, no conception of the wealth and diversity within the genus *Rosa*, this book, *Classic Roses* by Peter Beales, an English nurseryman, was at hand to bring forth the many races of roses that stretch back into history and are still here to fill the special needs of home garden-makers as well as public garden displays and botanic garden collections.

Many gardeners in this country look to England for garden inspiration, but fear they cannot grow the same plants, nor grow them as well, as in English gardens. While it is true that only in a small section of our country, the coastal Pacific Northwest, are gardening conditions similar, there is still a wide selection of plants that can be adapted to our own gardens, in whatever part of this great diverse country, and in no division of plants is there more choice and diversity than in roses. Native, wild roses have been discovered growing everywhere throughout the northern temperate hemisphere, native roses of Asia have adapted and naturalized here in America, and the old European garden roses of past centuries were brought to our shores by the earliest colonists, where they quickly became garden plants of our own tradition and were passed down in families, and given local names.

The trick is to find the right roses for our own garden situations. Peter Beales, in this lovely book, points the way. Roses are so easy to grow! But one must know a little something about them. This book is a delightful way to learn about them. The choice may still be difficult, if only because there is, in fact, so very much to choose from among all the roses available to us. You may wish to get in touch with other rose lovers in your locality.

The Heritage Roses Group was formed in the mid 1970s to exchange information and share together their love for the Old Garden Roses and other unusual kinds. There are six Heritage Roses Coordinators throughout the country, and many subgroups have formed. If you will drop me a card, I'll be happy to send you complete information about the Heritage Roses Group, and put you in touch with someone near you. Or you could write to the American Rose Society for this information. There is no affiliation between the two organizations, but there has always been generous support and mutual cooperation between them and many rose lovers are members of both. My address and that of the American Rose Society may be found in Appendix B of this book.

Hundreds of rose lovers have contacted me since this book was first published here in America, and they told me how they were inspired by Peter Beales in *Classic Roses* to plant these wonderful roses. Some of them had 'given up on roses,' but could not resist trying them again because of Peter's book; and because their eyes were opened up to roses they didn't know existed, roses that would adapt themselves so beautifully to their own garden situations, they have found success in using roses in many ways. In rose gardens and in gardens with roses mixed with other plants, in special groupings, in shrub borders, around patios, as climbers on trellises and pillars, as scramblers and ground-covers over steep or awkward sections of garden, as specimen plants for a garden focal point, in many ways, just about any way you could imagine, hundreds of readers of *Classic Roses* have kindly let me know what they did in their own gardens after reading Peter's book.

In the mid 1970s there were very few sources for these roses, these Heritage or Classic or Old Garden Roses, and the other unusual roses, including the marvelous new developments in shrub roses. But since then more and more commercial sources have come into being; and while it is still important to order early, and sometimes to plan ahead for the coming year in order to fill in with the varieties we want that we were not able to obtain this season, we do now have many sources throughout the USA and Canada, and each season more varieties are offered. One great help in getting roses to do well in gardens in severe winter climates as well as in harsh summer ones, desert gardens really, is the option of obtaining roses on their own roots. For some varieties, this is the answer to garden persistence. And many people have found that once roses are well established in gardens, they can survive, not only winter cold, but severe drought situations when extra water for plants cannot be spared. People are amazed that roses not only survive such difficulties, but continue to offer so much beauty at the same time. I have heard so many success stories. They are as inspiring as Peter's book!

You are in for a treat! Here are classic roses for you to learn about and dream over and grow in your own garden.

Berely Dobson

BEVERLY R. DOBSON
Irvington-on-Hudson, New York,
July 1988

Preface

Fate introduced me to roses at an early age and over the years I have built up a comprehensive collection, the greater part of which is made up of the older roses; I make no apology for being heavily biased towards them since I have fallen completely under their spell. If, with this book, I am able to impart some of this enchantment to my readers then I will be content.

In my writing I have tried to answer the many questions I have been asked about roses over the last thirty years or so and have also tried, with my publishers, to quench the insatiable thirst that rose lovers seem to have for faithfully reproduced photographs.

I have accordingly written a brief history of the rose and discussed its evolution, followed by my ideas on how some of yesterday's and our present day roses can be fitted into the landscape of today's gardens, together with some practical advice, gleaned over the years, on their cultivation.

Bearing in mind the need to conserve and perpetuate many of the charming old varieties from the past, without taking the narrow minded view that all that is old is necessarily good. I have tried to describe, in the dictionary section and where appropriate, and to express personal opinions on, a wide range of species and varieties from the past and the present.

If, as you turn the pages of this book, a few of my muddy footprints emerge then perhaps the odd rose petal along the way will compensate.

P.B.

August 1985

'Narrow Water'   [AB]

Climbing Bourbon Rose 'Blairi No. 1' at Mottisfont Abbey, Hampshire [VP]

PART I
History and Evolution of the Rose

The first roses

The genesis of roses and their subsequent evolution must inevitably be a matter for conjecture, but there is good reason to suppose, on the basis of fossil evidence and the present day distribution of species, that the rose has flourished in some form since remote prehistoric times, long before the evolution of *Homo sapiens*. It is likely that the garden cultivation of roses began only some 5000 years ago, probably in China. It is tempting to believe – romantic fancy though it may be – that the practical uses and attractions of the rose were recognized by early man, perhaps widely separated on different continents long before, possibly in Neolithic times.

Indeed, it seems likely that the edible properties of the rose would have been appreciated even before it became prized for its aesthetic qualities. The nutty, sweet, succulent young tips of the shoots of such species as *R. canina*, the common Dog Rose for example, are as I remember from childhood, quite tasty; and later in the year much nourishment and, as we now know, vitamin C supplement could have been extracted from the fleshy skin of the fruit of this and similar species. We would be arrogant indeed if we assumed that our primitive ancestors were not capable of deriving pleasure from the scent, form and colour of what, even in those far-distant days, must have been an incomparably beautiful flower.

Moving forward in time we may suppose that the earliest gardeners of history had a choice, depending on where they lived, of many of the 150 or so species of the genus *Rosa* which had then evolved and laid the foundations for the many thousands of natural mutations and man-manipulated varieties of our present time.

Whether or not you take the view that the rose has undergone too much and too frequent manipulation by human hand and that the garden flower we know today is too far removed from that which nature intended, it is evident that our modern rose is the product of a truly multi-racial plant society.

The original wild or pure roses of nature – then, of course, nameless – would have been single flowers comprising five petals, except for *R. sericea*, the only species with four petals; and all would, in their natural

Above: R. *foetida*
Below: 'Frühlingsgold'

[RCB]
[VP]

habitat, have reproduced readily and true to type, from seed. Earlier evolution would have guaranteed their survival in hostile conditions by providing thorns to deter predators, and furnishing them with scent and colour to attract insects, vital for the reproduction process.

These earliest species may conveniently be divided into four main groups, all from the regions of the northern hemisphere where almost all roses probably evolved, namely Europe, America, Asia and the Middle East.

European species

European species would probably have included *R. canina* (Dog Rose) and some of its related species, *R. eglanteria* and *R. villosa*, growing as shrubs, and *R. arvensis*, growing into trees. Also from Europe, but from the less fertile areas and coastal regions, would have come *R. pimpinellifolia* or *R. spinosissima*, as it was known until recently. Perhaps even then the occasional natural mutation had occurred in this species, either by subtle changes of colour from its natural white or by the formation of additional petals to create double flowers.

Whereas it is possible to isolate the main groups of species quite easily, it is not so simple to identify the numerous subdivisions of the genus *Rosa*. It is fairly safe to assume that various forms of *R. gallica* existed, for it is unlikely that a species of such importance could emerge merely as a subdivision of another race. Its ubiquity is probably accounted for by its deep colour, scent and agreeable nature, which, when communications improved much later, would have made it widely popular. Its origins are probably rooted in Southern Europe or the Middle East where there was a greater appreciation of aesthetics than in the more barbarous regions of the North. Despite obscure origins, a form of *R. moschata*, although probably flourishing on both shores of the Mediterranean and in Asia, would have been the one European species to provide flowers late in summer.

American species

One of the most important of the small group of species native to the American continent was probably the clear pink *R. virginiana*, a tidy plant with attractive, light but rich green foliage, which, like most of the American species, flowered slightly later than many of those from Europe. The small, deep pink flowers and tiny leaves of the moisture-loving *R. nitida*, from the north-eastern regions, must have been distinctive; and another rose which enjoys moisture, *R. palustris* (Swamp Rose), would have created more interest for its finely toothed leaves than for its indifferent flowers of clear pink. As for *R. setigera* (Prairie Rose), this was not unlike the European Dog Rose but with a slightly deeper pink flower, fewer thorns, and leaves made up of three to five leaflets and not seven to nine, as is usual with *R. canina*.

A relatively short-growing species probably inhabiting America at an early date was *R. carolina*. The petals of this rose are small, clear pink, and when the flower is fully open, it nestles into a 'hand' of long, thin sepals.

From the more temperate parts of the American continent might have come two relatively thornless, pink species, the large-flowered *R. blanda* and the smaller-flowered but equally interesting *R. foliolosa*, with its unusual, grass-like foliage.

Whilst all the native American species may lack strong perfume and colour variation of flower, they all possess the great attribute of richly toned autumn foliage. Much later these attributes prompted Wilhelm Miller, a landscape architect from Chicago, to write in the 'American Rose Annual 1917' –

"About ninety per cent of the commonest landscape problems can be solved with the aid of nine species of wild roses." Six of these were the American species already mentioned, the other three were *R. rugosa*, *R. multiflora* and *R. wichuraiana* all from Asia. I am heavily biased of course but, even allowing for a change in 'commonest problems' since 1917, if ten per cent were solved by roses these days, some 'unimaginative', so-called 'landscape schemes' I know of could be, if not solved, made more interesting.

Species from Oriental Asia

The most important of the far more numerous species from Asia, and particularly the Orient, would have been *R. indica*, now, more correctly, *R. chinensis*, which undoubtedly existed during the early Chinese dynas-

R. eglanteria hips and *right: R. pimpinellifolia* hips (see text p. 17)

Above: R. canina   [RCB]
Above right: R. pimpinellifolia   [VP]
Right: R. moschata   [VP]

ties; and forms of this recurrent rose could well have been cultivated by gardeners there around 3000 BC. Much later genes from this species, when introduced to others by breeding, laid the foundations for our familiar modern recurrent roses. It is a sad paradox that such an important stud rose should, in its true form, have become extinct, even, it seems, in its native land. Its demise was probably the sin of nurserymen the whole world over, an arrogant assumption that new strains are essentially better than old.

Other fascinating species from the Far East could have been *R. laevigata* and *R. bracteata*, distinct but with similar characteristics. Both are climbers and have very large, single, white flowers with pronounced stamens, glossy foliage and large, cruel barbs. An early form of *R. banksiae* would likewise have caught the eye – a smooth, thornless species with light green foliage, long pliable shoots and clusters of white flowers; and observant plant collectors of a much later date were to find natural mutations of this species, the double white *R. banksiae alba plena* and the very attractive double yellow *R. banksiae lutea*.

The huge and abundant trusses of *R. multiflora* would have made a superb display, its legacy to later generations being its generosity, for it was subsequently to form the basis of modern Cluster-Flowered and Large-Flowered roses.

The medium-sized, white flowers of the procumbent *R. wichuraiana* would have made their mark as an early example of a ground cover rose.

This species was later to be used as a seed parent, yielding some of the best loved ramblers of this century, notably 'Albertine', 'Albéric Barbier', 'Emily Gray' and 'New Dawn'. Many other more obscure ancient species probably flourished in various parts of Asia – and another form perhaps of *R. moschata* from the Himalayas, and one or more of the several species which bear elongated or flagon-shaped hips, such as *R. moyesii* or *R. sweginzowii* from western and northern China. Southern Asia, too, must have been the home of a form of *R. rugosa*, for surely a non-selected species existed at a very early date, since it grows so freely from seed. Its promiscuity has since resulted in many and varied offspring a few of which have achieved great prominence, notably 'Roseraie de L'Hay', 'Blanc Double de Coubert' and 'Frau Dagmar Hartopp'.

Hips of *R. virginiana*; *right, R. foliolosa* and *below, R. foliolosa* flower and foliage   [VP/VP/PB]

Species from the Middle East

The yellow forms of the subgenus *pimpinellifoliae* are from the more fertile areas of the Middle East. Only from this region, in fact, do we find yellow species, as against a predominence of white and pink from the other principal areas. That a yellow rose existed is beyond doubt, for how

R. blanda   [PB]

R. multiflora   [PB]

could nature or man have produced *R. foetida*, *R. ecae* and *R. hemisphaerica* without the necessary yellow genes?

I think it is possible that *R. foetida* had developed latent partial sterility as part of the continuous evolution of roses, and that civilized man saved it, just in time, from total extinction by learning vegetative propagation. On this analogy, who knows whether we may not have arrived too late for the blue rose, its transient flowers to remain forever forbidden to us. Perhaps its seed lurks hidden beneath some glacier, awaiting resurrection. For only self-fertilizing plant species have the capacity to reproduce themselves in their own evolving image.

Two groups of roses, whose origins are shrouded in mystery are absent: Damask Roses *R. × damascena* and Provence roses *R. × centifolia* and their hybrids. Without doubt the origins of these are hidden amongst the species already discussed but since they have fully-double flowers and are incapable of self perpetuity, they could not emerge until man had perfected a means of assisting their continued existence. They could have occurred by chance of course and were simply given perpetuity by the use of grafting or by cuttings or could they have been the result of crosses made by a dedicated plantsman of an early civilization around the Mediterranean or Middle East? With great respect for the many theories, some based on scientific evidence, I find myself taking the somewhat romantic view of their birth, based if you like on the tenuous opinion that their

Hips of *R. sweginzowii* and *right, R. rugosa alba*

[VP/VP]

scarcity in numbers is compatible with the decline of the great empires of early history; and each can be attributed to the work of just one or two inquisitive, early botanists who will remain anonymous for ever. Their emergence in more northerly Europe in the sixteenth and seventeenth centuries coincides with the wider horizons of the voyages of discovery, undertaken by the Dutch in particular. Hybridizing and the germination of rose seeds, would have needed artificial heat in Northern Europe, a possible but unlikely aid for such experiments at that time. Whilst the ingenious Dutch undoubtedly worked on them, the climates of Italy, Greece, Turkey or Persia would have been far more conducive to success given the haphazard methods of breeding then in use.

The Greeks and Romans took great pleasure in the rose. It appears in their mythology and literature variously as the emblem of love, beauty and youth.

It was the fragrance of the rose that above all else made it so popular to the people of these early civilizations. They not only used its petals in their raw state as a sort of confetti on important occasions but manufactured perfume in the form of rose water and attar of roses. They also dried the petals to make a kind of 'pot-pourri'; and it had an important place in the practice of herbal medicines, as indeed it did in later history.

Little is known about the varieties or species that adorned the gardens of the Ancients. Some future archeological discovery may shed more light on the part that the rose played in the lives of such cultured peoples. Clues that do exist suggest they knew only a few varieties, probably early Damasks such as *R. × damascena* – 'the Summer Damask', and *R. × bifera* – 'the Autumn Damask' and, almost certainly, some form of Gallica. Without doubt, several species already discussed would have been around then but one can only speculate as to their importance. The Ancients, in common with people of other periods in history, would have been impressed by novelty and probably been oblivious, as we are today, to some of nature's more subtle beauties. We have no reason to suppose that these inventive people, who laid the foundation for modern language, thought of roads, actually used central heating and whose architects and craftsmen created such superb buildings, could or would not manipulate a few roses. After all they knew how to propagate. Roses definitely enjoyed the climate further east. In the fertile areas of Asia Minor and even further afield, roses would have grown in abundance. We must therefore assume that traders of this period would be keen to return with the odd specimen or novelty.

Centifolia and Moss Roses

It was in the fifteenth and sixteenth centuries that man began to interfere with the progeny of the rose to more effect. The Dutch, in particular, did pioneer work, especially in selecting improved strains of *R. × centifolia* and its hybrids. Proof of this comes from the frequent appearance of these blowsy, many-petalled roses in the works of the Old Masters, captured in perpetuity, sometimes with equally well proportioned ladies of the era.

R. × centifolia and *right, R. × damascena bifera* 'Quatre Saisons'   [JB/PB]

Examination by plant cytologists in recent years of the chromosomes of *R. × centifolia* prove beyond doubt that it is a complex hybrid and not, as previously thought, a true species. Apparently the Centifolias are made up of genes from *R. gallica*, *R. phoenicia*, *R. moschata*, *R. canina* and *R. × damascena*. The late Dr C. V. Hurst* declared that they were one of the youngest groups, developed in Holland some 300 years ago, contradicting the belief, based on references to 'hundred-petalled roses' as early as 300 BC, that they were among the oldest. When and how such a complex line of

* Dr Hurst's work is collated and documented in Graham Stuart Thomas's book *The Old Shrub Roses*.

hybridity occurred is open to speculation. If, as is said, the Dutch introduced over 200 variations or varieties of Centifolias between 1580 and
1710, this is a tremendous quantity of roses, suggesting a very fertile parent
stock. One wonders how much of the work done by the Dutch was wholly
original. Might they have used single or semi-double clones from warmer
climates, thus building on work done by earlier civilizations? And did they
perhaps witness the gradual extinction of originals in favour of over 200
novelties? There are no records to determine the origins of *R. × centifolia*,
which is likely to remain yet another fascinating horticultural mystery.

The Moss rose apparently emerged as a sport from a Centifolia prior
to the mid-18th century. In the early 19th century a few single-flowered
forms appeared in their ranks, enabling a few hybridists to cross them
with hybrids from other groups in an attempt to prolong their flowering
period, but this was soon discontinued.

Rivers', Woods' and Hooker's catalogues listed some thirty between
them and Paul listed thirty-two Moss roses in *The Rose Garden* (10th ed.,
1903). Many of these probably came about by seedlings raised hap-
hazardly and in large numbers, yielding a small proportion of moss-
bearing offspring which, in turn, were selected for this propensity – rather
than for the high quality of their flowers. Nowadays many of us still
appreciate the Moss rose but we are more selective when it comes to
quality.

The Gallicas and Damasks of the Middle Ages

With the decline of the Roman Empire, roses lost much of their importance, and it was not until the Crusaders of the twelfth and thirteenth
centuries brought back specimens from their travels to the East that they
once more became popular in Europe. When they proved sufficiently
hardy to withstand the rigours of a more northerly latitude, they soon
found their way into the gardens of noblemen and rich merchants, some
of whom turned them to profit. The petals were used for making perfume
and for their tenuous medical properties in the practice of apothecaries.
The 'Autumn Damask' known as 'Quatre Saisons' in France would have
been particularly valuable, producing two crops of flowers for exploi-
tation.

Until then the major source of production, especially of medicine, was
presumably the 'Apothecary's Rose' or 'Red Damask' *R. gallica officinalis*,
later the emblem of the Lancastrians. This was the rose which 'sported' –
the term used for a natural mutation in plants – to produce the legendary
striped rose *R. gallica versicolor*, better known perhaps as 'Rosa mundi',
named, it is said, after 'Fair Rosamund', mistress of King Henry II. If
this romantic legend has any validity – and it seems plausible that such a

'Chapeau de Napoléon'   [VP]

striking sport would have created quite a sensation at that time – this would date it from the mid-twelfth century; but it could well have been brought back to England as a novelty by some crusading knight, implying an earlier origin. Whatever the origin of 'Rosa Mundi', I have no doubt that a striped rose of some variety existed at the time of Henry II.

Alba Roses

Although I normally dislike putting roses into any sort of pecking order, since all have their own special attributes, faults, and appeal, according to taste, the Albas occupy a special place in my league table.

They are a beautiful and intrepid group, going far back in time and although there is some uncertainty about their origin and indeed their early parentage, a few varieties and perhaps the original form certainly existed in medieval Europe. Their foliage, fruit and stems are rather similar to, if more refined than *R. canina* which supports the belief that this group of roses has a common ancestry with this species and the other parent could be either *R. × damascena* or *R. gallica*. Both, I feel sure, would welcome the credit for so beautiful an offspring. All the dozen or so members of this group grown today are blessed with a strong constitution. They start to flower in late June, and few other types of rose can match

their refinement of texture and quality of perfume. All are of pastel shades, from pure white through to clear, deep pink.

An old gardening book of 1840, *The Flower Garden*, lists 42 distinct varieties. I suspect that a few of these, with names I have not seen recorded elsewhere, were simply variations of *R. × alba* 'Maxima' or 'Maiden's Blush', roses I frequently receive for identification each year. These two varieties have more alternative names than any others I know. 'Maiden's Blush' has been known over the years as 'La Royale', 'La Séduisante', 'La Virginale', 'Incarnata' and 'Cuisse de Nymphe', a slightly deeper form having the name 'Cuisse de Nymphe Emue'. It was surely this rose, growing prominently in the garden of my birthplace and affectionately known as 'Grandad's Rose', which first excited my curiosity and led me to my lifelong affinity with roses. I have a vivid childhood memory of seeing this rose, drawn to her no doubt by her 'expensive' perfume which seemed to pervade the air of the whole garden. Despite years of neglect, this old plant is still growing exactly where I remember it, and will undoubtedly outlive me. I derive pleasure from knowing that her offspring are now growing in many diverse places, since it was from this very plant that I first obtained budding-eyes of this variety when starting my nursery.

The several names for *R. × alba* 'Maxima' afford historical insights, for they include 'Bonnie Prince Charlie's Rose', 'Jacobite Rose', 'Cheshire Rose' and 'White Rose of York', indicating an auspicious rose. The true 'White Rose of York', however, was probably the specific and single form of *R. × alba* or even a white form of the common *R. canina*.

Subsequently, after the bitter years of war, the Houses of York and Lancaster fused their emblems, *R. × alba* and *R. gallica officinalis* respectively, and so emerged the Tudor Rose, emblem of England to this day. Was this an original concept by an unsung heraldic artist or could his inspiration have come from the undoubted existence at that time of two striped roses, 'Rosa Mundi' and/or *R. × damascena versicolor*?

Above and right: R. gallica officinalis   [JB/VP]

The influence of Empress Josephine

By the end of the eighteenth century, the foundation for present day roses was well and truly established. The French, in particular, played an important role and an array of diverse varieties emerged, inspired no doubt by the Empress Josephine, who not only filled her garden at the Château de Malmaison with a collection of her favourites, but by her patronage encouraged Pierre Joseph Redouté to make his masterly paintings of them. Redouté published his work in conjunction with Claude Antoine Thory, a botanist, who made the first serious attempt to sift the tangled genealogy of roses. Much of his work has been proved accurate and stands up, when tested, against the much more scientific methods employed today.

This period of rose history holds much fascination for me. To have been a French nurseryman at that time would have been fulfilling, both in job satisfaction and financial reward. How I would have survived in the Revolution I dare not speculate, but Redouté somehow managed to sit on the fence, working for both factions at various times throughout his career. I know nothing of his personality but his talents somehow isolated

R. × alba, 'Maxima'   [VP]

'Maiden's Blush'   [VP]   *R. × damascena*, 'York and Lancaster'   [JB]

'Empress Josephine'   [JB]

him from the politics, intrigue and bitterness of this turbulent period of
French history. Or was it his subject? Roses, at least in Europe, have
somehow always emerged from troubles and strife with enhanced values,
notably the Holy Wars, with the introduction of several new species, the
Wars of the Roses, with the birth of an emblem, and the Napoleonic Wars
and the French Revolution with a new found respectability created by
Empress Josephine, Thory and Redouté.

Josephine's garden at Malmaison brought together the biggest collection of roses ever assembled, and it continued to expand until her death
in 1814, when it quickly fell into neglect. It seems that in spite of the
strife, roses still managed to pass from Britain to France, and a recently
discovered irony is that one of the original designs of the rose garden at
Malmaison (although I think never used) is very close to that of the
Union Jack. A touch of sarcasm? A gesture of goodwill? Or patriotism
from an Englishman named Kennedy employed by the Empress to help
her lay out her rose garden? None of these I suspect – merely coincidence –
a rose garden can hardly be based on the design of the Tricolore. Happily,
I am told, work is now in hand to restore this rose garden to its original
design – an enterprise of historical importance that will afford deep
pleasure to rose lovers.

China Roses

The late Dr Hurst, already mentioned in relation to *R. × centifolia*, did considerable research on the China roses. Evidence of an advanced regime of China garden roses is seen in early Chinese paintings which depicted roses of considerable hybridity as far back as the tenth century. During the sixteenth century, occasional visitors to China and other parts of the Far East reported sightings of roses which bloomed for a very long season. Later, throughout the eighteenth century, as travels from Europe to the East steadily increased, plant material was being collected in ever greater quantities; it was therefore not surprising that the Chinas should find their way to Europe. In 1781 a pink form of *R. chinensis*, now known as 'Old Blush', was planted in Holland and soon reached England. Some eight years later a red form was found growing in Calcutta and brought to England by a captain of the British East India Company. It soon found favour and was variously named *R. semperflorens*, the 'Bengal Rose' and 'Slater's Crimson China'. This rose and 'Old Blush', then called 'Parson's Pink China', were between them responsible for the remontancy factors in most of our modern roses. Although 'Slater's Crimson China' is now seldom seen, having been superseded by such excellent red Chinas as 'Gloire de Rosomanes' in 1825 and 'Cramoisi Superieur' in 1832, 'Old Blush' is quite common, blessed as it is with considerable longevity and a fond liking, it seems, for neglect.

Some of my most recent acquisitions include a batch of cuttings and some seed from China labelled *R. chinensis*. These came at quite the wrong time of year for ideal propagation but some of the staff of the John Innes Institute in Norwich and Jim Russell of Castle Howard quickly agreed to help me spread the risk and consequently, between us, we have raised several plants. Although the seeds have yet to germinate, some cuttings, although purported to have come from the same plant, have now produced a few flowers as one-year cuttings, indicating a hybrid of reddish-pink colour but with an erratic petal number from five on some plants to up to eighteen on others.

These and one or two other China garden hybrids came to me through Mrs Hazel le Rougetel, who visited China in 1982. One, in particular, is a charmer with shapely flowers of sulphur-yellow-flushed pinkish-red. Hazel tells me that, translated, the name is 'The Tipsy Imperial Concubine'!

The Portland Roses

Towards the end of the eighteenth century a rose of much significance appeared in France. Its origins were obscure, as is so often the case but its habit of flowering almost continuously throughout the season won it instant favour. It arrived there by way of England with the name *R. portlandica* but later became known as 'Duchess of Portland', after the lady* who was reputed to have brought it to England from Italy, where it was said to have originated from a man-induced, or more probably, a chance cross between a Damask × Gallica seedling and an unknown China rose, probably 'Slater's Crimson', a mating which is thought to have established, at least in part, the invaluable remontancy habit of many of our present day roses.

Having observed 'The Portland Rose', as it has become known, for many years, I am of the opinion that no China rose was in any way involved in this scattering of pollen, although Damask and Gallica certainly played their part: Damask in the form of *R. × damascena bifera* ('Quatre Saisons') from which it inherits its remontancy and Gallica in the form of *R. gallica officinalis* (the 'Apothecary's Rose') from which it inherits its tidy, compact habit. Whatever its parentage this rose was immediately put to stud by the perceptive French hybridists, amongst whom was Comte Lelieur who was in charge of the Imperial Gardens in France at that time. It was he who raised 'Rose Lelieur', later renamed by request of Louis XVIII 'Rose du Roi'. To produce this rose it is said that Lelieur crossed 'The Portland Rose' with *R. gallica officinalis*. This is another curious fact since such a cross brought more Gallica genes into the little dynasty of Portlands and even more curious when one observes 'Rose du Roi' and its descendents closely. One would suspect a pollen parent or ancestor with a higher petal count. I don't doubt the use of a Gallica but why a common rose such as *R. gallica officinalis* when apparently the Empress Josephine had over 150 different varieties of Gallicas in her collection at the time the cross was made?

In order to compare any offspring and retrace this ancestry, I have tried several times, without success, to cross the probable parents, 'Quatre Saisons' and *R. gallica officinalis*, later perhaps to go further by introducing 'Slater's Crimson China' into the next generation, and so on. I shall keep trying.

In my small way I have dabbled with other Gallicas as both seed and

* Recent correspondence with Sally Festing, who has written a biography of the 2nd Duchess of Portland (1715–85), reveals that the rose was named after her and not the 3rd Duchess. Not only was the 2nd Duchess of Portland a keen rosarian but she never left England in her lifetime. Mr John C. McGregor, formerly of the US Huntington Botanic Garden, brought this fact to Sally Festing's attention, pointing out that the rose was listed in an old nursery catalogue of 1782 and appeared in France three years later. This must cast doubt on Italy as its country of origin.

'Old Blush', the 'China Monthly' Rose   [JB]
'The Portland Rose'   [PB]

'Bourbon Queen'   [JB]

pollen parents and, with few exceptions, their offspring have tended to be of shortish growth. Some years ago I crossed various named Gallicas with 'Scharlachglut', a very vigorous Gallica hybrid which seemed to contradict my theory. These yielded a number of seedlings, all of similar short to medium height; one of the taller of these has now been introduced and given the name of 'James Mason'. Judging from this and other crosses made, I cannot help feeling either that 'Scharlachglut' has somehow been wrongly classified or that its Gallica 'blood' is several times removed. Interestingly, the late Edward LeGrice used pollen from various purple Gallicas to breed his unusually coloured Floribundas. Most of these, many of which were never introduced, tended to a shortish habit with their remontancy not influenced by the introduction of Gallica genes.

Bourbon Roses

Soon after The Portland Rose appeared, another new race of roses came about by chance. It was the promiscuous old China rose 'Parson's Pink', now better known as 'Old Blush', which played its part by co-habiting, it is said, with the Damask 'Quatre Saisons' on the Ile de Bourbon, an island in the southern Indian Ocean, now renamed Réunion, where roses were used as partition hedges. The results of this union were localized plants of a rose commonly called by the islanders 'Rose Edouard'. M. Bréon, director of the island's small botanic gardens, collected seeds from this rose and sent them to his friends in France among whom was M. Jacques, head gardener to the Duc d'Orléans, who recognized the resulting seedlings to be the forerunners of a new race, naming the first one 'Bourbon Rose'. Although this is generally accepted as the means by which the first Bourbon rose was born, there is reason to believe that another 'Rose Edward' had been growing in the Botanical Garden, Calcutta, for some years before M. Bréon collected his seed. Perhaps the Réunion rose had first found its way to India, maybe as seeds which could easily produce variable offspring. Since last year I have had a 'Rose Edward' from Trevor Griffiths of New Zealand, which was originally obtained by Nancy Steen from a grower in New Delhi as the genuine Calcutta form. I have yet to see it flower. Whatever its origins, several French nurserymen recognized its potential and it was used extensively for crossing and recrossing, so giving rise to a range of mostly continuously flowering shrub roses which were to adorn gardens worldwide, with very little competition, well into the nineteenth century. Some of these remain favourites to this day. Notable Bourbons which still give excellent value as shrub roses are 'Bourbon Queen', 'Souvenir de la Malmaison', 'Louise Odier', 'Mme Isaac Pereire' and, of course, the thornless 'Zéphirine Drouhin'. Most Bourbons are fairly vigorous shrub roses but some make excellent climbers and should be used more widely for this purpose. Bourbons fall roughly into two types: those which have inherited the flower forms of the Chinas, the best examples being 'La Reine Victoria' and its paler sport 'Mme Pierre Oger', and those that follow the form of their Damask ancestors such as 'Bourbon Queen' and 'Souvenir de la Malmaison'. Conspicuous differences also appear in their growth habits and in the form and texture of foliage and thorn patterns. This suggests

'Parkzierde'   [VP]

that, through the years, other 'blood' has been introduced from time to time. As a rule, however, there is a correlation between flower style and growth habit which helps to isolate their respective ancestral leanings, those with few thorns and twiggy, pliable wood to the Chinas and those with thorny, stiffer growth, to the Damasks. Victorian writers, in particular William Paul, divided Bourbons into classes based on their predominent ancestral likenesses.

Victorian Roses

Such was the momentum of advance in rose cultivation during the Victorian era that it must have been difficult for nurserymen and gardeners alike to keep pace, not merely with the ever increasing numbers, but, more significantly, with the entirely new races now emerging from various parts of the world. Communications were improving and the affluence stemming from the Industrial Revolution had spread over into the horticultural trade, with nurserymen striving to satisfy the demands of more and more people who had newly discovered the delights of gardening. The revolution in roses is best illustrated in the comprehensive rose catalogues of the period, with each bigger and better issue introducing dozens of new and allegedly improved varieties.

Noisette Roses

Another family of roses to appear at about the same time as the Portlands and Bourbons was that of the Noisettes, which had their beginnings in America. Here again the China rose was involved, this time in conjunction with the Musk Rose, *R. moschata*.

'Parson's Pink China' or 'Old Blush', was crossed with *R. moschata* by a rice grower from Charleston, South Carolina, one John Champney who, in return for the original gift of 'Parson's Pink', passed on the remaining seedlings to his friend and neighbour Philippe Noisette, a French emigrant. Philippe then made more crosses, sending both seeds and plants to his brother Louis in Paris. The latter, seeing them flower, doubtless realized the importance of his brother's gift and named the first seedling 'Rosier de Philippe Noisette', subsequently shortened to 'Noisette'. The original 'Champney's Pink Cluster' and one of its first seedlings 'Blush Noisette' are still with us today and well worth garden space.

William Paul writes of his introduction to Noisettes –

"The peculiar features recommended to notice were its hard nature, free growth, and a large cluster of flowers, produced very late in the year, which were indeed recommendatious of no common order."

Descendants from the first Noisette rose vary both in stature and florifer-

'Blush Noisette'

ousness. Most start their flowering rather later than, for example, the Bourbons and many repeat or virtually continue flowering throughout the summer. Later in their history they were heavily interbred with other groups and some of their distinctive 'Noisette' characteristics were lost, not least their hardiness. Important varieties in the group include 'Blush Noisette', 'Aimée Vibert', 'Bouquet d'Or', 'Céline Forestier' and 'Mme Alfred Carrière' to name but a few. They are still available, and doing stalwart service in many gardens today.

Hybrid Perpetual Roses

As a result of a fusion between the Bourbons and, it would seem, any other parent that came along, a race of roses appeared which, following initial confusion, became known as Hybrid Perpetuals. They were accepted as a new group sometime in the 1820s and later many varieties were to fill catalogues. Their sheer numbers and very hybridity, however, proved to be the downfall of many, and only the best survived. Those that are still with us today are well worth their place as shrubs or climbing roses in the modern garden. Some, indeed, are truly beautiful, and most have a powerful scent. I like, in particular, 'Reine des Violettes', 'Baroness Rothschild', 'Baronne Prévost', 'Dupuy Jamain', 'Paul Neyron' and 'Ulrich Brunner Fils'. One of the latest to be raised and introduced was the indefatigable 'Frau Karl Druschki', later renamed 'Snow Queen'.

'Reine des Violettes'

[PB]

'Dupuy Jamain' and *right*, roses edged with hebe
and berberis at Castle Howard, Yorkshire   [VP]   [PB]

'Ardoisée de Lyon'   [VP]

Tea Scented Roses

At the time this somewhat haphazard and largely undocumented scattering of pollen was taking place to bring forth the Bourbons, Noisettes, Portlands and early Hybrid Perpetuals, a few new and hitherto unknown hybrids were finding their way into the hands of rose breeders. These had, like their very close relations the Chinas, originated in the Orient and were probably the result either of a much earlier programme of hybridizing by the Chinese or chance crosses between *R. gigantea* and *R. chinensis*. Like the Chinas, they had the desired characteristic of prolonged flowering. The first of these to arrive in Europe was *R. indica odorata* soon to become known as 'Hume's Blush' after Sir Abraham Hume to whom it was sent from the Fa Tee Nurseries of Canton in 1810. The second came in 1824 found during an expedition to China to collect plants for the Royal Horticultural Society. This was later classified as *R. odorata ochroleuca*, but its original name of 'Parks' Yellow Tea-scented China' after its collector, John Parks, has been used ever since. Yellow clouded sulphur and scented, it was this rose, in 1830, which brought forth the first of several yellow or near yellow Noisettes, beginning with 'Lamarque' and tapering off to the last important introduction, 'William Allen Richardson', in 1878. It was Parks' rose and 'Fortune's Double Yellow', found by Robert Fortune in a Chinese mandarin's garden in 1845, which brought the valuable yellow colouring into some of the many Tea Roses bred and introduced during the early 20th century. Although thought extinct for many years, I believe that thanks to the kindness of various donors I now have plants of all three of the above roses. I only hope they can endure our chilly Norfolk climate.

It seems that the early Tea Roses as well as the Chinas arrived in ships of the East India Company who were of course primarily concerned with the transporting of tea but since a small part of their cargo yielded another new race of roses, it is possible that this, coupled with their unusual scent, led to the term 'Tea-Scented Rose' as a nickname coined perhaps by the sailors whose job it was to tend them. I grow several varieties of 'Teas' and have yet to detect any real resemblance to the scent of tea in any of them.

Whatever the origins of the name, Tea Roses soon became quite fashionable, especially in the warmer parts of Europe. Many were not totally hardy, but this fact, coupled with their beauty, simply made them more sought after, and the Victorians proceeded to grow them in abundance, the hardiest outdoors, and the tender ones in conservatories and stove-houses. The blooms were borne on rather slender, weak stalks and most had high, pointed centres when in bud, which distinguished them from other roses of the day. The Victorians loved to wear roses in their buttonholes and many were grown specifically for this purpose.

Hybrid Tea Roses

It is not my intention in this book to cross the somewhat arbitrary boundaries dividing the modern bedding roses from the older and more modern
shrub roses; but no history of the rose, however summary, would be complete without at least a brief excursion into this territory. It was inevitable
that someone would cross a Tea Rose with a Hybrid Perpetual and thus
create yet another distinct race, the Hybrid Teas. The credit for this is
usually attributed to the French nurseryman, M. Guillot, who raised
'La France', its pointed bud and recurrent flowering habit undoubtedly
setting it apart at that time. From other crosses he made came a vast array
of tidy-growing, twice-flowering, apparently hardy roses which received
a warm welcome, especially as the ever increasing popularity of flower
shows was leading to a race for bigger and better exhibition blooms.

Henry Bennett of Stapleford, working along similar lines to M. Guillot,
did much early work on the development of the Hybrid Teas. In particular, he raised a rose called 'Lady Mary FitzWilliam' which later
figured in the parentage of many highly desirable varieties.

I cannot exclude a personal anecdote concerning this rose, as a result
of an illustration which appeared in a small book entitled *Late Victorian*

Above: 'Mabel Morrison' and *right:* 'Mme Caroline Testout'   [PB/PB]

'La France'   [PB]

Above: 'Lady Mary Fitzwilliam' and shown, *right*, in
a 19th century lithograph   [KM]

'Grace Darling', an early British Hybrid
Tea Rose   [JB]

Roses, written by myself, with photographs by Keith Money. This picture was of an unidentified variety discovered by Keith at Caston in 1975. We did not state dogmatically that it was 'Lady Mary FitzWilliam', but hoped it might create some interest, either confirming that it was the 'Lady Mary', or suggesting a suitable name. Two letters came from Australia, both expressing the opinion that the rose was indeed 'Lady Mary FitzWilliam'. One was from Deane Ross, a professional rose grower whose father had started their business in 1906, and who, when shown the photograph, was an alert gentleman of 87 years. Deane wrote: "When I showed him your book he said, 'Now that is Lady Mary Fitz-William'". Deane then went on to say that his father had grown this variety extensively in his early years as a nurseryman, and remembered it well. This does not necessarily authenticate the rose – photographs are not the easiest means of identification – but it is particularly interesting, since later I acquired a colour print of 'Lady Mary Fitzwilliam' which strengthens my belief that the rose could well have been rediscovered. It came from Mrs Margaret Meier, a niece of Henry Bennett's great- grand-daughter, Mrs Ruth Burdett; and Mrs Burdett herself added support to this belief by informing me that Henry Bennett's son Charles emigrated to Australia and started commercial rose-growing there at the turn of the century, doubtless taking with him ample stocks of his father's roses.

Even if 'Lady Mary FitzWilliam' is now lost, many early Hybrid Teas have survived, though few stand up to the competition of the modern

Above: R. *foetida bicolor* [PB]
Below: 'Arthur Bell' a modern yellow floribunda [VP]

'The Fairy' [PB]

Hybrid Teas. It is in their climbing form, that they come into their own, and some, such as the Climbers 'Caroline Testout', 'Lady Sylvia', 'Etoile de Hollande' and 'Crimson Glory' have few rivals even from the most recent creations.

Throughout the 19th century, breeders had searched for their ideal – a clear yellow rose. Several existed, at least with yellow in their make-up, but all had resisted passing on this colour to any of the Bourbons, Hybrid Perpetuals or Hybrid Teas. The breakthrough came towards the end of the century, and again thanks to a Frenchman, M. Pernet-Ducher, who, after much trial and error, eventually succeeded in crossing *R. foetida persiana* with a Hybrid Tea. The seedling from this cross, when recrossed with *R. foetida bicolor*, led to the first yellow Hybrid Tea, 'Rayon d'Or', now it seems, extinct. However, another yellow from the same cross, 'Soleil d'Or', has survived to this day. For a while, the siblings from Pernet-Ducher's work were called 'Pernettianas'; later they were to be classified with the Hybrid Teas. Whilst no one should deny him credit for this achievement, it has to be said that this breakthrough led to an epidemic of black spot – a legacy still with us today.

'Nathalie Nypels'

Above left: 'Plentiful' [JB]
Above: 'Albéric Barbier' [PB]
Left: 'Thisbe' [PB]

Floribunda Roses

As already mentioned, the modern Floribunda roses owe their large trusses of flowers to one of their early ancestors, *R. multiflora*, but like the Hybrid Teas they are of very mixed pedigree. Suffice it to say that their long flowering season was bequeathed to them by the same hybrid Chinas that begat the Teas. Their career began as charming little bedding roses known collectively as 'Dwarf Polyanthas'. These were crossed with the Hybrid Teas by Poulsen of Denmark in the early 1920s, producing the 'Hybrid Polyanthas', which were renamed 'Floribundas' in the 1950s, providing massed colour throughout the summer.

During the last twenty or so years, Floribundas and Hybrid Teas have been interbred so much that it has become difficult to separate them in genetic terms. In 1971 a new rose classification was prepared, primarily for the benefit of the ordinary gardener. Two new terms were introduced, so that we now have 'Cluster-Flowered roses' for Floribundas and 'Large-Flowered roses' for Hybrid Teas.

Wichuraiana Roses

If I were just embarking upon a career of breeding roses I would pursue the development of *R. wichuraiana*, and of *R. luciae* (see page 257), parent or parents of many of our garden ramblers. Most of the impressive results achieved by Barbier (in France), by Jackson and Perkins, and by Brownell (both in the USA), came to a dead end over sixty years ago. Apart from nature herself giving us 'New Dawn', a sport from 'Dr Van Fleet', in 1930 the work initiated by these hybridists was, until recently, largely neglected. It is a testimony to their work that ramblers such as 'Albéric Barbier', 'Albertine', 'Sanders White' and 'Excelsa', raised in the early years of the present century, are still widely grown and still listed in most rose catalogues.

The chance birth of 'New Dawn' was indeed a happy event, for not only did it provide us with perhaps the best-ever remontant climbing or rambler rose but, when used as a parent by modern hybridists, has also given us several very good modern long-flowering climbers such as 'Bantry Bay', 'Coral Dawn', 'Pink Perpétue', 'Rosy Mantle' and 'White Cockade', and at least one procumbent variety, by the late Edward LeGrice, who applied its pollen to 'Mermaid' to produce 'Pearl Drift'.

'Trier' and *right:* 'Ballerina'   [RCB/VP]

Above: 'de la Grifferaie'   [RCB]

Below: 'Russelliana'   [VP]

The Hybrid Musks

An important development in shrub roses occurred during the first quarter or so of the 20th century. Tucked away in rural Essex, a clergyman, Joseph Pemberton, worked at rose-breeding and came up with a complete breakthrough – a distinct strain of long-flowering shrub roses, with substantial flowers borne in clusters and in quantities equal to those of the Polyanthas. As the foundation for these, he used two closely related roses, 'Aglaia' and 'Trier', which he had acquired from Germany a few years earlier. By crossing these two roses, both of *R. moschata* and *R. multiflora* parentage, with selected Teas, Hybrid Teas and Hybrid Perpetuals, he produced a unique strain, initially known as 'Pemberton roses'. They are now called Hybrid Musks, and are still invaluable both as specimen shrubs and for use in group planting schemes. The Rev. Pemberton bequeathed his entire stock to John and Ann Bentall, his gardeners, who set up in business as rose growers and subsequently introduced more Pemberton roses as well as some of their own varieties.

'Rose Marie Viaud' and *top right: R. arvensis*
Right: an unknown double Ayrshire Rose

[VP/PB/IL]

Multiflora Ramblers

R. multiflora has been mentioned several times in relation to its influence on other roses or strains of roses, but deserves mention here for its own sake. William Paul listed twenty-seven varieties, many of which are still available today. Most of these have their place as camouflage for unsightly buildings or decrepit trees; others would be well placed both on pergolas and on walls. Most Multifloras root readily from cuttings and because of this, some varieties were used extensively as understocks for other roses, especially during World War I and the 1920s. A variety particularly favoured for this purpose was 'de la Grifferaie', a persistent rose which is often sent to me for identification, for having shed its more delicate enforced charge of the budded rose, it seems to thrive on neglect.

The Ayrshire Roses

I make no apology for devoting some space to another interesting diversion from the main line of rose development, *R. arvensis*. I have always been interested in this rose and its few offspring, and since authors have tended to neglect it, this is an opportunity to redress the balance slightly.

In its wild habitat it has great charm and is the only native climbing rose in Britain, and climb it will, to the top of the tallest thicket or hedge. No matter how coarse its competition or support, it remains graceful by cascading its long, thin, dark-coloured shoots back towards the ground, for it is quite at home scrambling through undergrowth or simply creeping along the ground or banks. Of its hybrids, 'Ayrshire Splendens' is now the most common; and an excellent example of this, some 10 ft (3 m) tall and 10 ft (3 m) wide can be seen at Castle Howard in Yorkshire, where it has been grown as a specimen shrub with support. Most of the other members of this race of superb climbers, known collectively as Ayrshires, have somehow been lost, overwhelmed presumably by the popularity of the Wichuraiana hybrids with their stronger colouring. I am, however, hopeful that a double, pure white Ayrshire variety sent to me from Scotland by Mrs McQueen of Dunfermline will turn out to be a happy rediscovery.

Good climbers were, of course, very scarce before the mid-19th century, but when they became more plentiful the Victorians used them extensively, as is evident from some of the monochrome photographs in Jekyll and Mawley's *Roses for English Gardens*, published in 1902.

Lack of authentic records once again prevents us from tracing the first double 'Ayrshire' back to its precise source. Various stories connect the rose with places as far apart as Germany, Canada and Yorkshire; but

Above: 'Mrs Colville'. *Right:* autumn foliage on *R. pimpinellifolia*
Below: Burnet Rose 'Double Pink' form

[RCB/PB]
[PB]

if not actually bred in Scotland, it certainly started its career there. I am inclined to feel, however, in spite of the work done on these roses by Mr Martin of Dundee, that had it originated there local pride would have prohibited the name 'Ayrshire', as it seems to have been called from its beginning. Of all the stories surrounding this rose, I think the following is the most plausible. It was first seen in 1776 by a Mr J. Smith of Monksgrove Nurseries, Ayrshire, growing in the garden of a Mr Dalrymple of Orangefield, near Ayr. It had been planted there by Mr John Penn, a huntsman who was a keen gardener. Penn told Smith that he had brought the rose from his native Yorkshire where he had found it growing in a garden, having supposedly been introduced there from Germany. The 'Orangefield Rose' attracted much local attention and found its way to Loudon Castle, from where it was eventually widely distributed.

Some of the other stories about the origin of the Ayrshires only make sense if one recognizes an understandable confusion with other climbers of this period, namely the evergreen roses.

Sempervirens Roses

The 'evergreen roses', as they were known by the Victorians, are hybrids of *R. sempervirens*, bred in France in the first half of the 19th century. They are less vigorous and have fewer thorns than the Ayrshires, although the latter are not themselves over-thorny. Furthermore, the Ayrshires produce their flowers singly, or in small clusters, while the evergreens produce theirs in large trusses some two weeks later. Varieties worth special mention in this small group are 'Félicité et Perpétue' and 'Adélaide d'Orléans'.

Pimpinellifolia Roses

I have already made a brief reference to the Pimpinellifolias. These charming little roses were very popular at the beginning of the 19th century, only declining in popularity when superseded by longer-flowering roses. Although only a few varieties now remain, I find them delightful to grow. They are not fussy about soil and can be reproduced easily from cuttings. When grown on their own roots, they sucker freely, but in so doing never outgrow their welcome. The so-called Burnet or Scotch roses were almost as preponderant in 1824 as the Cluster-Flowered rose is today. Although there is little doubt that the 'double' Pimpinellifolias flourished long before 1800, it is worth recalling Joseph Sabine's account of their introduction, which was published while he was Secretary of The Royal Horticultural Society in 1822. Two brothers named Brown, one of whom was a partner in a nursery trading as 'Dickson & Brown' of Perth, were apparently the first to realize the potential of these roses when one of them, Robert, found a malformed, wild 'Scotch Rose on the hill of Kinnoul' near Perth, in 1793. From this one rose, which they planted in the nursery, they collected seed. These seeds produced plants with semi-double flowers. Eventually, by continuous seed-sowing and selection, they assembled some good, double forms which included a marbled pink-and-white variety. From these they increased stock and supplied nurseries on both sides of the border. In Scotland, Robert Austin of Glasgow had, by 1814, 'upwards of 100 varieties of new and undescribed sorts'. In England, William Malcolm of Kensington and Messrs Lee & Kennedy of Hammer-

Above and below: 'Red Blanket'   [PB/VP]

smith had, between them, purchased most of Dickson & Brown's stock, and as a result these roses soon won deserved popularity in the south and subsequently spread far and wide. I have collected about ten varieties at present but, apart from a few, I fear most will be impossible to name.

Burnet roses were formerly known as 'spinosissimas' from *R. spinosissima*, which has recently been changed to *R. pimpinellifolia*.

In the 1830s a Mr Lee of Bedfont succeeded in crossing one of these varieties with the 'Autumn Damask' to produce 'Stanwell Perpetual'. This rose bears a close resemblance to the Burnets in foliage and thorns but is taller and more straggly. Flowering almost continuously and superbly scented, it is still quite a favourite today.

With the notable exception of Wilhelm Kordes in Germany, who used forms of *R. pimpinellifolia* in the 1930s and 1940s to give us 'Frühlingsgold' and 'Frühlingsmorgen' among others, few other breeders have used them, at least not successfully, since their heyday, although Roy Shepherd of America produced a worthwhile hybrid Pimpinellifolia shrub, 'Golden Wings', in 1956.

Procumbent Roses

The most recent development, obviously through demand, has been a steady increase in the number of spreading or prostrate roses which have been bred to cover the ground. They are usually termed 'ground cover roses', a term I do not like because I believe it exaggerates their potential, and implies that they can be used as dense, spreading shrubs to suppress weeds and take the backache out of gardening. Perhaps one day such roses will be bred but until then I propose to call them 'Procumbent' varieties. After all, many much older roses can be used to cover ground and only their voracious nature has prevented their widespread usage for this purpose. I am thinking, in particular, of the Wichuraiana climbers and ramblers. Nevertheless, the recent procumbent roses are excellent garden plants, not requiring too much labour, when massed in groups, to keep tidy. Several of them also have the advantage of a much longer flowering season. Notable among these are the delightful 'Snow Carpet', with tiny leaves and dense growth, 'Smarty', a more vigorous, spreading variety of soft pink, and 'Red Blanket', again vigorous but rosy-red and with persistent foliage.

Reflections on the future

We have now discussed the main avenues taken by the rose in its journey from prehistoric times to the 20th century. Who knows what rose breeders will get up to next? I suspect that a writer in fifty years time may well be using a wholly new vocabulary to discuss the results of our present endeavours. Already we talk of 'genetic engineering', 'tissue culture', 'cloning' and 'microbiology'; all this, together with the computer's capacity for detailed analysis, will certainly play its part in our future quest for 'the perfect rose'. Already, too, we see new types emerging, with breeders searching scientifically for some of the elusive qualities that will make the rose an even better garden plant.

Enlightened breeders will no doubt realize as they strive to find the 'perfect rose' that the re-awakened interest in old-fashioned roses is not just a passing fad. Although nostalgia unquestionably plays a part; their rise in popularity over these past twenty or so years could not have been sustained had it not arisen from an appreciation of their more subtle and refined attributes by a very discerning public, who are not always willing to believe that something new is necessarily something better, at least until such superiority has been proved.

Above: an informal rose hedge at Albion House, Little Waltham, Essex   [RCB]
Below: 'Bobbie James' on a pergola at the Garden of the Rose, St Albans, Hertfordshire   [JB]

PART II
Roses in the Landscape

For several centuries roses have enjoyed a dual role, being the most popular and the most versatile of all outdoor garden plants. Rose breeders over the years have successfully produced not merely pretty faces but a range of garden plants which, used correctly and imaginatively, can meet almost any landscaping challenge. I doubt whether so many of the now-called old-fashioned roses would have survived had they not fulfilled both roles so effectively. Yet post-war trends in landscaping seem largely to have ignored shrub and old-fashioned roses. Only since Graham Thomas revived interest in them during the late 1950s and 1960s have they become increasingly popular. To some extent this has been a cult and they have been enjoyed for their intrinsic beauty as flowers rather than for their wider value as garden plants; but the reverse is true for, in particular, the Rugosas which are now almost 'stock in trade' for municipal landscapers, and more imaginatively, some of the more vigorous climbers are now enjoying a popularity they have not experienced since Gertrude Jekyll used them so cleverly in many of her gardens.

Although there is usually a rose to fit any situation, this is not to advocate roses for their own sake. Good landscaping should always take all possibilities into account. The best schemes are achieved by the harmonious use of a variety of subjects in sympathy with the buildings they serve, and the wider boundaries surrounding them. The role most often, given to climbers and old-fashioned roses in smaller and medium-sized gardens is that of 'supporting' plants, i.e. to provide background to other plants or to beds of modern roses, or as individual shrubs for additional height or colour. In larger gardens, on the other hand, they usually find themselves playing the entire cast, segregated from the landscape into separate communities to form the complete rose garden. Both roles are admirable and should be encouraged, but this is 'type casting' and many landscape schemes would benefit considerably if old-fashioned and shrub roses were given the chance to prove themselves 'good mixers'. Presumably fashion plays its part in all this but one suspects that it goes deeper than simple vogue. Rather, it is a question of 'image'. All are inexorably linked by their given name, 'roses', and the long reign of modern Hybrid Teas and Floribundas have resulted in confusion of purpose between these and other types of roses. If we try to remember that modern Hybrid Teas and Floribundas are, in their widest sense, bedding

'Nevada' in the gardens at Mannington Hall, Norfolk   [PB]

plants and old-fashioned roses shrubs, then their virtues would not be confused merely because of a generic name. Also, many beautiful, old-fashioned roses would not be rejected for the sin of having a short flowering season, and should, perhaps, receive the same consideration as other shrubs with equally short flowering seasons, instead of living a life of inferiority simply because their shorter-growing sister, with the same family name, can produce flowers all summer. No one after all rejects a Lilac because it flowers only once each season. Obviously modern bush roses should, and do, play an important part in the garden. Too often, however, roses with short flowering seasons are discarded simply on the grounds of 'value for money'. We all have our own tastes and sense of values, thank heaven. Given the choice, I would never exchange one bloom of 'Mme Hardy' for an armful of 'Iceberg'. Nor would I plant a bed of 'Mme Hardy' in the middle of my lawn.

To a lesser extent, once-blooming, climbing roses suffer the same fate. With few exceptions, nature has decreed that her finest blooms come in small doses; consequently, some of her most beautiful climbers are overshadowed by more flamboyant subjects whose only claim to fame is a longer flowering season.

All roses are really equal, but some, for the wrong reasons, are more equal than others. Of course a long flowering-season is important but is it as important as beauty, charm or fragrance? Some roses combine all these things but are difficult to grow. Others, with one or more of these

'Rambling Rector' at the Garden of the Rose, St Albans, Hertfordshire [PB]

'Iceberg' and *right:* 'Mme Hardy' [VP/PB]

virtues perhaps, grow like weeds, or may have other faults. It is this very unpredictability that makes them so fascinating both for their own sakes and as landscape shrubs.

Another probable reason why they are used so sparsely in landscape schemes is, paradoxically, their sheer weight of numbers. With such a vast array of characteristics, the choice of roses for specific tasks is daunting both to the uninitiated and expert alike. This is further complicated by photographs of the same variety which look quite different and by descriptions in catalogues and books that often contradict one another. When choosing roses, bear in mind these small discrepancies and avoid, if

The new rose gardens at Elton Hall, Peterborough   [PB]

possible, falling into the trap of choosing from photographs alone. Read about the ones you like, preferably from more than one book, and try to see them growing either at a nursery or in one of the many gardens that are open to the public. Advice, based on experience, from rose-growing friends is also invaluable. Do not be afraid of making mistakes; all the best gardens have developed by trial and error. So if a particular old rose fails to come up to expectation, does not suit a particular spot or, equally important, does not fit into a preconceived colour scheme, find another home for it or just give it away and start again with another rose.

Old and shrub roses for an established garden

Old roses can be mixed with most other garden subjects with comparative ease, although as a matter of personal taste, except for some of the short-growing or procumbent varieties, I do not consider that they mix well with heathers or conifers. They can, however, cohabit happily with herbaceous plants, especially grey foliage types. I will discuss the various plants to grow with roses in a later chapter, but as a general rule, when mixing old roses with herbaceous perennials, the best effect is achieved if, when viewed from a distance, the rose blends with the border both in terms

'Brenda Colvin'

Above: 'Lady Penzance', and *right*, hips of *R. pomifera*   [PB]

'Excelsa' weeping standard at Warren Place, Newmarket   [PB]

of form and colour. Often this is best done by planting in groups of three. One group of roses, strategically placed, can add strength and maturity to flimsy areas of the border, whereas another of graceful shape will reduce the coarse lines of the more robust border plants. Try, where possible, to use upright-growing shrub roses in the taller, upright areas of the border, and more pendulous ones in the shorter zones. These are not golden rules but sensitivity in such matters can be most rewarding. Colour, too, is important. Soft pinks, purples and whites go very well with grey foliage plants, buffs, creams and magentas with dark green or purple foliage, and the stronger colours of red, yellow and flame with the brighter green

Pillar roses growing at the Bagatelle Gardens, Paris   [RCB]

and variegated foliage. Another important factor is the timing of flowers. Try, where possible, to achieve continuity in particular areas. Plan, too, for scent, placing a scented rose in an area where scent is absent in the other plants.

Standard roses are often difficult to position, especially in the more informal gardens, but the herbaceous border is an ideal place for them, since they often provide the extra height required to give the border better contours, without seeming to intrude, as might be the case with a shrub rose. Climbing roses on pillars are also effective in the same way, though care must again be taken to choose colours sympathetic to the herbaceous plants.

Rustic trellis placed behind herbaceous borders to support climbers and ramblers can look effective. Remember, however, that throughout the winter most roses will lose their leaves, so that care should be exercised in designing the trellis in order for it not to appear too unsightly when the roses are dormant.

In larger gardens very pleasant walks can be created by using a combination of old-fashioned roses, climbing roses and herbaceous plants. I am not too much in favour of walks that go nowhere, so it is better if they have a purpose, such as leading to another part of the garden or to a summerhouse or some such feature. These can, of course, be created from old roses alone, but they are more interesting if compatible perennials and flowering and foliage shrubs are used in moderation. The climbers can be placed on rustic trellis at the back of the border.

Smaller gardens, especially those of modern style, are often surrounded by closeboard fencing or interwoven panels. These, often by necessity, form the background to mixed or herbaceous borders, and climbing roses, with the additional help of wire, can make an ideal backdrop to the border and camouflage for the fence.

'The Garland' at Lime Kiln, Claydon, Suffolk   [PB]
Right and below: 'New Dawn'   [PB/PB]

Old-fashioned roses in mixed shrubberies

Species, old-fashioned and shrub roses fit perfectly into mixed shrub borders and, in my opinion, are very much under-used for this purpose. I would omit a few stalwarts such as 'Canary Bird', 'Frühlingsgold', 'Nevada', *R. moyesii* and some of the Rugosas – not that these are unsuited to shrubberies, but simply because there are so many other ideal varieties

Top left: 'Mme Sancy de Parabère' [RCB]
Above: 'Canary Bird' [PB]
Centre left: 'Nevada' at Mannington Hall, Norfolk [TW]
Bottom left: 'Nevada' [VP]

of diverse size and habit which are never given the chance, except occasionally by more adventurous landscape designers. The colour range of
roses is vast when compared with that of flowering trees and shrubs. True,
if left to their own devices, the more vigorous varieties can get out of hand,
and some will take over if permitted to do so. Many, however, will fit
comfortably amongst shrubs and provide a variety of attributes such as
scent, autumn colour and hips. In the front of the shrubbery, too, numerous short-statured shrubs, both flowering and evergreen, have grey,
purple or variegated foliage, and are primarily grown for this reason;
short shrub roses, planted in groups of three, can enhance such shrubs by
providing a longer flowering season.

Roses for parks and municipal planting

A few parks departments, to their credit, already use shrubs and old-
fashioned roses for municipal landscaping schemes; and more would
perhaps follow suit if they could obtain them in sufficient numbers. By
and large, however, with the exception of the traditional Rugosa varieties,
they tend to be neglected in favour of the modern bush roses. Admittedly,
many local authorities grow their modern roses quite well, but others,
where soil is less favourable, persist in growing them when common sense
dictates that they should be scrapped and replaced with shrub and old-
fashioned roses. Costs are doubtless a factor in such decisions, but surely

Top left: 'Scabrosa', and *left:* 'Schneezwerg' [VP/VP]
Below: 'Schneezwerg' at Mannington Hall,
Norfolk [PB]

Autumn foliage of *R. virginiana* and *right: R. woodsii fendleri*   [PB/VP]

most people would much prefer to see successful plantings of these types rather than some of the ailing apologies for rose beds so frequently encountered – probably due to an insistence on bright colour, often orange, to the exclusion of everything else. In any case, on the basis of cost-per-square-metre, shrub roses are probably less expensive, since their planting density is lower. I suspect, however, that the biggest responsibility for lack of imagination in rose planting schemes by local government rests with some nurserymen, offering large numbers of modern roses at very low prices and fewer varieties of old-fashioned roses and shrub roses.

The Rugosas, of course, have their fair share of space in parks, municipal gardens and industrial planting schemes. These are often used as 'barrier plants' between dual carriageways and also to furnish roundabouts, providing greenery and flowers without the need for expensive maintenance. Yet there are several other species roses which would serve this purpose admirably, notably *R. virginiana*, *R. woodsii fendleri*, *R. pimpinellifolia* and *R. wichuraiana* to name but four. I accept that *R. rugosa* and its hybrids are excellent subjects for industrial and roadside planting, but to my mind they emit a somewhat urban aura and, perhaps because of their Japanese origin, look out of place in rural schemes where European or American species roses would be more congruous.

There are some very good modern shrub roses which are already used in high-density planting, particularly the newer prostrate varieties, and obviously these, too, have considerable future potential. I can, neverthe-

Above: Hips of 'Frau Dagmar Hartopp'   [VP]
Below: Climbing 'Mme Caroline Testout' at Hatfield House, Hertfordshire   [TW]

less, think of several ramblers, which would make admirable prostrate roses, especially for use on banks and mounds both of which are now an almost compulsory part of the contour ground-work in modern industrial developments and roadworks. I wish, too, that climbing roses were used more freely to adorn public buildings. This is probably ruled out on grounds of cost and possibly on the basis of likely structural damage. This may have been true in the days of soft bricks and mortar, but I cannot really believe that modern building materials will come to much harm in the arms of a rose. Many new buildings cry out for greenery, if not for flowers, and it should not be too difficult to make provision for rose supports even at the design stage.

Standard roses, too, could be used effectively in many formal plantings, although admittedly they require good maintenance and in open spaces make ideal targets for vandals and thieves.

Roses for woodland, the wild garden and partial shade

Roses are not too happy if planted in dense shade, but several species and varieties will tolerate partial or dappled shade. They usually look somewhat out of place in coniferous woodland, but some species combine well with deciduous plantings or even mixed plantations where conifers are in the minority. This is not to advocate turning such areas into rose gardens, but a few groups planted here and there in glades, clearings and along paths can provide added interest to a woodland walk. Apart from the pleasure offered to the eye, they attract, in season, insects to their flowers, provide thickets for nesting birds, and, in due course, edible fruit for them. Many species also have attractive autumn foliage.

The wild garden is frequently an area designated as such within the garden proper, and here the single-flowered wild species can be a considerable asset by providing added interest when the wild spring flowers are gone.

In more open spaces such as parkland, groups of species roses, if not overdone, can also look effective. On golf courses, too, they can provide interesting hazards, grouped here and there along the edge of the fairway.

It is important to use group planting in all these situations. By groups I mean a minimum of five plants, but often, depending on the space, considerably more than this should be used in one area. If more than one variety is wanted, plant a single variety per group and allow ample space between each group. The density of planting within a group will depend upon the ultimate dimensions of each species, but they should be planted in such a way as to intermingle within two or three years. Soil condition is not normally a problem, but it may help to feed the soil well at the initial planting and, of course, keep the roses free of such competitors as brambles and ivy especially for the first year or two.

N.B. Roses suitable for woodland are marked W in the Dictionary section. Those suitable for partial shade are marked ⦿.

R. multiflora at the Botanic Gardens, Madrid

[RCB]

Roses for hedges

In addition to the natural hedgerow roses, which are better grown in hedges rather than to form them, small roses for hedging fall roughly into two groups, formal and informal, the demarcation line being somewhat ill-defined, but with the majority belonging to the latter group.

Formal hedges

The majority of formal rose hedges seen today are made up of modern roses. There are many excellent Cluster-Flowered (Floribundas) roses which are ideal for this purpose and, almost without exception, these make attractive, short-growing, dividing hedges within the garden. The best known and by far the most popular hedging variety is 'Queen Elizabeth'. I have no wish to decry this excellent variety but its dominance as a formal hedge rose over the last two decades has been at the expense of several other good hedging roses of almost equal ability.

When planting a formal rose hedge, consideration should be given to any upright-growing variety capable of reaching the desired height. Bushes should be planted either in a single row with 18 in (45 cm) spacing between each plant or, for a really thick hedge, a double row of staggered bushes with 12 in (30 cm) between each row and 24 in (60 cm) between each plant. It is essential to prune the bushes very hard in the first year to

'Roseraie de l'Hay' and *right*, 'Queen Elizabeth' [JB/VP]

encourage basal growth for later years, when such hard pruning will not be possible. If formality is desired from some of the old-fashioned and species roses, traditional methods of pruning have to be abandoned in favour of shears; and since not all types take kindly to such treatment, the choice of variety is particularly important. Such clipped hedges can look very attractive, but these must be pruned very hard both in the first year and in the second year as well. Once the hedge is growing well, clipping can start but, if this is not timed correctly, flowering may be affected. Clipping should be practised after flowering so that the hedge has time to make growth for the following year. Throughout the rest of the summer it should only be necessary to remove extra vigorous or 'awkward' shoots as they appear. Only the 'once-flowering' varieties are suitable for treatment in this way. So if you require more from your hedge, such as autumn flowers and/or hips, then informality must be accepted. Planting distances for old-fashioned and species roses will depend on the variety but few will need to be closer than 24 in (60 cm) and most make satisfactory hedges planted 36 in (90 cm) apart.

Informal hedges

The scope of varieties for informal hedging is vast. In fact, almost any variety can be used for this purpose, depending upon the degree of informality required. Some of the Hybrid Musks, for example, make quite neat plants as hedgerows, whereas the Centifolias will form wide, impenetrable, untidy jungles. The secret of good informal rose hedges, no matter what the type, is, as already stressed, hard pruning in the first year and light clipping or tidying when the hedge is matured. Feeding, too, is important to keep them at their best.

Just a note of warning. Beware of misleading claims. All rose hedges need attention, perhaps more than some traditional hedging shrubs. Low-cost rose plants, advertised as unsurpassable, may prove a considerable disappointment. Some of those on offer are no more than simple understocks which, in spite of their apparent cheapness, are, in fact, sold at highly inflated prices.

N.B. Roses suitable for hedging are marked H in the Dictionary section.

Shrub roses and old-fashioned roses with water

Assuming that water, in some form, is present in the garden, there are usually roses that can be planted by or near to it. Roses, however, should not be planted in boggy areas, so if there is danger of frequent flooding from a natural water feature, they should be ruled out in favour of plants that enjoy high water tables.

It is possible to select several species roses to grow on the banks of

R. wichuraiana with water at Mannington Hall, Norfolk   [PB]

natural water features such as rivers, streams, ponds and lakes. I say
species deliberately, for with few exceptions it is better to use natural
plants in natural landscapes. Where water exists naturally in a garden
setting, its presence should be harnessed as a natural habitat for trees and
shrubs which grow in sympathy both to the water and its surroundings.
Where grassy banks or open spaces permit, a group of semi-pendulous
species roses drooping towards the water can be quite enchanting when
viewed from the opposite bank. Equally, if you can persuade a vigorous
climber such as *R. helenae*, or *R. filipes* 'Kiftsgate' to grow into overhanging
trees and cascade towards the water, the effect can be very rewarding.

Man-made lakes, moats and lily ponds can all accommodate the
quieter hybrids as well as species roses along their banks. Again, however,
shape and ultimate dimensions of the bushes relative to other plants
should provide the criteria rather than colour, important though this is.
Paradoxically, the smaller the water feature, the longer the list of suitable
roses. For stone or concrete ponds or small pools, perhaps with statuary,
stronger colours and the more upright-growing roses may be used. In
my opinion, though, any rose planted within 'reflection' distance of the
water, no matter how small the pool, should at least have a semi-pendulous
habit of growth; and any rose planted directly by the water's edge should
be pendulous.

N.B. Roses likely to look attractive in proximity to natural water are
marked with a ≋ in the Dictionary section.

Old roses in pots and tubs
for terraces and patios

Many gardens, especially those in towns, have paved areas suitable for pot-grown roses. Ideally, of course, roses are best grown directly into the ground, so it is a good idea, when designing such features, to make provision to accommodate the odd rose or two simply by leaving small, unpaved areas in strategic places, by surrounding a patch of soil with a low stone wall or even building double walls and filling the space between with soil. This last option will provide an admirable opportunity for growing shorter or cascading varieties; and space can usually be left unpaved, too, at the base of these walls for growing suitably selected roses. Patios and terraces, especially those close to the house, often look incomplete simply as extensions to living rooms. With a little care and thought they can also provide a 'lived in' part of the garden.

Roses are far happier in pots and tubs than many of us realize. The cultivation of these are discussed in a later chapter but the choice of suitable varieties is almost as important as the choice of receptacle in which they are to grow. Many garden centres offer a good choice of ornamental

'The Fairy' with water at The Garden of the Rose, St Albans [JB]

containers in all sizes. Rose bush and container should, however, be in sympathy with each other; thus, broad, dumpy roses are best accommodated in broad, dumpy pots, whereas slender, upright pots are best for taller, erect roses, or for pendulous, cascading varieties. Where space or walls permit, and a sufficiently large container can be provided, even climbing roses are feasible. These may never reach their full dimensions but, if properly looked after, can reach to the eaves of a two-storey house or be trained to cover the side wall of an average sized garage adequately. Climbers, suitably staked, can also be grown in good-sized tubs as small pillar roses. Patios and terraces, especially in modern and town gardens, are often designed on fairly formal lines, as are rooftop gardens, and for these standard shrub roses in square, wooden tubs are most effective.

N.B. Roses recommended for growing in pots are marked with ▽ in the Dictionary section.

Climbing roses for pergolas, trellises, pillars and arches

Read any gardening book from the Victorian or Edwardian era and it will be noticed immediately that a variety of structures were used as props for their roses. These came in a wide range of building materials. Brick

'Gruss an Aachen' growing in a pot and *right:* Flowers and plant of 'Cupid'   [RCB] [TW/VP]

piers were highly favoured, elaborately designed wrought-iron was popular for arches and railings, sophisticated timber structures were used as pergolas, gazebos and trellises. In those days, of course, labour was plentiful and materials relatively inexpensive. To indulge in such things today would be costly. Of course these are not always to our modern taste and structures of this nature are scarcely ever built today. Perhaps we have become frugal in our attitudes in this direction, open-plan gardens, lawns and the inevitable curved shrubbery being the vogue, with plants acting their part upon this stage without support or other props.

Leaving aside the capital and maintenance costs, all sorts of structures can be built quite easily with rustic poles, and provided the main posts are substantial, these can last for many years. Indeed, they can be designed and built to suit almost any type of garden. Most timber for this purpose comes from the thinning of plantations and woodlands. Spruce and larch are by far the most common. Birch can look attractive though it lasts less well than other species. Of the hardwoods, ash is particularly good. The cost of such posts and poles will depend on what is locally available, but in comparison with prepared timber, it is never expensive. It is best bought ready-treated under pressure with preservatives, thus giving the timber longer life.

For those seeking a more formal structure, rough-sawn timber is the least expensive of the prepared materials and should likewise be ready-treated with preservative. Upright poles or posts should be a minimum

'Dorothy Perkins' and *right:* 'Albertine'   [PB/PB]

thickness of 4 in (10 cm) and should always be sunk at least 2 ft (60 cm) into the ground. Rails and cross-members can be thinner than this but not less than 2 in (5 cm). Since the principal purpose of such structures is to provide support for climbing roses which will eventually cover them almost completely, the pattern created by the criss-crossing timber need not – unless so desired – be very elaborate. What is important, in order

American Pillar at the Garden of the Rose, St Albans [JB]

to ensure long life, is the quantity and quality of the upright poles placed in the ground. The spacing of these poles is therefore crucial. The best rustic trellis has uprights placed at about 6 ft (1.8 m) intervals. Rustic arches should be well anchored in the soil at each corner upright.

A more simple form of support for climbers and ramblers is post and wire. Posts can be set, say 10 ft (3 m), with straining wire stretched across at approximately 12 in (30 cm) vertical intervals. Remember that the roses, when fully grown, will be of considerable weight and the wire used must be of sufficient thickness to support them. All end or corner posts should have additional straining posts to enable the wire to be stretched tightly.

Although they will eventually hold one another upright, posts for pillar roses should be placed at least 2 ft (60 cm) into the ground.

Tripods are an excellent means of giving support to some of the more awkward, old shrub roses, and make it possible to use climbers and ramblers within a shrubbery to good effect. Such tripods can be of any size, and indeed built with specific roses in mind; three posts of rustic timber are simply placed in 'wigwam' fashion and secured at the top with wire.

The possibilities using rustic timber are unending and, with a little time and thought, structures built from it can provide the opportunity to grow a range of climbers and ramblers which, in many gardens, would be impossible.

Roses on supports. *Left:* 'Amy Robsart', *right:* R. *foetida*   [PB/VP]

'Vanity' on a flint wall   [PB]

Roses on walls and fencing panels
and for northerly aspects

Walls and fencing come in all shapes and sizes but the one thing they have in common is the provision for a third dimension to gardening. All the best gardens I know possess walls that are well-clothed with a variety of climbing plants. Some walls may be worth admiring for their own sake, but many are not, and these could be considerably improved, even if only partially covered with plants. Builders and architects will throw up their hands in horror, but walls should be used for more purposes than that of 'retaining space'. We adorn interiors, why not exteriors? I agree that some of the most pernicious such as the more rampant species of Ivy and Virginia Creeper can play havoc with guttering, get under tiles and spoil the face of bricks. With few exceptions, however, no such charge can be levelled at the rose. In any case, modern building materials are far more impervious to damage from plants than were their older counterparts and few buildings less than a century old can be seriously damaged by climbing plants of any type. More care should be taken, of course, on buildings of very soft brick, clay-lump, sandstone or timber. It boils down to common sense.

Climbing roses, if grown on walls, will need support. The commonest method is to use wire fixed to the wall by special nails with clips, or screws with eyes, which can be bought especially for this purpose. On soft walls, these are best held in with the aid of wooden plugs which, when placed into pre-drilled holes, expand when the nail or screw is driven in. Wires should be stretched parallel to the ground at 12 inch (30 cm) intervals. Each wire should be held an inch or so (2.5 cm) from the wall by placing the special nails or screws approximately every 3 ft (90 cm) along its length. As the climbers grow, the main shoots can be fixed to the wire, training some shoots along and others upwards; the more twists and turns the better. The shoots are usually quite pliable and a dense covering can be achieved by this means. A soft twine should be used for fixing the shoots, otherwise they can be strangled as they grow. Another method of training climbers to walls is to fix an adequately sized piece of trellis about an inch (2.5 cm) away from the wall and to train the rose as it grows, as already described. This method is probably more suitable for modern buildings since trellis can look rather out of place on an older house. Walls facing east and west, blessed with a minimum of four to six hours of sunshine daily, are probably the best for climbing roses. Roses can also be grown on south-facing walls but there temperatures can get extremely high and, unless they are well-nourished and kept watered, they will have difficulty giving of their best in high summer.

The north wall is the problem wall and, I may add, not just for roses. Few worthwhile plants enjoy such a situation. Most roses will grow on such a wall but only a few will flower to their full potential. Because they show up better Nature has decreed that the best of these will be white or cream in colour. The additional problem with a north wall and, to a lesser extent, the east wall, is hardiness. So this restricts the choice even further.

Recent years have seen the rise to prominence of the fencing panel or close-board fence, which springs up everywhere when new developments take place. Before condemning this phenomenon, it is worth asking what could be used in its place at comparable cost. Hedges, perhaps, but that is another argument. At the cost of a few strands of wire and a few nails such panels can make admirable supports for the less vigorous climbers which, when fully grown, will themselves help support the fence.

N.B. Climbing roses for colder, northerly aspects are marked with an N in the Dictionary section. Those that are shade tolerant are marked ◍.

Climbing roses for trees

When I was a child, our garden was relatively devoid of roses, but being fairly old, it was well-populated with ancient apple trees, none of which had any real character and all were rather out of condition. Their names were not known, except for one which my grandfather called a 'snout' I know not why, except that when the tree deigned to produce apples, each had a nose-shaped protrusion at the stalk end. Year after year these trees produced varying quantities of fruit most of which was blown down by

'Kiftsgate' at Lime Kiln, Claydon, Suffolk and *below*: showing its hips and autumn foliage   [PB][VP/PB]

the wind to rot on the ground. Few were edible and, apart from making strong cider which I was never allowed to sample officially, they had little real use. The point of this somewhat sudden deviation is to contemplate how many other such trees, of dubious purpose, exist throughout the world. All could be put to the admirable use of supporting a climbing rose. I am against growing roses up into trees which, in themselves, have character but many country gardens have trees which could well be improved in partnership with a rose; and not just trees, some rather boring stretches of hedgerow, attractive only for their bird population, could well be enhanced by the addition of a few well chosen vigorous climbing species.

Not all the vigorous, climbing roses are suitable for this purpose of course but many are, and many more could be. Nature has her own way, she does not provide for growing and flowering at the same time; thus, without exception, all the vigorous tree-climbing roses flower only once each season. Some, though, do have good autumn foliage and produce abundant hips to give colour later. As with the climbers for north walls, the most suitable, with one or two exceptions, are white, cream or yellow in colour. Size of tree should not present a problem since some of the very vigorous climbers can reach thirty feet (9 m) with ease, although it will take a number of years for these to flower very freely; probably because, until their heads appear above the branches, they are growing in relative shade.

Dead tree trunks, and trees which are past their best, can also make ideal supports for less vigorous ramblers and climbers. Even unsightly trees, perhaps awkward to remove, can become more congenial if supporting a rose.

It is best to plant these roses a little distance, about 2 ft (60 cm), from the trunk on the side of the tree with most light giving them a helping hand initially with string or wire, until they can scramble their own way up, through the branches. Bear in mind that being vigorous, they need to make big roots. If soil is poor, as so often under trees, give them a good

'Rambling Rector' and *right*: growing in a tree at Castle Howard, Yorkshire   [PB/VP]

start by adding a pocket of good soil at planting time and apply plenty of water at the height of summer.

N.B. Roses suitable for tree-climbing are marked with a T in the Dictionary section.

Procumbent and Semi-procumbent Roses

As already mentioned, I wish to avoid the term 'ground-cover roses'. This can be misleading and wrongly equates these roses with plants better described as such. Certainly there are several shrub roses and species roses which grow broader than tall and some that prefer simply to creep along the ground, but none, to my knowledge, that do ground-cover work by excluding light and suppressing weeds in the same manner as prostrate evergreen shrubs and conifers. Nevertheless, prostrate and semi-prostrate roses will, if planted fairly close together, form impenetrable mounds over large areas of ground, so reducing maintenance to the minimum, and provide an effective display in the process. Breeders now realize the potential of such roses and are working hard to enlarge the range.

A use can be found for these roses almost anywhere where spread rather than height is an advantage – as among other shrubs, to hide a manhole cover or to camouflage, if not conceal unsightly tree stumps. Some, if

Procumbent roses at the Garden of the Rose, St Albans   [RCB]

chosen with care and given space, can even be used effectively and attractively in large rockeries.

N.B. Procumbent roses suitable as ground-creepers are marked with G in the Dictionary section.

Above and right: R. paulii with its autumn foliage

[VP/PB]

'Frau Dagmar Hartopp'

[VP]

An informal arrangement of old roses

[PB]

Old roses for flower arranging

Devotees of flower arranging will not need telling that old roses make ideal subjects for their art; nor will they need reminding that these roses are amongst the most difficult flowers to arrange.

My own experience of arranging such roses extends only to their use in fairly large numbers on our trade stands at flower shows, not to the intricacies of floral art, so I have no intention of stepping into this province. I know that many people enjoy arranging flowers more for simple pleasure than from any artistic aspirations. Old-fashioned roses, in almost any context, make ideal companions in the home, the range of their colours, shapes and flower formation being adaptable to vases of all types, from the single rose on the dressing table to the large pedestal in the hall.

Two or three carefully chosen bushes, growing in even the smallest garden, can usually provide enough flowers for taking indoors without any detriment to the outdoor display; and their scent will pervade the entire house, rivalling both sweet peas and ten-week stocks.

The problem with old roses as cut flowers is their relatively short life. To get the best from them they should be placed up to their necks in fresh clean water immediately after picking and left, preferably overnight, but certainly for two or three hours, before they are arranged. Being woody subjects, it is also an advantage to remove some of their lower leaves and thorns and to crush or slit the bottom of the stem to help them take up water. For our exhibition work we use a substance in the water which, if it does not keep them fresh, helps arrest premature petal-fall. I have heard that aspirin or even sugar will have the same effect. An old lady with a stall at our local flower market swears by a pint of lemonade in a bucket of water to keep her roses fresh.

Old roses are better displayed by themselves, but this is a matter of taste. Some species and varieties have very attractive foliage which can be used effectively with other flowers, as can their hips in the autumn.

Most of the double old-fashioned roses will need to be picked at the almost-open stage, for few will open indoors from the tight-bud stage. To give of their best, old roses need at least one-third of their stem in water at all times. They will last longer in a dry atmosphere if their leaves are sprayed occasionally with clean water from a hand sprayer.

Old shrub roses under glass

Although the very old roses such as Centifolias, Damasks and Gallicas can be grown under glass, it does not really make much sense to do this, except for exhibition purposes. In such conditions their flowering season is further shortened and their ungainly growth habit becomes difficult to tame. However, there are a number of interesting old varieties, originating in warmer climes, notably the Teas and the Chinas, which can be very rewarding when grown in this way. No extra heat is necessary. Roses are quite happy in cold greenhouses where they will flower from early May onwards. Those with larger greenhouses or conservatories can indulge themselves by growing one or two of the more tender but very beautiful climbing Teas and Noisettes, like vines on wires, about 12 in (30 cm) inside the glass. This method was often used by Victorian gardeners, for in addition to providing early flowers, the foliage provided shade for other plants growing in the conservatory in high summer.

The older Tea roses, apart from those which grow happily out of doors, actually prefer the protected environment and can give much pleasure even in the smallest of greenhouses. They are best grown in 10 in (25 cm) pots which make them sufficiently portable to move around. In fact, they are probably better after flowering from late spring inside, spending the summer out of doors.

Treatment is much the same as for outdoor roses except that the demands of early flowering will need consideration when feeding, and watering will be necessary every day as they start to grow. Pruning, too – which in the case of Teas should be sparing – is essential, otherwise, in such an environment, they will soon become 'leggy'.

N.B. Roses which grow and flower particularly well under glass are marked Gh in the Dictionary section.

Above: 'Dr Grill' [PB]
Below: 'Devoniensis' [PB]

'Fritz Nobis' growing under glass [PB]

Old roses for their hips

Whatever may be said by the critics of old and shrub roses, the faculty of some to produce ornamental hips is one attribute which cannot be denied. Such is their attraction that several varieties are well worth growing for their hips alone. In some cases the fruits far excel the flowers. Most of the species bear some form of fruit, varying in shape from plump and round to long and slender, and ranging in colour from bright orange to deep purple and black. They may be highly polished, or bristly. Some are borne erect, others pendulously; and many – presumably those that taste bitter to birds – last well into winter to brighten an otherwise dull time of year.

Whilst species are the main fruit bearers, some hybrids better known for their flowers also bear hips. 'Scharlachglut' for example, produces huge, urn-shaped fruit of rich scarlet and 'Mme Gregoire Stacehelin', a beautiful climbing rose, will produce a good crop of large hips in a good summer.

N.B. Roses which produce a good crop of ornamental fruit are marked F in the Dictionary section.

R. glauca (R. rubrifolia)

[VP]

Roses for their ornamental foliage

Although autumn colouration is not, as a rule, a major feature of shrub and old-fashioned roses, it is sufficiently important to be taken into account when planning a garden. Several species, and indeed hybrids, display richly toned foliage which will harmonize pleasingly with other trees and shrubs at the end of summer. Amongst these are most of the better known varieties of the Rugosas whose leaves change with the shortening days to mustard tints deepening to russet before falling early in winter. 'Roseraie de l'Hay' is a particularly good example of these.

The small, almost fern-like foliage of the Burnet roses, *R. pimpinellifolia* and its hybrids change to russety-red which adds further to the attraction of their black hips. Outstanding, especially after a dry, hot summer with a display of rich coppery-red are the thornless Boursault climbing roses; of this group 'Morletti' is particularly striking. As mentioned earlier, most of the American native species are conspicuous for their autumn display. *R. virginiana* is perhaps the best example, its naturally shiny leaves changing to burnished-gold before the early frosts of winter persuade them, inevitably, to fall.

Autumn colour in roses is, of course, a bonus yet a wide gamut of colours can be found both in foliage and stems throughout the flowering season. Variations though often subtle range from the bright rich green of *R. banksiae*, the greys of *R. brunonii* 'La Mortola' and the Albas such as 'Celestial' and 'Maiden's Blush' to the rich plum colouring of *R. glauca* better known erroneously as *R. rubrifolia*, not to mention the Moss roses with their distinctive, variably toned, mossy stems and such hybrids as the lovely 'Albertine' with its rich bronzy-red young shoots and leaflets.

Many of the species have vicious thorns, a problem when attempting to prune, but even these can be an additionally attractive, ornamental feature. Such a useful species, often planted specifically for the ornamental value of its thorns is *R. sericea pteracantha* whose young stems, in common with others of its group, are covered with broad, wedge-shaped, cherry-red, translucent thorns which when mature become an almost impenetrable armour and give considerable character to what would otherwise be a rather dull shrub in winter. Another interesting shrub, this time for its dense population of tiny thorns is *R. farreri persetosa* 'The threepenny bit rose'; after it drops its numerous small ferny leaves in winter, this semi-procumbent shrub becomes a tawny-coloured thicket of arching, hairy branches, enhanced even more by hoar frost on a winter's day.

N.B. Old-fashioned and shrub roses with colourful autumn foliage are marked with an A in the Directory section.

Hips of *R. jundzillii* (*top left*), *R. pisocarpa* (*top right*),
R. setipoda (*centre right*), and 'Scharlachglut', with
autumn foliage of a Gallica rose

[VP]

Autumn foliage of 'Mme Louis Lévêque'
and *below:* of 'Morletti' and *R. × kochiana*

[PB]
[VP/VP]

R. sericea pteracantha with its translucent thorns and
right: 'Anna Pavlova'

[PB/PB]

Roses and their perfume

The principal attribute that distinguishes the old roses from modern counterparts is their fragrance. This is not to say that modern roses are not fragrant. In fact, more perfumed roses are probably being introduced than ever before; 'Anna Pavlova' for example, a recent introduction, has a stronger perfume than any other rose I know. Scent, of course, being intangible, can only be evaluated subjectively, and perfume manufacturers would be out of business if this were not so. I happen to think that quality is more important than quantity, and that for sheer beauty of fragrance the old roses still have the edge.

The variations of scent are of course fascinating. The heady, all pervading, almost intoxicating perfume of the Centifolias is in no way similar to the refined elegance of that of the Albas; the spicy, somewhat lingering perfume exuded by the Damasks differs completely from the softer, more delicate fragrance of the Gallicas. Fragrance is not confined to flowers; foliage too can be scented. *R. primula* for example has leaves that smell distinctly of incense and many of the Mosses exude the strong odour of balsam from their moss, especially when touched.

High on my list of favourite perfumes from roses is that of the Sweet Briar *R. eglanteria*. The scent comes from the foliage, especially the young foliage, after rain. Of all our senses smell is probably the most evocative.

My first job as an apprentice nurseryman was to weed a large patch of Sweet Briars and a whiff of its scent even now never fails to transport me back to that time.

Shrub and climbing roses as standards

Roses have been grown in this somewhat contrived way for many years, and it seems they have been quite popular throughout that time. I came across a delightful little snippet in *A Shilling Book of Roses* by William Paul, published in the 19th century:

> 'The late Colonel Calvert once told me that he was present at an auction sale of standard roses in London when the "Village Maid" Rose was first introduced. Twenty plants were sold at one Guinea each. When they came to be distributed only nineteen could be found. Two purchasers seized the nineteenth plant, fought over it and paid half a Guinea each to the Auctioneer as compensation for the mischief done'.

If nothing else, this should put the cost of a present-day standard rose into perspective.

Except for a few varieties of weeping standards very few old-fashioned roses are today grown in this way, for although such plants are technically feasible, demand is so low as to make them uneconomic for modern nurseries. A few shrub roses, however, do make excellent standards and by searching around or ordering early, it is still possible to obtain stocks of these. Their greatest asset is that they enable other plants to be grown underneath.

Standard roses are produced by budding two. or three buds at the top of a stem, usually of *R. rugosa*. Their height varies slightly from nursery to nursery, but the usual height for full standard shrub roses is four feet (1.2 m), with half-standards, when available, at about $2\frac{3}{4}$ ft (85 cm). The reason for the slight variation is interesting. Budders are usually people in a hurry who find it quite a chore to use a measuring rod, thus the relative height from the ground of parts of the body are often used for measuring the stems as they proceed along the rows, weeping standards at shoulder height, shrub standards at chest height, modern standards of Large-Flowered and Cluster-Flowered roses navel height and half-standards a little lower and so on.

With regard to half-standards, it has always baffled me why these are not more popular. Their relative height to other plants makes them much less ungainly. The cultivation and growing of weeping standard roses is discussed later in the book.

Old-fashioned roses, Species and Shrub roses which make ideal standards are as follows. For full descriptions see Dictionary section.

'Rose à Parfum de l'Hay' and
right: *R. primula* [PB/RCB]
Below: 'Meg Merrilees' and 'Excelsa' weeping
standard [JB/PB]

'Nozomi' grown as a weeping standard
Right: 'Alfred de Dalmas' in a mixed border   [PB]

Shrub roses as standards
'Ballerina', 'Marjory Fair', 'Canary Bird', 'Nozomi', 'The Fairy', 'White
Pet', 'Yvonne Rabier', 'Yesterday'.

Weeping standards
'Albéric Barbier', 'Albertine', 'Dorothy Perkins', 'Excelsa', 'Emily Grey',
'Félicité et Perpétue', 'François Juranville', 'Golden Glow', 'Minnehaha',
'Sanders White'.

Pegging down

It is sad, though understandable, that the practice of 'pegging-down' has
now largely died out as a means of getting the best from roses, for it is a
most effective and tidy way of persuading masses of flowers from otherwise ungainly and sometimes reluctant varieties. Nowadays, however,
the cost of this practice, where space might permit it, as in parks and large
gardens, would be prohibitive; furthermore, with the advent of newer
types of procumbent roses, such areas as lent themselves to pegged-down
roses can now be furnished with relative ease. Nevertheless, there are
still strong arguments for pegging, which comes into its own in herbaceous

and mixed borders, especially near the front of such borders when one bush, if pegged down correctly, can cover quite a large area among other short-growing plants at very little extra cost and effort. The mechanics are quite simple. In the first year, having pruned the roses hard at planting time, the shoots should be allowed to grow up naturally. In the second year, instead of pruning, train these shoots as near to parallel to the ground as possible and also in as many directions as they will permit, holding each shoot in position some 12 in (30 cm) from the ground by wire pegs. The ends of the shoots should be pruned off to an eye. Such training will encourage each parallel shoot to send up numerous vertical shoots, most of which will flower. At the end of each season, these shoots, having flowered, can be shortened and spurred, like fruit trees. In this way – especially if new, main shoots, as they appear, are trained into position to replace less productive older ones – the plants will go on flowering quite efficiently for many years.

The main problem encountered by this method of growing roses is weed control, but if the soil is initially clean and given a generous mulching of peat or bark chippings, any weed growth should be manageable.

Some of the Bourbons and Hybrid Perpetuals are almost custom-built for this purpose. In the past 'Frau Karl Druschki' and 'Hugh Dickson' were two great favourites for pegging-down, both fairly free-flowering and with long, strong shoots.

Companions for Old and Shrub Roses

Whether or not roses should be grown in association with other plants is a matter of some argument. As will by now be clear, my own opinion is that roses, admirable though they can be on their own in an enclosed area, should form part of the overall garden scheme. Sometimes roses should even play a minor role, enhancing rather than dominating the landscape. Conversely, where they are dominant, their presence can be enhanced by other plants in less commanding roles. In this sense, planning a garden is rather like casting a play.

In the formal setting, old-fashioned roses are often grown in beds separated by paths and lined with edging plants; such edging should be quite formal in habit and not too tall. In the 19th century, clipped dwarf box, *Buxus sempervirens suffruticosa*, was used extensively for this purpose, and this can still be effective in re-creating the atmosphere from that period, especially in conjunction with crazy-paved paths. Dwarf lavender *Lavendula* var 'Munstead' especially also makes a good natural edging to borders, but careful pruning is necessary to keep it in good condition. Catmint, *Nepeta mussinii*, with its lavender-blue flowers and grey foliage is the least expensive edging plant but looks bedraggled and dead in winter, unless clipped back each year. If allowed to do so, it will also over-reach into the rose bed. Other small, shrubby plants suitable for

Roses with mixed foliage plants at Castle Howard, Yorkshire   [PB]

edging are some of the varieties of dwarf hebes, not all of which are fully hardy, and *Santolina*, with grey foliage but yellow flowers, which needs careful placing. One of my particular favourites is *Berberis thunbergii atropurpurea nana*, with bronzy-red foliage, which looks particularly good with roses of most shades of pink.

It is in the more informal areas where shrubby plants can be combined with shrub and old-fashioned roses with some measure of abandon. A few combinations for shrubberies, worth consideration, are as follows:

Shrubs for use with white, pink and deep red roses

Berberis *thunbergii atropurpurea* and its various purple forms. Buddleia 'Royal Red', Caryopteris × *clandonensis*, Ceanothus, Ceratostigma *willmottianum*, Cistus × *crispus*, Daphne, Deutzia, Escallonia various, Fuchsias, Hebes – grey foliage varieties, Hydrangea *paniculata grandiflora*, Kolkwitzia, Lavender, Olearia *haastii*, Philadelphus, Pittosporum, Potentilla, Prunus *cistina*, Romneya *coulteri*, Rosemary, Vibernum × *burkwoodii*, and Weigela *florida foliis purpureis*.

Some perennial plants ideal with white, pink and deep red roses

Aquilegia, Artemisia, Astilbe – soft colours, Campanula – all varieties, Dianthus (pinks) most colours, Geranium – Cranes Bill types, Gypsophila, Hosta *fortunei*, Paeonia – especially the soft coloured varieties, Phlox – soft colours, Scabiosa, Sedum, Stachys.

Smaller trees suitable as a background for white, pink and deep red roses

Amelanchier, Arbutus *unedo*, Betula *purpurea*, Cercis *siliquastrum*, Eucalyptus *gunnii*, Fagus *purpurea pendula*, Malus (Crab Apple) 'Golden Hornet', 'John Downie' and *tschonoskii*, Morus *niger* (Black Mulberry), Populus *alba*, Prunus *pendula rosea*, Prunus 'Amanogawa', Pyrus *salicifolia* 'Pendula' (Willow-leafed Pear), Salix *caprea* and Salix *caprea pendula* (Pussy Willows), Sorbus *aria lutescens*, Sorbus *aucuparia* (Mountain Ash) and Stranvaesia *davidiana*.

Shrubs for use with bright red, orange and yellow roses

Berberis *thunbergii*, *candidula* and × *stenophylla*, Chimonanthus *praecox* and *fragrans*, Choisya *ternata*, Cornus *stolonifera* 'Flaviramea', Corylopsis *pauciflora*, Cytisus (Broom) – bright coloured varieties, Euonymus – variegated varieties, Genista – most varieties, Hypericum – most varieties, Ilex (holly) – variegated varieties, Ligustrum (privet) – variegated varieties, Mahonia – all varieties, Potentilla – most shrubby varieties, Pyracantha, Sambucus *nigra aurea* and Weigela *florida variegata*.

Perennials for use with bright red, orange and yellow roses

Alchemilla *mollis*, Alyssum *saxatile*, Euphorbia – various, Paeonia – brighter colours, Rudbeckia and Saxifraga (London Pride).

Small trees for use with bright red, orange and yellow roses

Acer *negundo* 'Variegatum', Acer *pseudoplatanus* 'Brilliantissimum', Acer *platanoides* 'Drummondii', Cotoneaster × *rothschildianus*, Cytisus *battandieri*, Liquidambar, Parrotia *persica*, Populus *candicans* 'Aurora', and Salix *alba* 'Chermesina'.

Mixed climbing roses

Many delightful combinations can be achieved by mixing climbing roses with other climbing plants. The scope for this is practically limitless and, provided care is taken to ensure the marriage will work much pleasure can be derived from experimenting with various combinations. If an interesting colour effect is desired, it is obviously important that all the plants will flower at the same time. Clematis (except the *montana* types, which are too vigorous) and roses flowering together are a superb combination, particularly white clematis with purple or dark red roses and vice-versa. Summer jasmine also combines well with purple roses.

Roses and daffodils at Albion House, Little Waltham, Essex   [RCB]

Roses with bulbs, corms etc.

Spring-flowering bulbs can always be used with shrub and old-fashioned roses, helping to give colour to rose borders at a time of year when roses are at their least interesting. Combining and blending colours is not so important with bulbs since they come into flower well before the roses. As a matter of personal taste, I prefer to keep tulips away from the old-fashioned roses, and to plant them in beds of Cluster-Flowered and Large-Flowered varieties; and even then I would only use the shorter growing varieties and some of the species. Daffodils and narcissi are quite at home among old roses, and clumps or groups of these go well among, underneath and alongside them. However, despite their different flowering seasons, I feel that species roses are best paid the compliment of being grown with the less flamboyant bulbs.

Other bulbous plants which make good bedfellows for the older roses are allium, camassia, chionodoxa, crocus, grape hyacinth, galtonia, puschkinia, scilla and snowdrop. Most lilies are happy growing with roses, but I sometimes find their upright stance slightly incongruous among the taller shrub roses and therefore feel that they should be planted in fairly large groups for best effect. Most lilies also prefer to keep their heads in the sun and feet in the shade, so this is a good reason to plant them with the shorter growing roses; and for the same reason I would exclude gladioli altogether, although the shorter growing montbretia can be effective. The tuberous rooted forms of anemone are happy growing in the partial or dappled shade of shrub roses, as are hardy cyclamen. Aconites, if naturalized, give a refreshing lift to a group of rather dull, dormant shrub roses in early spring. Both the bulbous and tuberous rooted iris flourish in most soils, and groups of these will grow harmoniously with shrub roses. All the above-mentioned flowers are, of course, suitable for growing beneath climbers and ramblers.

Annuals and biennials with roses

Annual bedding plants conjure up pictures of massed beds of brightly coloured salvias and french marigolds, but this need not be the case, for several of the annuals can combine well with old-fashioned roses if planted in random groups among the bushes. Petunias, clarkias, ten-week-stocks and, among the taller roses, nicotiana, all blend quite well especially if you can obtain the seed in specific colours. Old-fashioned roses grown in pots, especially those of paler shades, will not object to a few plants of lobelia and alyssum shading their roots and falling gently over the edge of their containers, nor will they object to the company of such upright plants as petunias.

Biennials, too, can look quite at home with old-fashioned roses, especially in cottage gardens where such flowers as hollyhocks, foxgloves, brompton stocks, aubretia, forget-me-nots, violets and pansies, all help to evoke a feeling of Victoriana.

Old-fashioned roses with herbs

Old-fashioned roses make superb companions for culinary herbs. When strategically placed in the herb garden such roses can add colour, height and scent to a visually rather drab area. Old roses have much in common with herbs, both historically and aesthetically, and a few well chosen varieties will help capture an atmosphere from the past.

Conversely, herbs placed in groups among old roses can look most effective and, at the same time, keep the kitchen well supplied throughout the year.

Fruit and vegetables with old roses

To consider growing fruit and vegetables among roses may seem contrary to all the laws of gardening; but when ground space is limited, and with careful choice of subjects, there is no reason why they should not be grown together. Beetroot, for example, has lush dark red foliage, and a few plants, either in clumps or at random, cannot look out of place; nor do clumps of purple broccoli, spinach or parsley. Marrows and ridge cucumbers, provided the soil is good and fertile, will happily crawl about the shrub rose border without causing offence, least of all to the roses; and the same goes for the odd clump of rhubarb, or bush of white currant, redcurrant and/or gooseberry. I would avoid blackcurrants because of their distinctive smell, but strawberries, especially the delicious alpine species, can make quite a cheerful and useful ground cover.

Wild flowers with old roses

I have already mentioned the use of species roses in the wild garden; conversely, wild flowers can make a most effective ground cover in which to plant both species and many of the less hybrid varieties of old roses. Wild flowers or even weeds, provided they are not too pernicious, would certainly be welcomed by such types of roses as the Gallicas, Centifolias and Damasks, although the more modern hybrids might well resent too many intrusions of this kind. Wild flowers can arrive naturally and be encouraged to spread by the removal only of those weeds that offend the eye, or which, at a later date, may infest other parts of the garden by their seeds or roots; in particular, couch grass, ground elder, bindweed, thistles, docks and fat hen. Alternatively, wild flowers can be introduced by the sowing of seed or, in some cases, planting; both may be obtained from specialist seedsmen or nurserymen. The list of suitable wild flowers is endless and, in any case, I do not know enough about them to be too specific. If you choose to introduce some wild flowers among your roses, do be sure to purchase your seed. It is not worth plundering our countryside for seed or plants. There are few enough left growing there.

PART III
The Cultivation of Roses

Buying and Planting Roses

Shrubs, old-fashioned and climbing roses fall roughly into three groups, as will soon be discovered when setting out to purchase them. Firstly, there is a nucleus of about twenty varieties which are available from most commercial rose growers and garden centres and therefore generally available. These may not necessarily be the best varieties but, generally speaking, they have been tried and tested and are likely to give good service in most gardens. The second group consists of about fifty to seventy varieties which are usually offered by most good commercial rose growers and by some of the better garden centres. The fact that a variety may be listed in several catalogues is in itself a good test of its popularity and hence its reliability. The third group of many hundreds of less common varieties are available only from specialist growers of old-fashioned roses. It must be remembered however, that although some of the established garden centres will take the trouble to find the rarer varieties, especially if you are buying in substantial quantities, they can hardly be expected to oblige in this way if requirements are very modest.

Roses are no exception to the adage 'you get what you pay for'; and unless buying from a specialist with a good reputation, it is wise to inspect the goods before purchase. There is no substitute for recommendation, so if gardening friends have bought satisfactorily from a particular firm, it would be wise to follow their example.

Virtually all the nurserymen of my acquaintance have chosen this profession because they enjoy it and hope to make a living from it. As businessmen, too, this tends to be their order of priorities and they feel, probably rightly, that their customers should have the same attitude, putting interest in their gardens ahead of commercial considerations. If buying shrub and old-fashioned roses from a local garden centre, inspect the goods before purchase. If buying from a specialist by mail order it is a good idea to become familiar with their stated terms of business before ordering. Roses take two years to produce and growers usually start sending out their orders at the beginning of the dormant season in mid-October. These are despatched in rotation, as received. So if orders are placed early, say May, June or July, bushes will usually arrive for November planting. Given the length of time needed to produce a rose bush, the grower's biggest headache is to forecast likely sales of each variety in advance. Not even a computer can get it right. Thus if rare and unusual varieties are required, order early in the season or be prepared to be put on a waiting list.

It is safe to plant rose bushes throughout the dormant season. Growers will usually send instructions with the order, and if upon opening the parcel there is reason to complain, this is the time to do so; do not wait to see how the rose gets on later in the growing season. If the weather is unsuitable for planting when the bushes arrive, find a spot where they can be 'heeled-in' (see page 100) until they can be planted; or if the weather is really terrible, with frost and snow, place the roots in a bucket or box, covering them with peat, soil or even damp sand, and store in a garage or suitable outbuilding until they can be heeled in when the weather improves. If none of these remedies can be adopted, simply leave them covered with a damp sack or old blanket in the garage until they can be handled properly. Never keep them in a centrally heated area for any length of time. They will think it is spring and start to shoot, or they may become dry and quickly dehydrate.

When buying roses, look for, and expect to receive, a rose of reasonable quality. They will normally be maiden plants, i.e. bushes with one year's growth behind them in the nursery. In the case of modern roses, bushes should have three or more shoots coming from the 'union' (where the roots and shoots join) or from the same axis-point above the roots; and as a rule this should apply to old-fashioned, shrub and climbing roses. Nevertheless, there are some varieties of these which are much more difficult to grow, at least in the nursery; consequently, no matter how good the nurseryman, it is impossible to produce plants with this number of shoots. Other varieties of shrub roses grow in a different way and tend to make more shoots as they reach maturity later in their life; these, too, will frequently have fewer than three main shoots. The criteria for judging quality tends to vary according to the type and variety you may have ordered. Look firstly at the size of the roots; there should be a well-developed main root and a number of fibrous, smaller roots. Look secondly at the condition of the shoots; the thickness and number of these will, of course, depend on the variety and type of rose.

One reason why some of the more beautiful older roses, especially the Teas and Hybrid Teas, are no longer widely grown by nurserymen is that as maiden plants they are smaller than their modern counterparts, and thus few attain the standard set for modern bush roses. An old 1920s or 1930s Hybrid Tea variety from a specialist will not only be more expensive but probably considerably smaller as a maiden plant. It is more costly because of its rarity and because it is more difficult to produce.

There are several other factors that govern the size of maiden roses, not least the type of understock on which they are grown. Consumer organizations in most countries issue guidelines to consumers and growers on the quality of roses and I do not wish, in any way, to imply that these guidelines are wrong. In compiling the above guide I have simply drawn on my own experience in the nursery trade and stated what, in my opinion, is the optimum quality old-fashioned, climbing or shrub rose that, given reasonably good soil and proper care, will develop into a good garden shrub.

Buying container grown roses

Roses can be bought, already flowering, in containers. They are naturally slightly more expensive than bare-root stock because of the extra work and material needed to produce them. Many garden centres offer a small range of shrub and old-fashioned roses in this form. Some people refuse to buy such roses and whereas I agree there is no substitute for traditional winter planting, container-grown roses are certainly here to stay and will become available in increasing numbers. Provided we learn to adapt to the new techniques of planting and aftercare, buying shrub roses in full flower can be a worthwhile and pleasant experience.

Suckers and understocks

A rose plant purchased from the nursery actually comprises two different roses, the roots being one species, usually *R. laxa* or *R. multiflora*, and the shoots another, i.e. the variety chosen. So when planted the root sometimes decides to become independent and send up a shoot of its own, this being known as a sucker. Since the roots are usually more vigorous than their enforced guest, the shoot or shoots, if allowed to grow, will eventually take over and smother the variety being cultivated. Suckers, when they appear, should be removed before they have a chance to grow to any size. Experience will enable a gardener to recognize them as slightly different from the young shoots which sprout from the stems above the ground, for suckers always appear from below ground level and often some little distance from the plant. It used to be said that shoots from the rootstock had leaves which were constructed of seven leaflets and that the leaves of the proper rose were made up of five. This has never been a very reliable guide to the recognition of suckers even on modern Hybrid roses and should be treated almost as an old wives' tale. It is even less true in the case of the species, old-fashioned shrub roses, climbers and ramblers, since many of them have the same number of leaflets per leaf as those of the rootstock. If doubtful, scrape a little soil away from the rose bush and try to find the original union of stock and scion. If the shoot is coming from below this point, then a sucker it is. Remove it at the

Above: Examples of a good quality and poor quality plant
Below: A badly planted rose with suckers

point where it joins the root; if cut higher up, even more suckers will be created in misplaced gratitude for pruning. Pulling suckers from the root is more effective than cutting them, especially when they are young. If this is not possible, a blunt instrument is sometimes more efficient in tearing the sucker from the root than a knife or secateurs. In days now gone, gardeners and rose-growers used a special tool called a 'spud' for removing suckers. Shaped like a miniature, blunt spade, it could be pushed into the soil close to the rose bush in a downward tearing fashion, thus eliminating any possibility of secondary growth.

Apart from removing suckers as and when they appear, the best remedy for their prevention is to ensure that the roses are planted sufficiently deep to cover the complete rootstock. Suckers sometimes grow from wounded roots, so avoid inflicting damage when hoeing or digging around roses.

The understock used in modern rose production is chosen according to the soil and to the experience of the nurseryman. *R. coriifolia froebelii*, commonly known as *R. laxa*, a strong rooting species which produces few suckers, is by far the most widely used today. The other one in common use is *R. multiflora*, with a vigorous root system. The common Dog Rose, *R. canina*, has now largely disappeared as an understock; a blessing both to nurserymen and to gardeners, for it was very prone to suckering. Standard roses are usually grown on *R. rugosa* stems, largely because they are the

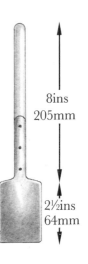

8ins
205mm

2½ins
64mm

easiest type to grow straight and firm. These can send up both root and stem suckers especially in their early years after transplanting, and a wary eye should be kept open for these as the plants grow.

Heeling-in

The term 'heeling-in' simply means the digging of a trench large enough to accommodate the roots of roses so as to retain them temporarily in good condition until they can be planted in their permanent position. Place the bushes in the trench about 3–6 in (7.5–15 cm) apart and replace the soil to cover the roots, firming with the heel. They can remain here until the weather is right for planting. Roses will keep this way for weeks, even months, and many nurserymen do it as a temporary measure. It is not necessary to place the bushes vertically as for planting; they will be quite happy at an angle of 45°, which helps to prevent them being blown about in strong wind. It is important when heeling-in to ensure that the union, or junction of roots and shoots, is about 2 in (5 cm) below ground level. This will further help to avoid wind-rock and will ensure, if the weather is really severe, that the union is well protected from frost. Roses are very hardy plants and usually quite difficult to kill, unless maltreated. The two best ways to kill them before planting is by allowing the roots to become frosted while they are out of the ground and, especially when planting in spring, exposing them to drying winds with their roots unprotected. In extreme climates, such as North America, only the hardiest roses will survive outside during the winter months and it may be necessary to protect them by earthing them up, or insulating the roots. Once a bush starts to lose its moisture, it is very difficult to arrest dehydration, a condition which quickly results in the death of the plant.

Planting roses

The most common reason for the failure of new roses is bad planting. Planting should not be a difficult task, but it is of prime importance to do the job well. The only implement needed is a good, clean spade. Gloves, too, are essential to give protection against thorns. Other requirements are a supply of bonemeal in a bucket or bag and some damp peat in a wheelbarrow. If several roses are to be planted, keep them covered with sacking or polythene until the holes are dug. Ideally, soil should have been prepared well ahead of planting If well-rotted farmyard manure or mature compost can be incorporated into the soil before planting, so much the better. Roses tend to do rather better in slightly acid soils and have a definite preference for clay. It is a good idea, in very acid soils, to spread an ounce or two of lime over the ground after planting. Obviously, performances will vary. They will grow in all types of soil, and in the last resort are as good as their gardener.

Planting bush, shrub and old-fashioned roses

Holes should be large enough to take the root of each plant without cramping; about one spade's depth is usually enough. A couple of good, open handfuls of damp peat should be sprinkled into the bottom of each hole, together with a closed handful of bonemeal, then with the spade, mixed thoroughly with the soil at the bottom of the hole. Scatter another closed handful of bonemeal on the heap of soil which is to go back into the hole, together with a couple more handfuls of damp peat, and partially mix. Alternatively, of course, mix the bonemeal and peat in a bucket or wheelbarrow before starting the operation. Having prepared the hole, the rose should be stood in the centre, ensuring that the roots are well spread out; enough soil is then placed around the roots to hold it in an upright position, thus enabling more soil to be added with both hands on the spade. When half the soil has been replaced, the bush should be given a little shake to ensure that soil falls between the roots, then tread the soil with the feet, firmly enough to hold the rose tight but not so firm as to compact the soil. The lighter the soil the more heavily it will need to be pressed or trodden. With the rose standing upright in the hole, replace the rest of the soil, leaving the last half-spadeful for a tilth around the rose after treading again with the feet. Having made sure that the label is firmly attached, tidy up any footprints and leave the rose to settle in. If the rose has been planted in the autumn or winter, it may need a light retreading a few weeks later or in the spring before it starts to grow.

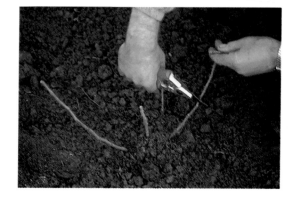

Planting and pruning a new rose

Depth of planting

When planted the union should end up about 1 in (2.5 cm) below the surface, so that when planting is complete, the shoots appear to come from below soil level. Depth of planting is important for at least four good reasons. Firstly, it keeps the rose anchored against undue wind-rock; secondly, it helps reduce the incidence of suckering; thirdly, the plant, if so inclined, can make its own roots independently of its root stock; and fourthly, especially in the case of the more tender roses such as the Teas and the Noisettes, the vulnerable union is protected against very severe frost. I am convinced that planting deeply helped save several of my plants from total extinction during the particularly bad winters of 1981-2 and 1984-5.

Large-Flowered and Cluster-Flowered roses

are usually planted between 18 in (45 cm) and 24 in (60 cm) apart, but all except the smallest shrub roses need more space than this, and judgement of planting distances depends on their ultimate size. If several roses are to be planted in the same border or bed, or planted to a prepared plan, it is best to mark out their positions first, with canes.

Planting specimen roses in grass

When planting specimen roses in lawns or shrub roses in grass, it is important to leave an ample circle of soil around the bush. Roses do not like the competition of tall uncut grass, especially in their early years; and apart from looking untidy, it is difficult to remove from around an established plant and makes mowing difficult.

Planting climbing roses

Adopt the same method for planting climbing roses, but when these are to grow on walls, remember that the soil is often poorer near the house or building and that a little extra organic material will be needed at planting time. Newly planted climbing roses are often the first to suffer from drought, since they have extra foliage to support. Frequently, too, they miss out on some of the rain, especially those on south-facing walls or fences. If planning to plant on pillars or tripods, the structure should be erected in advance of planting, so ensuring that the roots are not disturbed as the holes are dug for the posts.

Planting and staking standard roses

For standard shrub roses and weepers, stout, tall stakes should be positioned in advance of planting and inserted at 18 in (45 cm) into the ground. At least two rose tree ties will be needed to fix the stem to the stake. For weeping standards, which are sometimes 5 ft (1.5 m) tall, three ties may be necessary. Stakes of course usually have a shorter life than the standard rose itself so, at some point in its life, it will need restaking. Provision for this can be made at planting time by placing a drain pipe,

of sufficient size to take the stake, vertically into the ground to the correct depth and placing the stake into this before planting the rose. This will enable the replacement of stakes to take place later without too much disturbance to the soil surrounding the roots. Should a dry or hot spell of weather arrive during the first season, or indeed in succeeding seasons, the rose will need water. The fact that it is deep-rooted and does not show obvious signs of suffering is no reason for neglecting its thirst.

Specific replant disease

Roses hate 'stepping into other people's shoes'. This is because of a soil condition known as 'rose sickness'. The soil apparently becomes contaminated by chemical secretions from the rose roots, which newly planted bushes find offensive. Such a condition, called 'specific replant disease', manifests itself in stunted, rather reluctant bushes that never develop satisfactorily, no matter how well they are tended. It is for this reason that commercial rose producers never grow successive crops of roses on the same land without at least a two-year break between each crop. Therefore, if planning to plant roses where other roses have been growing, first change the soil. This is very important and should not present much of a problem. It is simply a matter of the juxta-positioning of two lots of soil, one, say, from the vegetable garden or from any spot where the soil is good and has not previously grown roses, and the other from the site of the old rose, i.e. where the new rose is to be planted. There are no short cuts; soil must be changed even if you are replacing a young bush. If this is not possible, old bushes should be removed and the soil in which they were growing rested for a period of at least twelve months before new bushes are planted. The vacant plot can, of course, be used for another catch crop, such as vegetables or bedding plants whilst resting from roses.

Planting roses into pots

In an earlier chapter I discussed the growing of roses in pots, tubs and urns; so it is worth describing how these should be planted. Whatever the type of rose, a good, large container is important. Free drainage is essential, so in addition to drainage holes, shingle or broken bricks should be placed in the bottom of the container. A thin layer of coarse, damp peat should be placed over the drainage material, followed by John Innes Potting Compost No. 3. If this is dry, dampen it slightly before use, since once in situ it is much more difficult to moisten thoroughly. The peat layer over the drainage material is to stop the soil sifting through and blocking the drainage holes. The container should be filled to about 2 in (5 cm) from the top to allow watering without spilling both water and soil over the edge. The rose should be planted deep enough for the shoots to appear to come from below the soil surface. If a wooden container is used, its life can be prolonged by lining the inside with thick polythene before filling with soil, remembering to allow sufficient drainage holes in the bottom. If the roses are already in containers or pots the latter should be removed before planting, taking care not to disturb the ball of soil around the roots. This will be easier if the container is well soaked beforehand. Most containerized roses are not really set sufficiently deep in their pots, so they will require transplanting much more deeply when placed in their permanent position. For several weeks after planting they will sustain themselves from the ball of soil in which they have been growing and, until they start making additional roots, will need liberal and frequent watering. Like all pot plants, roses grown in containers will need repotting from time to time. This should be done only in the dormant season, and some of the existing soil should be retained around the roots, especially in the case of older plants.

Soils for roses

Roses, by and large, prefer clay-based loam, but this is not a luxury enjoyed by all gardeners, and it is possible to grow roses on most types of fertile soil. Some species and varieties will – if

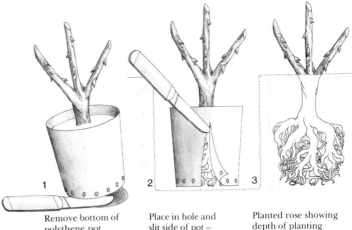

1 Remove bottom of polythene pot

2 Place in hole and slit side of pot – remove polythene

3 Planted rose showing depth of planting

Planting container-grown roses

not thrive – adapt happily even to the poorest soils. Whatever the soil, however, there are a few basic conditions to observe if they are to thrive. Good drainage is very important. With the exception of one or two species, such as *R. nitida* and *R. palustris*, roses detest having to stand for too long with their feet in water. Therefore, although they enjoy moisture, if the soil is waterlogged through bad drainage, it is better to correct this by incorporating drains before planting. Roses prefer slightly acid-to-neutral soils spanning the 6 to 6.5 pH range; if soil is more alkaline, this is not a disaster. Many varieties of old-fashioned roses will tolerate chalk, especially if they can be given a good start by planting them in a pocket of imported neutral soil amply laced with peat. By the time the lime content has risen to that around it, the rose will be settled, and although it may not exactly romp away, it will make quite a worthwhile shrub where many of the more hybrid roses will struggle. Conversely if your soil is very acid, a dressing of an ounce or two of lime at planting time and in succeeding springs will be beneficial.

Pruning

No subject provokes more friendly disagreement among my gardening friends than that of pruning. So, relating some of my experience in this controversial area, will, I am sure, cause some eyebrows to be raised among those who hold other opinions.

I recall an occasion, when as a very young man, having just been taught to prune, seeing a neighbour pruning his roses with shears, I remarked precociously that if he wished I would teach him how to prune his roses correctly. He simply carried on snipping and replied, 'I am doing them the way I've always done them and my roses have always been the best in the village.' My pride being somewhat hurt, I let the matter rest; but for years afterwards I always felt a pang of embarrassment when passing his garden in summer, for indeed he did have the best roses for miles around. I am not advising people to prune their roses with garden shears, but it is worth remembering that pruning roses is not an exact science and there are many valid arguments as to how and when it should be done.

The two most important aids to good pruning are firstly as with planting, a strong pair of

A newly planted rose correctly pruned

gloves and secondly a good pair of secateurs. Gloves come in all types but only the strongest will protect hands from some of the more vicious shrub roses, and give the confidence to prune positively. Modern secateurs are well-made, precision instruments and it is important to choose only the best. These should have a good, clean cutting edge and a design that provides maximum cutting action with a mini-

mum of effort. For older, more mature shrub roses and climbers, a pair of long-handled pruners, suitable for operating with both hands will also be needed.

Having said this, if a decision is made to prune, there are two golden rules which apply to all roses, both ancient and modern, be they climbers or shrubs. The first is that no matter what size plants received from the nursery, they should always be pruned very hard after planting. No matter how great the temptation to leave them unpruned or to treat them lightly, adopt the maxim of 'being cruel to be kind', this sometimes applies, too, to pruning in later years.

The reason for such treatment is to encourage all new shoots to grow from the base, or near to the base of the young bushes. If left unpruned or pruned lightly, the first season's growth will start from the top end of the plant and it will be difficult to induce basal growth in succeeding years.

The second golden rule is to prune at the correct time. In most parts of the British Isles this will be in late February or early March. If they are pruned much earlier than this, there is a danger of frost damage to exposed tissue, especially in the top 2–3 in (5–7.5 cm) of the pruned shoots. If pruned later, it will mean removing lots of young shoots, made by the bush as it responds to the first flush of spring. These rules apply, of course, to roses growing for general garden purposes. Gardeners endeavouring to produce roses for exhibition or wishing to time their blooms for a specific event, may well wish to choose other times for pruning, but this is outside the scope of this book.

Pruning once-flowering roses

Pruning can undoubtedly benefit some shrub roses but it must be stressed that others are best left unpruned, except on a general maintenance basis. It is often far more difficult to decide whether or not to prune than how to prune. When in doubt, the best policy to adopt for the vast majority of old-fashioned and shrub roses is, do nothing. I believe that many of the older roses, such as Albas, Centifolias, Damasks and

Gallicas, are best pruned in summer after flowering. This enables them to refurbish themselves with flowering wood during the same season and give a better display the following year. To prune these roses, remove any dead or diseased wood and any weak shoots that look incapable of supporting flowers the following season. Get rid, too, of any shoots that are chafing or rubbing one another, and thin out overcrowded areas likely to give the plant a leggy appearance. Care should be taken, however, not to destroy the general character of the shrubs. Furthermore, try not to overdo the summer pruning, since this will result in much loss of sap, and the plants will not recover in time to make growth for the following year. If severe treatment is necessary, this should be done in the dormant season.

The Species roses, Burnets and Sweet Briars are, by and large, best left to develop their own personalities until they risk getting out of hand, when it does no harm to prune them fairly hard to keep them within bounds.

Pruning shrub roses

The Portlands are usually repeat or continuous flowering, an attribute which in my opinion is positively encouraged if they are pruned whilst dormant each season and deadheaded in summer when necessary.

Except in the largest gardens where they can be given their heads, Hybrid Musks, Bourbons and Hybrid Perpetuals are best pruned every winter. If done sensibly, this will keep them replenished with young shoots and stop them becoming leggy and unkempt. I also believe that intelligent, moderate pruning will help prolong their life. Prune them in February by removing all superfluous shoots, i.e. those too thin to support many flowers. Remove, too, any wood that is overcrowding the shrub, usually from the centre of the bush; and reduce the length of some of the main shoots by one-third, so as to encourage early flowers. The remaining shoots can be reduced by up to two-thirds or more; these will not only produce flowers but usually provide the foundation for strong growth and replacement wood for future seasons.

Whether grown as a hedge or as individual specimens, Rugosa roses should only be pruned lightly to keep the hedge or shrub in shape. For the first year, of course, they need to be pruned hard. But should they get out of hand in later years they will tolerate harsh pruning and easily recover. The Chinas and older Hybrid Teas should be pruned in the same way as modern roses by removing twiggy, thin or dead wood, and cutting back the stronger shoots to about one-third of their length each year, aiming if possible to encourage basal growth. Tea roses prefer to be pruned more sparingly; they need to be pruned, of course, in order to keep them in shape, and to prevent them developing too much old unproductive wood, but not pruned for pruning sake.

Pruning climbing roses and ramblers

Climbing roses fall roughly into two categories, those that flower on wood produced in the same year and those that flower on wood produced in the previous year. In the first category are the Noisettes, especially the larger flowering varieties, the climbing Hybrid Teas, climbing Teas and the Hybrid Perpetuals; these flower on lateral growths and at the same time send up long, strong shoots. They need help and support to be effective as wall plants, especially in their early years. The dual object, therefore, in pruning these types of climbing roses is to encourage ample climbing shoots and to persuade those shoots to produce as many flowers as possible by the development of laterals from the stems. Thus, the method of pruning climbers alters somewhat as the plant ages and settles into its chosen position. Over the first few years, the strong, climbing shoots should be trained in as many directions as possible without giving the plant too much of a contrived look. They can be twisted, turned and bent into position by securing them to trellis or wires fixed to the wall. The lateral growths produced by these shoots can then be cut back each year to about one-third of their length. These 'spurs' will then each produce several flowering shoots which, when similarly pruned in their turn the following year, will produce more, and so on. The same treatment applies to climbing roses growing on pillars, pergolas and arches. Species such as *R. bracteata* and *R. laevigata* and their hybrids are likewise best pruned by this method.

In the second category are the ramblers or

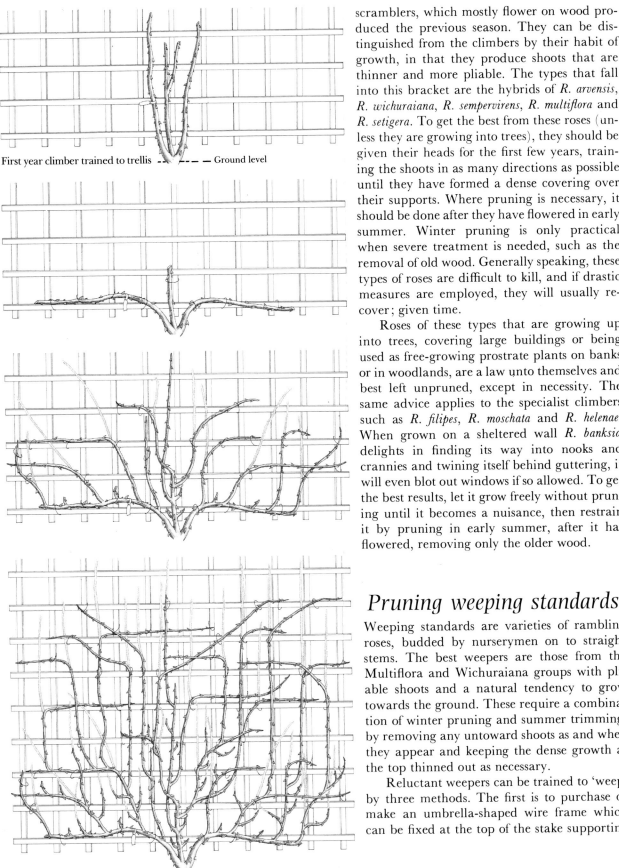

First year climber trained to trellis ------ ----- Ground level

Pruning climbing or rambler roses

scramblers, which mostly flower on wood produced the previous season. They can be distinguished from the climbers by their habit of growth, in that they produce shoots that are thinner and more pliable. The types that fall into this bracket are the hybrids of *R. arvensis*, *R. wichuraiana*, *R. sempervirens*, *R. multiflora* and *R. setigera*. To get the best from these roses (unless they are growing into trees), they should be given their heads for the first few years, training the shoots in as many directions as possible until they have formed a dense covering over their supports. Where pruning is necessary, it should be done after they have flowered in early summer. Winter pruning is only practical when severe treatment is needed, such as the removal of old wood. Generally speaking, these types of roses are difficult to kill, and if drastic measures are employed, they will usually recover; given time.

Roses of these types that are growing up into trees, covering large buildings or being used as free-growing prostrate plants on banks or in woodlands, are a law unto themselves and best left unpruned, except in necessity. The same advice applies to the specialist climbers such as *R. filipes*, *R. moschata* and *R. helenae*. When grown on a sheltered wall *R. banksia* delights in finding its way into nooks and crannies and twining itself behind guttering, it will even blot out windows if so allowed. To get the best results, let it grow freely without pruning until it becomes a nuisance, then restrain it by pruning in early summer, after it has flowered, removing only the older wood.

Pruning weeping standards

Weeping standards are varieties of rambling roses, budded by nurserymen on to straight stems. The best weepers are those from the Multiflora and Wichuraiana groups with pliable shoots and a natural tendency to grow towards the ground. These require a combination of winter pruning and summer trimming, by removing any untoward shoots as and when they appear and keeping the dense growth at the top thinned out as necessary.

Reluctant weepers can be trained to 'weep' by three methods. The first is to purchase or make an umbrella-shaped wire frame which can be fixed at the top of the stake supporting

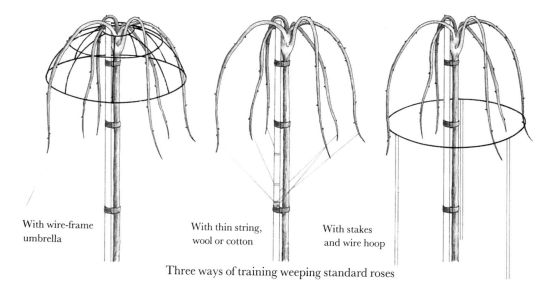

With wire-frame
umbrella

With thin string,
wool or cotton

With stakes
and wire hoop

Three ways of training weeping standard roses

the rose, thus enabling the shoots to be trained downward as they grow. The trouble with this method is that the frames are unsightly and will often spoil the overall appearance of the garden. Far better is the method of attaching cotton to the end of the branches which are not naturally weeping and either pegging this to the ground, thus pulling the shoots downward, or attaching a heavy stone to the end of the cotton to keep the shoots angled downwards. The third method is to attach a hoop on to three equally spaced stakes around the stems. The hoop should be about 3 ft (90 cm) above the ground. The shoots are then tied to the hoop, thus training them downwards to give a good weeping effect.

Old-fashioned roses, species roses or shrub roses growing as standards need the same treatment as afforded to their shrub counterparts; but because they are grown in this way they will need tidying more frequently to keep them in shape.

Dead-heading

Dead-heading is in many ways far more important to some varieties than pruning, although this can be rather a nuisance where large numbers of old roses are concerned. It is less of a drudge, however, if the habit of carrying secateurs at all times is adopted whilst walking round the garden, and snipping off any unsightly dead heads as and when they occur. It is best to make the cut at the first true leaf below the flower stalk. Only dead-head

those varieties which retain their dead petals and become unsightly. Many others will eventually produce hips – pleasing to all, including the birds.

Pruning neglected roses

Old, neglected rose specimens pose yet another difficult pruning problem. Breathing new life into old shrub roses and climbers, however, is often impracticable, so it would be misleading to suggest ways of attempting this. Roses do not live for ever and their longevity is often related to the treatment they receive throughout their lives. Broadly speaking, the nearer a rose is to a true species, the longer it will live. It follows,

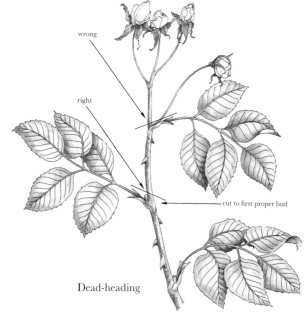

wrong

right

cut to first proper bud

Dead-heading

therefore, that it is easier to rejuvenate an old-fashioned rose than a modern hybrid. Sentiment plays an important part in these decisions but where a rose is obviously approaching its twilight years, it is better to put it out of its misery and replace it with another. As mentioned earlier, the soil will need changing but provided the variety can still be obtained, this is the most economical procedure. If its name is unknown and identification has proved impossible, some specialist nurseries will produce new plants from stock taken from the old plant. By this means direct offspring can be replanted and an old variety may possibly have been saved from extinction.

Feeding roses

Good preparation of soils before planting is always rewarded by more contented roses. It is advisable, therefore, to dig over the soil well in advance of planting, incorporating some form of organic material. Well rotted farmyard manure is undoubtedly the best, but failing this, a mixture of coarse, damp peat and bonemeal can be used or, better still, well rotted compost from the compost heap. If the soil is very poor, a balanced fertiliser with added trace elements can be broadcast over the soil ahead of planting. Special rose fertiliser can be bought from most garden centres – a worthwhile investment when you consider that the roses being planted are to last for many years; the same type of fertiliser can be used as top-dressing after the roses are established, preferably before the start of the growing season, usually at the time of pruning. This gives the nutrients the chance of penetrating the soil, prior to the beginning of maximum root activity as the days lengthen in early spring. On good soils, one top-dressing should be enough to sustain the rose throughout the summer, and no further feeding should be necessary until the following spring. For impoverished soils, however, a second dressing should be applied in early summer, by which time the rose will be seeking further nourishment to provide a second flush of flowers or secondary growth, depending on its habit.

The proprietary brands of fertiliser are specially prepared for roses and will usually contain the proper mix of nutrients in the most beneficial proportions. Should any other type of balanced fertiliser be used – and there is no reason why not – it should be low in nitrogen and high in potash, with a good mix of the major trace elements. Iron is particularly important, especially if your soil is alkaline; so is magnesium, which is frequently deficient in many soils. Those who believe in organic gardening can supply nutrition by means of liquid seaweed, spent hops, farmyard manure, fish meal, etc., but the levels of potash must be kept up by the use of soot or wood ashes. All soils, of course, are improved by the incorporation of organic materials, but I do not greatly favour constant mulching of rose beds with farmyard manure. This practice, apart from looking unsightly for much of the year, tends to harbour the spores of diseases by giving them a perfect environment from which to launch themselves at the rose each spring. Mulching, if considered necessary, should be to suppress weeds rather than as a source of nutrition. Coarse peat or bark chippings are ideal for controlling weeds, especially if applied to the depth of about 1 in (2.5 cm), to fairly clean ground. Nor do I consider the use of lawn trimmings a good practice; in any event, they should only be applied in moderation. They are best composted and spread at a later date; again, this should be done sparingly, for the high nitrogen content of such compost can lead to abundant growth, fewer flowers and less immunity to disease.

The nutritional requirements of roses growing in pots or tubs are the same as for those growing in open ground; remember however, that nutrients leach from potted soil far more quickly than they do from natural soil, so more frequent applications of fertiliser are necessary. Liquid fertiliser can be applied at the time of watering. Roses also respond to foliar feeding, but this should not be done in hot sunshine, remembering not to overdo the nitrogen unless the bushes are badly stunted.

To sum up, if you love old-fashioned roses, it is worth growing them whatever your soil, provided you do not expect rewards out of proportion to the loving care you give them.

Weed control

Gardeners fall into two categories where weeds are concerned; those who tolerate weeds and are prepared to live happily with them, and those who insist upon their removal from every nook and cranny. Both schools tend to frown at each other's philosophy. From a nurseryman's point of view wild flowers or wild plants growing rampant among roses are a problem, and they have to be kept under control. However, as I said earlier, I favour leaving weeds until they become a nuisance and start to hamper the performance of the roses.

The most troublesome weeds are the perennial and deep-rooted types, especially couch grass and thistles, which have a habit of taking refuge among the bushes themselves and growing up through the lower branches. If this is permitted the rose definitely suffers and the weeds become almost impossible to eradicate. It is therefore important for roses to start in soil which is as free as possible from perennial weed infestation. Thus in the initial preparation of the ground, it is essential to make sure that such weeds are dealt with severely. This can be done very successfully with hormone-based herbicides, applied several months in advance of planting and while the weeds are still growing. For those who prefer not to use chemicals, it is a case of backache and blisters, forking out all the roots and rhizomes from the soil all around the area to be planted. Any small piece of root left in the ground will

rapidly take hold and reinfest the soil with renewed vigour.

Annual weeds, which usually invade in large armies, are not quite such a problem since, apart from reinfestation by seed, they succumb to the hoe pretty quickly on a hot day. There are chemicals that will deal with these both at the pre-emergent stage and whilst they are growing. Such chemicals must be used with great care, not only for the wellbeing of the roses but, more importantly, for the good of the soil, the animal and bird population, and not least ourselves. This is no place to discuss the rights and wrongs of their usage; but before any chemicals are used, read specific instructions carefully and carry these out to the letter. There are a number of available herbicides, and advice can best be obtained from those experts who supply them.

One of the most effective ways to control weeds is to use other plants as companions to old-fashioned and shrub roses, especially some of the ground-hugging perennials and shrubs; this subject has been dealt with earlier in the book. It is worth remembering that weeds only become a problem if allowed to take hold, and the best form of control is hoeing or treating the ground with suitable herbicides before they emerge as seedlings.

Propagation of roses

Vegetative propagation as a means of reproducing plants has probably been known since civilisation began. If man had not learned to work with nature and use such means of reproduction, many of our oldest varieties, incapable of self-perpetuation, would have been lost in the remote mists of time.

Species, of course, can reproduce themselves from seed. So from the beginning they have been relatively independent, needing man's assistance only to develop their hybrids and to help them multiply by producing them from cuttings or by grafting or budding. Although a form of grafting is still practised in the commercial production of roses, this is now done on a limited scale in the case of old-fashioned roses, usually in the form of bench-grafting to propagate difficult subjects such as 'Mermaid', *R. banksia lutea* and a few other

varieties which do not lend themselves readily to the technique of budding.

Grafting

Bench-grafting is a fairly sophisticated means of propagation and its success depends mainly on the skill and experience of the nurseryman. Grafting involves placing a branch or shoot from a preselected variety on to the root or shoot of another, thus creating a union between the two and the eventual growth of a complete plant in its own right. The host plant providing the root is termed the 'stock', and its enforced guest which supplies the branches is called the 'scion'. By careful selection of compatible species and varieties, each will influence the other and so enable hybrids to perpetuate in their exact form. The choice of stocks with specific attributes enables them to influence the scion and, to some extent, vice-versa. These reciprocal influences are not so pronounced in roses as they are, for example, in apples, when the ultimate size of the tree is controlled by the stock on which the variety is grafted. Stocks are usually grown from seed by specialist growers. In recent years, as mentioned earlier, the most commonly used stock has been *R. laxa*.

For bench-grafting roses, suitable stocks are selected each year in early January and plunged, in bundles of fifty or so, into damp sterile peat, under glass. These are forced into early growth for about two to three weeks until root activity is well under way. Scions are then taken from dormant plants of the variety to be propagated, and grafted on to each active stock, the top of the stock having first been removed at a point a few inches above the roots. The scion selected is usually of one-year wood, between 3–4 in (6.5–10 cm) long, with three or four buds. The top end of the scion is usually cut straight across, immediately above a growing point or bud. The bottom is cut into a half-wedge shape and an inverted cut

made upwards into the wedge on the exposed-tissue side of the cut. A similar cut is made to match the slant of the scion on one side of the stock, and a reverse cut made, so the two can be joined together in a neat and tidy fashion. Care is taken to ensure that the two cambium layers, which are situated under the bark, are placed together. This done, the joint is bandaged with grafting tape or raffia and waxed watertight, either with grafting wax or petroleum jelly. The top of the scion is also sealed to reduce dehydration.

The stock with scion attached is then potted with enough nutrients in the compost to see it through one season. It is then placed in a heated greenhouse. Within a few weeks the two will fuse together and the scion will begin to grow. Fairly soon, after it becomes obvious that the graft has taken, a 2–3 ft (60–90 cm) cane should be placed in the pot with the plant. This should be fixed firmly to both stock and scion by raffia to provide a splint for support during the crucial few weeks whilst complete fusion takes place. By early summer the join should be secure enough to release the grafting-tape or raffia

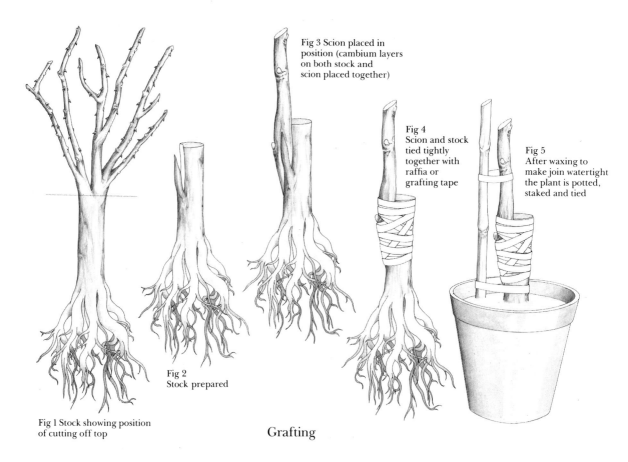

Fig 3 Scion placed in position (cambium layers on both stock and scion placed together)

Fig 4 Scion and stock tied tightly together with raffia or grafting tape

Fig 5 After waxing to make join watertight the plant is potted, staked and tied

Fig 2 Stock prepared

Fig 1 Stock showing position of cutting off top

Grafting

from the union, thus avoiding strangulation as both stock and scion swell with growth. This method of grafting is known as 'whip and tongue', but there are a number of variations on this, such as 'wedge-grafting', 'saddle-grafting', 'chip-grafting' and so on. All rely on the compatibility of stock and scion and the alignment of their respective cambium layers. The result should be a sizeable plant by the end of the first growing season.

Budding

Budding is by far the most widely used method of producing roses. Success with budding, even on the smallest scale, gives one a very satisfactory feeling of achievement and there is no reason why the amateur should not try to produce a few rose bushes by this means. All that is needed is a budding knife with specially shaped blade and handle, available, in various designs, from good gardening shops and ironmongers. Most rose nurserymen will sell a few stocks, knowing that however successful, no threat is posed to their businesses.

Budding is an acquired technique, and nurseries employ skilled propagators who are capable of working very rapidly, handling up to 400 bushes an hour. Speed is essential since budding is usually done at the peak growing season with both stock and scion in active growth. Stocks for this purpose are normally planted as one-year seedlings in rows during the preceding winter. By mid-June these are ready for budding and will remain in this state of readiness for about two months. The stocks are planted in such a way as to leave 1–2 in (2.5–5 cm) of root protruding above ground level. The scions or buds are selected by taking a ripe flowering-shoot from a ready-made rose bush. The shoot is usually ripe when the flower has started to open. The flower and the top 2 in (5 cm) of the stem are removed together with the leaves, to facilitate later handling. It is a good idea to leave about $\frac{1}{3}$ in (1 cm) of leaf stalk attached to the stem, depending upon the variety. Most rose 'sticks' will have between four and eight buds. At no time must the stick be allowed to become dry. It can be kept fresh for several days if necessary by placing it in damp newspaper and polythene.

To perform the budding operation first make sure that the stock is clean and free of soil at

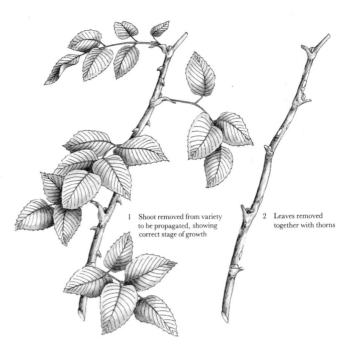

1 Shoot removed from variety to be propagated, showing correct stage of growth

2 Leaves removed together with thorns

Preparation of wood for budding

ground level. Open the bark of the stock with the knife to form a T-shaped cut, taking care not to damage or scrape the tissue inside the bark. A vertical cut about 1 in (2.5 cm) long is enough to tease back the bark at the top of the 'T'. The stock prepared, the scion is then placed in the free hand and held by the index finger and the thumb, palm uppermost, with the thin end or top of the scion pointing towards the wrist. The index finger should be placed directly under the first or top bud on the stick to give support. The first bud is then cut from the stick with one cutting motion of the knife. With the thumb of the knife hand, press the 'sliver' that is being removed firmly on to the knife blade. Having made a clean cut to about $\frac{1}{3}$ in (1 cm) above the bud, the bark can then be torn back to remove it completely from the stick, still holding it between knife blade and thumb. Experts retain the stick in their hand as they complete each budding operation but at this point the novice is best advised to place the stick aside and retain only the bud between finger and thumb. The wood from the bud is then separated from the bark, usually in two stages. Holding the blunt end between thumb and finger, with the thumbnail for support, remove half the wood from the top downwards and the other half from the bottom upwards,

Budding

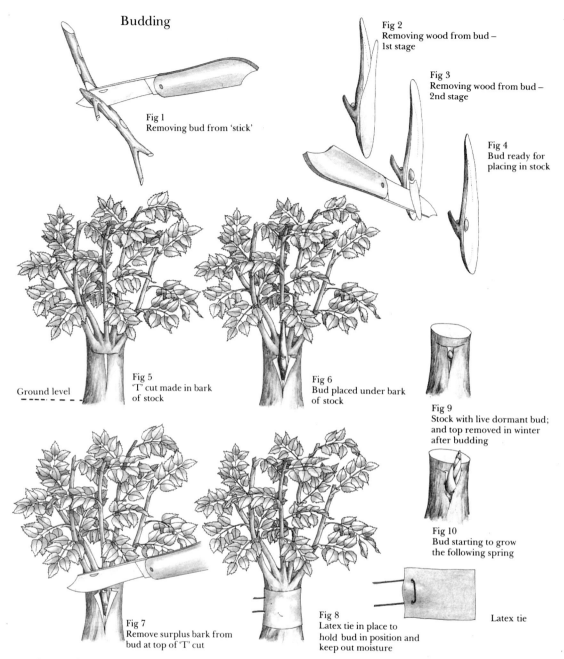

Fig 1
Removing bud from 'stick'

Fig 2
Removing wood from bud –
1st stage

Fig 3
Removing wood from bud –
2nd stage

Fig 4
Bud ready for
placing in stock

Ground level

Fig 5
'T' cut made in bark
of stock

Fig 6
Bud placed under bark
of stock

Fig 7
Remove surplus bark from
bud at top of 'T' cut

Fig 8
Latex tie in place to
hold bud in position and
keep out moisture

Fig 9
Stock with live dormant bud;
and top removed in winter
after budding

Fig 10
Bud starting to grow
the following spring

Latex tie

exposing a plump little bud on the inside of the bark. If there is a hole instead, throw it away and start again.

The next stage calls for dexterity. Hold the top end of the bud with one hand, and use the other to hold open the bark of the stock with the handle of the budding knife; then carefully slide the bud into position under the bark of the stock, finally cutting off any spare bark from the bud at the top of the 'T'. Lastly, the wound has to be bandaged, both to hold it together and to prevent moisture getting in.

Nurserymen use special, inexpensive latex patches for this, but if these cannot be obtained, use some thin raffia, winding it around the cut; beneath the bud three times and above the bud four times, and knotting it carefully at the top. After three or four weeks the 'bandage' can be removed; success or failure will be immediately obvious. If the bud has failed to take and there is still time, another attempt can be made on the other side of the stock. If it has taken it should be left untouched until mid-winter, when the complete top of the stock should be removed at about ⅓ in (1 cm) above the bud. The following summer, lo and behold, a rose! This can either be left where it is for life or transplanted to another position in the following dormant season.

Roses from cuttings

Many gardeners, having had success at rooting roses from cuttings, are mystified by the fact that this is not done commercially, enabling them to purchase roses which will be free of troublesome suckers. A few types of roses lend themselves readily to this method of propagation, notably *R. rugosa* and its hybrids, and these are sometimes offered commercially on their own roots, as are some of the species and unusual hybrids which have proved resistant to budding or grafting techniques. But most attempts at commercial production over the years have failed. Nowadays, with sophisticated hormone rooting powders and mist units, getting them to root is not a problem; in fact, many varieties root readily without such aids. The difficulty is growing enough stock plants to provide the cuttings. With the budding method, six buds are the equivalent of only one cutting, so a nurseryman would need six times as many stock plants to produce plants for sale. Although recent developments in tissue culture might provide the answer, I can see no way around the difficulties which arise later when the bush has to be transplanted. Except for some species, the root systems are small when compared with budded roses, and they do not take readily to transplanting. Thus there is a high failure rate for open-ground, bare-root plants produced from cuttings. To counteract this, they have to be grown in pots from an early age, so enabling them to be transplanted complete with soil. This is fine where plants can be sold locally and in garden centres, but it presents a problem for despatch by mail order. Another difficulty is to produce bushes large enough to satisfy the long-established pattern of quality demanded by the public. An own-root rose needs to be at least one year older than its budded counterpart to get anywhere near its size. I recall vividly an occasion several years ago when a customer asked me to produce for her thirty different roses on their own roots. I explained all the

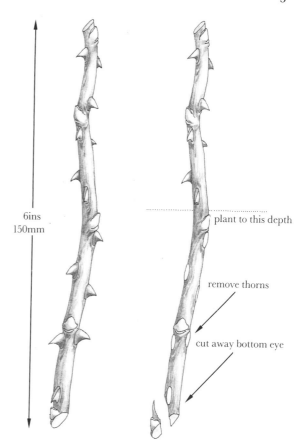

6ins
150mm

plant to this depth

remove thorns

cut away bottom eye

Hardwood cuttings taken in autumn

pros and cons and she said that she was prepared to wait. In order to be sure of enough plants I produced six of each, which took two years of patient work. When she received them, she promptly returned the lot, saying they were too small! The only consolation, apart from not seeing that lady again, was a lot more experience at growing roses from cuttings.

Despite all this, Malcolm Lowe of Nassau, New Hampshire, USA, has established a system of 'own-root roses' whereby plants are produced to order. He roots his cuttings under glass in early autumn and plants the rooted plants straight into the ground the following spring. His success rate is apparently high, but I think the climate of New Hampshire is more conducive to such a method of rose production than ours in the UK.

The best time to take hardwood cuttings is when the leaves begin to fall and the wood has had all the summer to ripen. For cuttings of this type, select mature, one-year wood,

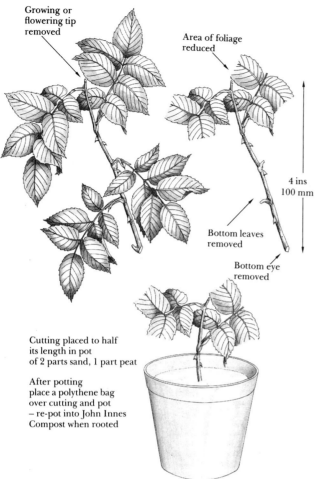

Growing or
flowering tip
removed

Area of foliage
reduced

4 ins
100 mm

Bottom leaves
removed

Bottom eye
removed

Cutting placed to half
its length in pot
of 2 parts sand, 1 part peat

After potting
place a polythene bag
over cutting and pot
– re-pot into John Innes
Compost when rooted

Softwood cutting taken in summer

preferably the thickness of a pencil or more, though this will depend somewhat on the variety. The ideal cutting should be about 6 in (15 cm) long and cut to a growth bud at both the top and bottom. For heel cuttings, the bottom should have a small slice of two-year wood still attached. Leaves, where present, should be removed before placing the cutting straight into the ground to a depth of half its length, preferably in a sheltered, warm part of the garden. If the soil is heavy, a little sand placed in the bottom of the trench before planting, will help rooting, having dipped the bottom $\frac{1}{3}$ in (1 cm) or so of the cutting into rooting hormone. Alternatively, the cuttings can be placed directly into a pot containing equal parts of sand and moist peat, and placed in a cold frame or cold greenhouse.

By early spring these cuttings should start to root and will grow into reasonable small bushes by the following autumn, when they can be transplanted into a permanent position.

If preferred, cuttings can be taken from late June onwards, but these need slightly more coddling. Shoots of the current year's wood should be cut from the bush and cuttings made to a length of about 4 in (10 cm), again cutting to an eye, top and bottom. Remove all leaves except for the top two, which if needs be, should be reduced to just two leaflets to reduce transpiration. The prepared cuttings should then be placed in pots in a mixture of peat and sand, watered, and covered with a polythene bag, held in position with a piece of cane acting as a tent peg and a rubber band to anchor the bag around the top edge of the pot. By this system, cuttings should root quite quickly, especially if the pots are kept in a warm place such as a greenhouse or on a windowsill. During this period very little watering is necessary since moisture builds up within the sealed environment of the polythene. Placing the pot in a saucer of shingle, into which water can be poured periodically, will ensure that the cutting never dries out before it makes root. When the cuttings have made some small amount of growth, the polythene can be removed and the plant slowly hardened-off before winter. During the winter, the plant can be repotted into better nourished soil and eventually planted into a permanent situation.

These are just two of the ways of producing roses from cuttings. Remember however, that not all varieties will root successfully and that others will not make such large plants or grow as quickly as those produced from budding.

Tissue culture

Tissue culture is a recent development, not yet as fully adapted for roses as it is for some other plants. Undoubtedly it has a future, but it is still uncertain whether it can be of substantial benefit in the production of old-fashioned roses, apart from shortening the time required to increase the numbers of certain varieties. The process is, in any case, outside the scope of this book. It is sufficient to say merely that the technique involves using very small sections of tissue and persuading these to grow into true plants in sterile laboratory conditions. It departs from previously accepted horticultural principles in that only the growth points of plants were formerly thought to be capable of developing roots and shoots.

Layering

Layering is not often practised with roses but, depending upon the variety, it is quite a feasible method of propagation. Although it is not possible with sturdy, upright growers, since they will refuse to bend to the ground, it is a fairly efficient way of propagating the more flexible old-fashioned roses, climbers and ramblers.

Simply arch a one-year-old shoot to the ground and place the point of contact – about 12 in (30 cm) from the tip – into a shallow trench, tethering it with a wire pin or similar aid. A knife wound in that part of the bark which is placed underground will sometimes aid rooting; then cover with soil. This can be done at almost any time of the year but rooting is naturally quicker in spring, just before seasonal growth begins.

Once rooting has occurred, the protruding tip will start to grow and the parent shoot can be cut away. The new rose can then be transplanted into a permanent position at any time during the dormant season.

Division

Division as a means of propagation is common practice with many plants, though this is not normally associated with roses; nevertheless, there are some species and varieties where such a method can be adopted quite successfully. The only necessary condition is that candidates for such treatment should actually be growing on their own roots and not grafted or budded on to an understock.

Several species of roses and their hybrids are naturally free-suckering plants; if these suckers are removed from the bush with a section of root attached they become new plants in their own right. The Burnet roses or Scotch briars are perhaps the best subjects for this form of propagation; indeed it may be their propensity for free-suckering that accounts for their longevity. One frequently comes upon such roses in old gardens, having way outlived their companions from an earlier age and multiplied themselves by suckers several times over and retaining none of their original root systems; in fact, they were probably planted as suckers in the first place. Other types of roses which can be multiplied in this way are *R. wichuraiana*, *R. palustris*, *R. nitida*, *R. virginiana*,

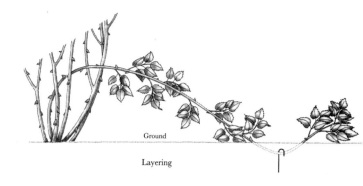
Ground

Layering

R. eglanteria and, of course, the ubiquitous *R. rugosa*. Most forms and hybrids of all these species lend themselves to division, provided, as already said, that they are growing on their own roots.

Roses from seed

All true species will of course grow from seed, but to be sure of identical offspring, parent seed plants need to be grown in isolation in order to avoid becoming 'chance hybridized' with other compatible species or hybrids. Such chance hybrids occur sometimes with only minor differences from their parents, having been fertilized by bees or by some other natural pollen-carrying agent.

Hybrids sometimes pop up in gardens from seeds which have either simply dropped off the plant or have been distributed by birds, *R. glauca* and *R. filipes* being just two species which have produced foundlings in this way. Some hybrids, too, in particular the Rugosas, if growing close to other roses, will sometimes produce interesting if not startling variations from their self-sown seeds.

All root stocks used in modern rose production are grown from seed. Parent plants of suitable species such as *R. laxa* and forms of *R. multiflora* are grown in relative isolation, usually in the warmer parts of the Eastern Mediterranean. The seed is collected from parent plants and sold to specialist rose stock growers in Europe, in particular Holland and Germany but lately in the UK as well. Seeds are sown in very early spring and the seedlings are produced, all in one growing season, by the tens of millions. These are then sold to rose nurserymen who produce saleable bushes two growing seasons later by budding. Thus the roots of bought roses are well-travelled; excluding the age of the seed, they are three years old by the time they are planted in the garden.

Economics is not the only reason why rose stocks are grown from seeds. Viruses are less likely to be transmitted by this means than by vegetative propagation. Seeds gathered from garden hybrids, even those which have been self-pollinated, yield rather different results from those collected from species, in that none will come true and each seedling produced will differ from its parents, only one of which, of course, will be known. Seed pods from most garden hybrids need a long summer to ripen. Only those from hips provided by the earliest flowers of summer are usually viable in the UK and similar latitudes; this is why hybridizing, north of about latitude $45°$, is carried out in greenhouses.

Growing seed from garden hybrids can be interesting, if not particularly fruitful. An unsophisticated method is to collect ripe hips in early winter and to place them in flower pots full of sharp sand, keeping these outdoors where the greatest fluctuations in temperature can be obtained until about February. Choose a position which can be protected from mice, for these little creatures seem to enjoy the flavour of rose seeds.

The number of seeds in each hip will vary from one or two, to as many as fifty in some varieties. Seeds should be taken from the hips in early February, by which time the fleshy part of the pods will have rotted away. They should then be washed and sown about $\frac{1}{4}$ in (0.5 cm) deep in good compost in a seed tray or flower pots; then placed in a warm greenhouse with bottom heat to warm the soil to a temperature of about $45°F$ (about $6°C$). Haphazard germination will start a few weeks later as the days lengthen and may continue spasmodically until early summer. Transplant any seedlings into a good potting compost in 3 in (7.5 cm) pots soon after germination and keep them in the greenhouse. Shade them for a few days until they take root. They should flower within a few weeks, depending on the type of rose. Climbers etc. may not flower until the following summer. If budding is not possible, repot them into larger pots and await a second flowering the following year. There is little point in planting them into the garden until they have proved worthwhile.

All this has little to do with rose growing, but it is enjoyable, and no matter how poor the seedlings, at least they will be unique, which may be encouragement to progress to a little real hybridizing.

Seeds packed into rose hip

Pests and diseases

The belief that shrub and old-fashioned roses are less troubled by pests and diseases than some of their modern cousins may not bear close analysis. The fact that this often appears to be the case is probably more due to their vigour and ability to overcome affliction than any inherent resistance to contracting disease. This is further borne out by the fact that many have come down to us from the distant past. Frequently, too, the once-flowering varieties will have finished their main flush of flowers before diseases or pests have a chance to affect them seriously, whereas in modern roses, if left unchecked, such afflictions as black spot and rust can cause havoc in late summer and autumn. There is undoubtedly a correlation between the vigour of a rose and resistance to disease; some of the larger shrub roses, and in particularly the vigorous climbers, are usually more healthy than their shorter counterparts.

Good cultivation, adequate feeding and, especially, good drainage and irrigation are the best methods of avoiding severe problems from diseases. Contented bushes will always give better rewards. Black spot and rust, probably the two worst diseases, have both been given a new lease of life since in the late 1950s in the UK when Clean Air legislation was passed – hence less healthy roses – a small price to pay, admittedly, for the improvement to our own health. Most other countries now have similar legislation and their rose growers similar problems. Our best hope in the control of rose diseases comes from the breeders who are becoming ever more conscious of raising healthier stocks. To achieve this they will have to search back among old-fashioned roses and species to find the elusive, disease-resistant genes.

Greenflies

When conditions are right, aphides of many types attack roses but by far the most common are greenflies and a severe infestation can be very troublesome. Aphides have a number of natural predators, in particular the delightful and harmless ladybird, although it is unlikely that she alone will provide any measure of control. Ants, too, are often seen in company with aphides, but these are attracted to the sticky deposits left behind rather than to the pests themselves. Aphides multiply rapidly if left unchecked. In days gone by gardeners used

soapy water to control these pests, they also sprayed tobacco water on infested shoots. Some even purchased special aphide brushes to remove them, cleverly designed to avoid any damage to the roses. Nowadays we use insecticides, some so sophisticated that they are harmless to birds and predatory insects. The most effective of these are 'systemic', which work from within the plant thus preventing infestation before it occurs. Such sprays need applying at about 10 to 14 day intervals. Contact insecticides actually kill aphides after infestation, and such sprays need repeating as and when aphides are seen to be present.

Capsid bugs

These are less common than aphides and can be quite elusive little pests, quickly moving on from one bush to another. They damage succulent growing tips, leaving them stunted, withered and peppered with tiny holes. Systemic insecticides are the best preventative measures, although the capsids will often cause some damage before succumbing to their effects.

Caterpillars

Various caterpillars occasionally attack the leaves of roses. Evidence of their presence is usually the disappearance of whole sections of leaf or the growing tips of young tender shoots. A search through the foliage usually finds them, for removal and instant disposal.

Caterpillars are the larvae of moths which themselves do not feed on roses, so chemical control is more difficult. Specific chemicals for caterpillar control are nevertheless available. Advice on these should be sought from experts if the infestation is troublesome.

Cuckoospit

The unsightly appearance of this pest is probably more offensive than the pest itself, at least on roses. It is more common on roses with heavy weed infestation or those growing in herbaceous borders than on roses in the open. The spittle-like substance surrounding the froghopper nymph can usually be washed away by an extra strong jet from the sprayer, whilst spraying against other pests or diseases.

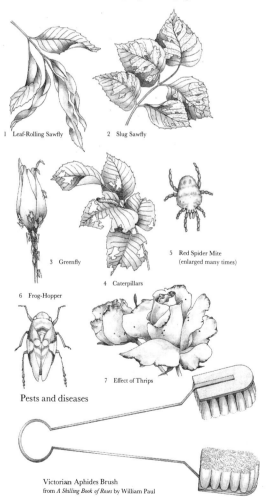

1 Leaf-Rolling Sawfly   2 Slug Sawfly

3 Greenfly   4 Caterpillars   5 Red Spider Mite (enlarged many times)

6 Frog-Hopper   7 Effect of Thrips

Pests and diseases

Victorian Aphides Brush
from *A Shilling Book of Roses* by William Paul

Leaf-rolling sawfly

Damage caused by this insect usually manifests itself too late for any remedy. The only answer – and this rather hit-and-miss – is to start spraying with contact insecticides very early in the year to try to catch adult flies whilst they seek out suitable young leaves to infest with their eggs. Not all damaged leaves will have fertile eggs; most, it would seem, are injected by the sawfly with a chemical which causes the leaf to curl, thus protecting the larvae when they hatch. Heavy infestation can look very unsightly in early summer, but the bush, although suffering slightly from the interruption to its natural process, soon recovers. No real harm is done, except perhaps to render it more prone to diseases such as mildew. Spraying with the same chemical as that used for caterpillars will give some measure of control over the developing larvae, but the curled leaves make this extremely difficult.

Another species of sawfly following the same life cycle is known as the slug sawfly. This is less common but can be devastating if an infestation occurs. The larvae feed on the surface tissue of the leaf, leaving just a skeleton structure behind. Control of this is the same as that for the leaf-rolling sawfly.

Red spider

This very difficult little curse is more troublesome on roses under glass than on those outdoors. The mites are almost invisible to the naked eye and live on the underside of the leaves. They multiply very quickly and often have a severe hold over the roses before an infestation can be diagnosed, causing leaves to lose colour, become limp and eventually fall to the ground; the eggs then lie in the soil throughout the winter. Control is difficult and more effective before severe infestation occurs. Perimiphos-Methyl seems, at present, to be the most effective chemical if applied whilst the mites are active in summer. If the presence of this pest is suspected without actual evidence, give the ground around the bushes a good winter-wash with old-fashioned tar oil while the roses are dormant. This will destroy any eggs before they hatch.

Thrips

This pest is more troublesome on modern roses than on old-fashioned roses, preferring the tighter buds of the Large-Flowered roses. It usually occurs in hot, thundery weather and is seldom nuisance enough to warrant spraying, except perhaps on some of the Climbing Hybrid Teas and the more doubled Bourbons, Noisettes and Teas. Again prevention is better than cure, and spraying with a systemic or contact insecticide just before the flower buds begin to open will usually stop the tiny little flies from nibbling at the edges of the petals and disfiguring the flowers.

Rabbits and deer

Rabbits can be quite a serious pest to roses in country gardens, especially in winter, and particularly in those situated near golf courses and heathland, and open acres of farmland, where they are more numerous. Their activities are unpredictable. In spring baby rabbits, in particular, find the young, succulent tips of roses most acceptable; and in winter rabbits of all ages indulge in what appears to be malicious vandalism, stripping the bark completely off shoots of any age, to tiptoe height. If planting old-fashioned roses in the country, take the precaution of fencing off the garden against rabbit invasion; failing this, encircle each bush, at least during its early years, with small-mesh wire. There are chemicals, offensive to rabbits, which are supposed to keep them off, but these, in my experience, provide only flimsy defence.

Deer, too, enjoy a good meal of roses especially when hungry in deep mid-winter; but they are shy creatures and should only present a problem to roses growing near woodlands or on parkland. Roses are sometimes grown around paddock fences and the like, and it should be remembered that most grazing animals will, at some time, sample the taste of any roses they can reach. The most positive precaution here is to plant only the most thorny varieties and species.

Above: Black spot
Below: Rust on leaves in summer

Above: Mildew on leaves in summer
Below: Mildew and rust on a branch

Black spot

Of all the diseases to affect roses, with the possible exception of rust, black spot is the most pernicious. Granted, it is much more of a problem to modern hybrids than to old-fashioned roses; but this should not make lovers of old roses complacent, for persistent attack on some varieties can leave the shrubs somewhat jaded each year and ultimately reduce them to a fraction of their true selves.

This disease attacks the leaves, usually from mid-summer onwards, often resulting in complete defoliation. Even a partial or mild attack will render bushes unsightly. It can be recognized easily by the black or dark brown patches which spread rapidly over leaves and often extend to the young stems, causing them initially to become mottled and later to die. Each leaf that falls carries with it millions of spores which overwinter in the soil, ready for an attack the following season.

The removal and burning of infected leaves, both from the bush and from the surrounding ground, will therefore help prevent the disease spreading to less susceptible varieties. Black spot is a fact of life in roses and little can be done remedially once the disease has taken hold. A number of chemicals are available which, if sprayed in advance of the infection, will keep the disease at bay, at least until the first flush of the flowers is over. Manufacturers' claims as to the degree of control can only be justified if their instructions are strictly followed and accompanied by good husbandry and cleanliness.

Experience has convinced me that regular overhead irrigation will control black spot, provided it is done overnight to avoid scorching the foliage. This should be done, at a minimum interval of ten days, for about five hours on each occasion. From the point of view of cleanliness, a winter wash both of the plant and the surrounding ground with a solution of Jeyes Fluid helps to kill off any spores lurking on decaying leaves or in the soil and helps delay infection from the disease in early summer.

Powdery mildew

Powdery mildew attacks roses from early summer onwards and, if allowed to flourish, can be quite a serious problem on some varieties. The first signs of mildew are small patches of greyish-white powder, usually near the top of the young growing shoots and on the succulent young leaves. If not checked, these patches spread rapidly to cover the entire plant. In severe epidemics it will also extend to the more mature leaves and flower buds. The young leaves curl, distort and fail to develop, thus preventing the plant from functioning satisfactorily. Attacks of mildew on otherwise healthy plants weaken their resistance to other diseases; black spot, in particular, flourishes when mildew has been allowed to take hold. Well-nourished plants, while not rendered immune, will suffer less from an epidemic than under-nourished ones. Equally, the 'prevention is better than cure' rule applies to chemical control of the disease. A number of contact fungicides are available, but in order to be efficient they must contain a wetting or spreading agent to enable sufficient chemical to adhere to the leaves. Systemic fungicides are the best method of combating mildew. These should be sprayed on to known susceptible varieties well in advance of the appearance of the disease. Mildew is very persistent and has a very rapid life cycle, enabling spores to develop resistance to specific chemicals very quickly. For this reason, if the effectiveness of spraying starts to wear off, change to something else for a while. The over-use of nitrogenous fertilizers is often the cause of mildew, especially when mid-summer application leads to excessive growth in the autumn. Mildew may also follow summer drought, so try to keep the roses well watered during such periods.

Downy mildew

This form of mildew affects roses grown under glass, especially those grown in pots. It takes the form of dull brownish or sometimes bluish patches on the surface of mature leaves, which can also spread to the stems. Infected leaves become limp and fall. Severe attacks may cause the death of whole plants. The disease is usually brought on by extremes of day and night temperatures, especially when linked to bad ventilation in greenhouses and conservatories. Some control can be achieved by the use of similar fungicides to those used against powdery mildew and black spot. The disease seldom attacks outdoor roses.

Rust

Of all rose diseases, a bad infestation of rust can be the most devastating. If conditions are right – it enjoys moist warm weather – susceptible varieties will deteriorate rapidly and die from its effects. Signs of infection are often not noticed until the disease is established but if spotted early enough the disease can be controlled. Small orange pustules attach themselves to the underside of leaves and multiply rapidly until they have spread all over the plant including, on occasions, the stems and thorns. As the spores age, they turn to dark brown and eventually to black, killing the leaf in the process. In some extra susceptible varieties where the stem has also been affected, the lifeless, brown leaves hang on to the plant as it dies. In others, they fall to the ground where the spores overwinter in readiness for the following season.

At the first sign of the disease, all infected foliage should be removed and burned. Chemical control is difficult because spray has to be directed upwards on to the underside of the leaves. The same fungicides as used for black spot have some preventative qualities but, if an attack is diagnosed at an advanced stage, oxycarboxin, a chemical available under several trade names, is quite effective. Varieties most prone to this disease tend to act as hosts, thus causing the less susceptible ones to become infected. If rust is found to occur repeatedly on the same plants it is best to remove and burn them. 'Conrad F. Meyer' and 'Sarah Van Fleet', both Hybrid Rugosas, are particular culprits and should be kept out of gardens where rust has proved a problem.

Stem canker

This is not a serious problem on good, well-nourished bushes, and is more frequently seen on older plants which have been allowed to develop lots of old wood, much of which has outlived its usefulness. It also appears on very old climbers, where constant pruning over the years has permitted the disease to enter the plant through exposed tissue. The disease takes the form of large, irregular shaped lesions, usually parched brown, sunken near the edges and swollen in the centre. Sometimes the bark is slightly lifted at the edge and rather gnarled in appearance. If infection occurs on expendable branches, these should be removed and burned; but older plants frequently develop the disease in awkward places. Careful removal of the lesions with a sharp knife and painting the wound with grafting wax or a similar substance will sometimes succeed. Such surgery is only worth trying if the bush or climber has great sentimental value. The best course is to destroy the old badly infected plant and replace it with another.

Viruses

Much has still to be learned about viruses in plants. There is little doubt that many of these live with roses, and have varying effects on their well-being. Even apparently healthy varieties may be contaminated by viruses, almost as part of their make-up. Viruses are transmitted by aphides moving from one plant to another or even by means of secateurs whilst pruning. The disease is certainly spread by constant vegetative propagation.

The most virulent virus to affect roses is known as rose mosaic. Leaves become mottled or streaked with yellow and fall prematurely. Growth is often stunted and the flowers small. Little can be done to control this disease; if an infection occurs and is diagnosed, the plant is best removed and burned before other plants are infected. This virus is sometimes confused with chlorosis, which is actually a trace element deficiency, usually iron.

Mineral deficiencies

Iron deficiency is probably the most common nutritional ailment of roses; this manifests itself in a yellowing of the leaves, especially younger leaves either on the margins, or along the veins, or both. The leaves eventually turn completely yellow and drop off. Since the deficiency commonly occurs in calcareous soils, an application of sequestered iron to the soil in early spring should correct it. In the longer term, it is worth applying potash to the soil to help release locked up iron.

The other common deficiency is that of magnesium, which, in the case of roses, is probably a major requirement for successful performance. Symptoms of deficiency are not easily recognizable, but the leaves, especially the older ones, show chlorosis and are sometimes badly developed, especially at their apex. Epsom salts, applied to the soil once or twice a season in liquid form, will help rectify this. Where symptoms are markedly obvious, a solution of this can be applied as a foliar feed.

Other ailments

Other minor ailments can, from time to time, trouble roses. The most common of these stem from our own careless use of chemicals, particularly herbicides. Great care must be taken with these, especially the hormone variety. By far the most common diagnosis I make is that of spray damage. Always use a separate sprayer for weedkillers. No matter how carefully you think you have washed weedkiller from a machine, there could be just enough left inside to kill or disfigure your plants.

Malformation of flowers

Proliferation

Some of the more double flowered old-fashioned roses will occasionally sprout a malformed bud from their centre. This is known as proliferation, and is a most unpleasant sight. The phenomenon usually occurs in the early flowers, and in the case of the repeat-flowering shrubs, seldom reappears on autumn blooms. Close inspection of the misshapen flowers reveals that for some reason, probably genetic, the reproductive organs, in particular the pistils or female parts, have become fused, and instead of developing normally have changed into another complete flower bud, which grows out of the centre of the bloom. Close examination of this secondary bud shows that it appears to be complete in every way; sometimes it is even carried on a stalk and protrudes by up to as much as half an inch (1.5 cm). I have occasionally seen this in less obvious form in the very first blooms of some modern Large-Flowered roses, but this is rare.

Although some authorities consider it to be a virus, this has not been proved. I know of no other scientific explanation, but since its incidence does not seem to be related to the soil in which a variety is grown, at least out of doors, nor to any noticeable geographical location, we must assume it to be a form of genetic mutation, inherent in particular varieties and perpetuated by careless selection of budwood. I believe that the severity of the malformation is in some way influenced either by temperature or sunlight or both. Flowers appear to be more severely affected following a dull, cold spring, and bushes growing in partial shade are invariably worse than those in the open. I have noticed, too, that the problem is less severe on plants growing under glass. I find it interesting that 'Mme Isaac Pereire' is more prone to this problem than her sport 'Mme Ernst Calvat'. The same applies to 'Souvenir de la Malmaison', which sometimes suffers, and her sport 'Souvenir de St Annes', which does not. Apart from some of the more double Bourbons, one or two Damasks, and Centifolias, including a few Mosses, are worst affected. One or two Hybrid Perpetuals, which are closely related to the Bourbons, are also troubled from time to time; as is the China 'Cécile Brunner'. Little can be done by way of prevention or cure

Proliferation

beyond the removal of affected blooms as they appear.

Balling of flowers

Some old-fashioned roses, in common with some modern roses, do not like wet weather in summer. This is particularly true of the many-petalled, fully-double varieties with tightly folded flowers. They can usually endure it when open, but if prolonged rain occurs during the late bud stage, their outer petals will rot and congeal, thus preventing the flower from opening. Balling can become worse if strong sunshine follows rain, causing the petals to become encased in a crisp cocoon of decay, from which there is no escape. The whole flower then rots and falls off or, worse still, remains on the plant in a ruined, unsightly mess. There is not much to be done about this beyond cursing the weather, although in smaller gardens, where an individual rose is suffering, the outer petals can be teased carefully from the bud with thumb and forefinger before the rot has gone too deep, thus allowing the flower to unfurl without hindrance. Varieties particularly prone to this are the Bourbons 'Souvenir de la Malmaison' and 'Boule de Neige', and the Hybrid Perpetuals 'Baronne Prévost', 'Georg Arends' and 'Frau Karl Druschki'. Some of the Centifolias and Mosses are also prone to balling.

Above: A balled flower
Below: A balled flower after being teased open

Breeding new varieties

Plant breeding and hybridizing is a subject in itself and an elementary knowledge of botany is probably necessary for it to be fully understood.

Of all facets of roses and rose growing, it is probably fair to assume – judging by the questions I am asked – that breeding new varieties holds the most mystery. Many people appear to confuse this process with that of vegetative propagation, which I have already discussed. The breeding of roses is achieved by manual, sexual fertilization and is concerned only with the flowers of the two roses which are being crossed; and the resulting seeds.

Propagation, on the other hand, is achieved by inducing parts of plants to produce roots, as in cuttings; or to join with other plants, as in grafting or budding, thus increasing their numbers by non-sexual means; it therefore concerns only the shoots and roots of plants, not the flowers.

Beauty, fortunately, is in the eye of the beholder, so no one will ever know if the perfect rose is produced; perhaps, if we judge on flowers alone, all roses are perfect; hybridists, however, seek much more than perfection in flower. They nowadays look for health, vigour, attractive foliage, scent, resistance to weather, and an agreeable habit of growth.

The first step for a hybridist is to select potential parent roses with care. This choice will depend upon the type of rose he wishes to breed. A professional will give first consideration to parents likely to satisfy public demand. The present vogue for so-called ground cover roses is the hybridists' reaction to the modern preference for labour-saving, cost-effective plants. In Victorian times, fashion demanded large, shapely flowers for the show bench and in the Edwardian era, ramblers and climbers for arches and pergolas. This is not to say, of course, that hybridists merely follow fashion; they sometimes create it, as, for example, the brightly coloured Floribunda roses of the 1950s and 1960s, and the Miniature roses of the 1970s.

The selected breeding stock will either be planted in cold greenhouses or grown in pots. Hybridizing begins as soon as the roses start to flower in late spring or early summer. The first stage is to remove all petals from the selected seed parent. This must be done just before the petals unfold, thus ensuring no previous cross-fertilization. The next stage is to render the seed parent totally female by removing the stamens very carefully, usually with small scissors or tweezers. The stamens can be kept in small containers for use later as a male parent. Removal of stamens is a delicate operation, and any damage caused to the young seed pod will quickly result in the failure of the cross. The prepared potential mother is then left for about 24 hours, during which time the stigma will be seen to have become 'receptive' by deepening in colour and becoming slightly sticky. It is then ready for fertilization. Ripe pollen (visible as fine powder on the anthers) is then selected from a pre-chosen, compatible variety, and dusted on to the receptive female with a fine, soft brush. It should then be labelled and recorded. If pollen is plentiful, a further application the next day may benefit germination. Particular care must be taken with pollen to ensure that it does not become mixed; and any brushes used should be reserved for each individual batch of pollen and cleaned thoroughly after use. When pollen of selected parents is plentiful, commercial hybridists often dust it straight on to the stigma from a fully open rose.

After about two weeks, a successful mating will manifest itself in a healthy green hip which will eventually ripen to rich red or orange. If the cross has failed, the pod and stalk will start to wither and eventually turn brown or, in some cases, just drop off. Sometimes, fertile hips which have gone through the ripe stage become brown and rotten, but these are still good and will contain seeds.

The pods should be taken from the plants in late autumn and stored in readiness for sowing in early spring.

When the seedlings come into flower, any that are worth keeping should be either potted on, for another year's growth and testing, or budded in the nursery. If many eventually useless seedlings are kept, it can become a very expensive waste of time; so for commercial purposes only about one in fifty seedlings are taken to a second year of testing. After that time any seedlings with potential can be propagated in larger numbers for further trial. This is never more than one in every five hundred or so, and by the third year of trial this could well be reduced to one in five thousand. Consequently, unless hybridizing is done on a very large scale, the chances of breeding a top-selling rose are very remote.

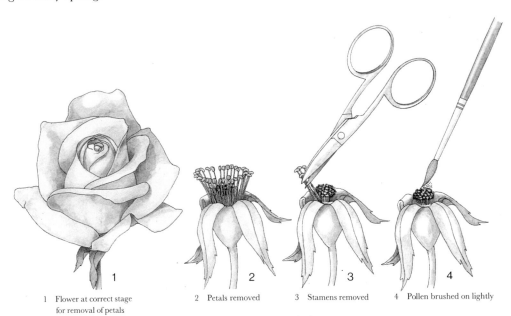

1 Flower at correct stage for removal of petals 2 Petals removed 3 Stamens removed 4 Pollen brushed on lightly

Breeding new varieties

PART IV
The Dictionary

Plant systematics are constantly undergoing change, so the place of the genus *Rosa* within the plant kingdom depends upon which published system one accepts. This is particularly true within the genus itself, for since Thory's work was published in the early 1800s* all subsequent classifications have been somewhat fragmented and there is no definitive system to follow.

All plant life is classified into divisions and then into subdivisions, each of which is split again into classes. After classes come various subclasses, which are again divided into orders. These orders are then grouped into families, the families into tribes and the tribes into genera. Thus the genus *Rosa* is part of the tribe Roseae, itself part of the family Rosaceae which, in addition to roses, contains diverse other plants such as potentilla and apple trees. At the genera stage all species with the same characteristics are grouped together; in the case of roses they are known botanically as genus *Rosa*. Then, to complicate things further, the genus, in common with other genera, is split into subgenera; for roses – subgenus I, *Hulthemia*; subgenus II, *Rosa (Eurosa)*; subgenus III, *Platyrhodon*; and subgenus IV, *Hesperhodos*. Subgenus II, *Rosa*, is by far the largest; and although *Hulthemia* is still included in this book as subgenus I, strictly botanically, it has now been reclassified outside the genus *Rosa*. The reason for these subgenera is that botanists consider each group, though still roses in every sense, to be sufficiently different in make-up to warrant separate classification. In turn, each subgenus is further subdivided into sections and subsections according to predominant characteristics and recognizable relationships. In this dictionary I have placed the various species into the sections to which they belong under their subgeneric heading. The subsections have been ignored since at this stage their different, definable characteristics are small.

Over the years, earlier by chance mutation or natural hybridity, and later by deliberate manipulation or by a combination of all these factors, hybrids occurred, or were developed, with the genealogy of the various sections. These lead us to what are loosely termed the garden groups of roses, viz: Albas, Bourbons, Gallicas, Damasks. Teas, etc.

*See page 27.

These garden groups are here placed in their rightful position under the species to which they most owe their lineage. The species themselves appear in alphabetical order under the subgenus and section to which they belong.**

Listed and described are many Species, Old Hybrid roses, Modern Shrub roses, Climbing and Rambling roses, most of which are, or should be, available today from the many thousands which have been discovered or raised and introduced over the past few hundred years.

**Works with more emphasis on botanic systematics and taxonomy usually credit those who work or have worked in these fields by placing their names against species which they have discovered, classified or named. This is a gardening book and I have not done this, largely in the interest of simplicity, and not from any lack of respect for those whose names are omitted. In compiling this dictionary I have referred frequently to Bean's *Trees and Shrubs* Volume IV 1984; *Roses* by Gerd Krüssman; the works of Graham Thomas and Jack Harkness; and *Modern Roses* 7, by McFarland.

Letters and symbols used throughout the dictionary to indicate the special usage of each species or variety.

(SP) Spring-flowering only – usually May/early June.

(S) Summer-flowering only – usually mid-June to the end of July.

(R) Recurrent or repeat-flowering.

(C) More or less continuous-flowering throughout summer.

N Suitable for north walls (though roses only 'tolerate' this situation).

G Procumbent roses (ground cover, in modern idiom).

T Vigorous roses suitable for growing up into trees.

P Tolerant of poorer soils.

A Good autumn foliage.

H Suitable for hedging.

W Suitable for woodland planting.

F Worth growing for the ornamental value of their fruit.

Gh Suitable for growing under glass as well as outdoors.

▽ Suitable for growing in pots, urns or tubs, etc.

◍ Shade tolerant (though no rose really enjoys full shade).

≋ Suggested for growing adjacent to water.

☼ Needing a sunny, warm position to thrive.

Table comparing Seasons in the Rose Cycle in the Northern and Southern Hemisphere

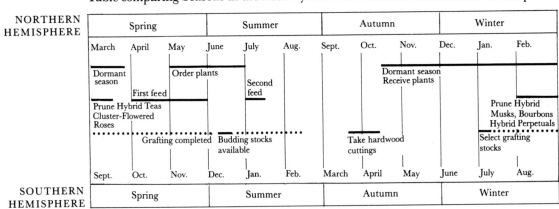

ROSA Subgenus I
Hulthemia (Simplicifoliae)

Although included here, this subgenus has now been reclassified by botanists and is no longer part of the genus *Rosa*. However, except for foliage, which consists of simple individual leaves without stipules, rather than composite ones with stipules, it grows and behaves just like a rose; so much so that to discriminate against it and omit it on grounds of race would be quite wrong. Note. For further information on these fascinating plants see Jack Harkness' excellent book *Roses*.

SPECIES

Hulthemia persica
× *Hulthemosa hardii*

ORIGIN AND DISTRIBUTION

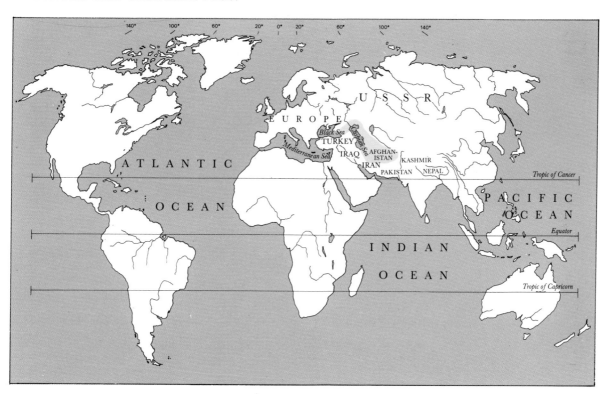

Hulthemia persica

[RCB]

Hulthemia persica, R. persica, R. berberifolia

CENTRAL ASIA 1789

Difficult to grow but worth some perseverance.
Leaves slender with no stipules. Small, single
flowers of bright clear yellow with a browny-
crimson splodge in the centre of each; usually
borne at end of twiggy, downy, angular shoots
with hooked thorns which are arranged in pairs
below the leaves. Flowers spasmodically for a
fairly long season.

[☼ ▽ (S)]   2′ × 2′   60 × 60 cm

× *Hulthemosa hardii,   R. × Hardii*

Hardy FRANCE c. 1830

Hulthemia persica × R. clinophylla

A medium-growing rose, very unusual with small,
single, buttercup-size flowers of deep, golden
yellow with a striking, bright, reddish-brown eye
in its centre. Growth twiggy but dense with spiteful thorns and numerous pinnate leaves without
stipules. Supposed not to be hardy. A potted bush
in my possession seems to have thrived on neglect
but this is probably exceptional.

[☼ ▽ (SF)   6′ × 4′   1.8 × 1.2 m

ROSA Subgenus II Rosa (Eurosa)
SECTION I *Pimpinellifoliae*

Growth mostly upright, varying from 3 ft to 12 ft, 1 m to 4 m.
Stems prickly with many thorns.
Leaves small, some 7 to 9 leaflets, others 9 to 11. *R. sericea* 13 to 17 leaflets.
Flowers mostly produced singly on short stems.
Sepals always persist on ripe hips.

SPECIES

R. × cantabrigiensis
R. dunwichensis
R. ecae
R. foetida (R. lutea)
R. foetida bicolor
R. foetida persiana
R. × hemisphaerica
R. × hibernica
R. hugonis
R. × involuta (R. gracilis, R. rubella,
R. wilsonii)

R. koreana
R. pimpinellifolia (R. spinosissima)
R. primula
R. × pteragonis
R. × reversa
R. × sabinii
R. sericea
R. xanthina

GARDEN GROUPS

Austrian Briars
Burnet and Scotch Roses

ORIGIN AND DISTRIBUTION

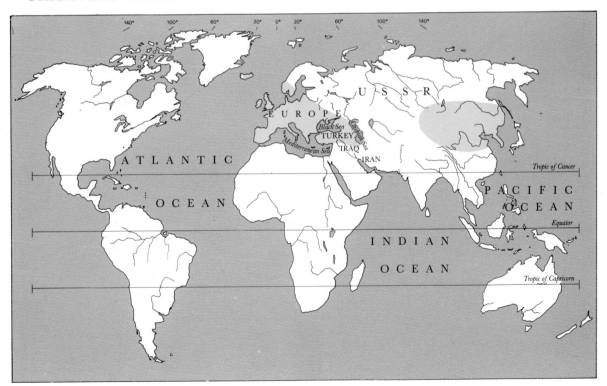

R. ecae 'Golden Chersonese'

R. ecae

R. ecae

AFGHANISTAN 1880

A small, very prickly shrub with reddish-brown twigs and small, fern-like leaves. Numerous buttercup-size single flowers of deep, rich yellow with pronounced stamens. Needs extra special care when it can be spectacular.

[(S)]   4′×3′· 1.2 m × 90 cm

'Helen Knight'

F. P. Knight UK 1966

R. ecae × R. pimpinellifolia altaica

A useful hybrid with large, slightly cupped, single, deep yellow flowers produced in late spring amid fern-like foliage. Vigorous shrub with darkish stems and thorns.

[P ⬤ (S)]   5′×4′   1.5×1.2 m

FORMS AND HYBRIDS OF
R. ecae

'Golden Chersonese'

E. F. Allen UK 1963

R. ecae × 'Canary Bird'

A fine shrub with single, rich golden-yellow flowers produced profusely early in the season. Upright growth with dark brownish wood and thorns. Foliage fern-like, individually small but abundant.

[N P ⬤ (S)]   6′×4′   1.8×1.2 m

'Helen Knight'   [VP]

R. foetida

R. *foetida*, R. *lutea*, 'Austrian Briar',
'Austrian Yellow'

ASIA 16th century or earlier
Large, single flowers of rich golden-yellow with
prominent stamens produced in early June. Erect
growth with large, blackish thorns. Wood chestnut brown. Foliage bright green and firm in
texture. An important rose, being largely responsible, with its cousin R. *foetida persiana* for the
yellow colour in our modern roses. The rather
unusual specific name comes from the slightly
unpleasant smell of the flowers.

[P (S)]   8′×5′   2.5×1.5 m

R. *foetida bicolor*   [RCB]

R. *foetida bicolor*, R. *lutea punicea*, 'Austrian
Copper'

ASIA 16th century or earlier
A sport from R. *foetida* which occurred at some
time in the distant past. In this form the flowers
are rich copper-orange, dazzling when at their
best. The flower occasionally reverts to the
original yellow and sometimes both colours
appear on the plant simultaneously. Like its
cousins, rather prone to black spot.

[P (S)]   5′×4′   1.5×1.2 m

R. *foetida persiana* 'Persian Yellow'

S.W. ASIA 1837
Very double, globular flowers of rich, golden-
yellow. Has all the attributes and faults of both
previous species, except that I believe it to be
rather less vigorous.

[P (S)]   6′×4′   1.8×1.2 m

FORMS AND HYBRIDS OF
R. foetida

'Lawrence Johnston', 'Hidcote Yellow'

Pernet-Ducher FRANCE c. 1920 Introduced 1923
'Mme Eugène Verdier' × R. *foetida persiana*
An early flowering, climber with clusters of semi-
double, yellow flowers with prominent stamens.
Fragrant. Very vigorous with abundant, lush,
light green foliage.

[P N ◍ (R)]   25′×20′   7.5×6 m

'Le Rêve'

Pernet-Ducher FRANCE c. 1920
'Mme Eugène Verdier' × R. *foetida persiana*
Similar to 'Lawrence Johnston', in fact, from the

'Lawrence Johnston'   [VP]

R. foetida and *R. foetida bicolor* on the same plant   [RCB]

same cross. Slightly less vigorous and perhaps a shade less bright in colour. Very fragrant. Both are excellent varieties which should be grown more often.

[P N ◍ (R)]   20′×15′   6×4.5 m

'Star of Persia'

Pemberton UK 1919

R. foetida × 'Trier'

An interesting hybrid from Pemberton proving that he explored other avenues of breeding while working on his Hybrid Musks. Tall, vigorous bush, or small climber. Semi-double, bright yellow flowers which, when fully open, display deep golden stamens to effect. Its parent, *R. foetida* shows through in its growth habit and foliage. Not often seen these days.

[☼ (S)]   8′×4′   2.5×1.2 m

'Star of Persia'   [RCB]

R. × *hemisphaerica*, 'The Sulphur Rose'

S.W. ASIA Pre-1625

The globular, fully-double, luminous, rich sulphur-yellow flowers nod amid plentiful, greyish-light green foliage. They seldom open properly in damp weather but are well worth perseverance, since when they do open the flowers are most attractive. Prefers a warm, sheltered position to thrive. Is 'smelly' rather than scented.

[☼ ▽ (S)]   6′×4′   1.8×1.2 m

R. hugonis

R. hugonis, 'Golden Rose of China'

CHINA 1899

Large quantities of medium-sized, primrose-yellow flowers on an upright growing bush. Densely thorny, the stems are bronzy-brown in colour. Its leaves are plentiful with a fern-like quality both in appearance and to touch, turning bronzy-orange in autumn. This rose also bears small, dark red fruit in late summer.

[P W A F ☼ (SP)] 8′ × 5′ 2.5 × 1.5 m

R. × cantabrigiensis, *R. pteragonis cantabrigiensis*

Cambridge Botanic Gardens UK c. 1931
R. hugonis × R. sericea

Less upright than *R. hugonis*. The flowers are larger and slightly paler. They also withstand the weather in a more determined fashion. The shoots are graceful, arching and of a fawny-brown colour as are the numerous thorns. Foliage is fern-like but not as colourful in autumn as its parents.

[P W F ☼ (SP)] 7′ × 5′ 2 × 1.5 m

FORMS AND HYBRIDS OF
R. hugonis

'Earldomensis'

Page UK 1934
R. hugonis × R. sericea

A spreading shrub, with flat reddish thorns which are translucent when young. Attractive fern-like foliage. Its flowers are rich yellow, single and produced from late May to early June. Difficult to propagate.

[☼ W A F ◍ (SP)] 7′ × 5′ 2 × 1.5 m

'Headleyensis'

Warburg UK
R. hugonis × unknown, possibly *R. pimpinellifolia altaica*

A handsome shrub, more compact than *R.*

R. cantabrigiensis   [RCB]

hugonis. Foliage is particularly good being rich clear green and produced in profusion from thorny, brownish stems. Flowers soft primrose yellow with good perfume.

[P W A ◍ (SP)] 7′ × 4′ 2 × 1.2 m

R. × involuta, *R. gracilis*, *R. rubella*, *R. wilsonii*

N. EUROPE C. 1820

Thought to be a natural hybrid between *R. pimpinellifolia* and *R. villosa* but the pollen parent could possibly be another species of its habitat region such as *R. tomentosa* or *R. sherardii*. Flowers of small to medium size, white on a spiny, free suckering plant with smallish, grey-green leaves. Stems, especially the older ones are fawnish-brown. Hips oval to round, slightly bristly. Frequently seen in the wild in parts of Scandinavia.

[W P ◍ (S)] 3′ × 3′ 90 × 90 cm

R. koreana

KOREA 1917

A shrubby, fairly dense, bristly plant with reddish wood. Single, white to blush-pink flowers followed by small, pendulous oval, orange hips. Leaves dark green and numerous, made up of 7 to 11 leaflets.

[W P ◍ (S)] 3′ × 3′ 90 × 90 cm

R. pimpinellifolia
Burnet Roses

R. pimpinellifolia, *R. spinosissima*, 'Burnet Rose', 'Scotch Briar'

EUROPE Pre-1600

Charming, single flowers, creamy-white, sometimes with subtle hints of pink, borne freely early in the season. Pronounced stamens. Foliage small and coarsely fern-like. Stems very densely populated with long, needle-like prickles. Globular, almost black fruit. Suckers freely when it is grown on its own roots. Happy in most soils, particularly sandy soil. This species has given rise to many and varied hybrids over the years.

[P W H A ⊕ (SP)]   3′ × 3′   90 × 90 cm

R. pimpinellifolia altaica, *R. pimpinellifolia spinosissima*

ASIA C. 1818

Dark brownish wood with numerous spiney thorns and soft-textured, well-serrated, greyish-light green foliage. Flowers white, large and beautiful, single with pronounced golden-yellow stamens. A useful, healthy shrub with maroon-purple hips in the autumn.

[H W P A F ⊕ (SP)]   5′ × 3′   1.5 m × 92 cm

R. pimpinellifolia hispida

N.E. ASIA, SIBERIA C. 1781

An upright growing shrub with slightly larger foliage than *R. pimpinellifolia altaica*. Flowers large and soft yellow to white with prominent stamens. Shoots darkish green to brown with numerous spiney thorns. Very hardy.

[H W P ⊕ (SP)]   6′ × 4′   1.8 × 1.2 m

R. pimpinellifolia lutea

ASIA Date unknown

Single deep yellow flowers on an upright bushy plant. Similar to *R. pimpinellifolia altaica* in growth habit but less vigorous and with smaller flowers.

[H W P ⊕ (SP)]   4′ × 3′   1.2 m × 90 cm

DOUBLE FORMS AND HYBRIDS OF
R. pimpinellifolia

BURNET ROSES

Many double forms of *R. pimpinellifolia* have existed over the years since the first were introduced around 1800. These came in many colours and all were named. Some of these charming little roses are still with us but their names have become lost in time.

The Royal National Rose Society has a good and varied, representative collection of these which are well worth seeing in May and June, at St Albans. Only the most important are described here, otherwise the list could be endless.

'Double White', 'Double Pink', 'Double Marbled Pink', etc.

All these have globular flowers, produced in profusion on tidy, well-foliated, thorny plants. Most produce globular, dark, almost black hips in late summer and all make useful, tidy, rounded shrubs or attractive, thick hedges.

[G F P H A ⊕ (S)]   3′ × 3′   90 × 90 cm

[PB]
Above: R. *pimpinellifolia altaica*
Below: R. *pimpinellifolia*, 'Frühlingszauber' (see text p. 142) [VP]

Burnet rose 'Double Pink' (see text p. 139)   [PB]

Double Yellow Forms

Several exist with the yellow in their make-up obviously derived from *R. foetida*. The most important are:

R. × harisonii or 'Harison's Yellow' (Yellow Rose of Texas) – very double USA 1846

'Williams' Double Yellow' – semi-double UK 1828

I find both of these rather coarser in growth than the other colours and prefer an old, double form which I call, simply – 'Old Yellow Scotch'. This is more compact in growth, pleasingly scented and of very ancient origin.

[G P H ⦿ (S)]   4′ × 3′   1.2m × 90 cm

Burnet rose 'Double White' (see text p. 139)   [TW]

R. × hibernica (see text p. 144)   [TW]

R. × harisonii

[RCB]

OTHER FORMS AND HYBRIDS OF
R. pimpinellifolia

'Andrewsii'

Origin and parentage unknown c. 1806
Semi-double flowers of deep pinkish-red and cream, displaying yellow stamens when fully open. A dense, well-foliated and well-prickled plant. Sometimes repeating in the autumn, a rare feat for any of the Pimpinellifolia roses.

[G W P ⦿ (R)]   4' × 3'   1.2 m × 90 cm

'Dunwich Rose', *R. dunwichensis*

Date and parentage unknown
A procumbent form, found fairly recently at Dunwich in Suffolk. Flowers creamy-yellow with typical *R. pimpinellifolia* foliage, thorns and hips. A superb prostrate rose which is quite beautiful.

[P G F ▽ ⁘ (S)]   2' × 4'   60 cm × 1.2 m

'Falkland'

UK
Parentage and date unknown
Lovely, semi-double, cupped flowers of soft lilac-pink, paling with age to blush white. Compact growth. Typical Pimpinellifolia foliage. Good-sized, deep maroon hips in late summer and autumn.

[H W P F ⦿ (S)]   3' × 3'   90 × 90 cm

'Frühlingsanfang'

Kordes GERMANY 1950
'Joanna Hill' × *R. pimpinellifolia altaica*
Superb, medium-sized, pure white flowers with prominent stamens and a strong scent. Dark green foliage on an upright and healthy plant.

[P W H ⦿ (S)]   10' × 6'   3 × 1.8 m

'Dunwich Rose'

[RCB]

'Frühlingsduft'

Kordes GERMANY 1949
'Joanna Hill' × *R. pimpinellifolia altaica*
A vigorous, healthy plant with rather crinkled,
dark green, glossy foliage. Flowers large, fully-
double, soft lemon-yellow, heavily flushed with
pink and highly scented.
[P W H ⬤ (S)]   10′ × 6′   3 × 1.8 m

'Frühlingsgold'

Kordes GERMANY 1937
'Joanna Hill' × *R. pimpinellifolia* hybrid
Large, almost single flowers of rich golden-yellow
paling to primrose. Very profuse blooms on a
vigorous, upright plant with dark green foliage.
Stems also darkish green and rather thorny.
[P W H ⬤ (SP)]   7′ × 5′   2 × 1.5 m

'Frühlingsmorgen'

Kordes GERMANY 1942
('E. G. Hill' × 'Cathrine Kordes') × *R. pimpinellifolia altaica*
Large, single flowers of cherry-pink and white
with primrose centres and golden stamens.
Sweetly perfumed. Starts flowering early and is
occasionally recurrent. Upright. A well-foliated
shrub with dark green leaves.
[P W H ⬤ (SP)]   6′ × 4′   1.8 × 1.2 m

'Frühlingsschnee'

Kordes GERMANY 1954
'Golden Glow' × *R. pimpinellifolia altaica*
Large, single, pure white flowers opening early
in the season. Upright in habit with plenty of
thorns and dark green foliage.
[P W H ⬤ (SP)]   6′ × 4′   1.8 × 1.2 m

'Frühlingstag'

Kordes GERMANY 1949
'McGredy's Wonder' × 'Frühlingsgold'
Clusters of large, open, semi-double flowers of
rich golden yellow paling to soft yellow with age.
Fragrant. Dark leathery foliage. Dark greenish-
brown very thorny stems. Upright.
[P W H ⬤ (SP)]   7′ × 4′   2 × 1.2 m

Above: 'Frühlingsmorgen'   [RCB]
Below: 'Glory of Edzell'   [PB]

'Frühlingszauber'

Kordes GERMANY 1942
('E. G. Hill' × 'Cathrine Kordes') × *R. pimpinellifolia altaica*
Large, almost single flowers of silvery-pink with
abundant dark green foliage. An upright, rather
thorny plant. Very healthy.
[P W H ⬤ (S)]   7′ × 5′   2 × 1.5 m

'Glory of Edzell'

Origin, date and parentage unknown
Single, clear pink with paler, almost white centres
and pronounced stamens. Flowering very early
each season. Foliage small but dense, growth upright, spiney.
[P W H ⬤ (SP)]   5′ × 4′   1.5 × 1.2 m

'Golden Wings'

Shepherd USA 1956
('Soeur Thérèse' × *R. pimpinellifolia altaica*) ×
'Ormiston Roy'
Large, clear golden-yellow flowers, almost single

'Golden Wings' [VP]

Above: 'Maigold' [VP]
Below: 'Ormiston Roy' (see text p. 144) [VP]

with pronounced golden-brown stamens, produced abundantly both in clusters and singly,
amid rich light green foliage. Flowers almost continuously from June to October, sweetly scented.
An accommodating shrub in all respects.

[P H (C)] 5′×4′ 1.5×1.2 m

'Karl Förster'

Kordes GERMANY 1931
'Frau Karl Druschki' × *R. pimpinellifolia altaica*
A showy shrub. Large, semi-double flowers with
prominent golden stamens when fully open.
Bushy in growth with greyish light green foliage.
A most useful, underrated rose with intermittent
flowers produced later in summer.

[P W ◍ (R)] 5′×4′ 1.5×1.2 m

'Maigold'

Kordes GERMANY 1953
'Poulson's Pink' × 'Frühlingstag'
A superb climber. One of first to flower each
season. Non-recurrent but spectacular when in
full flush. Fragrant semi-double flowers, rich
golden-yellow flushed-orange. Foliage rich green
and glossy. Strong stems covered in reddish-
brown thorns.

[T P N ◍ (S)] 12′×8′ 3.5×2.5 m

'Mary Queen of Scots'

Origin, date and parentage unknown
A beautiful rose. Single flowers with prominent
stamens. Creamy-white in the centre with lilac
and reddish brush marks which deepen towards

the edge of each petal. These are followed by
globular, blackish-maroon fruit on a tidy, twiggy,
well-foliated little plant.

[P F ▽ ◍ (SP)] 3′×3′ 90×90 cm

'Mrs Colville'

Origin and date unknown
Thought to be *R. pimpinellifolia* × *R. pendulina*
A fascinating little shrub with single, crimson-

'Mary Queen of Scots' (see text p. 143)   [RCB]

purple flowers, having pronounced stamens and a prominent white eye in the centre. Less thorny than most of its type, with reddish-brown wood and small but plentiful foliage.

[H P F ▽ ◍ (SP)]   4' × 3'   1.2 m × 90 cm

'Ormiston Roy'
Doorenbos HOLLAND 1953
R. pimpinellifolia × *R. xanthina*
Single bright buttercup-yellow flowers on a thorny, dense plant with light green, fern-like leaves. Large purple to black globular hips in the autumn.

[H P F ▽ ◍ (SP)]   4' × 3'   1.2 m × 90 cm

'Single Cherry'
Origin, date and parentage unknown
Very bright, cherry-red, single flowers with paler, blended blotches of pink. Foliage grey-green and plentiful on a short, bushy plant. Small, rounded, blackish hips later.

[H P F ▽ ◍ (SP)]   3' × 3'   90 × 90 cm

'Stanwell Perpetual'
Lee UK 1838
R. × damascena bifera × *R. pimpinellifolia*
A prickly, arching but graceful shrub with numerous, greyish-green leaves, sometimes becoming mottled-purple as though diseased. Though unsightly, this discolouration is not serious, nor, as far as I know, contagious, and it should not put you off this superb, old variety. The long flowering season – so rare in this group – amply compensates for a few discoloured leaves. Flowers fully-double, quartered, soft blush-pink and scented.

[H P W ◍ (C)]   5' × 5'   1.5 × 1.5 m

'William III'
Origin, date and parentage unknown
Semi-double flowers of rich maroon paling to magenta, followed by dark chocolate-brown hips. Dense foliage on a tidy upright plant. Scented. An exquisite little rose.

[P W F ◍ ▽ (S)]   3' × 3'   90 × 90 cm

R. × hibernica
Templeton IRELAND 1795
R. pimpinellifolia × *R. canina*
A most interesting rose, discovered in Ireland at the end of the 18th century but now thought to be extinct there in the wild. The shrub is of medium size with leaves midway between those of *R. pimpinellifolia* and *R. canina*. A special feature of this shrub is its superb hips which are coloured like those of *R. canina* and shaped like those of *R. pimpinellifolia*, retaining its sepals in the same fashion as the latter. The flowers are single, medium-sized and bright pink in colour. I have not found it remontant as is claimed for the Irish clone but it is possible – since the two parent species are obviously compatible – that other clones exist. Professor Nelson of Dublin Botanic Gardens has recently drawn my attention to the fact that a plant, known to have come from Templeton's original, is alive and well in Belfast. In due course I intend to compare this with mine.

[P F W ☼ (S)]   4' × 4'   1.2 × 1.2 m

Above: 'Stanwell Perpetual'   [TW]
Below: 'William III'   [RCB]

R. primula, 'Incense Rose'

CENTRAL ASIA, CHINA 1910

Beautiful species with strong, upright, dark brown thorny stems supporting arching laterals. The glossy fern-like foliage has a strong aroma of incense. The flowers, which appear early in the season, are single and soft buttercup-yellow with pronounced stamens; they are strongly scented. A most useful and interesting shrub which sometimes sets small reddish fruit.

[W P A (SP)]   5′×4′   1.5×1.2 m

R. × pteragonis

GERMANY 1938

R. hugonis × R. sericea

A medium/tall shrub with broad, dark red prickles similar to those of R. sericea but with primrose yellow, five petalled flowers after those of R. hugonis.

[W P ⓜ (SP)]   6′×4′   1.8×1.2 m

R. × reversa

S. EUROPE 1820

R. pendulina × R. pimpinellifolia

Flowers variable from pink to white, mostly pink. Medium sized oval to round, pendulous, deep red hips. Growth slightly angular with purple shoots, often quite bristly.

[W P ⓜ (S)]   4′×3′   1.2 m×90 cm

R. × sabinii

N. EUROPE C. 1850

Very similar to R. × involuta, different in having longer flower stamens, large hips and less brown stems. Probably a cross between R. pimpinellifolia and R. mollis.

[W P ⓜ (S)]   3′×3′   90×90 cm

R. sericea, R. omeiensis

HIMALAYAS, W. CHINA 1822

A vigorous shrub with fern-like foliage and stout branches armed with large, hooked thorns and numerous small spines. Thorns bright translucent red while young. Flowers white with pronounced, pale yellow stamens; unlike any other species of the genus, these are comprised of four petals only. Fruit bright red, almost oval but slightly pear-shaped. In some works R. omeiensis is listed as a separate species. Perhaps this is so, but they are so alike that one species is enough here.

[P F W A (SP)]   10′×6′   3×1.8 m

R. sericea chrysocarpa

HIMALAYAS Actual date of introduction not known

The same in all respects to R. sericea except that its fruit is bright yellow.

[P W F A ⓜ (S)]   10′×6′   3×1.8 m

FORMS AND HYBRIDS OF
R. sericea

R. sericea pteracantha, R. omeiensis pteracantha

CHINA Introduced 1890

Delicate, fern-like foliage contrasting with brown stems clad with huge, wedge-shaped thorns. When young these thorns are quite spectacular, being translucent, glowing like rubies against morning and evening sun. The small – at first sight rather insignificant – flowers are quite beautiful on close inspection being white, single and made up of four petals only. These are followed by small, oval to round, variable yellow to bright orange-red hips.

[P F W A ⓜ (SP)]   10′×6′   3×1.8 m

R. sericea pteracantha   [VP]

R. sericea pteracantha atrosanguinea

As above, but with slightly deeper red, translucent thorns and darker red, almost black hips.

[P F W A ⓜ (SP)]   10′×6′   3×1.8 m

'Red Wing'

Origin and date unknown

R. sericea pteracantha × *R. hugonis*

A gracefully-growing plant with beautiful, red, wedge-shaped thorns. Flowers creamy-yellow, single. A lovely shrub, not difficult to grow, but difficult to produce in the nursery.

[A W ◐ (SP)] 6′×4′ 1.8×1.2 m

'Heather Muir'

Sunningdale Nurseries UK 1957

R. sericea hybrid

Pure white, single flowers produced, for such a rose, over a long season. Foliage fern-like and stems heavily covered with wedge-like thorns. Upright growth. Produces rich orange fruit.

[W F A ◐ (SP)] 8′×6′ 2.5×1.8 m

'Hidcote Gold'

Hilling and Co. UK 1948

R. sericea hybrid

Bright yellow, single flowers in small clusters on a robust plant. Stems liberally covered with broad wedge-shaped thorns and ferny foliage.

[A W ◐ (SP)] 8′×6′ 2.5×1.8 m

R. xanthina

CHINA 1906

An angular shrub with dark stems and thorns and dark green, fern-like foliage. Flowers small, loosely and raggedly semi-double, scented, rich yellow, produced early in the season.

[H (SP)] 10′×6′ 3×1.8 m

FORMS AND HYBRIDS OF
R. xanthina

'Canary Bird', *R. xanthina spontanea*

CHINA C. 1908

Tall, angular-growing shrub with dark wood and thorns, and dark green, fern-like foliage. Produces laterals of a graceful, pendulous habit on which the flowers are borne, making it a useful standard rose in good soils. Single flowers, rich canary yellow with prominent stamens, well scented. Sometimes rather temperamental, suffering partial die-back for no apparent reason; but if the dead wood is removed, it frequently recovers. Flowers sometimes appear intermittently in the autumn.

[H (SP)] 8′×6′ 2.5×1.8 m

R. xanthina, 'Canary Bird'

[PB]

ROSA Subgenus II Rosa (Eurosa)
SECTION II *Gallicanae*

Growth between 3 ft to 6 ft, 1 m to 2 m, upright or arching.
Stems variably armed.
Foliage large, usually made up of 5 leaflets.
Flowers solitary or in threes or four on long stems.
Sepals reflex and drop from hips when ripe.

SPECIES

R. × *centifolia*
R. × *centifolia alba*
R. × *centifolia muscosa*
R. × *damascena*
R. × *damascena bifera*
R. × *damascena trigintipetala*
R. × *damascena versicolor*
R. *gallica*
R. *gallica officinalis*

R. *gallica versicolor*
R. *macrantha*
R. *richardii*

GARDEN GROUPS

Gallicas
Cabbage Roses (Centifolias)
Damasks
Portlands

ORIGIN AND DISTRIBUTION

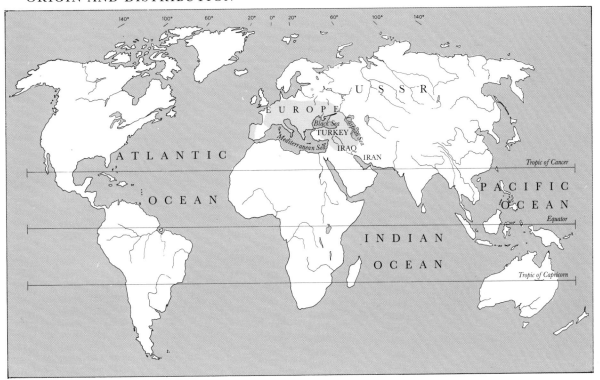

R. gallica 'Henri Foucquier' (see text p. 158)   [VP]

R. gallica

This group has a considerable influence on the evolution of modern roses, as is explained in more detail elsewhere in the book. These quietly unobtrusive garden hybrids, although seldom, if ever, remontant, deserve to be far more widely used.

Note: Included in this section are the few forms of *R. franco-furtana* which are closely related to the Gallicas. In some books these are listed as a separate group.

R. gallica, R. rubra, 'French Rose'

EUROPE, S.W. ASIA Of great antiquity
A rather insignificant rose considering that its genes permeate – to a greater or lesser extent – many modern garden hybrids. Small shrub with upright habit, bearing medium to large, single flowers with pronounced powdery-yellow stamens, petals varying from deep to soft pink. Useful for group planting, perhaps in the wild garden.

[W P ◍ (S)] 4′ × 3′ 1.2 m × 90 cm

R. gallica officinalis, 'The Apothecary's Rose', 'Red Rose of Lancaster', 'Rose of Provins', 'Double French Rose'

EUROPE, S.W. ASIA Of great antiquity
A showy shrub with erect yet bushy growth and coarse, dark greyish-green leaves. Flowers light crimson, semi-double, quite large, highly scented and profuse in June. In a good summer, when fully ripe, the small, oval hips are attractive. In the Middle Ages its scent-retaining properties were much valued by apothecaries.

[P F H ◍ ▽ (S)] 3′ × 3′ 90 × 90 cm

R. gallica versicolor, 'Rosa Mundi' (see text p. 152)

[RCB]

R. gallica versicolor, 'Rosa Mundi'

EUROPE, S.W. ASIA Of great antiquity
A striking rose. A sport from *R. gallica officinalis* to which it is identical except in colour. Probably the oldest and best known of the striped roses, it is a varied mixture of light crimson and white. The most romantic of various legends surrounding this rose is that it was named after 'Fair Rosamund', mistress of Henry II.

[F P H ◑ ▽ (S)]   3′ × 3′   90 × 90 cm

FORMS AND HYBRIDS OF
R. gallica

'Agatha', *R. × francofurtana agatha*

EUROPE, S.W. ASIA
Possibly *R. gallica × R. pendulina*
Although somewhat taller, this charming rose is thought to be a relative of 'Empress Josephine'. Flowers slightly smaller and of a deeper pink shade than those of the 'Empress' and with a stronger scent. Densely arching in growth, the leaves are soft to touch, yet appear quite crisp. Has few thorns of significance.

[P H ◑ (S)]   5′ × 4′   1.5 × 1.2 m

'Agathe Incarnata'

EUROPE C. 1800
Origin and parentage unknown
A highly scented rose with soft pink flowers. When fully open, the irregular petals form a tight, quartered effect, reminiscent of crumpled and torn crêpe paper. Foliage is grey-green and soft to touch. Growth dense, slightly arching and somewhat thorny. My particular clone seems fairly distinct but occasionally similar varieties crop up for identification, suggesting that others once existed as garden varieties. Graham Stuart Thomas suggests Damask influence in the 'Agathe' type Gallicas.

[P (S)]   4′ × 4′   1.2 × 1.2 m

'Alain Blanchard'

Vibert FRANCE 1839
Probably *R. centifolia × R. gallica*
Large flowers, slightly more than single in form, crimson smudged purple with pronounced golden stamens. Foliage dark green; growth dense and bushy. A most pleasing rose with a good scent.

[P ◑ (S)]   4′ × 4′   1.2 × 1.2 m

'Alain Blanchard'   [PB]

'Anaïs Ségalas'

Vibert FRANCE 1837
Parentage unknown
A shortish growing, arching shrub, rather more Centifolia-like than Gallica. Perhaps the main feature is the superb form of the flowers, each one seeming carefully groomed. Highly scented. Colour cerise to crimson, paling towards edges with age. Foliage small and dark green.

[▽ P (S)]   3′ × 3′   90 × 90 cm

'Antonia d'Ormois'

From the Roseraie de l'Hay collection FRANCE
Parentage and date unknown
Flowering slightly later than some other Gallicas. Fully double cupped flowers, the colour is of soft pink paling to almost white with age. This is not a rose I know well but its foliage is of a good clear green colour.

[P (S)]   5′ × 3′   1.5 m × 90 cm

'Assemblage des Beautés' [PB]

'Assemblage des Beautés', 'Rouge Eblouissante'

Originated in Angers FRANCE c. 1823
Parentage unknown
Double, bright crimson flowers changing to purple with age. Flowers scented and produced in abundance on a compact, bushy shrub. Foliage rich dark green; shoots bear few thorns. One of the nicest of the Gallicas.
[P ▽ ⦾]   4′ × 3′   1.2 m × 90 cm

'Belle de Crécy'

Mid-19th century
Origin and parentage unknown
Fairly reliable as a grower but temperamental in flower. At best can be one of the most beautiful in its group; at worst, horrid. Flowers are a pleasing mixture of pinks, greys and mauves, flat and quartered, often with a clearly defined, green eye in the centre. Highly scented. Growth upright, foliage grey-green. Stems almost thornless.
[P H ▽ (S)]   4′ × 3′   1.2 m × 90 cm

'Belle Isis'

Parmentier BELGIUM 1845
Parentage unknown
A small to medium-growing shrub with tidy, up-right growth and grey-green foliage. The flowers, which are fully double, opening flat, are a lovely delicate shade of pink with a strong perfume.
[P (S)]   4′ × 3′   1.2 m × 90 cm

'Boule de Nanteuil'

Mid-19th century
Origin and parentage unknown
A charming rose. Fully double flowers opening flattish and quartered. Colour deep pink, almost

Above: 'Oeillet Parfait' (see text p. 161)   [VP]
Below: 'Belle Isis'   [VP]

cerise with silver overtones. Like most Gallicas, it is scented. Growth robust and upright. Foliage dark green.

[P H (S)] 4′×3′ 1.2 m×90 cm

'Camaieux'

Vibert FRANCE 1830

Parentage unknown

Striking, double, pale pink blooms striped purplish-crimson changing with age to a pleasing mixture of lavender and purple. These open rather loosely and are borne on arching stems amid grey-green foliage on a shortish bushy plant.

[P H ▽ (S)] 3′×3′ 90×90 cm

'Cardinal de Richelieu'

Laffay FRANCE c. 1840

Parentage unknown

Beautifully formed rich purple flowers, borne mostly in clusters and of a delicate velvety texture. Sweetly scented. A compact bush with thin stems which are almost free of thorns. Foliage abundant, smooth and dark green, sometimes edged with maroon.

[P H ▽ (S)] 4′×3′ 1.2 m×90 cm

'Cardinal de Richelieu'   [PB]

'Charles de Mills'

From the Roseraie de L'Hay collection. An old variety

Parentage unknown

A rose of uncertain origin but one of the best, especially in good soil. Vigorous, with dark green leaves. Large flowers open to a mixture of purple and deep red. Sometimes, the petals form perfect edges as if the rose were enclosed by an invisible, circular frame. When fully open, the flower is quartered and sometimes exposes a dark green eye in the centre.

[P H (S)] 4′×4′ 1.2×1.2 m

'Camaieux'   [PB]

Above: 'Charles de Mills' [PB]
Below: 'Complicata' [VP]

'Complicata'

Origin, date and parentage unknown
An exceptional rose, good, even in poor soils. Vigorous with arching branches bearing flat, single flowers of bright pink with paler centres and gold stamens, produced freely about mid-June. Foliage matt grey-green, growth quite vigorous. This rose can range in use from a specimen shrub to an effective pillar or climbing rose, or even a tall hedge. In some works it is attributed to *R. macrantha*.

[P H ◍ (S)]   10′×6′   3×1.8 m

'Conditorum'

FRANCE An ancient variety
Date and parentage unknown
A very useful rose. Rich ruby-red double flowers abundantly produced on a tidy, upright, well-foliated bush. Scented. Foliage dark green.

[P H ▽ H P (S)]   4′×3′   1.2 m×90 cm

'Cosimo Ridolfi'

Vibert FRANCE 1842
Parentage unknown
Shapely cupped flowers of smoky lilac, opening fully double and flat. Scented. Foliage greyish-green. Growth compact. A little known but delightful Gallica.

[P H ▽ (S)]   3′×3′   90×90 cm

Above: 'Conditorum' (see text p. 155) [PB]
Below: 'd'Aguesseau' [JB]

'Cramoisi Picoté'

Vibert FRANCE 1834
Parentage unknown
An unusual rose. Compact, upright growth with thin, almost thornless shoots full of closely-packed, small, dark green leaves. Flowers fully double, small and pompon-like when open. Initially crimson later changing to deep pink with deeper flecks and markings. Sadly, little or no fragrance.

[▽ P (S)] 3′ × 2′ 90 × 60 cm

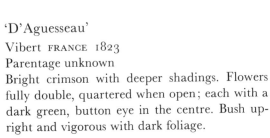

'D'Aguesseau'

Vibert FRANCE 1823
Parentage unknown
Bright crimson with deeper shadings. Flowers fully double, quartered when open; each with a dark green, button eye in the centre. Bush upright and vigorous with dark foliage.

[P (S)] 4′ × 3′ 1.2 m × 90 cm

'Duc de Fitzjames'

c. 1885
Origin and parentage unknown
For some years I have grown a beautiful, deep pink Centifolia under this name. This must now remain a mystery. James Russell of Castle Howard has recently sent me the correct variety which is, of course, a Gallica. I have yet to see this rose flower but understand it to be deep maroon-purple and vigorous.

[P (S)] 4′ × 3′ 1.2 m × 90 cm

'Duc de Guiche' [VP]

'Duchesse d'Angoulême', 'Duc d'Angoulême'

Vibert FRANCE 1835, perhaps earlier
Parentage unknown
Deep pink buds opening to fully double, small, delicate, saucer shaped, blush-pink flowers. These appear suspended from tops of smooth, light green shoots. Foliage crisp and bright green. Related to the Centifolias.
[P H ▽ (S)] 4′×3′ 1.2 m × 90 cm

'Duc de Guiche'

Prévost 1835
Origin and parentage unknown
An outstanding Gallica. Highly scented. Double, beautifully formed, rich violet-crimson flowers opening to a charming cupped shape. When fully open it reveals a pleasing central green eye. Foliage dark green. Rather sprawly in growth.

[P (S)] 4′×4′ 1.2 × 1.2 m

Right: 'Duchesse de Montebello' (see text p. 158) [PB]
Below: 'Duchesse d'Angoulême' [PB]

'Empress Josephine'   [RCB]

'Duchesse de Buccleugh'

Robert FRANCE 1860
Parentage unknown
Almost thornless with rich grey-green foliage.
This vigorous shrub flowers rather later than
some of its group. Well-formed flowers opening
flat; their colour is rich magenta-red with pink
highlights.
[P (S)] 6′×4′ 1.8×1.2 m

'Duchesse de Montebello'

Laffay FRANCE 1829
Parentage unknown
A lovely member of the Gallica family. The
small, fragrant, fully double flowers of soft
feminine pink are produced on a tidy, upright
plant with good, dark green foliage.
[P H ⦾ ▽ P (S)] 4′×3′ 1.2 m×90 cm

'Empress Josephine', *R.* ×*francofurtana*

Early 19th century
Origin and parentage obscure but thought to be
R. gallica × *R. pendulina*
Heavily textured petals form large, loosely
arranged, double, deep pink flowers with the
added charm of heavy veining plus lavender and
paler pink highlights; only slightly scented. The
bush has ample foliage, is relatively thornless
and is rather sprawly, yet still remains dense.
[P H ⦾ ▽ (S)] 5′×4′ 1.5×1.2 m

'Georges Vibert'

Robert FRANCE 1853
Parentage unknown
Colour variously described from carmine to
purple but alters with the climate as do so many

'Georges Vibert'   [VP]

striped varieties. The stripes, however, are always
present amid an abundance of petals. A tidy,
compact rose which is suitable for small gardens.
Foliage dark green but rather coarse.
[P H ▽ (S)] 3′×3′ 90×90 cm

'Gloire de France'

Pre-1819
Origin and parentage unknown
Very double, medium-sized flowers of pale pink
with deeper pink centres, produced in great profusion, fading rapidly to soft pink, almost-white
in hot sunshine. Has dark, crisp foliage and is
fairly low growing, almost a spreading variety.
[G P ▽ ⦾ (S)] 3′×4′ 90 cm×1.2 m

'Henri Foucquier'

Early 19th century
Origin and parentage unknown
Fully double flowers of clear pink, reflexing
when open and exposing a small, button eye.
Scented. Rather sprawly, not over-tall, with
dark green foliage.
[H P ▽ (S)] 4′×4′ 1.2×1.2 m

Above: 'James Mason'
Below: 'Jenny Duval' (see text p. 160)   [PB]

'Ipsilanté'

1821
Origin and parentage unknown
Pale lilac-pink, this lovely old rose deserves more attention. Fully double flowers large, quartered and scented. Foliage, on prickly stems, dark green. Growth habit perhaps rather coarse but still quite dense.
[H P ▽ (S)]   4′ × 3′   1.2 m × 90 cm

'Hippolyte'

Early 19th century
Origin and parentage unknown
One of the nicest of the Gallicas. Flowers exquisitely formed, magenta-purple with softer highlights in the centre. Clusters of blooms on thin almost thornless stems, often arching downwards. Foliage plentiful, dark green and very smooth for a Gallica.

[P ▽ (S)]   4′ × 4′   1.2 × 1.2 m

'James Mason'

Beales UK 1982
'Scharlachglut' × 'Tuscany Superb'
A beautiful, new introduction to the Gallica group. Flowers slightly more than single, large, up to 4″ (10 cm) across. Scented. Profuse flowering in mid-June. Flowers sometimes hidden amid abundant dark green foliage.
[P ▽ (S)]   5′ × 4′   1.5 × 1.2 m

[PB]

'Jenny Duval'
Mid-18th century
Origin and parentage unknown
Fascinating mixture of bright crimson, mauve
and violet varying with weather and, one suspects, mode. Flowers fully double, made up of a
multitude of petals, opening flat, sometimes
quartered. Exquisite perfume. Foliage greeny-
grey. Upright, tidy shrub.
[P H ▽ (S)]   4' × 3'   1.2 m × 90 cm

'La Belle Sultane', *R. gallica violacea*
Of considerable antiquity – pre-Redouté
Origin and parentage unknown
Slightly more than single flowers, soft violet
smudged-purple with very pronounced golden-
yellow stamens, produced freely on an upright
shrub with rather sparse, grey-green leaves.
[P H ◍ (S)]   5' × 4'   1.5 × 1.2 m

'La Plus Belle des Ponctuées'
Origin, date and parentage unknown
A tall, vigorous Gallica with good and ample dark
green foliage. The fully double, slightly crumpled
flowers are clear rich pink with smudges of softer
pink throughout, giving an overall mottled effect.
[P H (S)]   6' × 4'   1.8 × 1.2 m

Above: 'La Belle Sultane'

'Marcel Bourgouin'
Corboeuf-Marsault FRANCE 1899
Parentage unknown
Rich, deep red to purple flowers, semi-double,
sometimes showing off yellow stamens. Petals
have a velvety texture. Upright with smallish,
dark green leaves. I was privileged to work for
the late Edward LeGrice when he crossed this
and 'Tuscany Superb', among others, with
modern roses to breed his famous range of unusually coloured modern varieties.
[H P ◍ (S)]   4' × 3'   1.2 m × 90 cm

'Maître d'Ecole'. *See* 'Rose du Maître
d'Ecole'

'Nanette'
Origin, date and parentage unknown
Double, bright crimson flowers opening flat,
with a green eye, blotched or striped with purple.
A short growing variety, ideal for the small
garden or for growing in pots. Stems almost
thornless, well foliated with dark green leaves.
[P ▽ ◍ (S)]   3' × 3'   90 × 90 cm

'Nestor'

c. 1846
Origin and parentage unknown
A fine old variety. Predominantly magenta but varying with weather, and perhaps soil, from deep pink to mauve. Double, opening flat. Almost free of thorns, foliage crisp and mid-green.

[P ▽ (S)]   4′×3′   1.2 m × 90 cm

'Oeillet Flamand'

Vibert FRANCE 1845
Parentage unknown
I have grown this rose for a number of years, but am still unsure of its authenticity. Vigorous, upright in growth, large, abundant, dark green, rather coarse leaves. Flowers fully double, on erect stems, pinky-white with deeper pink, almost magenta stripes. Not my favourite, but interesting.

[H ▽ P (S)]   4′×3′   1.2 m × 90 cm

'Oeillet Parfait'

Foulard FRANCE 1841
Parentage unknown
Small-to-medium, pure white flowers erratically striped with bright crimson. Clustered flowers opening rather raggedly but fully double. Large, coarse leaves with plentiful thorns for a Gallica. Rather straggly.

[P (S)]   5′×4′   1.5 × 1.2 m

'Ohl'

Vibert FRANCE 1830
Parentage unknown
A medium-sized plant but vigorous; large, fully double flowers with deep crimson petals in the centre and violet petals around the edge. Highly scented, it should be grown more widely, for it is a unique colour combination. Foliage dark with few thorns on stout, strong stems.

[H ▽ P (S)]   4′×3′   1.2 m × 90 cm

'Ombrée Parfaite'

Vibert FRANCE 1823
Parentage unknown
A lesser known but good rose. Heads of flowers comprising several blooms of differing colours from purple to pink, sometimes blush-pink. Each flower fully double and scented. A short-growing plant, tidy and accommodating, with good, mid-green foliage.

[P ▽ (S)]   3′×2′   90 × 60 cm

'Orpheline de Juillet'

Paul UK 1848
Parentage unknown
Probably related to the Damasks. Large, fully double flowers of crimson-purple turning to fiery red in the centre. Upright growth, moderately vigorous with greyish-green leaves.

[▽ H P (S)]   4′×3′   1.2 m × 90 cm

'Pompon Panachée'

Date unknown, quite old
Origin and parentage unknown
A short growing, wiry, upright plant with ample foliage. Double, shapely flowers of creamy-white to white with pronounced splashes and stripes of deep pink.

[▽ (S)]   3′×2′   90 × 60 cm

'Président de Sèze', 'Mme Hébert'

c. 1836
Origin and parentage unknown
Unique mixture of magenta and lilac with paler edges. The centre of its large flower is packed with inward-folding petals to form a neat cushion. A superb and interesting rose of manageable proportions. Leaves grey-green. Shoots more thorny than most of its group.

[▽ P (S)]   4′×3′   1.2 m × 90 cm

'Rose de Rescht'. *See* Portland Damasks

Above: 'Président de Sèze' (see text p. 161)   [JB]
Below: 'Rose du Maître d'Ecole'   [JB]

'Rose du Maître d'Ecole'

Miellez FRANCE 1840

Parentage unknown

The large, fully double flowers, opening flat and quartered, are unusual, being predominantly pink with lilac highlights and magenta shadings. Heavy, well spaced flowers, in trusses on an upright bush with lush green foliage and few thorns.

[H P ▽ (S)] 3′ × 3′ 90 × 90 cm

'Scharlachglut', 'Scarlet Fire'

Kordes GERMANY 1952

'Poinsettia' × 'Alika'

This rose is a staggering sight as a fully established shrub. The very large, single flowers are bright, velvety-red with pronounced golden stamens. Foliage large, dark green tinted brownish-purple. Stems also brownish-purple and smooth, with a few vicious thorns. Fruit large, urn-shaped and bright orange when ripe. The persistent calyx, not typical of a Gallica, has prompted some to believe this rose to have *R. pimpinellifolia* in its make-up; a possibility also suggested by the shape of its thorns and early flowering habit. In addition to making an excellent, solid free-standing shrub, this rose is also good climbing into small trees, demonstrated admirably by a fine specimen, now well established and growing up into a white flowering cherry tree at Mannington Hall, Norfolk.

[T P W F ◫ (S)] 10′ × 6′ 3 × 1.8 m

'Sissinghurst Castle', 'Rose des Maures'

Origin, date and parentage unknown

Discovered at Sissinghurst, reintroduced in 1947. Old variety. Semi-double, deep maroon petals with paler edges and lighter reverses. Prominently displayed golden anthers add to the attractions of this rose. Scented. Foliage small but abundant. Stems thin and brittle with few thorns.

[▽ P ◫ (S)] 3′ × 3′ 90 × 90 cm

'Tricolore de Flandre' (see text p. 164)   [RCB]

'Surpasse Tout'

Pre-1832

Origin and parentage unknown

I have never had any great success with this rose but perhaps it is temperamental. At its best it is fully double, opening reflexed with tightly packed petals in the centre. Colour deep cerise-maroon, paling to softer shades with age. Highly scented. I find the plant rather leggy and rather short of foliage.

[P (S)]   4′ × 3′   1.2 m × 90 cm

'Tricolore', 'Reine Marguerite'

Lahaye Père FRANCE 1827

Parentage unknown

Deep pink to crimson flowers with petal edges tinged lilac, shapely and fully double. Scented. Foliage dark green. Stems moderately thorny.

[H ▽ (S)]   4′ × 3′   1.2 m × 90 cm

'Tricolore de Flandre'

Van Houtte BELGIUM 1846

Parentage unknown

Heavily striped with purple, the pale pink flowers are shapely, almost fully double and scented. Growth upright and accommodating. Ideal for the small garden or as single rose in pot. Foliage plentiful, smooth and dark green.

[H P ▽ (S)]   3′ × 2′   90 × 60 cm

'Tuscany, 'Old Velvet Rose'

Origin, date and parentage unknown

Beautiful rich dark red flower with pronounced stamens, seldom seen these days because it has been superseded by 'Tuscany Superb', a slightly more vigorous, deeper red, with equally prominent stamens and better foliage. 'Tuscany' may date back well before 1500.

[P ▽ (S)]   3′ × 3′   90 × 90 cm

'Tuscany Superb'

Paul UK 1848

Sport from 'Tuscany'

A superb rose. Semi-double flowers large and rich velvety dark red, displaying a golden crown of stamens when fully open. Strongly perfumed. Large, dark green leaves. Strong stems with few thorns provide an upright effect, fitting comfortably into any small space.

[P H ▽ (S)]   4′ × 3′   1.2 m × 90 cm

'Velutinaeflora'

Date unknown, may not be very old

Origin and parentage unknown

Pointed buds with downy sepals open to fragrant, single, pinkish-purple flowers with pronounced stamens. A fascinating, short-growing shrub with dense, grey-green foliage. Stems thorny by Gallica standards.

[P ◍ ▽ (S)]   3′ × 3′   90 × 90 cm

'Tuscany Superb', flower 1½ times actual size

[VP]

'Rose de Meaux' (see text p. 170). Flowers twice actual size.

[VP]

R. × centifolia
Cabbage Roses

R. × centifolia, 'Cabbage Rose', 'Provence Rose'
EUROPE Pre-1600
The fully double flowers of R. × centifolia prohibit this rose from self-perpetuation from seed. Thus, although R. × centifolia is usually listed as a species, it is probably a quite complex hybrid with a genealogy comprising R. canina, R. gallica, R. moschata and others. A rose similar to the present form was cultivated before 1600. A rather lax, medium-sized shrub with thick, coarse, grey-green leaves and abundant thorns. Flowers deep pink, very double cupped or cabbage-shaped when open. Has a strong, heady perfume.
[P W (S)]   6′ × 5′   1.8 × 1.5 m

R. × centifolia alba. See 'White Provence'

R. × centifolia muscosa. See Moss Rose section

FORMS AND HYBRIDS OF
R. × centifolia

'Blanchefleur'
Vibert FRANCE 1835
Parentage unknown
Flat, very double, sweetly scented flowers of white with occasional pink tints. Slightly tidier than some other Centifolias but the weight of blooms sometimes gives the plant a lax, open gait when in flower. Greyish-green foliage, soft to touch.
[P ◍ (S)]   5′ × 4′   1.5 × 1.2 m

'Bullata', 'Lettuce-leaved Rose'
Cultivated in 16th century
Origin and parentage unknown
Very large leaves and fewer thorns distinguish this rose from others in the group. Leaves unique, being loosely crinkly both in appearance and touch. Flowers are almost identical to those of R. × centifolia as is its growth habit, except that the density of foliage gives the overall appearance of a tidier plant.
[P W (S)]   5′ × 4′   1.5 × 1.2 m

'Duchesse de Rohan', 'Duc de Rohan'
c. 1860
Origin and parentage unknown
A fine rose, although in typical Centifolia mould, is rather coarse in growth. I am not sure if it is a true Centifolia, but it fits. Many-petalled flowers fade slightly with age from rich, warm pink to lavender, exuding a characteristically heady, Centifolia perfume, and occasionally repeating, which is, of course, untypical. It could be an early Hybrid Perpetual.
[(R)]   5′ × 4′   1.5 × 1.2 m

'Fantin Latour'

Origin, date and parentage unknown

A superb mystery rose with records conspicuously absent. The soft, delicate pink flowers and their form puts it into this group, its foliage being smoother, darker green and more rounded than is typical. Its shoots too are less thorny. I find the pervading perfume rather more Alba-like than Centifolia.

[P (S)]   5′×4′   1.5×1.2 m

[JB]

'Fantin-Latour'   [PB]

'Juno'

1832

Origin and parentage unknown

Not large but nevertheless an arching shrub. The globular, double flowers of pale blush-pink are produced profusely and are highly scented.

[H P ▽ (S)]   4′×4′   1.2×1.2 m

'La Noblesse'

1856

Origin and parentage unknown

Exceptionally tidy for a member of this group and flowering rather later in summer. Highly scented, the well formed, fully double blooms open flat and are soft silvery-pink.

[P H (S)]   5′×4′   1.5×1.2 m

'Ombrée Parfaite'

Vibert FRANCE 1823

Parentage unknown

One of the more unusually coloured Centifolias. The blooms, not large but produced abundantly, have many petals of varying shades, from pink to purple, giving them a mottled effect. Scented. Leaves smallish and rich green. A useful shorter-growing shrub. Closely related to the Gallicas.

[P ▽ (S)]   3′×3′   90×90 cm

'Petite de Hollande', 'Pompon des Dames', 'Petite Junon de Hollande'

HOLLAND C. 1800

Parentage unknown

An attractive and compact small shrub produc-

Left and above: 'Juno' [PB]

ing many small, double flowers about 1½″ (4 cm) across. These are cupped until fully open, and clear pink with deeper centres. Scented.

[P ▽ (S)]   4′×3′   1.2 m × 90 cm

'Petite Lisette'
Vibert FRANCE 1817
Parentage unknown
Small pompon flowers, 1″ (2.5 cm) across, of deep rose pink, produced in considerable numbers in large, evenly-spaced heads. Small, deeply serrated, greyish-green pointed foliage. Makes a useful shrub for front of borders.

[H ▽ (S)]   3′×3′   90×90 cm

'Petite Orléanaise'
c. 1900
Origin and parentage unknown
Another Centifolia with small, pompon-like flowers but taller than the other small-flowered varieties. Ample foliage and tidy disposition make this a useful shrub for growing in large tubs.

[P H ▽ (S)]   4′×3′   1.2 m × 90 cm

'Pompon de Bourgogne', 'Parvifolia',
R. burgundica
Pre-1664
Origin and parentage unknown
A superb little rose. Pompon flowers of rosy-claret to purple, some flecked with pink. Growth erect with foliage packed closely along clustered, thin, stiff stems. An ideal miniature rose for terrace or patio.

[H ▽ (S)]   2′×2′   60×60 cm

'Reine des Centfeuilles'
BELGIUM 1824
Parentage unknown
Large, scented, double, clear pink flowers, reflexed when fully open, with spiky petals. Ample foliage, medium to tall and, in my experience, fairly disorderly in habit.

[P (S)]   5′×3′   1.5 m × 90 cm

'Robert le Diable'
FRANCE
Date and parentage unknown
A very useful and interesting small shrub rose, slightly procumbent and well endowed with

Above: 'Petite d'Hollande' (see text p. 168) [PB]
Below: 'Spong' [VP]

foliage. Colour of flowers – produced later than most – difficult to describe but on the crimson side of red, with lilac and grey highlights and dark-purple shadings. Often exposes a small, green eye in the centre of each bloom.

[P ▽ (S)] $3' \times 3'$ 90×90 cm

'Rose de Meaux'

Sweet UK Pre-1789
Parentage unknown
A short, erect, well-foliated bush with massed, small, double, pink flowers – not quite pompons, more like small Dianthus with slightly frilly petals. Scented. A superb shorter-growing rose, temperamental in some soils, but most rewarding once established in good soil.

[H ▽ (S)] $2' \times 2'$ 60×60 cm

'Rose de Meaux White'

Origin unknown
As 'Rose de Meaux', but white.

[H ▽ (S)] $2' \times 2'$ 60×60 cm

'Rose des Peintres', *R. × centifolia*, 'Major', 'Centfeuille des Peintres'

An old variety Pre-1800
Origin and parentage unknown
A slightly more refined form of *R. × centifolia*. Large flowers opening fully double with a lovely clearly defined button eye in the centre. Clear deep pink in colour, with a delicate texture to the petals. Good dark green foliage on a sprawly plant.

[P W (S)] $6' \times 5'$ 1.8×1.5 m

'The Bishop' [PB]

'Spong'

Spong FRANCE 1805
Parentage unknown
An unusual name for an unusual rose. Of medium stature, rather like 'Rose de Meaux' with larger flowers and taller growth. Scented. Flowers early and needs 'dead-heading' after flowering, especially in wet weather. Good plentiful greyish-green foliage.

[P H ▽ ⦿ (S)] 4′ × 3′ 1.2 m × 90 cm

'The Bishop'

Origin, date and parentage unknown
Full, rosette-shaped flowers of an unusual mixture of magenta, cerise and purple. Fragrant. Flowering rather earlier than most of this group. Upright in habit. An excellent rose although some doubt exists as to its proper classification and, indeed, its true name.

[P ▽ (S)] 4′ × 3′ 1.2 m × 90 cm

'Tour de Malakoff', 'Black Jack'

Soupert and Notting LUXEMBOURG 1856
Parentage unknown
A unique rose. Vivid magenta flowers flushed deep purple and fading to lilac-grey, each bloom large, double, but loosely formed. A lanky, lax plant which benefits from support.

[P (S)] 8′ × 5′ 2.5 × 1.5 m

'Unique Blanche'. *See* 'White Provence'

'Village Maid' [JB]

'Village Maid', 'Belle des Jardins', 'La Rubanée', *R. × centifolia variegata*

Vibert FRANCE 1845
Parentage unknown
A vigorous, thorny rose with strong shoots. Rather more upright than most taller Centifolias. Soft, off-white blooms liberally streaked and striped with pink. Very floriferous when it blooms in late June. Scented. In my experience it occasionally repeats with an odd bloom in late summer.

[P (R)] 5′ × 4′ 1.5 × 1.2 m

'White Provence', 'Unique Blanche', 'Vierge de Cléry', *R. × centifolia alba*

Discovery in UK 1775
Parentage unknown – probably a sport from another Centifolia
In good weather, the flowers of this rose are quite the most beautiful of all white roses. Indeed, if we only had one good summer in ten, it would be worth waiting for just one of its perfect blooms. White silk is the nearest I can come to a simile. The shrub itself is not the most elegant, but who cares, when it yields such rewards?

[P I (S)] 5′ × 4′ 1.5 × 1.2 m

R. × centifolia muscosa
Moss Roses

Nature decreed, at some point in the evolution of the Centifolias, that some of them should have whiskers. These whiskers take a variety of forms, from multiple, stiff bristles to soft, downy glands which resemble moss. As so often with roses, there is no record as to exactly when the first mossy mutation occurred. Probably they have been with us far longer than the 280 or so years since one was first recorded. Controlled breeding was made possible by a chance, single-flowered sport at the beginning of the 19th century. Thirst for novelty led to an abundance of Moss Roses and between 30 and 40 varieties were commonly listed in Victorian nurserymen's catalogues. Many of these, had they stood naked, without the novelty of mossy clothes, would never have survived the competition and would quickly have faded into oblivion. They are not over-popular today and apart from a few which are underrated, I am not sure they deserve to be. It would be sad, however, if they were to die out. The following are those still available today, some of which merit wider recognition.

R. × centifolia muscosa

17th century

Origin unknown

Mossed form of *R. × centifolia*. Identical in all respects except for the moss, which is really closely packed reddish-brown bristles, brighter on young shoots and covering both stems and calyx. Rather prone to mildew. I do not believe this to be the form generally sold as 'Common Moss' in this country.

[P (S)]   6′ × 5′   1.8 × 1.5 m

'Chapeau de Napoléon' (see text p. 175)   [JB]

Above: 'Mme Louis Lévêque' (see text p. 180) [JB]
Below: 'Capitaine John Ingram' (see text p. 175) [VP]

FORMS AND HYBRIDS OF
R. × centifolia muscosa

'Alfred de Dalmas', 'Mousseline'

Portemer FRANCE 1855

Parentage unknown

Any criticism made of Moss roses does not extend to this little charmer, which probably really belongs among the Portland Damasks. Blooms semi-double, creamy-pink and scented. It flowers continuously from mid-June to November. Foliage lush, growth tidy and manageable. Its moss is green, tinted pink, turning to russet on its older shoots. Can fulfil a variety of roles from massed planting to an ideal outdoor pot plant.

[P H ⓪ ▽ (C)] 3′ × 2′ 90 × 60 cm

'A Longs Pédoncules'

Robert FRANCE 1854

Parentage unknown

Soft lilac-pink double flowers on a vigorous sprawly shrub with ample, light greyish-green leaves. Flower stalks long with profuse green mossing around globular buds.

[P ⓪ (S)] 5′ × 4′ 1.5 × 1.2 m

'Baron de Wassenaer'

Verdier FRANCE 1854

Parentage unknown

Vigorous, with much dark foliage and considerable moss. Flowers rich bright red to crimson, fully double, cupped, often borne in clusters on strong stems, in the way of 'William Lobb'.

[P (S)] 7′ × 4′ 2 × 1.2 m

'Blanche Moreau'

Moreau-Robert FRANCE 1880

'Comtesse de Murinais' × 'Quatre Saisons Blanc'

The bristly, purple, almost black moss on this

'Alfred de Dalmas'

[JB]

rose is too often marred by mildew for it to get much attention, although it has beautiful, fully double, pure white, perfumed flowers. Perhaps worthwhile if mildew can be controlled, as it starts flowering rather later in the season than most Moss roses.

[P ▽ (S)]   4′ × 3′   1.2 m × 90 cm

'Capitaine Basroger'

Moreau-Robert FRANCE 1890
Parentage unknown
A distinct feature of this rose is its ability to produce a sparse, second flush of flowers in late summer. Double, deep crimson, scented flowers emerge from tight, globular buds, sprinkled rather than covered with moss. Vigorous, better with support.

[P (R)]   6′ × 4′   1.8 × 1.2 m

'Capitaine John Ingram'

Laffay FRANCE 1856
Parentage unknown
Not over tall, one of the most charming of the Moss roses, deserving more attention. Well endowed with reddish moss on stems, receptable

'Célina'   [PB]

and calyx. Colour of the fully double flowers varies with weather from dark crimson to purple. Very strongly scented.

[P (S)]   4′ × 3′   1.2 m × 90 cm

'Catherine de Würtemberg'

Robert FRANCE 1843
Parentage unknown
An upright growing plant with sparse reddish

mossing and ample small, red thorns. Flowers lilac-pink and double, with a faint scent.

[P (S)]   6′ × 4′   1.8 × 1.2 m

'Célina'

Hardy FRANCE 1855
Parentage unknown
Not exceptionally mossy. Flowers are quite distinctive, of good size, semi-double, and a mixture of cerise, pink and lavender, displaying golden anthers when open. A reasonably tidy shrub but somewhat prone to mildew later in the season.

[P H (S)]   4′ × 3′   1.2 m × 90 cm

'Chapeau de Napoléon', 'Cristata', 'Crested Moss'

Vibert FRANCE 1826
Chance discovery
Fully double, highly scented, cabbage-like, silvery deep pink flowers enhanced by a fascinating moss formation on the calyx. This is shaped like a cocked-hat, hence the name. Apart from that, it is a useful shrub of medium size, well dressed with foliage. Probably better with support.

[P (S)]   5′ × 4′   1.5 × 1.2 m

'Clifton Moss'. *See* 'White Bath'

'Common Moss', ('Old Pink Moss', 'Communis')

FRANCE Pre-1700
Parentage unknown
Presumably so called because of its ubiquity, but I suspect it applies to a number of pink Mosses, which were, of course, very common in the 19th century. The rose I grow under this name could well be something else but I find it better than *R. × centifolia mucosa* in several respects. It is softer in colour, more regular in shape and tidier in growth habit. From cuttings sent to me over the years I believe that a number of different clones exist, all derivatives of *R. × centifolia muscosa*, but selected as better plants because of their more manageable dispositions. All are very well mossed and have an exceptionally strong perfume.

[P (S)]   4′ × 4′   1.2 × 1.2 m

'Comtesse de Murinais'
Robert FRANCE 1843
Parentage unknown
A tall rose, needing support but with much to commend it. Flowers soft pink paling to creamy-white when open, fully double, opening flat, even in wet weather. Moss clear rich green and rather bristly; if touched, it exudes a powerful, lingering, balsam-like odour. Scented moss is by no means unique but in this rose it is stronger than in most others.
[P (S)]   6′×4′   1.8 × 1.2 m

'Communis'. *See* 'Common Moss',
'Four Seasons Moss', *See* Damask section

'Crested Moss'.
See 'Chapeau de Napoléon'

'Crimson Globe'
W. Paul UK 1890
Parentage unknown
This sounds more like a vegetable than a rose and, frankly, I sometimes wonder if it is. Probably better in warmer climes.
[(S)]   4′×4′   1.2 × 1.2 m

'Cristata'.
See 'Chapeau de Napoléon'

'Deuil de Paul Fontaine'
Fontaine FRANCE 1873
Parentage unknown
Deep red to blackish-purple best describes the colour of this rose. A relatively small, very thorny plant with somewhat coarse foliage. Will repeat in most seasons.
(H ▽ (R)]   3′×3′   90 × 90 cm

'Dresden Doll'
R. S. Moore USA 1975
Parentage unknown
I feel that this charming miniature Moss rose should be included although I am not sure it should be placed here; but presumably it has Centifolia genes somewhere in its make-up. Raised recently, it is quite exquisite, with heavily mossed buds and stems and lush green foliage. The small, pointed buds open to fully-double, cupped, scented flowers of soft pink. Ideal for pots on patios, or even in window-boxes.
[P ▽ (C)]   9″×6″   25 × 15 cm

'Duchesse de Verneuil'
Portemer FRANCE 1856
Parentage unknown
One of the more refined Moss roses. Medium-tall and well foliated with light green leaves and dense darker green moss. Flattish flowers composed of many folded petals, these reflex to expose pale pink beneath and brighter pink above. Foliage, moss and flowers combine to pleasing effect.
[P (S)]   5′×3′   1.5 m × 90 cm

'Eugénie Guinoisseau'
Guinoisseau FRANCE 1864
Parentage unknown
Scented flowers in a mixture of shades between violet-grey and purple, substantial and more cupped in shape than most Centifolia Mosses. Foliage is smooth with just a hint of gloss, moss is dark green. Bears a second crop of blooms in a good season, surprising in such a tall variety. Better grown with support.
[P (S)]   6′×4′   1.8 × 1.2 m

'Félicité Bohain'
c. 1865
Parentage and origin unknown
A little-grown variety, with plentiful but small foliage. Moss reddish, spreading on to the edges of its young leaves. Smallish flowers have a button eye, surrounded by folded and crinkled, bright pink petals.
[▽ (S)]   4′×3′   1.2 m × 90 cm

'Gabriel Noyelle'
Buatois FRANCE 1933
'Salet' × 'Souvenir de Mme Kreuger'
Sadly, this is a rose I have yet to see but I understand it is very good. Its colour is bright salmon with highlights of orange and yellow. Recurrent.
[▽ (R)]   4′×4′   1.2 × 1.2 m

'Eugénie Guinoisseau' [JB]

'Général Kléber' [PB]

'Général Kléber'

Robert FRANCE 1856
Parentage unknown

An excellent variety both for beauty of flower and garden value. Flowers very bright, almost shining pink, quite large with patternless petals, rather like small, crumpled, pink tissues. Foliage copious, large and lush bright green; thick stems covered in bright lime green moss extending to the tip of sepals. Very few thorns.

[P ▽ (S)]   4′×4′   1.2×1.2 m

'Gloire des Mousseux'

Laffay FRANCE 1852
Parentage unknown

This rose probably has the largest flowers of all the Mosses and, for once, big is beautiful. Huge, scented blooms of clear soft pink, fully double and reflexing, produced freely on a substantial plant with light green leaves and moss.

[P ▽ (S)]   4′×3′   1.2 m×90 cm

'Goethe'

P. Lambert GERMANY 1911
Parentage unknown

Several single Mosses existed in Victorian times

'Gloire des Mousseux'

[PB]

but this later variety is the only true single available today. Rich magenta pink with yellow stamens. Reddish-brown moss and dark bluish-green foliage. When young, the shoots are pinkish-red. Very vigorous.

[P (S)]   6′×4′   1.8×1.2 m

'Golden Moss'

Pedro Dot SPAIN 1932
'Frau Karl Druschki' × ('Souvenir de Claudius Pernet' × 'Blanche Moreau')
This relatively recent Moss rose has very little to commend it, apart from being the only yellow in its group. The flowers are pale yellow, cupped and fragrant, but it detests wet weather and can be rather shy. Perhaps I have never seen it at its best?

[(S)]   5′×3′   1.5 m×90 cm

'Henri Martin', 'Red Moss'

Laffay FRANCE 1863
Parentage unknown
Clusters of medium-sized, bright crimson, scented flowers on sparsely mossed stems. Well worth

growing for the sheer quantity of flowers produced.

[P H (S)]   5′×4′   1.5 m×1.2 m

'Hunslett Moss'

UK 1984
Discovery by Humphrey Brooke. Introduced by Peter Beales.
Undoubtedly one of the earliest English Moss roses. Known to have been grown by Humphrey Brooke's ancestors for several generations. Large, full and heavily mossed, deep pink with a strong

Above: 'Henri Martin'   [PB]
Below: The same rose at Castle Howard, Yorkshire   [PB]

perfume. Foliage dark on a sturdy upright plant.
[P ▽ (S)]   4′ × 3′   1.2 m × 90 cm

'James Mitchell'

Verdier FRANCE 1861
Parentage unknown
Medium-sized, double flowers of rich, bright pink, produced plentifully in early July. Scented. A healthy plant, perhaps slightly short of foliage and moss, but makes an excellent, tidy shrub.
[P ◍ (S)]   5′ × 4′   1.5 × 1.2 m

'James Veitch'

Verdier FRANCE 1865
Parentage unknown
A most interesting, short-growing Moss rose. Royal purple with slate-grey highlights. Flowers almost continuously throughout summer. But

'James Veitch'   [PB]

for mildew, which can be a problem, it is superb. Another Moss rose which could well be placed among the Portland Damasks.
[▽ (S)]   3′ × 3′   90 × 90 cm

'Japonica'. *See* 'Mousseux du Japon'

'Jeanne de Montfort'

Robert FRANCE c. 1851
Parentage unknown
One of the tallest Moss roses, needing support if placed in a shrubbery. Moss dark maroon, leaves dark green and almost glossy. Flowers clear rose pink, borne in large clusters and scented. Worth growing as a small climber or pillar rose.
[P (S)]   8′ × 5′   2.5 × 1.5 m

'Laneii', 'Lane's Moss'

Laffay FRANCE 1854
Parentage unknown
Very double, crimson flowers produced freely on a sturdy plant. Scented flowers initially cupped but opening flat and reflexed, exposing a large green eye in the centre. Moss slightly darker than the deep green foliage.
[P (S)]   4′ × 3′   1.2 m × 90 cm

'Little Gem'

W. Paul UK 1880
Parentage unknown
Very popular in late Victorian times, this tidy, useful little rose is very free flowering and colourful. Flowers in clusters, evenly spaced and pompon-like, bright crimson. Stems, which are amply clothed in moss, are provided with many small, closely packed, rich green leaves.
[▽ (R)]   3′ × 2′   90 × 60 cm

'Louis Gimard'

Pernet Père FRANCE 1877
Parentage unknown
The fully double flowers open flat with rich, deep pink centres, paling towards borders to soft pink. Foliage very dark green with reddish veins and margins. Bristly moss, almost purple.
[P H (S)]   5′ × 3′   1.5 m × 90 cm

'Ma Ponctuée'

Guillot FRANCE 1857
Parentage unknown
A very unusual little Moss rose. Small double flowers produced intermittently throughout summer, pinkish-red with white flecks. Well mossed. It needs good soil to flourish. I suspect the variety has deteriorated over the years, perhaps by hosting some form of hard-to-detect growth-retarding virus.
[▽ (C)]   3′ × 3′   90 × 90 cm

'Maréchal Davoust'

Robert FRANCE 1853
Parentage unknown
An effective rose where an unusual colour is desired. Each flower's many reflexing petals combine an extraordinary mixture of purples,

greys, and pinks. The flower sometimes reveals a little green eye in the centre. Fairly tidy with very dark moss and grey-green foliage.

[H P ▽ (S)]   4′×3′   1.2 m × 90 cm

Above: 'Maréchal Davoust' (see text p. 179)   [JB]
Below: 'Mme de la Roche-Lambert'   [JB]
Right: 'Nuits de Young'   [PB]

'Marie de Blois'

Robert FRANCE 1852
Parentage unknown
This free-flowering rose should be more popular. Shoots are well covered with reddish moss and bright green leaves. Flowers are really randomly-formed clusters of bright pink petals, heavily scented and produced freely each season.

[P (C)]   5′×4′   1.5 × 1.2 m

'Mme de la Roche-Lambert'

Robert FRANCE 1851
Parentage unknown
Globular flowers which open flattish with many deep purple petals, which hold their colour even in hot sunshine. Scented. Moss is also deep purple and leaves dark green. An interesting and useful medium shrub which sometimes repeats its flowers well into the autumn.

[P ▽ (R)]   4′×3′   1.2 m × 90 cm

'Mme Louis Lévêque'

Lévêque FRANCE 1898
Parentage unknown
I first saw this rose in Mr Maurice Mason's famous garden at Fincham, Norfolk. Probably then at its best, it was as near perfect as any rose I have ever seen. The flowers are cup-shaped until fully open, quite large and of soft warm pink. More important than the colour is the soft, silky texture of the petals in their nest of moss. The

flowers are held on an erect, mossy stem amid large, dark green foliage.

[P ⩴ (R)] 4′ × 3′ 1.2 m × 90 cm

'Monsieur Pélisson'. *See* 'Pélisson'

'Mousseline'. *See* 'Alfred de Dalmas'

'Mrs William Paul'

W. Paul UK 1869
Parentage unknown
Short, strong stems bearing mossy buds which open to double, bright pink flowers with red shadings. Quite vigorous for such a short-growing shrub. This useful rose should be better known especially as it is recurrent.

[⩴ (R)] 3′ × 3′ 90 × 90 cm

'Mousseux du Japon', 'Japonica', 'Moussu du Japon'

Origin, date and parentage unknown
Perhaps the most heavily mossed of all roses, the moss creating an illusion that the stems are far thicker than they actually are. Flowers semi-

double, soft lilac-pink with pronounced stamens. Leaves – with mossed stalks – darkish green.

[H ⩴ (R)] 4′ × 3′ 1.2 m × 90 cm

'Nuits de Young', 'Old Black'

Laffay FRANCE 1845
Parentage unknown
Compact, erect shrub with small, dark green leaves and small almost double flowers, of very dark, velvety maroon-purple emphasized by golden stamens. Although not heavily mossed, and with somewhat small foliage, this is certainly one of the best moss roses for general effect, especially where dark colour is needed.

[P H ⩴ (S)] 4′ × 3′ 1.2 m × 90 cm

'Old Pink Moss'. *See* 'Common Moss'

'Pélisson', 'Monsieur Pélisson'

Vibert FRANCE 1848
Parentage unknown
Double flowers, opening flat, red changing to purple with age. A vigorous, upright, shortish grower. Foliage coarse dark green, deeply

veined. Stems have stumpy thorns and darkish green moss.

[P ▽ (S)]   4′ × 3′   1.2 m × 90 cm

'Princesse Adélaide'

Laffay FRANCE 1845
Parentage unknown
Foliage dark green, often variegated. Sparsely mossed. Flowers large, shapely, double, soft pink and well scented. Sometimes classed as a Gallica.

[P ▽ (S)]   4′ × 3′   1.2 m × 90 cm

'Pélisson' (see text p. 181)   [VP]

'Reine Blanche'

Moreau FRANCE 1857
Parentage unknown
A lovely, short to medium Moss rose which, for some reason, is often ignored in favour of the taller 'Blanche Moreau'. 'Reine Blanche' has very good moss which is light green, as is its copious foliage. The fully double flowers, although on a weak neck, are shapely, pure white with creamy centres, each with a tight, button eye in the centre.

[P ▽ (S)]   3′ × 3′   90 × 90 cm

'René d'Anjou'

Robert FRANCE 1853
Parentage unknown
This rose is of the most feminine shade of pink, with quite an exquisite perfume. As a shrub, it is not too vigorous, making it ideal for the smaller garden, especially as both foliage and moss have bronze tints which are most marked when young.

[P ▽ (S)]   4′ × 3′   1.2 m × 90 cm

'Salet'

Lacharme FRANCE 1854
Parentage unknown
A rose with considerable character, especially useful for the smaller garden. Flowers clear rose pink, deeper in the autumn, double and somewhat muddled when fully open. Not very mossy but the leaves are bright green especially when young.

[P ▽ (R)]   4′ × 3′   1.2 m × 90 cm

'Shailer's White Moss'

Shailer UK c. 1788
Parentage unknown
Supposed to be the white form of *R. centifolia muscosa* but unless I have a different rose, I find it less sprawly and with darker green foliage. Well mossed, highly scented; full, flat and quartered flowers with the outer layer of petals rather spikey, mostly white but with occasional hints of pink. Very free-flowering.

[P ◍ (S)]   5′ × 4′   1.5 × 1.2 m

'Soupert et Notting'

Pernet Père FRANCE 1874
Parentage unknown
A useful, short-growing, dense bush with well mossed stems and buds. Flowers deep pinkish-red, fully double and quartered when fully open. Sadly, mildew needs to be controlled to get the best from the autumn blooms.

[▽ (R)]   3′ × 2′   90 × 60 cm

'Souvenir de Pierre Vibert'

Moreau-Robert FRANCE 1867
Parentage unknown
The fully double flowers are a mixture of red, deep pink and violet, and are produced throughout summer. The shrub is somewhat lax for such a short plant but effective if placed correctly. Ample moss and foliage.

[▽ (R)]   4′ × 3′   1.2 m × 90 cm

'Striped Moss'

Origin, date and parentage unknown
Not, I find, the most shapely of roses, the small flowers are various shades of pink with random red markings. Its small upright stature makes it an ideal pot plant.

[H P ▽ (R)]   3′ × 2′   90 × 60 cm

'Striped Moss' [PB]

'White Bath' [PB]

'White Bath', 'Clifton Moss', 'White Moss'

Salter UK c. 1817
Said to be sport of 'Common Moss'
Large fully double pure white flowers. Heavily scented. Foliage, stems and buds well mossed. Of medium vigour.

[P ▽ (S)]   4′ × 3′   1.2 m × 90 cm

'William Lobb', 'Duchesse d'Istrie', 'Old Velvet Moss'

Laffay FRANCE 1855
Parentage unknown
Very vigorous, often producing long stems each with large clusters of flowers, so heavy as to bend to the ground. Best with support, perhaps of another rose, say a climber of similar colour such as 'Veilchenblau' or a vigorous creamy-white rambler. Well mossed, with ample, large leaves. Flowers large, semi-double and scented, a mixture of purple, grey, magenta and pink, slightly paler on the reverse.

[P (S)]   8′ × 5′   2.5 × 1.5 m

'Zenobia'

W. Paul UK 1892
Parentage unknown
A tall-growing, rather lanky rose with well mossed buds and stems and thick, leathery foliage. Flowers fragrant, globular, reminiscent of an old Hybrid Perpetual in shape, even when fully open. Colour on the cerise side of pink.

[P (S)]   6′ × 4′   1.8 × 1.2 m

'William Lobb' [VP]

'Zoe'

Vibert FRANCE 1830
Parentage unknown
A free-flowering Moss rose with medium sized bright pink, fully double flowers opening flat and made up of many narrow, fluted petals. Scented. Well endowed with brownish red moss. Foliage mid-green. An excellent example of this rose can be seen at Castle Howard, Yorkshire.

[P H ▽ (S)]   4′ × 3′   1.2 m × 90 cm

R. × damascena
Damask Roses

There is little doubt that the Damasks have a close affinity to the Gallicas; the more I delve into the complex lineage of roses, the more confused I become about them. As a mere grower of roses I can only follow, or attempt to follow, the rules laid down by others.

R. × damascena bifera. See 'Quatre Saisons'

R. × damascena trigintipetala. See 'Kazanlik'

R. × damascena versicolor. See 'York and Lancaster'

'Autumn Damask'. *See* 'Quatre Saisons'

'Belle Amour'
Discovered by Miss Nancy Lindsay 1950
Original date and parentage unknown
Rich yellow stamens framed by two layers of crinkled, salmony-pink petals. Possibly related to the Albas but its foliage and growth, respectively greeny-grey and thorny, places it here among the Damasks.
[P H W (S)] 5′ × 3′ 1.5 m × 90 cm

Above: 'Blush Damask' [TW]

'Belle Amour' [VP]

'Celsiana'   [RCB]

'Blush Damask'

Origin, date and parentage unknown

A vigorous, dense but sprawly shrub, very floriferous when in bloom but to fleeting effect. The
double medium-sized flowers are rich pink,
paling to soft pink at the edges. Needs dead-
heading, as the decayed flowers are very reluctant to fall. Probably of ancient origin.

[P H W (S)]   4' × 3'   1.2 m × 90 cm

'Botzaris'

1856

Origin and parentage unknown

Flattish, fully double flowers of creamy-white,
often quartered when fully open. Another
Damask with affinity to the Albas, hence its
quality perfume. Wood thorny, foliage rich light
green. A superb rose which will never outgrow
its welcome, even if left unpruned.

[P W H (S)]   4' × 3'   1.2 m × 90 cm

'Celsiana'

Pre-1750

Origin and parentage unknown

An attractive shrub in full bloom, its downy, light
grey-green foliage and reasonably contained
habit help make it quite unobtrusive whilst
'resting' in late summer. Flowers highly scented,
borne in nodding clusters, semi-double, displaying yellow anthers to effect. Clear pink fading to
pinkish-white in hot sun.

[P H W (S)]   5' × 4'   1.5 × 1.2 m

'Coralie'

c. 1860

Origin and parentage unknown

A rather thorny shrub of medium stature with
small greyish-green leaves. Soft pink flowers
open flat, rather more than semi-double, petals

'Ispahan' [JB]

'Gloire de Guilan' [PB]

'La Ville de Bruxelles' [JB]

'Kazanlik' [VP]

inclined to fold backwards when fully open. Still attractive when faded to blush-white in hot sun.
[P H W ▽ (S)] 4′×3′ 1.2 m × 90 cm

'Gloire de Guilan'
MIDDLE EASTERN ORIGIN
Introduced by Nancy Lindsay 1949
The flowers which are very double, and flat when open, are often beautifully quartered, clear pink in colour and richly fragrant. Flowering early

'Leda' [JB]

'Marie Louise' [TW]

summer, inclined to sprawl without support. Foliage light green, wood densely populated with small thorns. Probably of some antiquity.
[P W (S)] 6′×4′ 1.8×1.2 m

'Ispahan', 'Rose d'Isfahan'
MIDDLE EAST Pre-1832
Parentage unknown
Flowering for a long season compared with others of this group, the semi-double, light pink flowers hold both their shape and colour well. Very fragrant. It has attractive foliage and its stems are not over-thorny.
[P H ⊽ (S)] 4′×3′ 1.2 m×90 cm

'Kazanlik', 'Trigintipetala'
MIDDLE EAST Very ancient
Parentage unknown
A vigorous rose originating in the rose fields of Bulgaria as one of varieties used in the manufacture of 'attar of roses'. Ideal for making potpourri. The soft-textured petals are warm pink and very fragrant. Flower opens to a somewhat shaggy, double bloom. Foliage dark green; although it makes a good shrub, it is better with support.
[P W ◐ (S)] 5′×4′ 1.5×1.2 m

'La Ville de Bruxelles'
Vibert FRANCE 1849
Parentage unknown
Large, full, pure pink blooms with quartered and incurving centres. Highly scented. A strong, vigorous and upright shrub, which is good for specimen planting.
[P W (S)] 5′×3′ 1.5 m×90 cm

'Leda', 'Painted Damask'
Probably early 19th century
Origin and parentage unknown
Double flowers, blush-pink to white, with interesting crimson markings on the margins of each petal. Scented. Tidy and compact for a damask, foliage downy grey-green. A pink form also exists as 'Pink Leda'.
[P H ⊽ (S)] 3′×3′ 90×90 cm

'Marie Louise'
c. 1813
Parentage and origin unknown
Glowing pink, double flowers full and flat when fully open, well perfumed. Shrub compact,

bushy with good foliage, fairly free of vicious thorns.

[P H ▽ (S)]   4′ × 3′   1.2 m × 90 cm

'Mme Hardy'

Hardy FRANCE 1832
Parentage unknown
An elegant and sumptuous rose which can hold its own against any in the shrubbery. Flowers pure white, fully double and quite large considering the number it produces. Centre petals are folded inwards, exposing a rich green eye. Strongly scented. Growth, although strong and vigorous, is accommodating. Foliage bright, almost lime-green especially when young.

[P ◍ (S)]   5′ × 5′   1.5 × 1.5 m

'Mme Zöetmans'

Marest FRANCE 1830
Parentage unknown
Deserving more attention. Soft pink, double, sometimes quartered flowers, paling to blush-white, each with a prominent, green eye. A tidy compact shrub for a Damask, with darkish green foliage.

[P H ▽ (S)]   4′ × 3′   1.2 m × 90 cm

'Omar Khayyam'

1893
Origin and parentage unknown
Undoubtedly of some antiquity. Propagated from a plant growing on Edward Fitzgerald's grave in Suffolk, planted there in 1893 from seed gathered from plants on Omar Khayyam's tomb in Nashipur. Medium-sized light pink flowers double and scented. Shrub shortish, foliage grey-green and downy.

[▽ (S)]   3′ × 3′   90 × 90 cm

'Quatre Saisons', R. × damascena bifera, 'Autumn Damask'

MIDDLE EAST Extremely ancient
Thought to be R. gallica × R. moschata
A very old rose, loosely double with large, sometimes rather cumpled, petals. Colour clear but silky pink, highly scented. Shrub rather sprawly, foliage greyish and downy. Remontant, it tolerates pruning better than most others in this group. Another rose good for making pot-pourri.

[P W (R)]   4′ × 3′   1.2 m × 90 cm

Left: 'Omar Khayyam'   [JB]
Below: 'Quatre Saisons Blanc Mousseux' [RCB]

'Quatre Saisons Blanc Mousseux'

Laffay FRANCE Date unknown
'Quatre Saisons' sport
A name sometimes applied to other remontant Moss roses. This variety is well endowed with brownish-green moss on both stems and buds. Otherwise, except for its white colour, the same as 'Quatre Saisons'. An ancient rose.

[P Q (R)]   4′ × 3′   1.2 m × 90 cm

Above and left: 'St Nicholas' and its hips

[VP/VP]

'Rose d'Hivers'

Origin, date and parentage unknown

An odd little rose, placed here as a sibling, for want of another home. Rather un-Damask-like, with small, grey foliage and twiggy, yellowish-green shoots. Its flowers are small, though quite shapely; they pale towards the margins from clear pink to white.

[P W ▽ ◍ (R)] 3′ × 3′ 90 × 90 cm

'St Nicholas'

James UK 1950

Possibly a chance seedling of an unknown Damask × *R. gallica*

An odd rose but none the less attractive for that. Short-growing, the shrub has downy grey leaves and vicious thorns. Flowers are almost single, pink with rich golden anthers. A charmer when seen in early evening sunlight. If not dead-headed, produces good, attractive hips.

[▽ (R)] 3′ × 3′ 90 × 90 cm

'Trigintipetala'. *See* 'Kazanlik'

'York and Lancaster',
R. × damascena versicolor

Pre-1551

Origin and parentage unknown

Inconsistent blush-pink and white flowers. Sometimes mottled, sometimes with two colours on different flowers on the same head, semi-double and scented. Inclined to be rather untidy. Foliage grey, thorns numerous. More a collector's rose than of real garden merit.

[P W ◍ (S)] 5′ × 4′ 1.5 × 1.2 m

Portland Roses

According to the accepted way of things, I include these roses under the heading 'Damask'. Having grown most of them for a number of years, however, I find them more and more of an enigma. Whatever their place amongst roses, the Portlands are ideal for the smaller garden.

'Arthur de Sansal'

Cartier FRANCE 1855

Parentage unknown

A short-growing rose, well foliated and very free-flowering, sadly marred by a strong desire to mildew. Flowers very double, rosette-form, dark crimson-purple and scented.

[▽ (R)] 3′ × 2′ 90 × 60 cm

'Blanc de Vibert'

Vibert FRANCE 1847

Parentage unknown

White, double flowers with a touch of pale lemon in the base and a strong scent. Bush upright, well clothed with Gallica-like foliage. Very useful but quite rare these days.

[P ▽ (R)] 3′ × 3′ 90 × 90 cm

Above: 'Arthur de Sansal'
Below: 'Comte de Chambord' [PB]
Right: 'Portland Rose' (see text p. 192)

[PB]

[RCB]

'Comte de Chambord'
Moreau-Robert FRANCE 1863
'Baronne Prévost' × 'Portland Rose'
An outstanding member of this group with plenti-ful, large, grey-green foliage which sometimes hides the buds, at least until the flowers are fully open. Flowers are also large – for such a small plant – with many petals of rich warm pink, exuding a strong, heady perfume.
[P H (C)] 3′ × 2′ 90 × 60 cm

'Delambre'
Moreau-Robert FRANCE 1863
Parentage unknown
Fully double, deep reddish-pink flowers freely borne on a compact plant. Dark green, healthy foliage.
[P H ▽ ◍] 3′ × 2′ 90 × 60 cm

'Jacques Cartier'
Moreau-Robert FRANCE 1868
Parentage unknown
Very much like 'Comte de Chambord', especially in growth habit. Flowers, however, less cupped and much flatter in appearance, both when in bud and fully open; shortish petals give it an attractive, ragged look. The colour is deep pink fading towards the edges to soft pink. It is blessed with a good perfume. Strong, leathery dark green foliage.
[P H ▽ ◍]   3′ × 2′   90 × 60 cm

'Marbrée'
Robert et Moreau FRANCE 1858
Parentage unknown
An interesting variety. Slightly taller than most of this group, with ample, dark-green foliage. Double flowers opening flat, deep pinkish purple, with paler mottling. Sadly, only slightly fragrant.
[H P ▽ (R)]   4′ × 3′   1.2 m × 90 cm

'Mme Knorr'
Verdier FRANCE 1855
Parentage unknown
Similar in stature to 'Jacques Cartier' and 'Comte de Chambord', with slightly fewer leaves. Semi-double flowers of bright pink. Has a good strong fragrance.
[H P ▽)   3′ × 3′   90 × 90 cm

'Pergolèse'
Moreau FRANCE 1860
Parentage unknown
A very good rose. Small to medium-sized, fully double, scented flowers, of rich purple-crimson sometimes paling to soft lilac-mauve, produced in small spaced clusters on a plant which is well endowed with darkish green foliage. If pruned regularly, will repeat in most seasons. Shows considerable Gallica influence.
[P H ▽ (R)]   3′ × 3′   90 × 90 cm

'Portland Rose', 'Duchess of Portland'
R. portlandica, R. paestana
ITALY C. 1790
Parentage obscure, said to be 'Quatre Saisons' × 'Slater's Crimson China'
A very useful rose, of ancient origin, important as the progenitor of its race. Single to semi-

'Jacques Cartier'

'Rose de Rescht' (see text p. 194)

double flowers freely borne on a short, well-foliated plant, cerise-red with pronounced golden stamens. Scented. Useful for group planting but needs dead-heading for best effect.

[P H ▽ (R)]   3′ × 2′   90 × 60 cm

'Rose de Rescht'
Obscure origin and parentage
Discovered by Miss Nancy Lindsay. Date unknown

This is a fascinating little rose. Very Gallica-like in foliage, the only concession to Damask being a short flower stalk. Highly scented. The flowers, which are rich fuchsia-red in colour with strong purple tints, changing with age to magenta-pink, are tightly-formed rosette shaped, almost pompon and produced in small, upright clusters amid lots of foliage. Well worth a place in any garden. Very remontant especially when young; needs hard pruning to remain so when over five years old.

[H P ▽ ◍ (R)]   3′ × 2′   90 × 60 cm

'Rose du Roi'
Lelieur FRANCE 1815
'Portland Rose' × *R. gallica officinalis*?
An important rose. See page 30. Sometimes classified a Hybrid Perpetual, but I prefer to place it here. Flowers are double, red mottled purple, loosely formed when open and highly scented. Short growing but slightly straggly. Foliage small, rather pointed and dark green.

[P ▽ (R)]   3′ × 3′   90 × 90 cm

'Rose du Roi à Fleurs Pourpres', 'Roi des Pourpres', 'Mogador'
1819
Said to be a sport of 'Rose du Roi'
An interesting rose, the red-violet-purple flowers are similar to those of 'Rose du Roi' and freely produced throughout season. Plant short, bushy and slightly straggly.

[P ▽ (C)]   3′ × 3′   90 × 90 cm

'Rose du Roi'   [PB]

R. macrantha

R. macrantha,
c. 1880
Possibly of Gallica origin
A vigorous spreading and arching shrub bearing many attractive single flowers of clear pink, fading to white, with prominent stamens and a good fragrance. Plentiful dark, veined foliage. Globular red hips in autumn.

[W F P G (S)]   4′×6′   1.2×1.8 m

R. macrantha   [PB]

FORMS AND HYBRIDS OF
R. macrantha

'Chianti'
Austin UK 1967
R. macrantha × 'Vanity'
Semi-double blooms of rich purple-maroon with pronounced golden anthers when fully open – produced in clusters on well-foliated plant. Foliage matt, dark green. Scented.

[P (S)]   5′×4′   1.5×1.2 m

'Daisy Hill'
Smith IRELAND Date unknown
R. macrantha hybrid
May not be wholly correct in this section but I cannot find another place for it. Large, slightly more than single, rich pink flowers, well perfumed. Vigorous, rather wider than high in habit. Abundant dark foliage and globular red hips.

[W F G (S)]   5′×8′   1.5×2.5 m

'Harry Maasz'
Kordes GERMANY 1939
'Barcelona' × 'Daisy Hill'
A good but little known spreading rose with dark, greeny-grey foliage. Very vigorous. Single flowers large and cherry-red, paling to pink towards centre, each with a prominent arrangement of stamens. Scented.

[P G S W (S)]   5′×8′   1.5×2.5 m

'Raubritter', 'Macrantha Raubritter'
Kordes GERMANY 1967
'Daisy Hill' × 'Solarium'
A trailing shrub of great charm. Excellent for banks and similar features. Trusses of clear, silvery-pink, semi-double blooms of cupped, Bourbon form. Flowers borne all along rather thorny branches amid dark, greyish-green, matt foliage. Inclined to suffer badly from mildew, but this can be excused as it usually occurs after flowering is finished in late summer.

[P G ◍ (S)]   3′×6′   90 cm×1.8 m

'Scintillation'
Austin UK 1967
R. macrantha × 'Vanity'
Clusters of blush-pink, semi-double flowers on a sprawly, useful-sized plant. Foliage grey-green and plentiful.
[P G ⊕ (S)]   4′×8′   1.2 × 2.5 m

R. richardii, *R. sancta*, 'The Holy Rose'
ABYSSINIA 1897
Origin not fully known, probably a Gallica hybrid of considerable antiquity
A low-growing, slightly sprawly plant with dark green, matt-finished leaves. Flowers single, beautifully formed, soft rose pink.

[P G W ⊕ ▽ ≋ (S)]   3′×4′   90 cm × 1.2 m

'Raubritter' (see text p. 195)   [PB]

R. richardii   [RCB]

ROSA Subgenus II Rosa (Eurosa)

SECTION III *Caninae*

Growth upright and arching. Thorns usually hooked and numerous.
Foliage medium-sized, mostly greyish-green, 7 to 9 leaflets.
Flowers usually in small clusters.
Hips generally oval to round.
Sepals no consistent pattern.

SPECIES

R. agrestis; *R. × alba*; *R. biebersteinii*;
R. britzensis; *R. canina*; *R. collina*;
R. corymbifera; *R. dumales*; *R. eglanteria*;
R. glauca; *R. inodora*; *R. jundzillii*;
R. micrantha; *R. mollis*; *R. orientalis*;

R. pulverulenta; *R. serafinii*; *R. sherardii*;
R. sicula; *R. stylosa*; *R. tomentosa*;
R. villosa; *R. villosa duplex*; *R. waitziana*

GARDEN GROUPS

Albas
Dog Roses
Sweet Briars

ORIGIN AND DISTRIBUTION

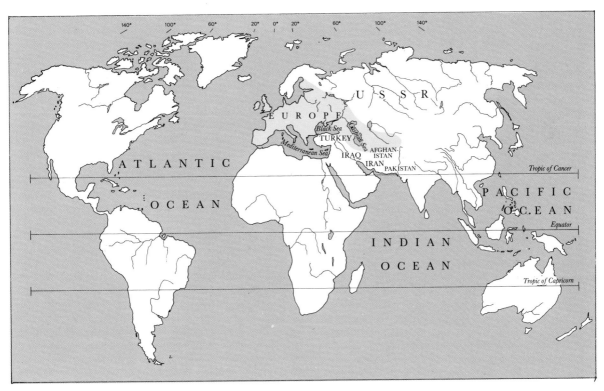

'Celestial'

R. agrestis
s. EUROPE 1878
A tall shrub related to the better known *R. eglanteria* to which it is similar in many respects

except that the foliage is without scent until the leaves are crushed.

[W P ◐ (S)]   10′ × 8′   3 × 2.5 m

R. × alba

As a garden group the Albas are exceptionally healthy and comprise some of the most beautiful roses from the past. They are mostly of pastel shades and without exception, are superbly scented. Notes on their history can be found on page 25.

R. × alba, 'White Rose of York'
EUROPE Pre-16th century
A lovely shrub, closely related to the 'Dog Rose' and in many ways similar, both in shape of flower and growth habit. Single flowers pure white and sweetly scented. Foliage matt-grey and smooth. Stems light green with an average population of stout thorns. Seldom seen in gardens today.

[P W H (S)]   6′ × 4′   1.8 × 1.2 m

FORMS AND HYBRIDS OF *R. × alba*

'Amelia'
Vibert FRANCE 1823
Parentage unknown
One of the less vigorous of the Albas with possibly some Damask influence. Large, semi-double, pink flowers up to 3″ (8 cm) with pronounced golden anthers. Superb scent. Grey-green foliage.

[P W H (S)]   4′ × 3′   1.2 m × 90 cm

'Blanche de Belgique', 'Blanche Superbe'
Vibert FRANCE 1817
Parentage unknown
Pure white flowers of good size and shape with a superb perfume. Foliage grey-green and healthy. Growth vigorous, bushy and upright.

[P H W ◐ (S)]   6′ × 4′   1.8 × 1.2 m

'Celestial', 'Celeste'
Origin, date and parentage unknown. Very ancient
Beautiful, semi-double, soft pink flowers combining well with leaden grey foliage. A healthy, robust yet charming rose with a superb, 'expensive' perfume.

[W P H ◐ (S)]   6′ × 4′   1.8 × 1.2 m

'Chloris', 'Rosée du Matin'
Origin, date and parentage unknown. Very ancient
Not seen as often as some other Albas, it has the darkest green leaves of all, and is comparatively thornless. Flowers double with incurving petals curling into a tight central button. Colour soft satiny-pink. Scented.

[W P H ◐ (S)]   5′ × 4′   1.5 × 1.2 m

'Cuisse de Nymphe'. *See* 'Maiden's Blush'

'Félicité Parmentier'
1834
Origin and parentage unknown
A tidy shrub bearing an abundance of flat, reflexing flowers similar in colour to pink coconut-ice. Good healthy dark greyish-green foliage.
[W P H ⓜ (S)]   4′×3′   1.2 m × 90 cm

'Jeanne d'Arc'
Vibert FRANCE 1818
Parentage unknown
Rather sprawly but nevertheless a very useful shrub. Darkish foliage shows off the creamy, rather muddled flowers to advantage; fading to white in hot sun.
[P W H ⓜ (S)]   6′×5′   1.8×1.5 m

'Königin von Dänemark', 'Queen of Denmark'
1826
Origin and parentage unknown
The individual flowers of this rose are slightly smaller than most other Albas and its colour a deeper pink. Shoots somewhat more than typically thorny and the foliage, although greyish-green is more coarse. Superbly scented, this rose is still an excellent ambassador for the Albas as a whole.
[P H W ⓜ (S)]   5′×4′   1.5×1.2 m

'Maiden's Blush Great', 'Cuisse de Nymphe', 'Incarnata', 'La Virginale', 'La Séduisante'
EUROPE 15th century or earlier
Parentage unknown
In France this rose is known by the very seductive name 'Cuisse de Nymphe', but, in England, Victorian prudery caused it to be known by the more refined but equally suggestive name 'Maiden's Blush'. This most lovely of roses combines all the best Alba attributes. Blush-pink, it has a refined perfume and is amply clothed with blue-grey leaves. 'Cuisse de Nymphe Émue' is the name applied to more richly coloured clones of this variety.
[P H W ⓜ (S)]   5′×5′   1.5×1.5 m

'Félicité Parmentier'   [PB]

'Maxima', 'Jacobite Rose', 'Bonnie Prince Charlie's Rose', 'White Rose of York, 'Great Double White', 'Cheshire Rose'
EUROPE 15th century or earlier
Possibly *R. canina* × *R. gallica*
Pure white, sometimes creamy-white, very double flowers in an upright cluster of 6 to 8 blooms. Healthy, grey-green foliage. Sometimes with good oval shaped autumn fruit.
[P W H (S)]   6′ × 4′   1.8 × 1.2 m

'Mme Legras de St Germain'
Early 19th century
Origin and parentage unknown
A relatively thornless rose. Medium-sized, very double creamy-white flowers produced in large clusters, highly scented, standing up well to inclement weather. Light grey-green foliage soft and downy to touch. Equally good as shrub or climber, when with support it will attain at least double its usual height.
[P W ◍ N (S)]   7′ × 6′   2 × 1.8 m

Above: 'Königin von Dänemark'   [JB]
Below: 'Mme Plantier'   [JB]

'Mme Plantier'
Plantier 1835
Parentage unknown
An interesting rose, best classified as an Alba. Probably an Alba/Moschata cross. Capable of climbing, when it will reach perhaps 20′ (6 m) into small open trees, but good as lax shrub or pillar rose. Flattish flowers, made up of many convoluted petals, pale cream, changing to pure white, borne in very large clusters on long, sometimes arching stems. Foliage and stems light greyish-green. Few thorns.
[T P ◍ N (S)]   12′ × 8′   3.5 × 2.5 m

'Pompon Blanc Parfait'
c. 1876
Origin and parentage unknown
An upright-growing variety not altogether typical of an Alba in growth habit, being rather stubby, apart from the occasional longer shoot. Smooth foliage and short leaf stalks. Scented, pure white flowers produced very freely in small clusters.
[P W H ◍ N (S)]   4′ × 3′   1.2 m × 90 cm

'Maiden's Blush Small'
Kew Gardens UK 1797
Parentage unknown, probably sport of 'Maiden's Blush Great'
Similar in all respects to its sister but slightly smaller, both in stature and size of flower.
[P H W ◍ (S)]   4′ × 3′   1.2 m × 90 cm

'Semi-plena' [VP]

'Princesse de Lamballe'

Origin, date and parentage unknown

An Alba seen mentioned from time to time but with which I am not familiar. Others, too, have become lost in the ravages of time. In fact, in one of my favourite old books, *The Flower Garden*, 1843, some 50 or so Albas are mentioned. Another old Alba which I have not seen is 'A Feuilles de Chauvre'. This is described as having small white semi-double flowers and growing to 3' (90 cm).

'Semi-plena', *R. × alba suaveolens*, *R. × alba nivea*

EUROPE 16th century or earlier

Semi-double, sweetly scented, pure white flowers with pronounced anthers borne on an upright but graceful bush with matt, grey-green leaves. Good autumn fruit. An underrated form of *R. × alba*, deserving more attention, especially as an informal hedge or lax shrub in the wilder garden.

[P W H (S)] 8' × 5' 2.5 × 1.5 m

R. biebersteinii, *R. horrida*

EUROPE AND W. ASIA 1796

A curious, almost gooseberry-like bush with small, white flowers followed by globular red hips.

[P F W ▽ (S)] 2' × 2' 60 × 60 cm

R. britzensis

MIDDLE EAST 1901

A tallish, upright shrub with bluish-green, relatively thornless branches and greyish-green leaves. Flowers large, up to three inches across, blush-white and scented. Hips biggish, oval and dark red with sparse bristles.

[F W P ◑ (S)] 8' × 6' 2.5 × 1.8 m

R. canina

R. canina 'Dog Rose'

EUROPE Ancient species

The most common wild rose native to Britain
and Europe, also occasionally found naturalized
in other temperate areas such as North America.
Although a coarse, somewhat awkward shrub, its
individual flowers are quite beautiful. Usually
pale or blush pink, they sometimes vary from district to district. I have recently found one of pure
white. They also have a sweet scent. A distinctive
feature is the abundance of orange-red hips produced in autumn. These are rich in vitamin C
and used in rose hip syrup; they also make a good
wine. Until superseded by *R. laxa*, the common
Dog Rose was the most widely used understock
for the production of modern roses. *R. canina
inermis* is a fairly thornless form now sometimes
used as such.

[F P N ◍ W]   Up to 10′×6′   3 × 1.8 m

R. canina   [VP]

FORMS AND HYBRIDS OF
R. canina

'Abbotswood', 'Canina Abbotswood'

Hilling UK 1954

R. canina × unknown garden variety

A chance hybrid with scented, double, pink
flowers, most useful where a well-armed, dense
shrub is needed for a specific purpose.

[P N ◍ W]   10′×6′   3 × 1.8 m

'Andersonii'

Hillier UK 1912

Chance hybrid of *R. canina* × possibly *R. arvensis*
or *R. gallica*

A deep pink, larger flowered form of *R. canina*
with fewer thorns and, in my experience, tidier
habit. Hips similar to those of its parent.

[F P N ◍ W]   8′×6′   2.5 × 1.8 m

'Andersonii'   [VP]

R. eglanteria

R. × collina
R. corymbifera × R. gallica
CENTRAL EUROPE 1779

A medium growing shrub with sparse, reddish thorns and pale, greyish-green leaves. Flowers mid to pale pink followed by oval, bright red hips.

[F W P ◍]   6′×4′   1.8×1.2 m

R. corymbifera
E. EUROPE AND ASIA 1838

Obviously related to *R. canina*, which it resembles both in size of plant and in foliage. Flowers are slightly larger in size, creamy white with hints of blush pink. Good orange-red hips, again similar to those of *R. canina*.

[P W F ◍ (S)]   10′×6′   3×1.8 m

'Amy Robsart' and, *right*, 'Amy Robsart' grown on a tripod at Mannington Hall   [VP]

R. dumales
E. EUROPE, MIDDLE EAST 1872

A medium shrub related, and similar to *R. canina*, found mostly in mountainous areas in southern Europe. Flowers large, 2½ ins (7 cms), clear rose pink, scented. Large oval to round red fruit.

[F W P ◍ (S)]   6′×5′   1.8×1.5 m

R. eglanteria, R. rubiginosa, 'Sweet Briar', 'Eglantine Rose'
EUROPE

Date unknown

Similar to *R. canina*, distinguished by its perfumed foliage and higher density of prickles. Flowers single, smallish and blush-pink. Fruits freely, the hips stay on the bush well into winter. Given its head it will reach 6′ or 7′ (1.8–2 m) in the open and twice this height if grown as hedgerow plant, which it prefers. In the garden, it is best clipped each year to encourage young growth, for the tips of growth exude the strongest scent. *R. eglanteria* is a native of Europe and has probably been appreciated for its perfumed leaves since civilization began. Many varieties are listed in 19th-century catalogues, but most of these seem to have disappeared now.

[P F H W ◍ ▽ (S)]   12′×8′   3.5×2.5 m

[PB]

FORMS AND HYBRIDS OF
R. eglanteria

'Amy Robsart'
Penzance UK c. 1894
Parentage unknown
Dull for most of year but spectacular in full bloom; a mass of scented, deep pink, almost single blooms in June on a vigorous bush. The hips, which do not always set, can compensate in late summer. Foliage only slightly scented.

[P F H W ◑ (S)]   10′×8′   3×2.5 m

'Anne of Geierstein'
Penzance UK c. 1894
Parentage unknown
This is a very vigorous member of its group with sweetly scented foliage and single, gold-centred crimson flowers, followed by oval scarlet hips in autumn.

[P F H W ◑ (S)]   10′×8′   3×2.5 m

'Catherine Seyton'
Penzance UK 1894
Parentage unknown
Lovely soft pink, single flowers with pronounced golden-yellow stamens. Rich green foliage on a vigorous shrub. Both flowers and foliage are scented. Orange-red hips in autumn.

[P W F H ◑ (S)]   8′×5′   2.5×1.5 m

'Edith Bellenden'
Penzance UK 1895
Parentage unknown
A good but little known Sweet Briar with well scented foliage. Its scented flowers are single, pale rosy-pink, produced very freely in season and followed by good, oval, red hips.

[P W H F ◑ (S)]   8′×6′   2.5×1.8 m

'Flora McIvor'
Penzance UK c. 1894
Parentage unknown
A medium tall vigorous shrub bearing single, deep pink flowers with white centres, followed by oval orange-red hips in late summer. Foliage scented, but leaves need to be rubbed between the fingers for this to be noticeable.

[P F H W ◑ (S)]   8′×6′   2.5×1.8 m

'Goldbusch'   [PB]

'Goldbusch'
Kordes GERMANY 1954
Parentage unknown
A most useful shrub which I would like to see grown more widely. Large, semi-double flowers produced freely in clusters amid an abundance of lush, light green, healthy, scented foliage. Flowers also well scented.

[P H W ◑ (S)]   8′×5′   2.5×1.5 m

'Greenmantle'
Penzance UK c. 1894
Parentage unknown
Single, rosy-red with golden stamens. Fragrant foliage. A lesser known sweetbriar which should be more popular.

[P H W ◑ (S)]   8′×5′   2.5×1.5 m

'Hebe's Lip', 'Rubrotincta', 'Reine Blanche'
W. Paul UK Introduced 1912
Thought to be *R. × damascena × R. eglanteria*
Of unknown but probably very ancient origin. Scented foliage. Flowers almost single, white, tinged with red at the petal edges. Thorny with coarse foliage. Open habit of growth.

[P H W ◑ (S)]   4′×4′   1.2×1.2 m

'Herbstfeuer', 'Autumn Fire'

Kordes GERMANY 1961

Parentage unknown

Clusters of large, semi-double, dark red, fragrant flowers which occasionally repeat in the autumn; these are produced on a vigorous bush with dark green, slightly scented foliage. Very large, elongated-pear-shaped, bright orange-red fruit. I have never understood why this rose is not better known.

[P W H F ◍ (R)]　6′ × 4′　1.8 × 1.2 m

'Janet's Pride', 'Clementine'

Paul UK Introduced 1892

Parentage unknown

Semi-double flowers, white with bright pink markings at petal edges. Scented. Not as vigorous as some of this group. Coarse foliage not unattractive. Interesting and unique.

[H P W ◍ (S)]　5′ × 4′　1.5 × 1.2 m

'Julia Mannering'

Penzance UK c. 1895

Parentage unknown

Bright, clear pink, heavily veined single flowers. Good, dark foliage, well scented as are the flowers.

[H P W ◍ (S)]　6′ × 4′　1.8 × 1.2 m

'La Belle Distinguée', 'Scarlet Sweetbriar', 'La Petite Duchesse'

Origin, date and parentage unknown

Probably a very old variety. A most interesting rose, not very tall and of an upright, bushy habit with numerous, small, slightly aromatic leaves. At first sight, the young bush is reminiscent of the Centifolia 'Rose de Meaux'. Flowers almost scarlet, fully double and produced freely.

[P H ▽ (S)]　5′ × 4′　1.5 m × 90 cm

'Lady Penzance'

Penzance UK c. 1894

R. eglanteria × R. foetida bicolor

A dense, vigorous shrub, probably the best known of the Sweet Briars, with by far the strongest-scented foliage. Flowers single, coppery-salmon and pink with pronounced yellow stamens, followed by bright red hips.

[F P W H ◍ (S)]　7′ × 6′　2 × 1.8 m

'Lady Penzance' grown on a tripod　[TW]
at Mannington Hall

'Lord Penzance'

Penzance UK c. 1890

R. eglanteria × 'Harrison's Yellow'

A vigorous, dense shrub with sweetly scented foliage. Flowers single, buff-yellow tinged pink, followed by bright red hips.

[F P W H (S)]　7′ × 6′　2 × 1.8 m

'Lucy Ashton'

Penzance UK 1894

Parentage unknown

Lovely, single, pure white flowers with the edges of each petal touched with pastel pink. Scented foliage. Makes a good vigorous shrub.

[P H W F (S)]　6′ × 5′　1.8 × 1.5 m

'Magnifica'

Hesse GERMANY 1916

'Lucy Ashton' seedling

A splendid shrub rose which should be more widely grown. Semi-double flowers purplish-red, of good size and quality. Foliage only slightly scented but dense and dark green. Makes a very good hedge.

[P H W ◍ (S)]　6′ × 5′　1.8 × 1.5 m

'Manning's Blush'

c. 1800
Origin and parentage unknown
A very good shrub rose. Flowers large, white flushed pink, fully double, opening flat, and fragrant. Foliage scented, small and plentiful suggesting *R. pimpinellifolia* influence. The shrub is bushy and dense and, although not generally recurrent, I have seen the odd flower in early autumn.

[P W H ⦿ ▽ (S)]   5′×4′   1.5×1.2 m

Above: 'Manning's Blush'   [PB]
Below: 'Meg Merrilees'

'Mechtilde von Neuerburg'

Boden GERMANY 1920
Parentage unknown
Semi-double flowers of an attractive pinkish-red. Foliage slightly aromatic, dark and plentiful. Has a vague Gallica look, belied by its size.

[P W ⦿ (S)]   10′×8′   3×2.5 m

'Meg Merrilees'

Penzance UK c. 1894
An extremely vigorous and prickly shrub rose. Bright crimson semi-double flowers followed by an abundance of good red hips. One of the best of its group, with scented flowers and foliage.

[P W H F (S)]   8′×7′   2.5×2 m

'Rose Bradwardine'

Penzance UK 1894
Parentage unknown
Clusters of single, clear rose-pink flowers on a vigorous, well-proportioned plant with good, dark green, aromatic leaves, good hips.

[P H W F ⦿ (S)]   6′×5′   1.8×1.5 m

[PB]

R. glauca

R. glauca, R. rubrifolia

EUROPE 1830

A very useful, ornamental shrub with glaucous-purple stems and foliage. Clusters of small, rather inconspicuous, yet rather beautiful flowers of soft mauve-pink. Oval reddish-purple hips in autumn. Useful for flower-arranging, one or two plants will give an almost unending supply of foliage for this purpose. For many years better known as *R. rubrifolia*. This is botanically erroneous, and the name *R. glauca* has now been accepted as more accurate.

[F N H W P A ◐ (S)]   6′×5′   1.8×1.5 m

R. glauca   [VP]

FORMS AND HYBRIDS OF
R. glauca

'Carmenetta'

Central Experimental Farm CANADA 1923

R. glauca × R. rugosa

Slightly more vigorous and consequentially less graceful than its seed parent. Foliage and stems glaucous-purple with numerous small thorns. Hips of similar size and colour, and flowers slightly larger than those of *R. glauca*.

[F N H W P A (S)]   7′×7′   2×2 m

'Sir Cedric Morris'

Sir Cedric Morris, introduced by Beales UK 1979

R. glauca × R. mulliganii

The male parent is an assumption by the late Sir Cedric. It was a foundling, growing among other *R. glauca* seedlings at his home, Benton End, Hadleigh, Suffolk, and introduced by me in 1979. A specimen of *R. mulliganii*, or what we know as such, was growing close by, flowering at the same time as *R. glauca*. I was staggered by my first sight of this rose. The glaucous-purple (not as purple as *R. glauca*) foliage is abundant and large. Stems are thick, also glaucous and very thorny. Flowers are evenly spaced in huge clusters and, when established, grow in massed profusion. These are single, pure white and display prominent golden anthers. The scent is strong, sweet and pervading. It bears a lavish crop of small, orange hips in autumn.

[F T P W A N (S)]   30′×20′   9×6 m   [JB]

'Sir Cedric Morris', at Benton End, Hadleigh, Suffolk

R. inodora, R. graveolens, R. obtusifolia

S. EUROPE 1905

A coarse, vigorous, thorny shrub with scented (sweetbriar) foliage, ideal for naturalizing or growing into hedgerows, almost a less refined form of *R. eglanteria*. Flowers single, soft pink to blush-white. Oval, bright red hips.

[F W P ◍ (S)] 8′ × 5′ 2.4 × 1.5 m

R. jundzillii, R. marginata

E. EUROPE 1870

A handsome rose. Flowers single, quite large, bright pink, produced freely on a medium-sized, moderately prickly plant bearing ample darkish green, serrated leaves. Smooth bright red round to oval hips in autumn.

[P F ◍ (S)] 5′ × 4′ 1.5 × 1.2 m

R. micrantha

E. EUROPE 1900

Similar to *R. eglanteria* but slightly less vigorous with smaller flowers and only slightly scented foliage.

[F W P ◍ (S)] 6′ × 4′ 1.5 × 1.2 m

R. mollis

N. EUROPE 1818

A small, shrubby plant with greyish to red stems and grey, downy foliage. Flowers mid-pink, borne mostly in small clusters of three or four fragrant blooms in mid-summer. Bristly, occasionally smooth, globular hips.

[F W P ◍ (S)] 3′ × 3′ 90 × 90 cm

R. orientalis

S. EUROPE/MIDDLE EAST 1905

A shrubby, short growing plant with slender, hairy branches. Leaves made up of five, seldom seven small, oval leaflets of bright green. Papery flowers of soft pink. Hips small, narrow, oblong and bright red.

[W P (S)] 2′ × 2′ 60 × 60 cm

R. pulverulenta, R. glutinosa

MEDITERRANEAN REGIONS Introduced 1821

Short growing and prickly, with small, pinkish-white, single flowers followed by small globular hips. Foliage smells of pine.

[P F ◍ ▽] 3′ × 3′ 90 × 90 cm

R. serafinii [VP]

R. serafinii

EASTERN MEDITERRANEAN REGION 1914

Small, single, pink flowers on a short-growing, thorny, rather sprawly plant. Rounded, bright orange-red fruit. Foliage serrated and glossy.

[P W F ◍ (S)] 2′ × 2′ 60 × 60 cm

R. sherardii, R. omissa

N. CENTRAL EUROPE 1933

Medium sized shrub with angular sometimes zig-zag branches and bluish-green foliage. Deep pink flowers usually in small clusters followed by smallish, almost urn-shaped hips.

[W P ◍ (S)] 6′ × 4′ 1.5 × 1.2 m

R. sicula

S. EUROPE AND N. AFRICA C. 1894

A short, free suckering shrub similar to *R. serafini* with reddish wood when young. Foliage is greyish-green and slightly scented as are the flowers which are soft pink in colour. Hips round to oval.

[H P ◍ (S)] 3′ × 2′ 90 × 60 cm

R. stylosa

EUROPE 1838

An arching shrub with small, narrow, oval, mid-green leaves. Its flowers are in small clusters, and individually are of medium size (1½ in, 5 cm) they are blush-pinkish-white followed by smooth, oval, red hips.

[F W P ◍ (S)] 10′ × 8′ 3 × 2.5 m

R. *villosa duplex*   [PB]

R. *tomentosa*

EUROPE Ancient species

Tall shrub rose, similar in many respects to *R. canina*. Medium-sized, clear, soft pink flowers with a good display of soft, creamy-yellow stamens. Scented. Foliage matt grey-green, softer in both appearance and touch to that of the 'Dog Rose'. Bright red, oval fruit. Grows wild in many parts of mainland Europe and the British Isles. I have come upon one or two in Norfolk hedgerows.

[F P W ⓪]   10′ × 8′   3 × 2.5 m

R. *villosa*, R. *pomifera*, 'Apple Rose'

EUROPE/ASIA 1761

Medium-sized shrub with greyish, downy leaves, which are said to be fragrant but this is barely perceptible in my plant. Flowers scented, clear pink and single. Fruit large, orange, apple-shaped and well covered with bristles.

[P F E N ⓪ (S)]   6′ × 5′   1.8 × 1.5 m

R. *villosa duplex*, R. *pomifera duplex*, 'Wolly Dodd's Rose'

First garden form discovered in the garden of the Rev. Wolly-Dodd, Cheshire, c. 1900
Parentage unknown

Similar in most respects to *R. villosa* but slightly shorter in growth. Flowers semi-double and clear pink. Sets hips only rarely but repeats flowers intermittently when growing in good situations suggesting hybrid origin.

[P F W N ⓪ (S)]   5′ × 4′   1.5 × 1.2 m

R. × *waitziana*

EUROPE 1874
R. canina × *R. gallica*

A medium to tall shrub with stems and armature similar to those of *R. canina*. Medium sized, deep pink flowers. Fruit seldom sets fully in the cultivated form.

[W P ⓪ (S)]   6′ × 4′   1.8 × 1.2 m

ROSA Subgenus II Rosa (Eurosa)
SECTION IV *Carolinae*

Growth shortish, upright. Thorns short, usually in pairs, hooked.
Leaves composed of 7 to 9 leaflets – usually good in autumn.
Flowers mostly singly on short stalks.
Hips mostly roundish. Sepals drop when ripe.

SPECIES

R. carolina
R. carolina alba
R. carolina plena
R. foliolosa

R. × kochiana
R. × mariae-graebnerae
R. nitida
R. palustris
R. virginiana

ORIGIN AND DISTRIBUTION

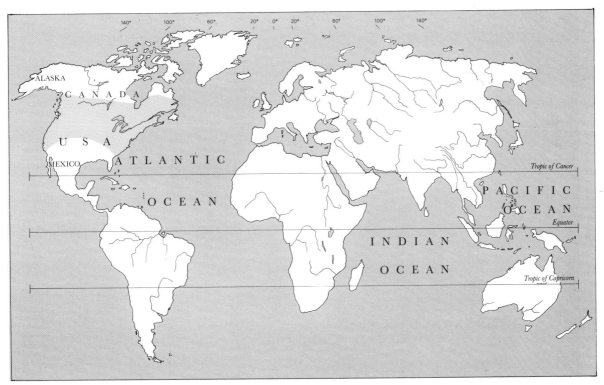

R. foliolosa

R. carolina

R. carolina

N. AMERICA C. 1826

A useful, free suckering rose – when on its own roots, with thin, relatively thornless shoots and completely thornless lateral branches. Ample, slightly glossy foliage. Flowers clear, soft pink borne solitarily, followed by roundish, red hips.

[⬤ F A P ▽ (S)]   3′ × 3′   90 × 90 cm

FORMS AND HYBRIDS OF
R. carolina

R. carolina alba, R. virginiana alba

Garden discovery USA 1867

But for its single, white flowers, it is similar in most respects to R. carolina. Slight differences in foliage suggest the influence of genes from another species or variety. This difference is most marked on the underside of leaves, with more numerous tiny hairs, making them appear greyer than those of the pink form.

[F A P W ⬤ ▽ (S)]   3′ × 2′   90 × 60 cm

R. carolina plena 'The Double Pennsylvanian Rose'

USA C. 1790 (Lynes rediscovery 1955)

Charming, small, double flowers of clear pink paling to almost white at the edges. Foliage smooth and dark green. Makes a tidy, short-growing, free-suckering plant when on its own roots, which is perhaps the best way it can be reproduced and grown. For more details of the rose and its re-discovery, see Graham Thomas's book *Shrub Roses for Today*.

[P ▽ (S)]   2′ × 2′   6′ × 60 cm

R. foliolosa

N. AMERICA 1880

Bright pink, solitary, slightly ragged flowers amid strange, narrow, elongated foliage. Free suckering when on its own roots. No thorns. Short-growing and tolerant of the wettest soils. Fruits small, widely spherical and bright red.

[P A F (S)]   3′ × 3′   90 × 90 cm

R. × kochiana

N. AMERICA 1869

Probably R. palustris × R. pimpinellifolia

I have become very fond of this little shrub. The pleasing, bright lime-green foliage remains healthy all summer and changes to a rich, russet-red in autumn. Few but strong thorns on stiff, thin, angular shoots. Flowers solitary and deep rose pink, reminiscent of those of the shrub *Cistus crispus*.

[P W ▽ A (S)]   3′ × 2′   90 × 60 cm

R. × mariae-graebnerae

H. Dabel GERMANY 1900

R. palustris × R. virginiana

A most useful, rare but striking little shrub. Bright rose pink flowers which are produced at first in profusion and then intermittently throughout the summer. Sparsely thorned shoots with almost shiny foliage. Small, round hips and good autumn colour.

[F A W P G ⬤ (R)]   3′ × 2′   90 × 60 cm

R. × kochiana

R. nitida

N. AMERICA 1807

A free-suckering, short shrub with thin, prickly stems and small, dainty, fern-like foliage turning to rich crimson in autumn. Flowers small, single, numerous and deep rose pink. A useful shrub. Hips small, oval and slightly bristly.

[G W F A ◑ ▽ (S)]   3′ × 3′   90 × 90 cm

R. palustris, 'The Swamp Rose'

N. AMERICA 1726

A vigorous rose with abundant, mid- to dark-green foliage, reddish stems and an upright habit. Single, deep pink flowers produced intermittently over a long season, followed by oval hips in the autumn. Will tolerate wet, boggy conditions.

[A P F W ▽ (S)]   4′ × 3′   1.2 m × 90 cm

R. nitida   [TW]

R. virginiana

R. virginiana

N. AMERICA C. 1807

At home in most soils, this very useful shrub does particularly well in light, sandy conditions. Well foliated with light green glossy leaves very colourful in autumn. Upright and bushy in growth. Blooms single, rich clear pink with yellow stamens and a good scent. Flowers appear later than in some species, followed by orange, plump, round hips remaining on the plant well into winter.

[H P W A F ◍ (S)] 5′ × 3′ 1.5 m × 90 cm

'Rose d'Amour'   [JB]

FORMS AND HYBRIDS OF
R. virginiana

'Rose d'Amour', 'St Mark's Rose',
R. virginiana plena

Pre-1870

Origin and parentage unknown

Taller than *R. virginiana* but the plant has many characteristics in common with this species. Flowers beautiful, quite small, high centred, and fully double with petals scrolled as they open, pastel pink deepening towards the centre of each bloom. An excellent example can be seen at The Royal Horticultural Society's Gardens at Wisley, Surrey, where it has grown quite tall as a wall plant.

[P A ◍ (R)] 7′ × 5′ 2 × 1.5 m

'Rose d'Orsay'

Origin, date and parentage unknown

Flowers, foliage and colour of wood are almost identical to those of 'Rose d'Amour', but its habit of growth and freedom of flower is quite different, being shorter, more branchy and untidy, and flowering for a much longer season. A superb rose, one fault being a reluctance to shed its dead petals, thus dead-heading is important for the best results.

[P A ◍ (C)] 4′ × 4′ 1.2 × 1.2 m

Note

For a number of years I have grown seedlings of *R. virginiana* from imported seed. When young, the plants look identical but in their second year become more varied, some almost thornless, some densely thorny, others growing much taller, with variation in colour and size of hips. The only constant and typical feature is their leaves. At least one of these seedlings – mistakenly sent to an anonymous buyer and presumably lost for ever – had a few more than the expected number of petals. One day, perhaps, I will track down the source of this seed. I suspect it comes from somewhere near the Eastern Mediterranean.

Mr Graham Thomas explained the difference between 'Rose d'Amour' and 'Rose d'Orsay', and the part he played in their respective identifications, in an article in The Royal National Rose Society's Rose Annual, 1977.

ROSA Subgenus II Rosa (Eurosa)

SECTION V *Cassiorhodon (Cinnamomeae)*

Growth mostly shrubby and upright. Variable from 3 ft–12 ft, 1 m–4 m.
Thorns often large and in pairs.
Leaves, 5 to 9, sometimes 11 leaflets.
Flowers mostly in groups, colours usually red or pink except in *R. wardii* and *rugosa*.
Hips are usually a special feature, large, variously shaped – sepals held erect when ripe.

SPECIES

R. acicularis nipponensis; *R. amblyotis*;
R. arkansana; *R. banksiopsis*; *R. beggeriana*;
R. bella; *R. blanda*; *R. californica*;
R. californica plena; *R. caudata*; *R. coriifolia*;
R. × coryana; *R. corymbulosa*; *R. davidii*;
R. davurica; *R. fargesii*; *R. farreri persetosa*;
R. fedtschenkoana; *R. forrestiana*; *R. gymnocarpa*;
R. hemsleyana; *R. holodonta*; *R. × kamtchatica*;
R. × kordesii; *R. × l'heritierana*; *R. macrophylla*;
R. majalis; *R. marretii*; *R. maximowicziana*;
R. melina; *R. × micrugosa*; *R. × micrugosa alba*;

R. mohavensis; *R. moyesii*; *R. multibracteata*;
R. murielae; *R. nutkana*; *R. × paulii*;
R. × paulii rosea; *R. pendulina*; *R. pisocarpa*;
R. prattii; *R. pyrifera*; *R. rugosa*; *R. rugosa
alba*; *R. rugosa rubra*; *R. rugosa typica*;
R. sertata; *R. setipoda*; *R. spaldingii*;
R. suffulta; *R. sweginzowii macrocarpa*;
R. ultramontana; *R. wardii*; *R. webbiana*
R. willmottiae; *R. woodsii fendleri*

GARDEN GROUPS

Boursaults; Rugosas

ORIGIN AND DISTRIBUTION

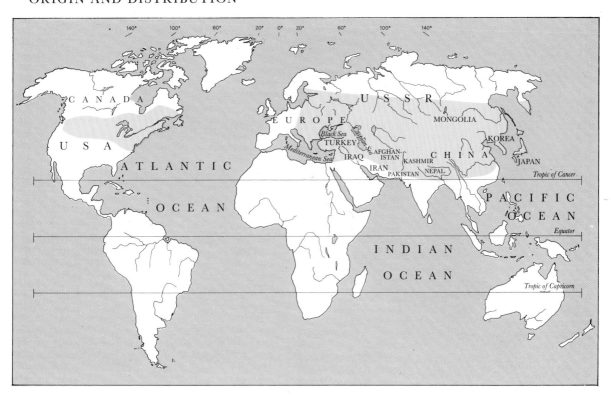

R. caudata (see text p. 221)   [VP]

R. acicularis

N.E. ASIA, N. AMERICA AND N. EUROPE 1805
Rich pink solitary flowers, 1½″ (4 cm) in diameter, occasionally in twos or threes. Bright red, plump, smooth, pear-shaped hips of approximately 1″ (2.5 cm) in length. Foliage mid-green to grey on a lax plant with thin shoots, an abundant amount of variably sized bristles and few real thorns.
[P W H (S)]   6′ × 5′   1.8 × 1.5 m

R. acicularis nipponensis

JAPAN 1894
Solitary flowers of 1½″ to 2″ (4–5 cm), deep pink, almost red, followed by plump, pear-shaped hips. Greenish-grey foliage. Flower stalks and hips bristly, with few real thorns.
[P W H (S)]   5′ × 4′   1.5 × 1.2 m

R. amblyotis

N.E. ASIA 1917
An upright, medium sized shrub similar to R. majalis to which it is obviously related. Medium sized, red flowers followed by medium sized, globular to pear-shaped, red hips.
[F W P ◍ (S)]   6′ × 4′   1.8 × 1.2 m

R. arkansana

USA 1917
A prickly, short growing, dense shrub with a fairly long flowering season in mid-summer. Foliage almost glossy and heavily veined. Flowers 1½ ins (5 cm), bright red with yellow stamens, usually in clusters. Small, round, reddish hips.
[P G ◍ (S)]   2′ × 2′   60 × 60 cm

R. banksiopsis

CHINA 1907
I lost my only plant of this in the severe winter of 1981 and never saw it flower. It is described in Hillier's *Manual of Trees and Shrubs* as being a medium-sized shrub with small, rose-red flowers followed by flask-shaped hips.
[P F W (S)]   5′ × 4′   1.5 × 1.2 m

R. beggeriana

CENTRAL ASIA 1869
Not the most auspicious of species but it has a long flowering season from mid-summer onwards when the early flowers, small and white, are followed by small, round, orange hips. Stems covered with lightish coloured, hooked thorns. Greyish-green foliage.
[P F W ◍ (S)]   8′ × 7′   2.5 × 2 m

R. bella

CHINA 1910
An upright growing rather prickly shrub with many of the characteristics of R. moyesii. Flowers single, bright pink. Medium sized flask shaped orange fruit.
[W P (S)]   8′ × 6′   2.4 × 1.8 m

R. blanda, 'Smooth Rose', 'Meadow Rose', 'Hudson Bay Rose', 'Labrador Rose'

N. AMERICA 1773
Subtly similar to R. canina except for fewer thorns and deeper pink flowers. Also less vigorous. Hips rather more pear-shaped than oval. A few other strains exist but none of great interest to the gardener.
[P W ◍ F]   5′ × 3′   1.5 m × 90 cm

R. californica

N.W. AMERICA 1878

Uncommon in UK. Described in McFarland's *Modern Roses*, as up to 8′ (2.5 m) with corymbs of single pink flowers 1½″ (4 cm) across. A large specimen is growing at the John Innes Institute near Norwich, but I have not seen it flowering.

[(S)]   8′×4′   2.5×1.2 m

R. californica plena

Date attributed, 1894

I have grown a species so named for a number of years without being able to compare it with the single form, *R. californica*. My suspicions were originally aroused when I acquired a plant of *R. nutkana*, which, in winter, looked remarkably like my *R. californica plena*. When it flowered the following summer both plants were indeed the same, except that the flowers of *R. nutkana* were single. I assumed that *R. nutkana* was wrong and was probably *R. californica*, and left it there. Two years later, Mrs Léonie Bell, an active member of the American Heritage Rose Society, wrote saying that she had received one of our plants of *R. californica plena* and, being suspicious, had compared it closely with *R. californica*. She could

Above: R. californica   [VP]
Below: R. californica plena   [VP]

find no valid reason to justify this name. Mrs Bell will obviously get to the bottom of this in due course. Meanwhile, pending research into its true identity, I will follow nomenclature rather than instinct and place the rose in this position. It is an excellent garden shrub with lilac-pink flowers, shaped rather like the individual bloom of a semi-double hollyhock. The shrub is healthy, upright in habit and amply foliated with grey-green leaves. The wood is dark and has few thorns.

[⊕ P W (S)]   8′×5′   2.5×1.5 m

R. caudata

CHINA 1907

Very similar to the better known *R. setipoda*, to which it could well be related. However, since usually listed as a separate species, I have followed that rule. It forms a dense shrub with thick, well armed branches. Flowers, produced in large clusters, are pale pink, followed by flagon-shaped, bristly hips.

[P W F ⓜ (S)] 7′ × 5′ 2 × 1.5 m

R. coriifolia froebelii, R. dumetorum laxa

EUROPE 1890

A dense shrubby rose, with greyish-green wood and foliage. Moderately thorny, flowers white, hips plump but oval. Of little use ornamentally but invaluable and widely used, especially in Europe, as an understock. Produces fewer suckers than most other understocks.

[W (S)] 5′ × 4′ 1.5 × 1.2 m

R. × coryana

Cambridge Botanical Gardens UK 1926
R. macrophylla × *R. roxburghii*
A medium-sized shrub with leaning towards *R. roxburghii* in appearance. An ideal woodland subject. Large, single, deep pink flowers produced in early summer. Interesting but not significant.

[P W (S)] 6′ × 4′ 1.8 × 1.2 m

R. corymbulosa

CHINA 1908

A medium, rather lax, almost thornless, thin-stemmed shrub; small leaves, with slightly hairy undersides, changing from green to deep purple in autumn. Flowers single, deep pinkish-red, with a white eye. Hips medium-sized, rounded and red.

[P W F (S)] 5′ × 4′ 1.5 × 1.2 m

R. davidii

CHINA 1908

A useful, late-flowering species with soft pink flowers borne, sometimes in clusters, along the length of each stem, sometimes singly. Upright and vigorous, with heavily veined, light green foliage and orange-red flagon-shaped hips in autumn.

[P F W ⓜ (S)] 10′ × 5′ 3 × 1.5 m

R. davurica

N. CHINA AND ASIA 1910

A shortish, averagely thorned shrub with small leaves and medium sized, pink flowers followed by small, oval hips.

[F W P ⓜ (S)] 3′ × 3′ 90 × 90 cm

R. farreri persetosa, 'Threepenny Bit Rose'

CHINA 1914

A charming, sprawly shrub with fine, fern-like leaves which turn purple and crimson in the autumn. Hips, produced in profusion, are bright orange-red. These features, together with its habit of growth are perhaps more important than its small lilac-pink flowers. Shoots biscuit-brown, densely covered in minute but fairly harmless thorns, giving an almost mossed effect. Rather enjoys partial shade.

[F G W P A ⓜ (S)] 5′ × 5′ 1.5 × 1.5 m

R. fedtschenkoana

S.E. EUROPE/ASIA C. 1880

A most useful shrub with single white, papery flowers, produced at first in profusion, then intermittently throughout summer. Foliage light grey-green and feathery. Sparsely bristled oval-to-pear-shaped hips.

[P H W A (R)] 5′ × 4′ 1.5 × 1.2 m

R. davidii [VP]

R. forrestiana

W. CHINA 1918

Pinkish-crimson flowers with creamy-buff anthers produced in small clusters, followed by bottle-shaped red hips. Ample, purplish-green foliage. Growth, also purplish-green, arching, dense and vigorous.

[P F G W (S)]   7′×7′   2×2 m

R. gymnocarpa

N. AMERICA 1893

Graceful, vigorous shrub with moderately thorny, wiry shoots and numerous small roundish leaves. Flowers small, single, pale pink. Small, red, pear-shaped, smooth hips in autumn. My stock came direct from seed collected by a friend in Nova Scotia where it grows wild.

[F P W ◍ (S)]   8′×10′   2.5×3 m

R. hemsleyana

CHINA 1904

Vigorous shrub similar to *R. setipoda*. Medium-sized, pink, single flowers borne in clusters, followed by bottle-shaped, bristly, orange-red hips.

[F P W ◍ ▽ (S)]   5′×4′   1.5×1.2 m

R. × kamtchatica, R. ventenatiana

Kamchatka USSR c. 1770

R. rugosa × R. amblyotis?

Often seen listed as a form of *R. rugosa*, but despite its obvious affinity to that species is distinct. Flowers smallish, single, pink touching cerise. Slightly scented. Mid-green foliage; stems well armed but less so than *R. rugosa*. Hips small to medium, round and bright red.

[W F P H A ◍ (C)]   7′×6′   2×1.8 m

R. fedtschenkoana (see text p. 221)   [TW]

R. kordesii

R. × kordesii
Kordes GERMANY 1950
'Max Graf' seedling
This rose was never introduced by Herr Kordes but he used it extensively in the breeding of some very important hybrids; hence its inclusion here. Offspring from this rose are particularly disease-resistant.

FORMS AND HYBRIDS OF
R. kordesii

'Dortmund'
Kordes GERMANY 1955
Seedling × *R. kordesii*
Large, single, crimson flowers with a pale, almost white, central eye. Produced in large clusters on a vigorous, thorny plant with dark green foliage.
[P N ⊕ (R)]   8′×6′   2.5 × 1.8 m

'Hamburger Phoenix'
Kordes GERMANY 1954
R. kordesii × seedling
Clusters of large, semi-double, rich crimson flowers on a spreading, vigorous shrub or short climber with dark green foliage. Hips good in autumn.
[P F N ⊕ (C)]   8′×5′   2.5 × 1.5 m

'Leverkusen'
Kordes GERMANY 1954
R. kordesii × 'Golden Glow'
Semi-double, lemon-yellow flowers which, when open, have attractively ragged edges. Sweetly scented, continues blooming all summer. Attractive glossy, light green, deeply serrated foliage. As so often with Kordes roses, rudely healthy.
[P N ⊕ (C)]   10′×8′   3 × 2.5 m

'Dortmund'

[RCB]

'Leverkusen' (see text p. 223)   [RCB]

'Parkdirektor Riggers'

Kordes GERMANY 1957
R. kordesii × 'Our Princess'
A very good climbing rose. Large clusters of deep
red to crimson, almost single, firm textured
flowers. Plant upright and vigorous. Foliage
healthy, dark green and glossy.

[P N ⬭ (C)]   10′×6′   3 × 1.8 m

The Boursault Roses

The Boursaults are but few and it was assumed until recently that *R. × lheritierana*, from which they descend, had occurred from a cross between *R. pendulina* and *R. chinensis*. Certainly their smooth stems, dark wood and leaf shape point in that direction.

Authoritative opinions vary, but chromosome counts do seem to prove conclusively the error of this assumption. Thus I have placed them here.

R. × lheritierana

PROBABLY EUROPE Pre-1820
Unarmed cane-like stems, variable from green to reddish-brown. Foliage dark green, rather blackberry-like, but smooth. Flowers double, opening flat, deep pinkish-red to blush-white. Smooth round hips, when and if they set.
[W P A (S)]   10′×8′   3×2.5 m

'Amadis', 'Crimson Boursault'

Laffay FRANCE 1829
Parentage unknown
A climbing thornless rose with long, arching shoots changing from green when young to almost chocolate-purple when mature. Smooth dark green foliage. Flowers semi-double, deep reddish-purple, rather ragged when open, produced both singly and in small clusters. Said to repeat but my plant has not done so to date.
[P A (S)]   10′×6′   3×1.8 m

'Blush Boursault', 'Calypso', 'Rose de l'Isle'

1848
Origin unknown – probably France
Parentage unknown
Flowers fully double, opening flat, with slightly ragged petals of pale blush-pink. Long, arching, thornless branches less purple than 'Amadis' but reddening with age. Foliage, dark green and plentiful, gives good display of autumn colour.
[P A (S)]   15′×10′   4.5×3 m

'Mme Sancy de Parabère'

Bonnet FRANCE c. 1874
Parentage unknown
A beautiful rose of rich pink. Fully double, opening flat, with the elongated outer layer of petals giving the effect almost of a ragged rose within a rose. Foliage handsome, darkish green. Thornless stems deepening from green to soft greeny-brown as they mature.
[P A ◐ (S)]   15′×10′   4.5×3 m

'Morlettii', *R. inermis morlettii*, *R. pendulina plena*

Morlet FRANCE 1883
Slightly less vigorous than other Boursaults although foliage and stems similar. Foliage particularly colourful in autumn. Flowers deep pinkish-magenta, almost double, rather ragged when fully open.
[P A (S)]   8′×6′   2.5×1.8 m

'Morlettii'   [VP]

Boursault Rose 'Mme Sancy de Parabère' (see text p. 225)

R. macrophylla

R. macrophylla
HIMALAYAS 1818

Medium-tall shrub with bright, cerise-pink flowers amid large, purplish-green leaves. Wood purple and smooth. Large orange fruits hang conspicuously, rather like small, slim bristly pears.

[P F W (S)]   10′×4′   3×1.2 m

laden with pollen. These start in mid-June and last well into July. Each flower is slightly concave. A special feature in autumn are the fiery-red hips which are in drooping clusters and flask-shaped. Foliage dark green with a dull gloss.

[P W F ◍ (S)]   10′×6′   3×1.8 m

FORMS AND HYBRIDS OF
R. macrophylla

'Arthur Hillier'
Hillier UK 1938
R. macrophylla × *R. moyesii*

An erect rose of considerable vigour. Masses of small clusters of large, single, rosy-crimson flowers with prominent yellow stamens heavily

'Auguste Roussel'
Barbier FRANCE 1913
R. macrophylla × 'Papa Gontier'

A vigorous climber or large arching shrub with large, semi-double, bright pink flowers. Apart from its flowers, which are beautiful, this shrub lacks the character of others in its group, especially in fruit.

[P F ◍ (S)]   15′×8′   4.5×2.5 m

'Doncasterii (see text p. 228)   [VP]

'Doncasterii'

E. Doncaster UK 1930
R. macrophylla seedling
A good rose, more arching than others of its type and less tall. Inherits dark, plum-coloured wood and purplish-green leaves from *R. macrophylla*, together with large, pear-shaped hips. Flowers pink verging on red.

[P F W ◍ (S)] 6′×4′ 1.8×1.2 m

'Master Hugh'

L. M. Mason UK 1966
R. macrophylla seedling
This rose provides us with some of the largest hips of all. They are orange-red in colour and flagon-shaped. The shrub is similar in other respects to its parent, except that its leaves are larger and it grows more vigorously.

[P F ◍ W (S)] 15′×8′ 4.5×2.5 m

'Rubricaulis', *R. macrophylla rubricaulis*

Hillier HIMALAYAS Of recent introduction
Similar to the species but wood darker and often covered in a greyish bloom. Said to be less hardy but I have no experience to prove this.

[F W ◍ W (S)] 8′×4′ 2.5×1.2 m

'Master Hugh' [PB]

R. majalis, R. cinnamomea, 'Cinnamon Rose'

N.E. EUROPE 17th century or earlier
An upright-growing, yet branching rose with slightly downy greyish-green foliage and mauvish-purple stems. The flowers, which are variable from pale to mid-pink, occur quite early in summer or, in good seasons late spring. Medium-sized rounded fruit.

[F W (SP)] 6′×4′ 1.8×1.2 m

'Rubricaulis' [VP]

R. marretii

MIDDLE EAST 1908

An upright growing shrub with purple wood and medium sized, mid-green foliage. Flowers mid- to pale pink usually in small clusters. Hips red, round and of medium size.

[F W P ◍ (S)]   6′×4′   1.8×1.2 m

R. maximowicziana

N.E. ASIA 1905

Single white flowers in small spaced clusters, sometimes hidden among soft-textured, serrated foliage. Not tall. Mine, after three years, admittedly in shady position, has reached 5′ (1.5 m), bushy with thin, sparsely spiny stems with many lateral branches on which flowers are produced. Perhaps a rogue hybrid, as none of its characteristics fit any other description I have found. Most similar is *R. fedtschenkoana*.

[P W ◍ (S)]   6′×4′   1.8×1.2 m

R. melina

N. AMERICA 1930

A short-growing, dense shrub with large, soft rose pink flowers. I have not met this rose as a mature shrub. As a maiden, it has greyish-green foliage with not much to commend it.

[P W ◍ (S)]   3′×3′   90×90 cm

R. × micrugosa

Foundling at Strasbourg Botanical Institute c. 1905

R. roxburghii × R. rugosa

A dense, medium-sized shrub with foliage recognizable as rugosa. Large, delicate, single, pale pink flowers followed by stubbled, round, orange-red hips.

[H W F P A ▽ ◍ (R)]   5′×4′   1.5×1.2 m

R. × micrugosa alba   [PB]

R. × micrugosa alba

Dr Hurst UK Date of introduction unknown

Very beautiful white flowers with pronounced stamens. Continuity of bloom should encourage its wider use. More upright in habit than its parent *R. micrugosa*, but otherwise similar in growth.

[◍ H W F P A ▽ (R)]   5′×4′   1.5×1.2 m

R. mohavensis

S. USA C. 1930

A short growing, dense shrub with numerous slender stems and an average population of thorns. Small, mid-green leaves. Flowers small, mid-to-soft pink. Rounded red hips. Enjoys moisture.

[F W P ◍ ≋ (S)]   3′×3′   90×90 cm

R. moyesii 'Eos' with foreground foliage of a Hybrid Tea

[PB]

R. moyesii

R. moyesii

W. CHINA Discovery 1890, introduction 1894
Despite the very attractive deep crimson flowers and distinctive dark green foliage, it is undoubtedly the fruit that makes this rose and its hybrids so popular. Although the hips are not as large as in some other species, the plant can usually be relied upon to yield a large crop each year. Produced pendulously, they are orange-red and flagon shaped, with a five-pointed crown at the bottom, formed from the retained sepals of the spent flower. As a shrub it is vigorous and solid but if allowed to grow for too long without pruning it gets gaunt and coarse at the base. I have seen this rose making a splendid, if unusual, wall plant. Beware of growing this rose from seed or purchasing seedling plants as many seedlings are sterile and never produce hips.

[P W F ⬤ (S)] 10′ × 6′ 3 × 1.8 m

R. moyesii, 'Pink form'

CHINA
Date unknown
Similar in most respects to R. moyesii except colour of flower which is, of course, pink. Several variable forms seem to have been distributed, presumably from seedlings, of R. moyesii or its forms, raised deliberately or by chance.

[P W F ⬤ (S)] 10′ × 6′ 3 × 1.8 m

FORMS AND HYBRIDS OF R. moyesii

'Eddie's Crimson'

Eddie CANADA 1956
'Donald Prior' × R. moyesii hybrid
A double, deep blood-red hybrid achieved by crossing the old red floribunda, 'Donald Prior' with a Moyesii hybrid. Foliage and bearing Moyesii-like, in full flower it makes an impressive, upright shrub. Fruit not so obviously Moyesii, spherical in shape and deep red in colour.

[P W F ⬤ (S)] 10′ × 6′ 3 × 1.8 m

'Eddie's Jewel'

Eddie CANADA 1962
'Donald Prior' × R. moyesii hybrid
Significant, in that I can vouch for this rose repeating in good seasons. Each double flower bright brick-red. Shoots dark browny-red. I have yet to see it set any fruit. Foliage in Moyesii mould. Achieved from same cross as 'Eddie's Crimson'.

[P W ⬤ (R)] 8′ × 6′ 2.4 × 1.8 m

'Eos'

Ruys USA 1950
R. moyesii × 'Magnifica'
An attractive shrub rose, very profuse in bloom with medium-sized, almost single flowers of bright pinkish-red with white centres, produced all along rather stiff but arching stems. Scented. Sometimes fails to set fruit.

[F P W ⬤ (S)] 8′ × 5′ 2.5 × 1.5 m

'Fred Streeter'

Jackman UK 1951
R. moyesii seedling
A denser shrub than any other Moyesii hybrid, with arching, spindly growth, bearing bright pink, single flowers along its length, followed by pendulous, large red hips.

[P W F ⬤ (S)] 8′ × 6′ 2.5 × 1.8 m

R. fargesii [RCB]

Above and below : 'Geranium' and its hips [RCB/VP]

'Geranium'

Royal Horticultural Society UK 1938
R. moyesii seedling
The most widely grown and best known of the Moyesii hybrids. Its single flowers are a beautiful, bright orange-red with a waxy texture. Its creamy anthers often powder the petals with pollen. Less vigorous than its parent and more angular in growth with lighter green leaves, paler stems, and larger, equally shapely but less deep red fruits.
[F P W ◐ (S)] 8′ × 5′ 2.5 × 1.5 m

'Highdownensis'

Hillier UK 1928
R. moyesii seedling
Arching branches of single, light crimson flowers on a bushy, dense, tall shrub with ample foliage. Fruit large, reddish-plum coloured and flagon-shaped.
[F P W ◐ (S)] 8′ × 6′ 2.5 × 1.8 m

'Hillieri ', *R. × pruhoniciana hillieri*

Hillier UK 1920
R. moyesii × *R. multibracteata*
Very dark red flowers, single with prominent anthers. Fewer thorns than others of this group with smaller and perhaps fewer leaves. Growth angular but stiff. Vigorously graceful. Not all the flowers set their fruit, which is large, orange and flagon-shaped.
[P W F ◐ (S)] 8′ × 6′ 2.5 × 1.8 m

R. fargesii

Veitch UK 1913
Very similar in stature to *R. moyesii* but slightly less vigorous. Flowers more pink than red and foliage smaller. Hips of the same shape but are usually larger and perhaps fewer.
[F P W ◐ (S)] 8′ × 5′ 2.5 × 1.5 m

R. holodonta

CHINA 1908
Glowing pink flowers in small clusters on an upright-growing, well-armed plant. Hips pendulous and flagon-shaped. This name is sometimes attributed erroneously to all pink forms of *R. moyesii*. It is now accepted that *R. holodonta* is

Above and below: 'Highdownensis' and its hips [RCB/VP]

R. holodonta [VP]

distinct and more akin to *R. davidii* than to *R. moyesii*. See Bean *Trees and Shrubs Hardy in the British Isles Vol. IV. 8th edition 1981.*
[P W F (S)] 10′×6′ 3×1.8 m

'Marguerite Hilling'
Hilling UK 1959
'Nevada' sport
This is a splendid, pink sport of the well-known 'Nevada', which it fully resembles except for its soft rose-pink colour. In first flush this rose is

'Marguerite Hilling' (see text p. 233)   [VP]

very showy and, like its parent, very floriferous from late May to mid-June, with intermittent flowers throughout the remainder of summer, and well into autumn.

[P W H (R)]   8′ × 7′   2.5 × 2 m

'Nevada'

P. Dot SPAIN 1927
R. moyesii hybrid?

A superb shrub. Large, single, slightly blowsy flowers produced in profusion on a vigorous, dense but tidy shrub in late May early June. Plentiful light green foliage. Dark chocolate-brown stems with sparse thorns. Usually flowers on intermittently throughout summer, and often gives a good display in the autumn. Opinions vary as to its proper parentage. It has some affinity in looks with *R. moyesii* and is usually placed here – a course that I follow despite tending to agree with Mr Jack Harkness, who suggests it might be better placed among the *R. pimpinellifolia* hybrids.

[P W H (R)]   8′ × 7′   2.5 × 2 m

'Nevada'   [PB]

'Sealing Wax'
Royal Horticultural Society UK 1938
R. moyesii hybrid
A fine hybrid, very similar in habit and foliage to 'Geranium' except for bright pink flower. Fruit bright red in the expected flagon shape.
[P W F ◍ (S)]   8′ × 5′   2.5 × 1.5 m

'Wintoniensis'
Hillier UK 1928
R. moyesii × *R. setipoda*
Of interesting parentage, giving rise to a vigorous shrub which romps away, both in height and girth. Its light grey foliage is slightly scented. Its flowers are single, deep pink and its fruit are large and very hairy.
[F P W ◍ (S)]   12′ × 10′   3.5 × 2 m

R. multibracteata

R. multibracteata
CHINA 1908
An elegant shrub with fern-like leaves from thick stems with numerous, spiky thorns, usually produced in pairs. Single flowers are produced in bunched clusters, often at the ends of arching shoots; these are lilac-pink and produced on thin petioles which have alternating bracts along their length. Has a long flowering season although is never very floriferous. The small hips, which retain their sepals, are rounded, bright red and sparsely bristly.
[F P W ◍ (R)]   6′ × 5′   1.8 × 1.5 m

'Cerise Bouquet'   [JB]

HYBRID OF
R. multibracteata

'Cerise Bouquet'
Kordes GERMANY 1958
R. multibracteata × 'Crimson Glory'
As so often with roses, one takes them for granted until a specimen is seen at its very best. At Helmingham Hall, Suffolk, Lord and Lady Tollemache have one shrub of this variety at least 12′ (3.5 m) high and 12′ (3.5 m) wide, standing alone in an open part of their garden and quite spectacular in full flush. Double flowers are produced in profusion on long, arching branches amid dense greyish-green foliage.
[P W ◍ (S)]   12′ × 12′   3.5 × 3.5 m

'Cerise Bouquet' growing at Helmingham Hall, Suffolk [PB]

R. murielae

W. CHINA 1904

A rare, medium growing, widish shrub with thin
stems of red-brown, mid-green to greyish foliage.
White flowers in small corymbs. Hips small,
flagon shaped and a bright orange red.

[F W P ◍ (S)]   8′×6′   2.4×1.8 m

R. nutkana

R. nutkana

N. AMERICA 1876

A strong-growing shrub liberally endowed with dark greyish-green foliage and strong, relatively thornless, nut-brown stems. The single flowers are clear lilac-pink with a touch of lilac, followed by smooth, rounded fruit untouched by birds until well into winter. I grow to like this species more and more.

[P W F ⦿ (S)]   6′×4′   1.8×1.2 m

R. nutkana, and *left*, its autumn foliage   [VP/PB]

FORMS AND HYBRIDS OF R. nutkana

'Cantab'

Hurst UK 1939

R. nutkana × 'Red Letter Day'

A lovely rose which should be more widely used where a medium-sized shrub is required. The flowers which appear in July are large, single and deep pinkish-lilac with pronounced creamy-yellow stamens. These are followed by plumply-oval hips of clear deep red when ripe, which remain on the plant well into winter. The dark stems are moderately armed and the foliage greyish-green.

[P W F ⦿ (S)]   8′×5′   2.4×1.5 m

'Schoener's Nutkana'

Schoener USA 1930

R. nutkana × 'Paul Neyron'

Vigorous shrub with large, single, clear rose-pink flowers. Quite fragrant. Growth arching but dense, with few thorns on darkish wood with grey-green foliage.

[P H W ⦿ (S)]   5′×4′   1.5×1.2 m

R. pendulina   [VP]

R. × paulii, R. rugosa repens alba

c. 1903

Origin unknown. Thought to be *R. arvensis* ×
R. rugosa.

A very prostrate, almost creeping shrub with
thick, thorny growth and coarse, leathery, dark
green foliage. Flowers single with five long, well-
spaced, pure white petals. Non-recurrent.

[P G W ◍ (S)]   3′ × 10′   90 cm × 3 m

R. × paulii rosea

c. 1910

Origin unknown. Possibly sport of *R. paulii*
Similar to *R. × paulii* in habit but with slightly
darker wood and foliage. Flowers clear rose pink,
single, with petals more closely arranged than in
the white form.

[P G W ◍ (S)]   3′ × 10′   90 cm × 3 m

R. pendulina, R. alpina, 'Alpine Rose'

EUROPE C. 1700

Arching, reddish-purple stems form a short,
slightly spreading, almost thornless bush. Foliage
is dark green and varies in shape from elongated
to oval and in size from small to medium large.
Single deep pink flowers with pronounced
yellow stamens, followed by handsome, elongated but plumpish hips.

[A P F W ◍ (S)]   4′ × 4′   1.2 × 1.2 m

R. pisocarpa

N. AMERICA 1882

A medium-sized shrub with a dense, slightly procumbent habit; plentiful smallish leaves and
shoots covered in spines. Flowers in little clusters,
single and lilac-pink. Fruit small, round, sometimes slightly elongated, bright red.

[A W F ◍ ▽ (S)]   3′ × 3′   90 × 90 cm

R. prattii

W. CHINA 1908

An almost thornless, short to medium shrub with
purple stems. Thorns that exist are yellow. Foliage greyish-green. Flowers pink, in small corymbs
followed by small, oval, whiskery fruit.

[W P ◍ (S)]   4′ × 3′   1.2 m × 90 cm

R. pyrifera

W. USA C. 1931

A short to medium, quite dense shrub. In many
ways very similar to the better known *R. woodsii*.
Flowers white, usually in corymbs. Hips smallish,
deep red and almost pear shaped.

[F W P ◍ (S)]   3′ × 3′   90 × 90 cm

R. rugosa

R. rugosa

JAPAN/PARTS OF W. ASIA 1796

A vigorous, thorny shrub freely sending up long canes. Over the years various forms of this species have been used to produce standard roses. It is these which appear, almost from nowhere, in derelict gardens as the result of having either reproduced themselves from the original root of a standard rose, having long ago cast off its enforced, more delicate charge. Its willingness, too, to chance-hybridize with other roses and produce seedlings with minor variations has led to uncertainty as to which form is the true species. All the semi-wild forms have lightish to mid-green, sometimes wrinkled but always rough-textured foliage. The scented flowers are single and in most clones have prominent, soft yellow stamens, their colours ranging from clear deep pink to deep cerise red. The hips are globular, usually rich red, and variable in size according to clone.

[W F P H A ◍ (C)] 7′×6′ 2×1.8 m

R. rugosa alba

c. 1870

Garden origin not known

This is one of the best forms of R. rugosa, making a most useful garden plant. Flowers are large, pure white and scented. It is a vigorous, bushy plant with fine, deeply veined, coarse textured but slightly glossy leaves. Stems thick, buff-greyish and densely populated with small thorns of similar colouring. Fruit is large and tomato red in colour.

[W F P H A ◍] 7′×6′ 2×1.8 m

R. rugosa rubra, R. rugosa atropurpurea

JAPAN Date unknown

Large deep crimson-purple flowers with creamy-yellow stamens. Habit of growth and foliage not unlike that of R. rugosa typica though slightly more vigorous.

[W F P H A ◍ (C)] 6′×5′ 1.8×1.5 m

R. rugosa alba

[JB]

R. rugosa typica, R. rugosa rugosa

JAPAN C. 1796

Makes a dense, rounded shrub and probably nearest to the true, wild species. Single, scented flowers, deep reddish-carmine, followed by bright red, globular hips. This form makes a useful hedge and is frequently used in municipal planting schemes.

[W F P H A ◍ (C)] 5′×5′ 1.5×1.5 m

FORMS AND HYBRIDS OF
R. rugosa

The many attributes of the Rugosa hybrids set them a race apart. They are invariably healthy, will grow almost anywhere without molly-coddling, and provide flowers throughout most of the summer. They are becoming increasingly popular as subjects for massed planting in parks, as barriers for motorways and as trouble-free screens for factories. Yet in gardens, too, their versatility can be harnessed to great and varied effect.

'Agnes'

Central Experimental Farms
Saunders CANADA 1922
R. rugosa × *R. foetida persiana*
Bushy, dense rose with dark green, rather crinkled foliage on thorny stems, one of the few yellows of this group. Flowers fully-double and highly scented, amber yellow fading to white, repeated intermittently throughout season after a good first flush in June.

[P H ◍ (R)] 6′×5′ 1.8×1.5 m

'Belle Poitevine'

Bruant FRANCE 1894
Parentage unknown
Long pointed buds opening to large, almost double flowers of rich magenta pink. Foliage lush, heavily veined and dark green. Slightly angular in growth but bushy. Occasionally sets large dark red fruit.

[A P H F ◍ (R)] 6′×5′ 1.8×1.5 m

'Blanc Double de Coubert'

Cochet-Cochet FRANCE 1892
R. rugosa × 'Sombreuil'
One of the outstanding Rugosa hybrids. Pure white, almost fully double flowers, exuding a superb perfume. Foliage rich dark green, plant dense and bushy. Fruit, sometimes quite large, only sets intermittently. Good autumn colour.

[F A P H ◍ ▽ (R)] 5′×4′ 1.5×1.2 m

'Carmen'

Lambert GERMANY 1907
R. rugosa × 'Princesse de Béarn'
Very large single blooms with prominent stamens; deep, velvety crimson. Dark foliage on a bushy plant. A useful and under-used rose.

[A P H ◍ ▽ (R)] 4′×4′ 1.2×1.2 m

'Agnes' [VP]

'Belle Poitevine' [VP]

Above: 'Blanc Double de Coubert'   [VP]
Below: 'Conrad Ferdinand Meyer'   [PB]

'Conrad Ferdinand Meyer'

F. Müller GERMANY 1899
R. rugosa hybrid × 'Gloire de Dijon'
A very strong, robust rose with stout stems and
large thorns. Foliage rather coarse, dark green.
Flowers large and full, unchanging silver-pink.
Very highly scented. Unfortunately rather prone
to rust, which can invade very early in the season.
[P W H (R)]   10′ × 8′   3 × 2.5 m

'Culverbrae'

Gobbee UK 1973
'Scabrosa' × 'Francine'
Very full, crimson-purple flowers on a well-
foliated, bushy plant. Well scented. Size makes
it a useful variety. Slightly prone to mildew late
in the season.
[W H (R)]   5′ × 4′   1.5 × 1.2 m

'Dr Eckener'

Berger GERMANY 1930
'Golden Emblem' × *R. rugosa* hybrid
Huge, scented, semi-double flowers of pale yellow

and coppery-bronze changing with age to a
slightly muddy pink; pronounced stamens when
fully open. Well scented. Foliage rather coarse,
growth vigorous and also rather coarse. With
spiteful thorns.
[W P ◍ (R)]   10′ × 8′   3 × 2.5 m

'Fimbriata', 'Phoebe's Frilled Pink', 'Dianthiflora'

Morlet FRANCE 1891
R. rugosa × 'Mme Alfred Carrière'
Rather unlike a Rugosa hybrid. Small double

frilly petalled flowers reminding one of *dianthus*, white with pale pink shadings. Bushy, upright shrub with numerous light green leaves.

[P H W A ◑ ▽ (R)]   4′ × 4′   1.2 × 1.2 m

'F. J. Grootendorst'

De Goey HOLLAND 1918

R. rugosa rubra × 'Nobert Levavasseur'

Clusters of small, crimson double flowers with

'Dr Eckener' (see text p. 241)   [TW]

frilly petals. Copious and somewhat coarse dark green foliage on a vigorous, bushy plant. Continuous in flower throughout the summer.

[H P W ◑ ▽ (C)]   4′ × 3′   1.2 m × 90 cm

'Frau Dagmar Hartopp', 'Fru. Dagmar Hastrup'

Hastrup GERMANY 1914

Parentage unknown

Beautiful, clear, silver-pink flowers with pronounced stamens especially good in autumn. Scented. Foliage dark green. Plant bushy, growing wider than tall. Excellent tomato-like hips.

[P F W A ◑ G ▽ (C)]   3′ × 4′   90 cm × 1.2 m

'Grootendorst Supreme'

Sport from 'F. J. Grootendorst' with deeper-red flowers.

[H P W ◑ ▽ (C)]   4′ × 3′   1.2 m × 90 cm

'Hansa'

Schaum and Van Tol HOLLAND 1905

Parentage unknown

Very free-flowering. Double, highly scented,

'Fimbriata' (see text p. 241)   [PB]

reddish-purple flowers. Vigorous, medium-sized plant with dark green foliage. Excellent red fruit.

[H P F W ◑ ▽ (C)] 4′ × 3′ 1.2 m × 90 cm

'Hunter'
Mattock UK 1961
R. rugosa rubra × 'Independence'
Scented, fully double, bright crimson flowers on a rugged, medium-sized, bushy plant with dark green foliage. A useful rose.

[P W ◑ ▽ (C)] 4′ × 3′ 1.2 m × 90 cm

'F. J. Grootendorst'   [JB]

'Lady Curzon'
Turner UK 1901
R. macrantha × *R. rugosa rubra*
An arching shrub with very thorny wood and dark green foliage. Lovely large, single, pale rose-pink, fragrant flowers. Vigorous, procumbent variety. Favours its pollen parent in most characteristics except habit which is why I place it here rather than with *R. macrantha* hybrids.

[P G W ◑ ▽ (R)] 3′ × 6′ 90 cm × 1.8 m

'Martin Frobisher'
Department of Agriculture CANADA 1968
'Schneezwerg' seedling
Shapely, double, soft pink flowers. Well scented. Foliage dark green, growth upright and very prickly Not often seen but, if obtainable, should be more widely grown.

[H P W ◑ ▽ (R)] 4′ × 4′ 1.2 × 1.2 m

'Mary Manners'
Leicester Rose Company UK c. 1970
Probably sport of 'Sarah Van Fleet'
Pure white, semi-double flowers in profusion on

'Hunter'   [RCB]

an upright, thorny bush with ample, dark green foliage. Highly scented. A useful rose, if a little prone to rust.

[H P W ◍ ▽ (C)] 4′ × 3′ 1.2 m × 90 cm

'Max Graf'

Bowditch USA 1919
R. rugosa × *R. wichuraiana*
A trailing rose, ideal for banks, etc. Single, deep silvery-pink flowers paling slightly towards the centre with pronounced stamens. Very procumbent with long, trailing shoots. Heavily dressed with large, dark, slightly glossy leaves. Seldom sets any fruit.

[F P G ◍ (S)] 2′ × 8′ 60 cm × 2.5 m

'Mme Georges Bruant'

Bruant FRANCE 1887
R. rugosa × 'Sombreuil'
Loosely formed, semi-double, creamy-white, scented flowers. Ample, rather coarse, dark green foliage on a vigorous, very thorny bush. Makes an impenetrable hedge.

[W P H ◍ (C)] 5′ × 4′ 1.5 × 1.2 m

Above: 'Mme Georges Bruant'

'Mrs Anthony Waterer'

Waterer UK 1898
R. rugosa × 'Général Jacqueminot'
Semi-double, shapely, rich deep crimson flowers, freely produced on a vigorous, broad, thorny bush with dark green foliage. Well scented.

[W P H ◍ (C)] 4′ × 5′ 1.2 × 1.5 m

'Nova Zembla'

Mees UK 1907
Pure white sport of 'Conrad F. Meyer' with all the same characteristics except colour of flower.

[P W H (R)] 10′ × 8′ 3 × 2.5 m

'Nyveldt's White'

Nyveldt HOLLAND 1955
(*R. rugosa rubra* × *R. majalis*) × *R. nitida*
Large, pure white, single flowers on a vigorous, dense, thorny bush. Dark green stems and foliage. Produces an excellent crop of round, bright red hips unfailingly each autumn.

[F P W H A ◍ (C)] 5′ × 4′ 1.5 × 1.2 m

'Parfum de l'Hay'
See 'Rose à Parfum de l'Hay'

'Pink Grootendorst'

Grootendorst HOLLAND 1923
'F. J. Grootendorst' sport
This rose is soft pink, otherwise similar in all respects to its parent. Tends to revert to red, sometimes giving both colours on the same head of blooms.
[H P W ⬤ ▽ (C)]   4′ × 3′   1.2 m × 90 cm

'Robusta'

Kordes GERMANY 1979
R. rugosa × seedling
Large, single, rich scarlet-red flowers on a strong, robust, dense, thorny plant with good, dark if somewhat coarse foliage. Scented. Makes a very good, impenetrable hedge.
[P H ⬤ (C)]   5′ × 4′   1.5 × 1.2 m

'Rose à Parfum de l'Hay', 'Parfum de l'Hay'

Gravereaux FRANCE 1901
(R. damascena × 'Général Jacqueminot') × R. rugosa
Large, globular buds opening flat to rich, bright red flowers which turn deeper in hot sun. It is fragrant and, at its best, very beautiful. The foliage is dark green on a bushy plant with ample thorns. It has a tendency to mildew later in the season. Difficult to classify but best here on account of several R. rugosa characteristics.
[W ⬤ ▽ (C)]   4′ × 3′   1.2 m × 90 cm

'Roseraie de l'Hay'

Cochet-Cochet FRANCE 1901
Sport from unknown hybrid of R. rugosa
One of the best loved of all the rugosa hybrids. Splendid, semi-double flowers, large and opening loosely flat. Strongly scented. Makes a dense, vigorous, bushy shrub, and is almost constantly in flower. Foliage dark green. Sadly, only occasionally sets fruit, but compensates with very good autumn foliage.
[P W H A ⬤ (C)]   6′ × 5′   1.8 × 1.5 m

'Ruskin'

Van Fleet USA 1928
'Souvenir de Pierre Leperdrieux' × 'Victor Hugo'
Bushy, well-foliated, recurrent rose which deserves more attention. Flowers large, fully double, crimson and highly scented.
[P H ⬤ ▽ (R)]   4′ × 3′   1.2 m × 90 cm

'Nova Zembla'   [PB]

'Sarah Van Fleet'

Van Fleet USA 1926
R. rugosa × 'My Maryland'
Parentage unknown
Semi-double, silky-pink blooms produced in profusion on a well-foliated but viciously thorny bush. Growth upright but bushy. Foliage dark green. Seldom sets fruit. Rather inclined to rust, especially after its first flush of flowers.
[P W H ⬤ ▽ (C)]   4′ × 3′   1.2 m × 90 cm

'Scabrosa'

Harkness UK Introduced 1960
Parentage unknown
As often happens, foundlings turn out good. Jack Harkness tells the story of this rose in his excellent book Roses. Sufficient to say here that it came on the scene through good observation. One of my favourite Rugosas. Large, single, rich silvery-cerise flowers with prominent anthers, often accompanied by large, tomato-shaped hips which are produced as abundantly as its flowers. Foliage dark, of thick texture, heavily veined and almost glossy green. Makes a dense, upright shrub. Particularly good for hedging. Very sweetly scented.
[H P W A ⬤ (C)]   6′ × 4′   1.8 × 1.2 m

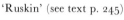

'Roseraie de l'Hay' and *below*, its autumn foliage
(see text p. 245)   [PB/PB]

'Ruskin' (see text p. 245)   [PB]

'Schneelicht'

Geschwind HUNGARY 1894

R. rugosa × R. phoenicia

Clusters of large, pure white, single flowers on a strong, impenetrable shrub with dark, viciously armed stems. Dark green foliage. Excellent as a dense hedge.

[P W H ⏣ (R)] 6′ × 4′ 1.8 × 1.2 m

'Schneezwerg', 'Snow Dwarf'

P. Lambert GERMANY 1912

R. rugosa × a Polyantha rose

An interesting, slightly smaller member of the Rugosas. Pure white, semi-double, well-formed flowers with pronounced yellow stamens when fully open. Plentiful greyish-dark green foliage. Rich red medium-size hips set intermittently, often appearing together with the flowers later in the season.

[F P W H A ⏣ (C)] 5′ × 4′ 1.5 × 1.2 m

'Scabrosa' (see text p. 245)

[VP]

'Sarah van Fleet' (see text p. 245)   [PB]
Below : 'Vanguard'   [JB]

'Souvenir de Philémon Cochet'

Cochet-Cochet FRANCE 1899
'Blanc Double de Coubert' sport
Like its parent in all but colour. Soft blush-pink
with deeper tones in the centre.

[P H W ◑ (C)]   5′×4′   1.5×1.2 m

'Thérèse Bugnet'

BUGNET CANADA 1950
(*R. acicularis* × *R.* × *kamtchatica*) × (*R. amblyotis* ×
R. rugosa plena) × 'Betty Bland'
A very hardy rose. Large, double flowers, clear
red paling to pink. Fragrant. Good foliage. *R.
rugosa* influence not immediately recognizable.

[P H ◑ (C)]   6′×6′   1.8×1.8 m

'Vanguard'

Stevens USA 1932
(*R. wichuraiana* × *R. rugosa alba*) × 'Eldorado'
A vigorous shrub, rather untypically Rugosa,
bearing semi-double flowers of salmon burnished
bronze. Very fragrant. Upright growth well-
foliated with glossy, burnished leaves.

[P W H F ◑ (R)]   8′×6′   2.5×1.8 m

'White Grootendorst'

Eddy USA 1962
'Pink Grootendorst' sport
Identical to other 'Grootendorsts', but with
white flowers and lighter green foliage.

[P W H ◑ ▽ (C)]   4′×3′   1.2 m×90 cm

R. sertata

W. CHINA 1904

A loose shrub with thinnish, arching, brownish branches with few thorns and greyish-green leaves. Deep pink flowers in small clusters followed by small, narrowly oval, dark red hips.

[F W P ⊕ (S)]   4′×3′   1.2 m×90 cm

R. setipoda

CENTRAL CHINA 1895

A medium-sized, shrubby rose with thick stems and well-spaced strong thorns. Scented foliage, noticeable only when leaves are crushed. Exquisite flowers, produced in large clusters, clear, pale pink, single and quite big, with yellow stamens. Flower stalks strangely purple. Finishes the season with large, pendulous plump, flagon-shaped, bristly, deep red hips.

[P W F ⊕ (S)]   8′×5′   2.5×1.5 m

R. spaldingii

N. AMERICA 1915

Medium shrub with yellowish-green stems and soft greyish-green foliage. Flowers pink and slightly crinkled when fully open, flowering rather shyly and intermittently for a long season. I have the white form, which is rather charming. Small, round, red fruit in autumn.

[P F W A ⊕ ▽ (S)]   4′×3′   1.2 m×90 cm

R. suffulta

Greene N. AMERICA 1880

Clusters of single, pink flowers followed by small orange hips. Short, dense plant with soft grey foliage and thin, spiney stems.

[W F ⊕ (S)]   4′×3′   1.2 m×90 cm

R. suffulta and its hips

R. sweginzowii macrocarpa

This garden form GERMANY

Original from N.W. CHINA

The thick, smooth, light brown stems viciously armed with thorns belie the beauty of this rose. Flowers numerous, single and bright pink, followed by large, shiny, plump, flagon-shaped hips of rich bright red. Well foliated and rather angular in growth.

[P F W A ◐ (S)]   10′×8′   3×2.5 m

R. ultramontana

S. USA 1888

A short to medium shrub with few or no thorns of consequence. Small to medium sized clusters of pink flowers in mid-summer. Small, smooth, rounded, red hips.

[W P ◐ (S)]   3′×3′   90×90 cm

R. wardii

TIBET C. 1924

A medium-growing, lax shrub which now appears to be extinct in its native form. *R. wardii* 'Culta' was raised at Wisley from seed, from the original form, and introduced in this name. Flowers single and white, rather like those of *R. moyesii*, with distinct brownish stigmas and yellow stamens. Shoots brownish, thorns sparse but sharp. Foliage bright green.

[F W ◐ ▽ (S)]   6′×5′   1.8×1.5 m

R. webbiana

HIMALAYAS, E. ASIA 1879

A good and interesting shrub with long, arching, almost trailing, pliable shoots, densely clothed with small grey-blue foliage and fairly harmless thorns – at least until they become old and more stubborn. Small, numerous, soft pink, scented flowers, followed by small, orange-red, bottle-shaped hips in the autumn.

[P F W ◐ ▽]   7′×7′   2×2 m

R. willmottiae

W. CHINA 1904

A superb shrub with arching stems of a darkish plum colour with a grey bloom. Grey-green, fern-like foliage, slightly scented when crushed. The plant, of arching angular habit, bears small, single, deep lilac-pink flowers with creamy-yellow anthers, followed by small, vaguely pear-shaped, orange-red hips.

[F W P ◐ ▽ (S)]   6′×6′   1.8×1.8 m

R. woodsii fendleri

N. AMERICA 1888

Makes a superb shrub of upright habit with numerous thin spiky thorns on greyish wood. The flowers plentifully produced on a well-foliated plant, are single, bright lilac-pink and followed by a crop of deep, waxy-red, globular hips which persist well into winter.

[H W P F ◐ (S)]   5′×5′   1.5×1.5 m

R. webbiana   [VP]

ROSA Subgenus II Rosa (Eurosa)
SECTION VI *Synstylae*

Growth vigorous, climbing and flexible, 6 ft–30 ft (2m to 10m).
Thorns variously sized, curved, some species sparse, others none.
Leaves mostly 5 to 7, sometimes 9, leaflets.
Flowers mostly in corymbs or clusters.
Hips mostly small, oval or round.
Sepals drop when hips are ripe.

SPECIES

R. anemoneflora; *R. arvensis*; *R. brunonii*;
R. × dupontii; *R. filipes*; *R. gentiliana*;
R. helenae; *R. henryi*; *R. longicuspis*; *R. luciae*;
R. moschata; *R. moschata nastarana*;
R. mulliganii; *R. multiflora*; *R. multiflora
carnea*; *R. multiflora cathayensis*; *R. multiflora
grevillii*; *R. multiflora watsoniana*; *R. multiflora
wilsonii*; *R. phoenicia*; *R. × polliniana*;

R. sempervirens; *R. setigera*; *R. sinowilsonii*;
R. soulieana; *R. wichuraiana*

GARDEN GROUPS

Ayrshires; Hybrid Musks;
Floribunda roses (Cluster-Flowered roses);
Modern Shrubs; Modern Climbers;
Polyanthas; Ramblers

ORIGIN AND DISTRIBUTION

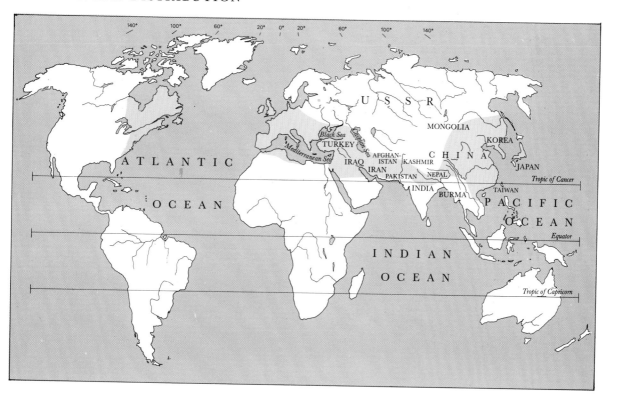

R. arvensis

R. anemoneflora, R. triphylla

E. CHINA 1844

A climbing rose, the garden form of which has small clusters of double, white flowers (in the wild, single). These are made up of large outer petals and many smaller ones in the centre. Quite interesting and unique. Growth is vigorous with few or no thorns. Needs mollycoddling for best results in colder climates.

[☼ T (S)]   12′ × 8′   3.5 × 2.4 m

R. arvensis

R. arvensis, 'The Field Rose'

EUROPE Date unknown

A beautiful, pure white single rose with medium-sized flowers and showy golden anthers. A ground-creeper or rambler with thin dark wood and foliage and well-spaced thorns. Frequently seen in hedgerows, especially in southern England

[P G ◍ F W P ≋ (S)]   20′ × 10′   6 × 3 m

FORMS AND HYBRIDS OF *R. arvensis*

'Ayrshire Rose', *R. capreolata*,
R. arvensis ayrshirea

c. 1790

Origin and parentage unknown

This semi-double form of *R. arvensis* seems now to be lost to cultivation, although I am hopeful that a plant may have been found (see p. 46).

[P G W (S) ◍ ≋]   20′ × 10′   6 × 3 m

'Ayrshire Queen'

1835

Origin and parentage uncertain

Sadly, another which seems to have become extinct. Descriptions suggest it was creamy-white with a purple throat.

[P G W (S) ◍ ≋]   20′ × 10′   6 × 3 m

'Bennett's Seedling', Thoresbyana'

Bennett UK 1840

Parentage unknown

Another double white. Said to be fragrant and very free-flowering.

[P G W (S) ◍ ≋]   20′ × 10′   6 × 3 m

'Dundee Rambler'

Martin SCOTLAND c. 1850

Parentage unknown

A double white with flower rather smaller than *R. arvensis* and growth more dense.

[P G W (S) ◍ ≋]   20′ × 10′   6 × 3 m

'Düsterlohe'

Kordes GERMANY 1931

'Venusta Pendula' × 'Miss C. E. Van Rossen'

Large, semi-double flowers of rich pink, paling towards centre. Foliage dark green and plentiful. Rather untidy but spreading to a dense wide shrub. Orange-red, plumpish, oval hips.

[F P G (S)]   5′ × 8′   1.5 × 2.8 m

'Ruga', *R. × ruga*

ITALY Pre-1830

R. arvensis × R. chinensis

Semi-double flowers in large, loose clusters. Pale pink and well scented. Darkish-green wood, well foliated with mid-green leaves. Very vigorous.

[W P N T (S) ◍ ≋]   30′×20′   9×6 m

'Splendens', 'The Myrrh-scented Rose'
Origin and parentage unknown

A good semi-double rose. Shapely buds opening to cupped flowers, white with hints of pink at the edges of each petal. Has an unusual perfume, and is sometimes called the 'myrrh-scented' rose. Stems dark purplish-green, foliage dark green.

[P G W ◍ ≋ (S)]   20′×10′   6×3 m

'Venusta Pendula'
Reintroduced Kordes 1928
Origin and parentage unknown

Clusters of cascading, small, white flushed pink, fully double flowers on spindly, dark plum-red shoots with dark, dull-green foliage. Moderately thorny, little or no scent.

[P G W ◍ ≋ (S)]   20′×10′   6×3 m

Above and below: R. arvensis 'Splendens'   [PB/VP]

Above: 'La Mortola'   [PB]
Below: *R. dupontii*   [PB]

HYBRID OF *R. brunonii*

'La Mortola'

La Mortola Gardens, Italy c. 1936
Introduced UK Sunningdale Nurseries 1959
Probably sport from *R. brunonii*
A more refined or less refined form, depending on your viewpoint, of *R. brunonii*. Foliage of the same texture but larger and more obviously grey. Flowers slightly larger and perhaps more numerous. Seems quite hardy here in Norfolk.

[N P T ⓘ (S)]   20′ × 12′   6 × 3.5 m

R. brunonii, *R. moschata nepalensis*

HIMALAYAS C. 1823
A densely foliated, vigorous climber. Leaves large, downy in texture and drooping, light grey-green. Shoots grey-green, with young wood a tarnished, pinkish brown. Extremely vigorous and armed with hooked thorns. Flowers are single, tissuey in texture, creamy white, produced in clusters in July. Until recently this species was thought to belong under *R. moschata* but is now accepted by most authorities as distinct.

[N P T ⓘ (S)]   25′ × 15′   7.5 × 4.5 m

R. × dupontii

EUROPE Pre-1817
Possibly *R. gallica* × *R. moschata*
Beautifully shaped pure white flowers with pronounced golden-brown stamens. Sweetly scented. Flowers rather later than many species, linking it perhaps with *R. moschata*. Also it has an occasional flower later in the summer. Growth is strong with light green wood and ample greyish-green foliage. Fruit, when set, ripens very late in autumn.

[P H W (S)]   7′ × 4′   2 × 1.2 m

R. filipes

R. filipes

CHINA 1908

A vigorous species capable of 30′ (9 m) or more into trees, large panicles of single, creamy-white scented flowers each with golden stamens. Lush, light green foliage, numerous hips in autumn. Now more commonly seen in the better garden form, 'Kiftsgate'.

[N P F G T A ◍ ≋ (S)]　30′×20′　9×6 m

FORMS AND HYBRIDS OF
R. filipes

'Brenda Colvin'

Colvin UK 1970

Probably 'Kiftsgate' seedling

Medium flowers of soft blush-pink to white, single, in clusters. Strongly perfumed. Very vigorous and healthy. Foliage dark green and glossy.

[P T ◍ ≋ (S)]　30′×20′　9×6 m

'Kiftsgate'

Murrell UK 1954　(Sport or form of *R. filipes*)

Found at Kiftsgate Court, Glos.

A strong, vigorous climber capable of climbing to considerable heights. The fragrant, creamy-white flowers with golden stamens are borne in huge, cascading trusses in mid-summer, followed by thousands of small, red hips in the autumn. The foliage is large, profuse and glossy, green tinted copper when young. It also changes to rich russet in autumn. It tolerates considerable shade and consequently it is an ideal subject for climbing into trees. Also an effective ground cover but only where its enthusiasm can be left unchecked.

[N P F G T A ◍ ≋ (S)]　30′×20′　9×6 m

'Treasure Trove'

Treasure UK 1979

'Kiftsgate' × Hybrid Tea

A superb seedling from 'Kiftsgate' with all the vigour and performance of its parent. Large trusses of semi-double creamy-apricot flowers changing with age to blush-pink. Quite outstanding, with a strong scent. Foliage changes from pinkish-red through to mid-green as it ages.

[N P F G T A ◍ ≋ (S)]　30′×20′　9×6 m

R. filipes 'Kiftsgate'

R. gentiliana, erroneously *R. polyantha grandiflora*

CHINA 1907

Single to semi-double, creamy-white flowers produced in dense, cascading clusters from an exceptionally vigorous climbing plant, followed by small, orange hips in autumn. Very large, dense, glossy foliage of light green with coppery overtones. Its stems which are similar in colour to its leaves are also shiny with a sparse mixture of broad, hooked thorns, and smaller, more numerous, bristles.

[P F T A ⓜ ≈ (S)]   20′ × 10′   6 × 3 m

R. helenae   [PB]

R. helenae

CHINA 1907

A vigorous climbing rose well worth its popularity as a climber into small trees. Foliage large, plentiful and grey-green. Stems thick, sometimes mottled brown. Single flowers, scented, creamy-white and borne in dense corymbs during mid-to-late June, followed by small, oval, red hips in early autumn, which alone can be quite spectacular.

[F P W T ⓜ ≋]   20′ × 15′   6 × 4.5 m

HYBRID OF *R. helenae*

'Lykkefund'

Olsen DENMARK 1930

R. helenae × unknown seedling

Huge trusses of single, scented, creamy-yellow flowers tinted pink. Foliage lush, light green tinted bronze. Shoots quite thornless and vigorous. Ideal for growing into trees and sturdy enough to make a large specimen shrub.

[P T W ⓜ (S)]   25′ × 15′   7.5 × 4.5 m

R. mulliganii   [JB]

R. henryi

CHINA 1907

A vigorous shrub or small climber with ample almost glossy foliage and large, hooked thorns. Dense corymbs of white flowers from early to midsummer followed by masses of small, round, dark red hips.

[P F T ⓜ]   15′ × 10′   4.5 × 3 m

R. longicuspis

F. Kingdom Ward W. CHINA C. 1915

Almost evergreen, this rose is very vigorous with profuse, long, leathery, serrated, dark green foliage, reddish-pink when young. Very floriferous the huge, cascading panicles of bunched, medium-sized, single, white flowers each with pronounced yellow stamens. The growth is as tall but not as coarse as, for example, 'Kiftsgate'. The strong, wiry stems are excellent in assisting it to achieve great heights into trees. The flowers have little or no scent and are followed by small, oval, orange-red hips. Not totally hardy but well worth trying in the south. The species grown and sold as this variety in most modern day catalogues is actually *R. mulliganii*.

[G P T F N (S)]   30′ × 15′   9 × 4.5 m

R. luciae

E. ASIA C. 1880

Very similar to the better known and more widely grown *R. wichuraiana*. A dense, spreading shrub with plentiful, almost glossy, dark green leaves. Clusters of medium-sized white flowers produced in late spring/early summer. Scented. It is now thought that this species was used to produce many of the hybrid Wichuraiana ramblers of late Victorian and Edwardian times.

[W T ⓜ ≈ (S)]   10′ × 8′   3 × 2.4 m

R. moschata
Musk Roses

'The Musk Rose'

Until recently this rose was thought to have become extinct. Species purporting to be this rose differed, and descriptions from botanists and plantsmen were equally variable. Over recent years various sightings have been reported. To relate this interesting saga would take many pages. At any rate, this quest appears to have ended happily. Graham Thomas pursued this rose relentlessly for many years, at last, it seems, with success. Two years ago he kindly sent me budwood and to my surprise these flowered as maiden plants in their first year, a feat climbers seldom achieve. Imagine my delight in watching, firstly, the leaves appear, and secondly, in late July, the flowers, both with the expected characteristics and timing. It seems we have the *R. moschata* again. Prior to this, I had been growing and selling a form of *R. moschata*, grown from seed, collected from I know not where. Foliage and growth were correct and therefore I had not bothered too much about the flowers which, since they never bloomed as maiden plants, I had not seen. I am now growing a few of these on to see what happens.

R. moschata

S. EUROPE/MIDDLE EAST

An ancient variety probably introduced during the reign of Henry VIII

Medium to short-growing climber with grey-green, slightly drooping foliage. Stems also grey-green, sparsely populated with hooked thorns. Flowers, produced in large spaced clusters, are cream until fully open when they change to white. Starts flowering in July and continues well into September. Hips, when produced, are small and oval.

[P W T N ◍ (S)]   10′ × 6′   3 × 1.8 m

FORMS AND HYBRIDS OF
R. moschata

This species has a few direct descendants, and many more a few generations removed, which are currently growing in our gardens. As discussed in an earlier chapter, it was father to the 'Noisettes'. Genes from *R. moschata* certainly inhabit the chromosomes of many of our modern roses. The newly adopted classification of 'Cluster-Flowered Roses' helps me depart from accepted practice at this point. For the roses listed in modern catalogues as 'Hybrid Musks' would, at least by name, normally follow on from here. However, their musk progeny is confused and somewhat distant, and they are better grouped with the 'Multifloras', i.e. 'Cluster-Flowered Roses'. The following are directly related to *R. moschata*; undoubtedly there were once others. Paul listed nine, excluding 'noisettes', in the tenth edition of *The Rose Garden*. I will therefore describe only those known to be available today and which are probably true to name.

R. moschata

R. moschata floribunda
Origin and date unknown
A very vigorous, spreading, dense, relatively thornless climber with large, long, lightish-green leaves and thick, green, slightly downy stems. The large, tightly packed clusters of single, white flowers are produced rather earlier in the season than other Moschata hybrids. Each flower has an attractive ring of yellow stamens and emits a pleasing musk scent; they are followed by oval to round, orange hips. This is a pleasing and under-used variety.
[P T F N ◍ (S)]   20′ × 15′   6 × 4.5 m

R. moschata grandiflora
Bernaix FRANCE 1866
An extremely vigorous climbing rose with typical Moschata-type foliage and extremely large clusters of single, white flowers, each with golden stamens. Very fragrant. Round orange hips in autumn.
[P T F N ◍ (S)]   30′ × 20′   9 × 6 m

R. moschata nastarana, 'Persian Musk Rose'
ASIA MINOR 1879
Possibly hybrid between *R. moschata* and *R. chinensis*

Similar in many respects to *R. moschata* but more vigorous in growth and with more numerous, smaller leaves. Flowers, although similar in form to those of the species, are slightly touched with pale pink, and can also be fractionally larger in some ideal situations. Flowers are provided well into autumn.
[P W N T ◍ (S)]   20′ × 10′   6 × 3 m

'Narrow Water'
Daisy Hill Nurseries IRELAND c. 1883
Parentage unknown
Not much is known about this rose, but it probably belongs in this section. A tallish shrub or small climber with dark foliage and large clusters of semi-double, lilac-pink flowers with a good scent. Particularly useful in that it flowers late into autumn. I grow more fond of it each season.
[P ◍ (R)]   8′ × 6′   2.5 × 1.8 m

'Paul's Himalayan Musk'
W. Paul UK Probably late 19th century
Parentage unknown
Perhaps nearer to *R. multiflora* or even *R. sempervirens* than its name suggests. Its drooping leaves (a clue to *moschata*) are slightly glossy and darkish green, with hints of copper when young. Broad,

'Narrow Water'

'Paul's Perpetual White' [PB]

hooked thorns on long, pliable wood. Very profuse when blooming in July. Flowers small,
double, pinkish-lavender, produced in drooping
clusters. Quite hardy, an outstandingly useful
climbing rose.

[P T ◍ ≋ (S)]   20′ × 12′   6 × 3.5 m

'Paul's Perpetual White', 'Paul's Single White'

G. Paul UK 1882

Parentage unknown

The flowers, large and single, and the way they
are displayed, solitarily or in small clusters,
suggest a liaison with *R. laevigata*. The foliage and
habit of growth, however, belie this. It is light
green and well spaced on relatively thornless,
almost lime-green shoots. Moderately vigorous.
From the first flush which occurs in July, flowers
continue to appear throughout the season until
well into autumn.

[P ◍ (R)]   15′ × 8′   4.5 × 2.5 m

'Princess of Nassau'

Probably early 19th century

Origin and parentage unknown

A recent rediscovery, I believe by Graham
Thomas, who sent me budwood in 1982. These
flowered as maiden plants, coinciding with *R.
moschata*, and going on well into autumn, fitting
Paul's descriptions almost perfectly: "Flowers,
yellowish-straw, form-cupped, very sweet". I add
to this, light green foliage, but can only hazard
a guess at its vigour, probably moderate. I can
now vouch for its hardiness since it survived the
severe winter of 1984/5 with only moderate frost
damage.

[◍ P (R)]   10′ × 8′   3 × 2.5 m

'The Garland'

Wills UK 1835

R. moschata × R. multiflora

Vigorous, spreading climber flowering in early
July in great profusion. Masses of small, semi-
double, daisy-like flowers, creamy-white, sometimes tinged pink. Very fragrant. Foliage mid-to-
dark green and not as large as in most other
Moschata hybrids. Stems are well armed with
stout, hooked thorns. An excellent rose.

[P N T ◍ ≋ (S)]   15′ × 10′   4.5 × 3 m

Above: 'Princess of Nassau' [PB]
Below: 'The Garland' at Lime Kiln,
Claydon, Suffolk [PB]

R. mulliganii

Forrest s. CHINA 1917
A medium vigorous species with broad, sharp, hooked thorns. Similar in many respects to *R. rubus*. Young shoots and foliage purplish-green; greyish-green when older. Flowers single in small spaced clusters, pure white and scented. Fruit small, red, round and conspicuous. Many of the plants grown and sold as *R. longicuspis* over recent years are actually this species and I confess myself in common with others to this error in identity.

[G P T F N ◍ (S)]   15′ × 10′   4.5 × 3 m

R. multiflora

R. multiflora

E. ASIA Late 18th, early 19th century
Very floriferous, at least for its relatively short flowering season. Flowers small, single, creamy-white grow in large clusters on wood produced in the previous season. When in full flush, they almost obscure the leaves which are smooth and lightish-green. Stems also smooth and fairly free of thorns. Fruit is small, round to oval, smooth and red in colour. Until recently it was popular as an understock both from seed and – as it roots easily – from cuttings.

[F P T N ◍ ≋ (S)]   15′ × 10′   4.5 × 3 m

R. multiflora carnea

CHINA 1804
A fully double form of *R. multiflora* with stronger shoots and larger leaves. Flowers tend to be globular, white faintly tinted pink.

[P W F T N ◍ ≋ (S)]   20′ × 10′   6 × 3 m

R. multiflora cathayensis

CHINA 1907
Pink form of *R. multiflora* with larger flowers and lighter-coloured foliage.

[F P T N ◍ ≋ (S)]   15′ × 10′   4.5 × 3 m

R. multiflora grevillei, R. multiflora platyphylla, 'Seven Sisters Rose'

CHINA 1816
A vigorous climbing rose with large, dark green, rather coarse foliage and stiff, dark green stems. Flowers are double, quite large, and borne in very big trusses; they vary from deep to soft pink with sometimes, lilac and even deep red blooms all produced together in the same truss. Scented. More common in Victorian times, when it was commonly-called 'Seven Sisters', derived from the seven different colours to be seen in each truss of flowers, another rose bearing this nickname being 'Félicité et Perpétue', which is actually a *R. sempervirens* hybrid.

[P T N ◍ (S)]   20′ × 10′   6 × 3 m

R. multiflora carnea   [PB]

R. multiflora watsoniana

JAPAN 1870
This unusual form of *R. multiflora* is probably an old garden hybrid. Slim, trailing stems with small, hooked thorns and small, narrow, light green leaves, often wavy at the edges. Large panicles of small, closely packed, single flowers of off-white to pale pink. Masses of small, globular, red hips in autumn and early winter. More of a novelty than a useful garden plant. Not fully hardy.

[F ☼ (S)]   5′ × 4′   1.5 × 1.2 m

R. multiflora wilsonii

Origin unknown 1915
Rounded trusses of medium-sized, single white flowers, produced very freely on a vigorous, moderately thorny plant which bears almost shiny foliage. Fruit orange, smooth, rounded but quite small.

[W P T N F ◍ (S)]   15′ × 10′   4.5 × 3 m

R. multiflora has had great influence in the development of the modern rose and I could almost fill two books of this size with hybrids which have *R. multiflora* somewhere in their lineage. I will place a number of important groups under this heading since this is where they are best placed in the family tree of roses. My selection may give rise to dissent but I am helped by the new rose classifications in that most of those listed under this heading are now termed 'Cluster-Flowered Roses'.

I have already dealt with the Multiflora Species and will subdivide the hybrids in this lineage into their garden groups, each with a brief note of introduction as follows: Hybrid Musks, Multiflora Ramblers, Modern Shrubs, Polyanthas, Floribundas and Modern Climbers.

Hybrid Musks

These are among the most useful of shrubs having, by and large, long flowering seasons and agreeable habits of growth. For notes on their history see page 45.

'Autumn Delight'

Bentall UK 1933
Parentage unknown
Soft, buff-yellow in colour from shapely, deeper coloured buds. The semi-double flowers are produced in large trusses on an almost thornless, upright but bushy shrub with dark green, leathery foliage.
[P H (C)] 4′×4′ 1.2 × 1.2 m

'Ballerina'

Bentall UK 1937
Parentage unknown
An outstanding rose with many uses from bedding to growing in pots. Huge sprays of small, single, pink flowers, each with a white centre. These are delightfully and daintily displayed throughout the summer on a bushy, upright, dense shrub with plentiful, mid-green foliage.
[P H ◍ ▽ (C)] 4′×3′ 1.2 m × 90 cm

'Bishop Darlington'

Thomas USA 1926
'Aviateur Blériot' × 'Moonlight'
Large flowers, semi-double, creamy-white to pink with a yellow base to each petal and a strong scent. Bush vigorous with mid to dark green foliage.
[P H (R)] 5′×5′ 1.5 × 1.5 m

Above: 'Ballerina' (see text p. 263)   [RCB]
Below: 'Buff Beauty'   [VP]

'Buff Beauty'

Probably Pemberton 1939 (perhaps 20 years
older)

Parentage unknown

One of the best of its group. A vigorous shrub
with spreading growth and dark green foliage.
Flowers fully double, opening flat from tight,
cupped buds and produced in large trusses.
Colour varies with weather and, I suspect, the
soil in which they are growing, from buff-yellow
to almost apricot, at times paling to primrose.
Strongly scented.

[P H ⓜ (C)]   5′×5′   1.5×1.5 m

'Cornelia'

Pemberton UK 1925

Parentage unknown

Conspicuous bronzy foliage produced on long,
dark brownish shoots. The small, fully double
flowers, which are produced in large clusters,
blend superbly with the foliage, being apricot-
pink flushed deep pink with paler highlights.
Particularly good in the autumn.

[P H ⓜ (C)]   5′×5′   1.5×1.5 m

'Cornelia'

[PB]

'Danaë'

Pemberton UK 1913

'Trier' × 'Gloire de Chédane-Guinoisseau'

Clusters of semi-double, bright yellow flowers changing to buff and then to cream with age. A healthy, vigorous plant with dark foliage. A most useful lesser known Hybrid Musk, well worth growing, where a shrub of this colour is sought.

[P H ⦿ (C)]   5′ × 4′   1.5 × 1.2 m

'Daybreak'

Pemberton UK 1918

'Trier' × 'Liberty'

Rather less than double flowers, lemon-yellow paling to primrose, produced on strong stems in medium-sized, well-spaced clusters. Foliage coppery, especially when young. Seldom gets very tall and seldom outgrows its welcome in any garden.

[P H ▽ (C)]   4′ × 3′   1.2 m × 90 cm

'Eva'

Kordes GERMANY 1938

'Robin Hood' × 'J. C. Thornton'

Trusses of good-size, almost single, bright carmine to red flowers which pale towards the centre to white. This lesser known variety is well scented. Dark green foliage on a fairly tall-growing plant.

[P H (C)]   6′ × 4′   1.8 × 1.2 m

'Felicia'

Pemberton UK 1928

'Trier' × 'Ophelia'

This rose is among the best of its group. The fully double flowers open rather muddled but even so remain quite a charming mixture of rich pink with salmon shadings; they pale slightly with age but I find this an added attraction. Foliage crisp, slightly crinkled at the edges and dark green. The bush retains its shape well with judicious pruning, making it ideal for specimen planting.

[P H ▽ (C)]   4′ × 4′   1.2 × 1.2 m

'Francesca'

Pemberton UK 1928

'Danaë' × 'Sunburst'

Large sprays of semi-double, apricot-yellow

Above: 'Felicia'   [PB]
Below: 'Francesca'   [PB]

flowers on strong, dark stems with glossy but dark green foliage. Useful, since its strong yellow colour is rare amongst shrub roses generally.

[P H ⦿ ▽]   4′ × 4′   1.2 × 1.2 m

'Kathleen'

Pemberton UK 1922

'Daphne' × 'Perle des Jeannes'

Very vigorous rose. Dark green foliage rather sparse for my taste. Stems greyish-green. Flowers almost single, medium-sized, best described as clear pink with deeper shadings.

[P] 8′ × 4′   2.5 × 1.2 m

'Lavender Lassie'

Kordes GERMANY 1960
Parentage unknown
Large trusses of beautiful, double, lavender-pink flowers, opening flat, produced throughout the summer on a healthy bush with dark green foliage. An ideal rose which can fulfil a variety of roles in the modern garden.

[P H ◍ (C)]   5′ × 4′   1.5 × 1.2 m

'Moonlight'

Pemberton UK 1913
'Trier' × 'Sulphurea'
Long, well-foliated stems with clusters of creamy-white almost single flowers with pronounced stamens. Scented. Vigorous and healthy.

[P H ◍ (C)]   5′ × 4′   1.5 × 1.2 m

'Nur Mahal'

Pemberton UK 1923
'Château de Clos Vougeot' × Hybrid Musk seedling
Large clusters of bright crimson, semi-double flowers, well perfumed. An interesting rose with much to commend it, not least its healthy dark foliage.

[P H ◍ (C)]   5′ × 4′   1.5 × 1.2 m

'Pax'

Pemberton UK 1918
'Trier' × 'Sunburst'
Very large semi-double flowers, creamy-white to pure white, with obvious golden stamens. Blooms produced in large, well-spaced clusters which, in turn, are on long, arching stems. Foliage crisp and very dark green. A superb rose.

[P H ◍ (C)]   6′ × 5′   1.8 × 1.5 m

'Penelope'

Pemberton UK 1924
'Ophelia' × 'Trier'
A favourite amongst the Hybrid Musks. This very pretty rose has large, semi-double flowers which, when open, show off to advantage the slightly frilled petal edges; creamy-pink with deeper shadings, especially on frilled edges. Scented.

'Pax'   [PB]

Foliage dark green with plum-red shadings, likewise the stems.

[P H ◍ ▽ (C)]   5′ × 4′   1.5 × 1.2 m

'Pink Prosperity'

Bentall UK 1931
Parentage unknown
Large trusses of small, clear pink, fully double blooms with deeper shadings on an upright bush with dark green foliage. Scented.

[P H ▽ (C)]   4′ × 4′   1.2 × 1.2 m

'Penelope' at Castle Howard, Yorkshire   [PB]

'Prosperity'

Pemberton UK 1919
'Marie-Jeanne' × 'Perle des Jardins'
Large, double, creamy white flowers produced in large even clusters on strong arching shoots with dark green foliage. The arching effect, caused largely by bending from the weight of flowers, rather than any tendency to sprawl, adds to its attraction. Well worth growing.

[P H ◍ (C)]   5′ × 4′   1.5 × 1.2 m

'Prosperity' (see text p. 267) [PB]

'Robin Hood'

Pemberton UK 1927
Seedling × 'Miss Edith Cavell'
Large clusters of medium-sized flowers, rather
more than single, bright scarlet aging to crimson. Good, dark green foliage with a bushy, tidy
growth habit.

[H ▽ (C)] 4′×3′ 1.2 m × 90 cm

'Sadler's Wells'

Beales UK 1983
'Penelope' × 'Rose Gaujard'
The newest member of this group. Makes fine
continuous-flowering shrub. Semi-double slightly
scented flowers produced in large, well-spaced
clusters on a vigorous but tidy bush. The background colour is silvery-pink, with each petal
laced with cherry red, especially at the edges.
The autumn flowers are particularly good, when
the enriched colouring seems almost impervious
to inclement weather. When cut, the sprays last
very well in water. Foliage is dark green, glossy
and plentiful.

[P H ◍ (C)] 4′×3′ 1.2 m × 90 cm

'Skyrocket' *See* 'Wilhelm'

'Thisbe'

Pemberton UK 1918
'Daphne' sport
Sulphur-straw coloured, the flowers are semi-
double rosettes borne in large clusters on a bushy,
upright shrub with glossy, mid-green foliage.

[P H ▽ (C)] 4′×4′ 1.2 × 1.2 m

'Vanity'

Pemberton UK 1920
'Château de Clos Vougeot' × seedling
Large sprays of fragrant, rose-pink, almost single
flowers of considerable size, produced freely on
a vigorous, bushy but somewhat angular shrub.
Rather short on foliage for my taste, but bright-
ness and density of flowers probably makes up
for this minor fault.

[P (C)] 6′×5′ 1.8 × 1.5 m

'Wilhelm', 'Skyrocket'

Kordes GERMANY 1944
'Robin Hood' × 'J. C. Thornton'
Clusters of crimson, almost single flowers on
stout, strong stems. A very useful rose since good
red varieties are scarce among the Hybrid Musks.
Foliage is dark green and healthy. Gives a good
display of hips if not dead-headed.

[H F P ◍ (C)] 5′×4′ 1.5 × 1.2 m

'Will Scarlet'

Hilling UK 1947
'Wilhelm' sport
Almost identical to 'Wilhelm' except being
brighter red.

[F H P ◍ (C)] 5′×4′ 1.5 × 1.2 m

Above: 'Sadler's Wells' [PB]
Right: 'Will Scarlet' [RCB]

Multiflora Rambler 'Ghislaine de Féligonde' (flower $1\frac{1}{2}$ times actual size). (see text p. 272)   [VP]

Multiflora Ramblers

'Apple Blossom'

Burbank USA 1932

'Dawson' × *R. multiflora*

Huge trusses of apple blossom-like, pink flowers with crinkled petals. Foliage rich green with copper overtones. Wood is similar in colour to its foliage with few or no thorns.

[P ◍ (S)] 10'×6' 3×1.8 m

'Aglaia', 'Yellow Rambler'

Schmitt FRANCE 1896

R. multiflora × 'Rêve d'Or'

Small, semi-double flowers of pale primrose yellow. Growth upright, stems almost thornless. Foliage rich light green with bronzy tints, especially when young. Important as one of the roses used initially by Pemberton in breeding his race of Hybrid Musks.

[P ◍ N (S)] 8'×6' 2.5×1.8 m

'Bleu Magenta'

c. 1900

Origin and parentage unknown

One of the daintiest of flowers. Rich deep purple with yellow stamens peeping from beneath folding, centre petals. Sweetly scented. Foliage dark and free of thorns. Although not recurrent, flowers later in summer than most.

[P N ◍ (S)] 12'×10' 3.5×3 m

'Blush Rambler'

B. R. Cant UK 1903

'Crimson Rambler' × 'The Garland'

A vigorous, almost thornless rose, popular as a cottage rambler in Edwardian days. Fragrant flowers blush-pink in colour, borne in cascading clusters. Foliage plentiful and light green.

[P (S)] 12'×10' 3.5×3 m

'Appleblossom' [PB]

'Bobbie James' [RCB]

'Bobbie James'

Sunningdale Nurseries UK 1961

Parentage unknown

A vigorous rambler capable of considerable climbing feats especially into trees and hedges. In fact, I rate this rose as one of the best for this purpose. The individual white flowers are cup-shaped and quite large, rather more than single, highly scented, and displayed in large, drooping clusters. The foliage is rich greeny brown and polished. Stems are strong and well equipped with sharp, hooked thorns.

[A P T N ◍ (S)]   30′ × 20′   9 × 6 m

'Crimson Rambler', 'Turner's Crimson', 'Engineer's Rose'

JAPAN 1893

Parentage unknown

More important as a stud rose in the development of ramblers than as a garden plant. Semi-double crimson flowers produced in clusters. Foliage light green. Rather disease-prone, which is the main reason for its virtual disappearance from modern gardens.

[(S)]   12′ × 10′   3.5 × 3 m

'Francis E. Lester'   [PB]

'De la Grifferaie'

Vibert FRANCE 1845

Parentage unknown

A vigorous, dark, rather coarse-foliaged plant, extensively used in the past as an understock, hence it is frequently found in old gardens. Trusses of spaced, fully double flowers of magenta fading to dingy white. Well scented, not of great garden value.

[P N ◍ (S)]   8′ × 4′   2.5 × 1.2 m

'Francis E. Lester'

Lester Rose Gardens USA 1946

'Kathleen' × unnamed seedling

Very large trusses of well-spaced, medium-sized, single flowers, white with splashes of pink on the edges of each petal. A special feature is its strong perfume. The shrub is vigorous but not overpowering, with lush, coppery-tinted, glossy foliage. Small red hips in autumn.

[T F P N ◍ (S)]   15′ × 10′   4.5 × 3 m

'Goldfinch'   [PB]

'Ghislaine de Féligonde'

Turbat FRANCE 1916

'Goldfinch' × unknown

A small climber or, if space permits, can be grown as a large shrub. Fully double, orange-yellow flowers in very large clusters. Healthy, large, glossy foliage. Almost thornless. I assume its long name has prevented this rose from gaining the popularity it deserves.

[P N ◍ (R)]   8′ × 8′   2.5 × 2.5 m

'Goldfinch'

W. Paul UK 1907

'Hélène' × unknown

Less vigorous than some but very useful where a small rambler or climber is required. Small cupped flowers a mixture of golden-yellow and primrose with pronounced golden-brown anthers, still charming even when fading to cream in hot sun. Almost thornless greenish brown stems and glossy foliage.

[P N ◍ (S)]   8′ × 5′   2.5 × 1.5 m

'Phyllis Bide' (see text p. 274) [PB]

'Hiawatha'

Walsh USA 1904

'Crimson Rambler' × 'Paul's Carmine Pillar'

Single, deepish pink to crimson flowers with paler, almost white centres. These are borne in clusters on a vigorous, free growing plant with lightish green leaves. Another rose awkward to classify, but probably best here, because of obvious Multiflora influence.

[P ⓘ T (S)]   15′ × 12′   4.5 × 3.5 m

'Leuchtstern'

J. C. Schmidt GERMANY 1899

'Daniel Lacombe' × 'Crimson Rambler'

Clusters of medium-sized, single deep pink flowers with centres paling to white. Good, mid-green foliage. Not often seen but a good, shorter rambler.

[P N ⓘ (S)]   10′ × 8′   3 × 2.5 m

'Mme d'Arblay'

Wills UK 1835

R. multiflora × *R. moschata*

Drooping clusters of small, flattish-topped yet slightly cupped flowers comprised of randomly arranged, shortish petals, fragrant, blush-pink paling to white. A very vigorous climber with darkish green foliage. Now quite rare.

[P T N ⓘ (S)]   20′ × 20′   6 × 6 m

'Madeleine Selzer'

Walter FRANCE 1926

'Tausendschön' × 'Mrs Aaron Ward'

Attractive, almost thornless rose with bronzy-green foliage, bearing trusses of fully double, scented, lemon to white flowers. Quite a spectacle when in full flush. An excellent medium-growing rambler.

[P (S)]   10′ × 6′   3 × 1.8 m

'Mrs F. W. Flight'

Cutbush UK 1905

'Crimson Rambler' × unknown

For some reason, this rose has escaped me. So I can only discuss it from a photograph and cribbed descriptions. Small, semi-double, rose-pink flowers in large clusters. On a short to medium-growing plant with large, soft mid-green foliage.

[(S)]   8′ × 6′   2.5 × 1.8 m

'Paul's Scarlet'

W. Paul UK 1916
Parentage unknown
Double, bright scarlet flowers in small spaced clusters. One of the brightest and most popular ramblers of its day. Foliage dark green, as are its relatively thornless stems. I am not sure it should be in this group, but where else to place it?
[P N ◍ (S)]   10′×8′   3×2.5 m

'Phyllis Bide'

Bide UK 1923
'Perle d'Or' × 'Gloire de Dijon'
Small, slightly ragged, large pyramidal clusters of flowers of mixed colouring including yellow, cream and pink, sometimes deepening with age and becoming mottled. Foliage plentiful but each leaf quite small. Growth vigorous and relatively thorn-free. A superb and important rose flowering continuously throughout the season, perhaps nearer to the *chinensis* subgenus than *synstylae*.
[P N ◍ (R)]   10′×6′   3×1.8 m

'Rambling Rector'

Very old variety
Origin and parentage unknown
Large clusters of fragrant, semi-double flowers, creamy to begin, then opening white to display rich yellow stamens. These are produced in abundance on a vigorous, healthy, scrambling shrub. Plentiful foliage, small, grey-green and downy. Superb as a tree or hedgerow climber, also useful for covering unsightly sheds. Produces a good display of small hips in the autumn. Many an old corrugated iron shed would become less of an eyesore if supporting 'Rambling Rector'.
[P W F T N ◍ (S)]   20′×15′   6×4.5 m

'Rose Marie Viaud'

Igoult FRANCE 1924
'Veilchenblau' seedling
Very double flowers of rich purple produced in small trusses on a vigorous rambler with light green foliage and relatively thornless, light green shoots.
[P ◍ (S)]   12′×6′   3.5×1.8 m

'Russelliana', 'Old Spanish Rose', 'Russell's Cottage Rose', 'Scarlet Grevillei'

Probably SPAIN 1840
Origin not known; probably a cross between *R. multiflora* and *R. setigera*
A rose of some antiquity with very double, small flowers borne in clusters. Its colour is a mixture of crimson and mild purple, giving an overall red appearance. Well worthy of garden space. Foliage dark green and stems rather thorny, belying its Multiflora ancestry. Good specimens can be seen at both Cranborne House, Dorset, and Mottisfont Abbey, Hants.
[P N T ◍ (S)]   10′×10′   3×3 m

'Seagull'

Pritchard 1907 Country of origin not known
R. multiflora × 'Général Jacqueminot'
Bright yellow stamens surrounded by a double layer of white petals. Highly scented flowers borne in large clusters on a vigorous, well foliated plant which has grey-green leaves. An established plant in full flush of flower is a sight to remember.
[P N T ◍ (S)]   25′×15′   7.5×4.5 m

'Tausendschön', 'Thousand Beauties'

J. C. Schmidt GERMANY 1906
'Daniel Lacombe' × 'Weisser Herumstreicher'
An interesting rose. The flowers which are large, double and borne in loose clusters, are pink with white towards their centre. Growth is strong with thornless shoots, amply clothed with mid-green foliage.
[P (S)]   12′×8′   3.5×2.5 m

'Tea Rambler'

W. Paul UK 1904
'Crimson Rambler' × a Tea Rose
Fragrant, double, soft pink flowers with brighter highlights on a vigorous plant with mid-green foliage.
[P T ◍ (S)]   12′×8′   3.5×2.5 m

'Tea Rambler'   [PB]

'Thalia', 'White Rambler'

Schmitt FRANCE Introduced by P. Lambert
GERMANY 1895
Quite a good rose, not often seen today. Flowers
white, smallish, double and highly scented, produced profusely in large clusters. Growth vigorous and only moderately thorny. Foliage mid-
green and mildly glossy.
[P T N ⊕ (S)]   12' × 8'   3.5 × 2.5 m

'Trier'

P. Lambert GERMANY 1904
'Aglaia' × unknown
An upright-growing climber or, if preferred, tall
shrub with small, creamy-yellow, single or near-
single flowers in clusters. Foliage small, almost
daintily so. Used much by breeders earlier this
century, especially in development of Hybrid
Musks.
[P ⊕ (R)]   8' × 6'   2.5 × 1.8 m

'Turner's Crimson'

See 'Crimson Rambler'

'Veilchenblau'

J. C. Schmidt GERMANY 1909
'Crimson Rambler' × unknown seedling
A vigorous rambler sometimes called 'The Blue
Rose'. Bears large trusses of small, semi-double
flowers of lavender-purple occasionally flecked
with white, especially in their centre. They
mature to bluish-lilac and fade to lilac-grey.
Scented. An ideal companion for cream and
white ramblers, when respective flowers can
merge to good effect.
[P T N ⊕ (S)]   15' × 12'   4.5 × 3.5 m

'Violette'

Turbat FRANCE 1921
Parentage unknown
Very double, cupped, rosette flowers of rich
violet-purple with hints of yellow in their base.
Flowers in clusters, scented. Foliage rich dark
green. Growth is vigorous and shoots have few
thorns.
[P T ⊕ (S)]   15' × 10'   4.5 × 3 m

'Veilchenblau'   [VP]

'White Flight'

Origin, date and parentage unknown
I have yet to find this rose described anywhere,
and suspect it to be wrongly named. It is perhaps
a sport from 'Mrs W. Flight' but I have never
seen this to check. Less vigorous than most of its
type. Huge corymbs of small, single, pure white
flowers amid an abundance of smallish, light
green foliage. Growth thin, wiry and yet dense.
Supplied to me by Mr Humphrey Brooke of
Claydon, Suffolk.
[P N ⊕ (S)]   10' × 8'   3 × 2.5 m

Modern Climbing Roses

In recent years a most useful trend has occurred in modern roses: the development of a number of continuous flowering climbers. To be more accurate, they are really large shrubs which, if placed by a wall or given support, will behave rather like climbers. They do not send up long climbing shoots as do, for example, climbing Hybrid Teas, and they usually flower on wood produced in the same season. As for classification, they are a mixed bunch and now very hybrid indeed. But much of their vigour and floriferous quality must derive from *R. multiflora*, which enables me to place them here.

Most have been raised as seedlings and are not climbing sports. I have again used the modern classification of 'Cluster-Flowered Roses' to justify my selection. More and more are coming in each year and it is difficult to keep up to date, but those chosen for inclusion are all well-tried varieties.

'Alchemist'

Kordes GERMANY 1956

'Golden Glow' × *R. eglanteria* hybrid

An unusual but beautiful medium-growing, climbing rose with rich green, healthy foliage and thorny wood. The very double flowers, mostly opening quartered, are a rich mixture of yellow and yolky-orange with a strong scent. These are produced quite early in the season; some of the first flowers are much paler than the later ones.

[P ◍ (S)] 12′ × 8′ 3.5 × 2.5 m

'Aloha'

Boerner USA 1949

'Mercedes Gallart' × 'New Dawn'

A sumptuous and most attractive rose comprising 60 or more rose-pink petals, each with a deeper reverse and shadings of magenta, strongly fragrant. Healthy, dark bronzy foliage. Has an upright habit and is seldom not in flower throughout the summer. In all respects a first-class rose.

[P (C)] 10′ × 6′ 3 × 1.8 m

Modern Climbing Rose 'Ritter von Barmstede' (see text p. 284)

[JB]

Above: 'Aloha' (see text p. 276) [PB]
Below: 'Altissimo' [PB]

'Altissimo'

Delbard-Chabert FRANCE 1967
'Ténor' × unknown
Large, bright red, single flowers borne in small-spaced clusters, sometimes singly amid dark green foliage. A superb rose for pillar work or trellis. Does not do well as a wall plant, at least for me.

[(C)]   10′ × 6′   3 × 1.8 m

'Ash Wednesday', 'Aschermittwoch'

Kordes GERMANY 1955
Said to be *R. eglanteria* hybrid
Although of Eglanteria descent, this rose is probably better placed here among modern climbers since I can detect no perfume from its foliage. Trusses of ashen-white to soft lilac, double blooms on a vigorous, thorny, well-foliated plant.

[P N (S)]   10′ × 6′   3 × 1.8 m

'Bantry Bay'

McGredy UK 1967
'New Dawn' × 'Korona'
Large, scented, semi-double flowers opening

'Ash Wednesday' [PB]

'Casino' [PB]

'Bantry Bay' [RCB]

rather blowsily, deep pink with quieter reflections. Foliage lush and dark green. One of the best and most free-flowering of its type.

[P (C)] 12′×8′ 3.5×2.5 m

'Breath of Life'

Harkness UK 1981
'Red Dandy' × 'Alexander'
Rich but not dazzlingly so. Apricot flowers are shapely, Hybrid Tea-like, and scented. Foliage dark green. A good and apparently reliable rose for those who like the orange shades, which are never the easiest of roses to grow.

[(C)] 10′×6′ 3×1.8 m

'Casino'

McGredy UK 1963
'Coral Dawn' × 'Buccaneer'
Clusters of large, full, globular, clear yellow scented blooms on strong, dark stems with contrasting light green, glossy foliage. Can be relied upon as a good pillar rose.

[(R)] 10′×8′ 3×2.5 m

'City of York', 'Direktor Benschop'

Tantau GERMANY 1945
'Prof Gnau' × 'Dorothy Perkins'
A good vigorous climber with ample glossy foliage. Flowers creamy-white with lemon centres, semi-double and cupped. Individually beautiful and produced very freely to give a superb, overall effect. Scented.

[P W N T ◍ (S)] 15′×10′ 4.5×3 m

'Clair Matin'

Meilland FRANCE 1960
('Fashion' × 'Independence') × unnamed Multiflora seedling
Free-branching, with large trusses of clear pink blooms, each with cream highlights. Each flower almost but not quite single. Free flowering habit makes this rose outstanding. Foliage dark green and stems chocolate-purple. Also makes a good free-standing shrub or tall hedge.

[P N ◍ (C)] 8′×4′ 2.5×1.2 m

'Compassion'

Harkness UK 1974
'White Cockade' × 'Prima Ballerina'
Dark green, glossy foliage on dark wood bearing shapely blooms of apricot and copper with yellow highlights. Scented.

[(R)] 10′×6′ 3×1.8 m

'Clair Matin' (see text p. 279)   [PB]

Above and below: 'Constance Spry' at Castle Howard,
Yorkshire   [PB/PB]

'Constance Spry'

Austin UK 1960
'Belle Isis' × 'Dainty Maid'
A beautiful rose in the old-fashioned style. Large,
clear, bright pink, very full with a myrrh-like
perfume. Copious grey-green foliage on a vigor-
ous, quite thorny plant. Ideal for most situations.
Particularly good on a tripod.
[P H ◍ (S)]   20′ × 10′   6 × 3 m

'Coral Dawn'

Boerner USA 1952
'New Dawn' × unnamed Yellow Hybrid Tea
Large, full, rather plump, coral-pink blooms
amid ample dark green, healthy foliage. Scented.
A first-class free-flowering rose.
[N ◍ (R)]   12′ × 8′   3.5 × 2.5 m

'Danse de Feu', 'Spectacular'

Mallerin FRANCE 1953
'Paul's Scarlet' × unnamed Multiflora seedling
So bright, this rose almost screams, which makes
it difficult to place with other climbers. Nevertheless, an excellent, free-flowering and double rose
with shapely buds opening flat. Colour bright

brick-red. Copious foliage but I find this variety rather prone to black spot.
[⏺ (C)]   12′ × 8′   3.5 × 2.5 m

'Danse des Sylphes'
Mallerin FRANCE 1959
'Danse de Feu' × ('Peace' × 'Independence')
Rich bright red, a seedling from 'Danse de Feu' and almost as bright.
[⏺ (C)]   12′ × 8′   3.5 × 2.5 m

'Handel' (see text p. 282)   [VP]

'Coral Dawn'   [VP]

'Danse de Feu'   [PB]

'Dreaming Spires'
Mattock UK 1977
'Buccaneer' × 'Arthur Bell'
Shapely, high-centred, deep yellow flowers with discreet touches of orange, fading to primrose with age. Fine, dark foliage on a vigorous plant.
[P (C)]   12′ × 8′   3.5 × 2.5 m

'Dublin Bay'
McGredy UK 1976
'Bantry Bay' × 'Altissimo'
A very good pillar rose with large, glossy leaves. Clusters of medium-sized, rich blood-red flowers. Almost constantly in flower throughout summer. Can also be grown successfully as large shrub.
[P (C)]   7′ × 5′   2 × 1.5 m

'Fugue'
Meilland FRANCE 1958
'Alain' × 'Guinée'
A very good but little known variety with fully double flowers of rich, deep red. Dark, glossy foliage and vigorous growth. Useful pillar rose.
[P (C)]   10′ × 6′   3 × 1.8 m

'Galway Bay'
McGredy UK 1966
'Heidelberg' × 'Queen Elizabeth'
Large, double, shapely flowers, of salmon-pink. Scented. Foliage profuse and glossy dark green. The plant is vigorous and has a tidy growth habit.
[P ⏺ (C)]   12′ × 8′   3.5 × 2.5 m

Above and below: 'Golden Showers' [PB/VP]

'Golden Showers'

Lammerts USA 1956
'Charlotte Armstrong' × 'Captain Thomas'
Large, loosely formed, rather ragged flowers,
of deep golden-yellow fading quickly to cream.
Flowers continuously from June to October.
Foliage rich dark green and glossy. Also capable
of making a good free-standing shrub.

[P ⦾ (C)]   10′ × 6′   3 × 1.8 m

'Handel'

McGredy UK 1956
'Columbine' × 'Heidelberg'
A good variety with dark stems and glossy, dark
green, almost purple leaves. Large, semi-double
flowers, cupped until fully open, silver-white with
pink to red markings especially on the petal
edges. These markings intensify with age. An
excellent rose, but somewhat 'pretty' for my taste.

[P (C)]   12′ × 8′   3.5 × 2.5 m

'Highfield'

Harkness UK 1982
A paler sport of 'Compassion', preferred by some
because it is less severe in colour.

[(C)]   8′ × 6′   2.5 × 1.8 m

'Ilse Krohn'

Kordes GERMANY 1957
'Golden Glow' × *R. kordesii*
Fully double, pure white flowers from shapely,
pointed buds. Slightly scented. Foliage rich
green and glossy. Growth vigorous.

[T N P ⦾ (S)]   15′ × 10′   4.5 × 3 m

'Köln am Rhein'

Kordes GERMANY 1956

Parentage unknown

Fragrant, double, deep salmon-pink flowers produced in clusters on a healthy, robust plant.
Foliage rich dark green and glossy. Not often
seen, but well worth garden space.

[P N ◑ (R)] 15′ × 10′ 4.5 × 3 m

'Malaga'

McGredy UK 1971

('Hamburger Phoenix' × 'Danse de Feu') ×
'Copenhagen'

Large, deep rose-pink flowers in good clusters on
a medium but vigorous plant with dark green
foliage. A special feature is the distinctive Sweet
Briar fragrance.

[P (R)] 8′ × 4′ 2.4 × 1.2 m

'Morning Jewel'

Cocker UK 1968

'New Dawn' × 'Red Dandy'

Large, semi-double flowers, fragrant, rich pink.
Very free flowering with glossy, clear green
foliage.

[P (R)] 10′ × 8′ 3 × 2.5 m

'Norwich Gold' [VP]

Kordes GERMANY 1962

Parentage unknown

Fragrant flowers of yellow shaded orange, very
full, opening flat. Foliage rather dull green.

[P (R)] 10′ × 8′ 3 × 2.5 m

'Norwich Pink'

Kordes GERMANY 1962

Parentage unknown

Semi-double, bright cerise flowers with a strong
fragrance. Foliage dark and glossy.

[P (R)] 10′ × 8′ 3 × 2.5 m

'Norwich Salmon'

Kordes GERMANY 1962

Parentage unknown

Fully double, soft salmon-pink flowers produced
in large clusters on a vigorous, bushy plant.
Foliage dark green and glossy.

[(R)] 10′ × 8′ 3 × 2.4 m

'Parade'

Boerner USA 1953

'New Dawn' seedling × 'World's Fair'

Cerise-red to crimson flowers, fully double and
scented. Foliage glossy, profuse and healthy.
Excellent both as pillar rose or free-standing
shrub.

[P ◑ (C)] 10′ × 8′ 3 × 2.5 m

'Pink Perpétue'

Gregory UK 1965

'Danse de Feu' × 'New Dawn'

One of the outstanding modern climbers. Its

'Parade' and *above right:* 'Pink Perpétue' [JB]

'Schoolgirl'   [PB]

colour is perhaps rather hard for some tastes, but it can be relied upon to produce masses of double, deep pink, rather cupped, semi-double flowers throughout the summer. Its very dark green foliage has glossy purple overtones which make an excellent foil for the flowers.

[P N ◍ (C)]   12' × 8'   3.5 × 2.5 m

'Ritter von Barmstede'

Kordes GERMANY 1959
Parentage unknown
Deep pink, double flowers in large clusters. Somewhat untidy in growth but has excellent, glossy dark green foliage.

[P ◍ (R)]   10' × 10'   3 × 3 m

'Rosy Mantle'

Cocker UK 1968
'New Dawn' × 'Prima Ballerina'
Silver-pink, fully double flowers with a strong perfume. Rather sprawly if not tethered, but very showy when in full flush. Good, glossy dark green foliage.

[N ◍ (C)]   8' × 8'   2.5 × 2.5 m

'Royal Gold'

Morey USA 1957
'Goldilocks' × 'Lydia'
Not the most free-flowering of climbers, but its flowers are usually of good quality, golden-yellow, almost non-fading, of classic Hybrid Tea shape, opening loosely-formed and quite large. Foliage glossy, mid to dark green. Needs a warm sheltered position to ensure against a slight tenderness.

[☼ (C)]   8' × 8'   2.5 × 2.5 m

'Schoolgirl'

McGredy UK 1964
'Coral Dawn' × 'Belle Blonde'
Rich, coppery-orange flowers Hybrid Tea-shaped in bud, opening loosely flat and semi-double. Highly scented. A little short on foliage and, in my opinion, rather overrated.

[(C)]   10' × 8'   3 × 2.5 m

'Soldier Boy'

LeGrice UK 1953
Unnamed seedling × 'Guinée'
A rose of considerable beauty. Flowers are single, rich scarlet with pronounced golden anthers. Foliage profuse and matt dark green. Repeats intermittently throughout summer.

[P N ◍ (R)]   10' × 8'   3 × 2.5 m

'Swan Lake'

McGredy UK 1968
'Memorium' × 'Heidelberg'
A beautiful rose, shapely in bud, opening large and fully double, white with a pale pink flush in the centre, and produced freely all summer. Rounded, dark green foliage, liberally produced on an upright, tidy plant.

[P (C)]   8' × 6'   2.5 × 1.8 m

'Sympathie'

Kordes GERMANY 1964
Parentage unknown
Fragrant, dark red, fully double and shapely blooms produced freely and continuously throughout summer. Foliage dark green and glossy.

[P (C)]   10' × 8'   3 × 2.5 m

'White Cockade'

Cocker UK 1969
'New Dawn' × 'Circus'
A thorny, upright climber with small but ample, dark, glossy foliage, combining well with fully double, pure white flowers which open into rather triangular shapes, hence its name. One of the best white climbers, but not the most vigorous; good grown as pillar rose.

[(C)]   8' × 6'   2.5 × 1.8 m

Modern Shrub Roses

An increasing demand for shrub roses has prompted breeders to produce and introduce many and varied tall varieties, all with long flowering seasons. These, as with modern climbers, are of very mixed progeny; and many, in addition to making excellent shrubs, may also be adapted to make admirable small climbers or pillar roses. Some also make very good hedging roses.

'Alexander'

Harkness UK 1972
'Super Star' × ('Ann Elizabeth' × 'Allgold')
Shapely pointed buds opening to large, slightly ragged flowers of a very bright luminous vermilion, displaying creamy yellow stamens to good effect. Foliage rich green and healthy. Growth upright, with strong thorny stems.
[P H ◍ (C)]   6′ × 4′   1.8 × 1.2 m

'Alexander'   [VP]

'Angelina'

Cocker UK 1976
('Super Star' × 'Carina') × ('Cläre Grammerstorf' × 'Frühlingsmorgen')
An extremely free-flowering, shortish shrub rose, not yet widely distributed but, as it becomes better known it is sure to become a firm favourite. The fragrant flowers are large, slightly fuller than single, and bright rose-pink. These are produced in large clusters on upright stems with dark green foliage.
[H P (C)]   4′ × 3′   1.2 m × 90 cm

'Anna Zinkeisen'

Harkness UK 1983
A shrubby rose with good mid-green foliage. Fully double flowers ivory-white with golden-yellow tones in the base, borne in clusters. Has a distinctive perfume.
[G P ◍ ▽ (C)]   4′ × 3′   1.2 m × 90 cm

'Angelina'   [PB]

'Ballerina' *See* Hybrid Musks

Above: 'Anna Zinkeisen' (see text p. 285)   [VP]
Below: 'Cardinal Hume'   [RCB]

'Berlin'

Kordes GERMANY 1949

'Eva' × 'Peace'

Large single flowers, bright, rich red, paling towards the centre to white. Pronounced yellow stamens. Upright but not tall. Foliage dark and crisp. The young wood especially is dark, with lots of thorns.

[P (C)]   5′ × 3′   1.5 m × 90 cm

'Bonica'   [M]

'Bonica'

Meilland FRANCE 1984

Parentage not recorded

The double flowers are made up of rather frilled petals of delicate pink with deeper centres; these are produced along strong arching stems throughout the summer. Foliage coppery-light green and glossy.

[P G (C)]   3′ × 6′   90 cm × 1.8 m

'Bonn'

Kordes GERMANY 1950

'Hamburg' × 'Independence'

Freely produced semi-double flowers of bright orange-red fading rather with age, though not offending the eye in so doing. A vigorous upright bush, with rich dark green foliage.

[P (C)]   6′ × 4′   1.8 × 1.2 m

'Butterfly Wings'

Gobbee UK 1976

'Dainty Maid' × 'Peace'

A beautiful rose. Large, refined, single flowers of blush-white with touches of red around their edges. Ample, dark green foliage. Not over-tall.

[▽ (C)]   4′ × 3′   1.2 m × 90 cm

'Cardinal Hume'

Harkness UK 1984

[('Lilac Charm' × 'Sterling Silver') × ('Orangeade' × 'Lilac Charm')] × [('Orange Sensation' × 'Allgold') × R. californica] × 'Frank Naylor'

A most unusual rose. The rich tyrian purple flowers, are double, made up of a multitude of many narrow petals, and borne in clusters which remain close to the plant, almost amongst the plentiful dark green foliage. Slightly wider than tall, but not wide enough to qualify as procumbent.

3′ × 4′   90 cm × 1.2 m

'Cocktail'

Meilland FRANCE 1959

('Independence' × 'Orange Triumph') × 'Phyllis Bide'

A bright rose with clusters of burnished red, single flowers each with yellow centres; the red intensifies with age. Upright, thorny growth with numerous, deep green, deeply serrated leaves.

[P H ◍ ▽ (C)]   6′ × 4′   1.8 × 1.2 m

'Copenhagen'

Poulsen DENMARK 1964

Seedling × 'Ena Harkness'

Double, scarlet flowers in clusters on an upright

'Cocktail'   [PB]

plant with good, bronzy foliage. Can also make a good, short-growing climber.

[(C)] 8′×4′ 2.5×1.2 m

'Dorothy Wheatcroft'

Tantau GERMANY 1960

Parentage unknown

Large, semi-double, bright red flowers, made up of petals that are slightly crimped on their outer edges. These are borne in large clusters on a vigorous, well-foliated, thorny shrub.

[P (C)] 5′×4′ 1.5×1.2 m

'Elmshorn'

Kordes GERMANY 1951

'Hamburg' × 'Verdun'

Large clusters of smallish, vivid pink, double flowers on a vigorous bush, carrying abundant, slightly crinkled, dark greyish-green foliage. A very good, free-flowering shrub rose, deservedly popular.

[P H ◍ ▽ (C)] 5′×4′ 1.5×1.2 m

'Erfurt'

Kordes GERMANY 1939

'Eva' × 'Réveil Dijonnais'

Single flowers of rich, cerise pink, paling towards the centre to almost white; prominent brown anthers. The rather beautiful flowers are enhanced by healthy, plentiful coppery-green foliage. Stems are coppery-brown with numerous hooked thorns. An outstanding shrub rose.

[P H ◍ (C)] 5′×4′ 1.5×1.2 m

'Fountain'

Tantau GERMANY 1972

Parentage unknown

Sizable, blood-red flowers in clusters on a medium-growing shrub with thick, dark green foliage. A good, healthy variety.

[P H ▽ (C)] 5′×4′ 1.5×1.2 m

'Erfurt'   [PB]

Above: 'Elmshorn' (flower 1½ times actual size) [VP]
Below: 'Fritz Nobis' [PB]

'Frank Naylor'

Harkness UK 1978
[('Orange Sensation' × 'Allgold') × ('Little
Lady' × 'Lilac Charm')] × [('Blue Moon' ×
'Magenta') × ('Cläre Grammerstorf' ×
'Frühlingsmorgen')]
Clusters of single red flowers with yellow centres.
Good, healthy, dense growth. Foliage long and
reddish-green. A very good shorter-growing
shrub rose where a bright colour is needed.
[P H ▽ (C)] 4′×3′ 1.2 m×90 cm

'Fred Loads'

Holmes UK 1968
'Dorothy Wheatcroft' × 'Orange Sensation'
Large, almost single blooms in large impressive
trusses, rich, bright, salmon-pink. A vigorous and
upright rose with large, leathery leaves.
[P H (C)] 5′×4′ 1.5×1.2 m

'Fritz Nobis'

Kordes GERMANY 1940
'Joanna Hill' × 'Magnifica'
A beautiful rose, flowering only once each
season, but nonetheless useful. A dense shrub,
extremely healthy, with small but numerous
grey-green leaves. Flowers are soft blush-pink to
quiet salmon, fully double and produced in great
abundance; followed in autumn by an impressive crop of small but colourful orange hips.
[P H F ◍ (S)] 5′×4′ 1.5×1.2 m

'Graham Thomas'

Austin UK 1983
(Seedling × 'Charles Austin') × (seedling × 'Iceberg')
Fully double, old-fashioned-type cupped flowers
of rich yellow, on a vigorous, slightly arching
plant with good foliage. Scented. I have not yet
had much experience of growing this rose, but
the name is recommendation in itself.
[(C)] 4′×4′ 1.2×1.2 m

'Grandmaster'

Kordes GERMANY 1954
'Sangerhausen' × 'Sunmist'
Pointed buds opening to large, semi-double
flowers of apricot-pink with lemon shadings.
Scented. Foliage light green on a bushy plant.
[(C)] 5′×4′ 1.5×1.2 m

'Heidelberg'

Kordes GERMANY 1958
'World's Fair' × 'Floradora'
Very bright rose, crimson-scarlet splashed deep
orange, fully double, produced in large trusses.
Foliage dark green and tough-looking.
[P (C)] 6′×5′ 1.8×1.5 m

'Heritage' [VP]

'Hero'

Austin UK 1982

Large, cupped, bright pink, fragrant flowers, of the old-fashioned style, produced on a strong-growing open shrub throughout the summer.

[P (R)]   5′×4′   1.5×1.2 m

'Heritage'

Austin UK 1984

Double, medium-sized, cupped flowers of pure blush-pink. A beautiful rose with a superb but unusual scent described by its raiser as reminiscent of lemon. A robust, bushy grower, with healthy foliage. Flowers freely throughout the summer.

[P (R)]   4′×4′   1.2×1.2 m

'Joseph's Coat'

Armstrong & Swim USA 1964

'Buccaneer' × 'Circus'

Often listed as a climber, I feel it is better as a free-standing shrub or, at most, a pillar rose. Loosely formed flowers from shapely buds, borne in large trusses on a thorny, upright plant with light green, glossy foliage.

[P H (C)]   5′×4′   1.5×1.2 m

'Kassel'

Kordes GERMANY 1957

'Obergärtner Wiebicke' × 'Independence'

Trusses of closely spaced, double flowers on

'Hero' [VP]

'Joseph's Coat'   [VP]

'La Sevillana'

Meilland FRANCE 1982
Parentage not recorded
Very healthy, abundant rich red, semi-double
flowers which hold their colour well, even in hot
sun. Rich dark green foliage.
[H P G (C)]   4′ × 5′   1.2 × 1.5 m

'Lady Sonia'

Mattock UK 1961
'Grandmaster' × 'Doreen'
A free-flowering, semi-double rose of deep

strong stems; orange-scarlet deepening with age
to bright red. Foliage leathery, slightly glossy.
Upright bushy growth. Stems brownish-red.
[P H (C)]   5′ × 4′   1.5 × 1.2 m

'Kathleen Ferrier'

Buisman HOLLAND 1952
'Gartenstolz' × 'Shot Silk'
Small clusters of semi-double, rich salmon-pink
flowers. Vigorous and upright growth with dark
green, glossy foliage.
[H (C)]   5′ × 4′   1.5 × 1.2 m

Above: 'Kassel' and *below:* 'Lafter'   [PB/JB]

'Lafter'

Brownell USA 1948
['V for Victory' × ('Général Jacqueminot' × 'Dr
Van Fleet')] × 'Pink Princess'
A most useful shrub. Clusters of semi-double,
rather loosely formed flowers of salmon pink and
apricot, with hints of yellow. Foliage dark green,
slightly glossy but leathery. Upright but bushy
growth.
[P H (C)]   5′ × 4′   1.5 × 1.2 m

golden-yellow. Shapely in bud and well formed when open. Foliage dark and leathery. Growth upright and free-branching.

[P (C)]   5′ × 4′   1.5 × 1.2 m

'Magenta'

Kordes GERMANY 1954
Yellow Floribunda seedling × 'Lavender Pinocchio'

A moderately vigorous shrub bearing double flowers of unusual shades, fawn and purple with pink and lilac highlights, opening flat in the old-fashioned form and produced in large clusters. Foliage dark green and growth openly bushy.

[H (C)]   5′ × 4′   1.5 × 1.2 m

'Märchenland'

Tantau GERMANY 1951
'Swantje' × 'Hamburg'

Very large trusses of well-spaced, almost single flowers, bright pink with deeper shadings. Very free-flowering. Foliage dark green, slightly glossy and plentiful. Upright bushy growth. This is a most underrated shrub rose.

[P (C)]   5′ × 4′   1.5 × 1.2 m

'Marjorie Fair'

Harkness UK 1978
'Ballerina' × 'Baby Faurax'

A good shorter shrub rose bred from 'Ballerina', and which could perhaps be included among the Hybrid Musks. The flowers, which are produced in large trusses, are small, single and red with a pinkish-white eye. Foliage plentiful and mid-green. Growth bushy and tidy.

[H P ▽ ◍ (C)]   4′ × 3′   1.2 m × 90 cm

Above: 'Magenta' and *below:* 'Märchenland'   [PB/PB]

'Marjorie Fair', and *right:* 'Nymphenburg'   [RCB/VP]

'Mary Rose'

Austin UK 1983
Seedling × 'The Friar'
Large, flesh to rose-pink flowers in the old-fashioned-mould. Highly scented. Bush robust and twiggy, with ample foliage, tolerating hard pruning if desired.

[▽ (C)]   4′ × 4′   1.2 × 1.2 m

'Nymphenburg'

Kordes GERMANY 1954
'Sangerhausen' × 'Sunmist'
A vigorous upright shrub or pillar rose. Semi-double flowers, salmon-pink with lemon and deeper pink highlights. Very free-flowering. Foliage dark green and glossy.

[P H (C)]   6′ × 4′   1.8 × 1.2 m

'Parkjuwel', 'Parkjewel'

Kordes GERMANY 1956
'Independence' × a red Moss Rose
A vigorous, shrubby plant with wrinkled, rather

leathery foliage and good well mossed buds. Flowers large, very double, globular, light soft pink. Loses nothing by not repeating.

[P H ◍ ▽ (S)] 6′×4′ 1.8×1.2 m

'Poulsen's Park Rose'

Poulsen DENMARK
'Great Western' × 'Karen Poulsen'
An outstanding shrub, vigorous, dense and broad in habit with trusses of large, shapely, silvery pink flowers and good clean dark green foliage.

[P ◍ (R)] 6′×6′ 2×2 m

'Rachel Bowes Lyon'

Harkness UK 1981
'Kim' × ('Orange Sensation' × 'Allgold') × *R. californica*
Semi-double, peachy-pink flowers of medium size in large clusters on medium-tall but bushy, well-foliated plant.

[P H (C)] 5′×4′ 1.5×1.2 m

'Radway Sunrise'

Waterhouse Nurseries UK 1962
'Masquerade' seedling
A striking, moderately vigorous shrub bearing clusters of single flowers; these are a mixture of flame, cerise-pink and yellow. The colours are suffused to give the general effect of glowing warmth, eye-catching but not gaudy. Foliage dark green and glossy.

[P H ▽ (C)] 4′×3′ 1.2 m×90 cm

'Roundelay'

Swim USA 1953
'Charlotte Armstrong' × 'Floradora'
An upright, free-flowering shrub with large trusses of cardinal-red flowers, fully double, opening flat. Has a good perfume. Healthy, dark green foliage. Deserves more attention.

[P H (C)] 4′×3′ 1.2 m×90 cm

'Sally Holmes'

Holmes UK 1976
'Ivory Fashion' × 'Ballerina'
A short-growing, almost Floribunda-type rose with an upright habit and good foliage. Trusses of single flowers of soft, pale pink to white.

[H ▽ (C)] 4′×3′ 1.2 m×90 cm

'Sparrieshoop'

Kordes GERMANY 1953
('Baby Château' × 'Else Poulsen') × 'Magnifica'
An interesting shrub with pointed buds opening to large, pale pink flowers, borne in trusses but sometimes singly. Upright bushy growth and healthy foliage.

[P ◍ (R)] 5′×4′ 1.5×1.2 m

'Till Uhlenspiegel'

Kordes GERMANY 1950
'Holstein' × 'Magnifica'
An arching tall shrub with large almost burnished, glossy green leaves. Large single flowers, glowing dark red with white centres. Scented.

[P ◍ (S)] 10′×8′ 3×2.5 m

'Uncle Walter'

McGredy UK 1963
'Detroiter' × 'Heidelberg'
Hybrid Tea-shaped flowers borne in clusters and opening to an attractively muddled shape; bright red, good for cutting. Foliage is dark green and plentiful. Often listed as a Hybrid Tea, but is much too vigorous and is better placed amongst shrub roses.

[P H (C)] 5′×4′ 1.5×1.2 m

'White Spray'

LeGrice UK 1974
Seedling × 'Iceberg'
A superb white variety deserving of more attention. An accommodating sized shrub with good, mid-green foliage. Flowers white to cream, fully double, shapely and produced in large clusters on a bushy plant.

[P H ▽ ◍ (C)] 4′×4′ 1.2×1.2 m

'Wife of Bath'

Austin UK 1969
('Mme Caroline Testout' × 'Ma Perkins') × 'Constance Spry'
Shorter-growing, small shrub rose of bushy habit with ample foliage. Fully double, old-fashioned-type flowers of warm rich pink. One of a range of very interesting roses bred by David Austin by crossing older roses with modern Hybrid Teas and Floribundas. David calls these, appropriately, 'English roses'. Many varieties in this range are shorter than shrubs in the accepted sense but have flowers in the old-fashioned style and many bloom for a very long season.

[P H ▽ (C)]   3′ × 3′   90 × 90 cm

'Yesterday'

Harkness UK 1974
('Phyllis Bide' × 'Shepherd's Delight') ×
'Ballerina'
An aptly named variety. Masses of small, almost single, rich pinky-purple, slightly scented flowers in large trusses on a sturdy, rather spreading bush.

[P G H ▽ ◍ (C)]   4′ × 4′   1.2 × 1.2 m

Above: 'White Spray'   [PB]
Below: 'Yesterday'   [VP]

Polyantha Roses

The first Polyantha rose issued from the marriage of a low-growing form of *R. multiflora* with an unknown hybrid China. This marriage was consummated with the help of Jean Sisley of Lyon, France, who raised several seedlings, the best of which was a white remontant rose introduced by the nurseryman Guillot, also of Lyon, under the name 'Paquerette' in 1875. 'Mignonette', sent out by Guillot in 1880, is probably the earliest of these roses still available; they were given the botanical classification *R. rehderiana*, now obsolete. Even enlightened rosarians such as Sisley and Guillot could not have realized the significance of this work, which was to lead on almost directly to the modern Floribundas or Cluster-Flowered Roses.

The Polyanthas were very popular in their day and, although their popularity has steadily declined since World War II, there are now signs of a well-deserved revival. They are happy-go-lucky

'Paquerette' [RCB]

little roses, producing clusters of small, slightly cupped, semi-double flowers throughout the summer. Many varieties have been introduced since 1875, but most of these have disappeared for ever. Of those that remain, I have selected the following seven as being representative. The others, which are equally attractive and garden-worthy, are too alike to be described in detail. From time to time a completely different colour will appear among the flowers of some varieties; this is because they frequently revert or sport back to others of their ancestry. These roses have many uses in today's gardens, from group planting to individual specimens at the front of borders and shrubberies. Some of the most relaxed types also make excellent subjects as partial ground cover. All are good for patios and growing in pots.

'Cameo'

de Ruiter HOLLAND 1932

'Orléans Rose' sport

Dense, clusters of small, semi-double, cupped flowers of soft salmon pink, deepening with age; these are produced on stocky, bushy plants which have strong shoots, these bearing a few large, cruel thorns and many smaller, kinder ones. Foliage plentiful and light greyish-green.

[P G H ◍ ▽ (C)]   2′×2′   60×60 cm

'Gloria Mundi'

de Ruiter HOLLAND 1929

'Superb' sport

Similar to 'Cameo' in flower shape and form, except with slightly fewer petals. Rich, scarlet-red with occasional flecks of white on the inner petals. Upright growth. Foliage dark green.

[P G H ◍ ▽ (C)]   2′×2′   60×60 cm

'Golden Salmon Superior'

de Ruiter HOLLAND 1926

'Superb' sport

Of similar flower formation and growth habit to the previous two but with a strong, orange-salmon colouring. One of the best for a massed, bright effect.

[P G H ◍ ▽ (C)]   2′×2′   60×60 cm

'Katharina Zeimet', 'White Baby Rambler'

P. Lambert GERMANY 1901

'Etoile de Mai' × 'Marie Parvie'

Rather different from others in that the flowers, although in large clusters, are more widely spaced. Growth too is more angular, the foliage darker and perhaps less dense.

[P G H (C)]   2′×2′   60×60 cm

'Mignonette'

Guillot Fils FRANCE 1880

R. chinensis × R. multiflora

Small, globular, double, blush-pink to white flowers, borne in large clusters. Plant dwarf and compact. Probably the earliest bred Polyantha still available.

[G P]   1′×1′   30×30 cm

'Miss Edith Cavell'

de Ruiter HOLLAND 1917

'Orléans Rose' sport

Rich red to scarlet sometimes overlaid crimson. Flowers in clusters, globular in bud, opening semi-double and flattish. Foliage dark green, stems slightly lighter. Like others of its race, has little or no scent.

[P G H (C)]   2′×2′   60×60 cm

1985 was the 70th anniversary of the execution of Nurse Edith Cavell. For a time we lived near her birthplace, the village of Swardeston, near

Norwich; in fact, I started my nursery less than a quarter of a mile from her house. As part of the planned commemorative events, the vicar of Swardeston, Rev. Philip McFadyen, asked me if I could obtain some plants of the 'Cavell' rose for him to plant in the village. After an initial search and enquiries in the rose trade, I was forced to conclude that the rose had become extinct.

Philip, believing that even a rose has a life hereafter, set about proving it by writing to the *Eastern Daily Press*, while I sped all over Norfolk looking at potential resurrections, none of them this elusive rose. Finally I called on a charming and spritely octogenarian, Mrs Doris Levine, at Brundall, a village adjacent to the Norfolk Broads. She and her late husband George had been given half a dozen plants of 'Miss Edith Cavell' soon after they were married in 1934. Two years later they moved house, taking the roses with them. Fifty years on, only one rather gnarled bush remained alive; from this I was able to propagate some ten plants and the life of another, almost extinct rose was rekindled, together with a little bit of Norfolk heritage.

'The Fairy'

Bentall UK 1932

'Paul Crampel' × 'Lady Gay' (not a 'Lady Godiva' sport, as often stated)

After a spell in obscurity, this rose is currently enjoying a new lease of life, and deservedly so. The small, globular, pink flowers are produced in profusion all over a dense, spreading bush with attractive foliage. It is procumbent enough to be used for partial ground cover as well as for group planting and patio work.

[P G H ◍ ▽ (C)] 2′ × 4′ 60 cm × 1.2 m

'Miss Edith Cavell' (see text p. 297)

[PB]

Floribunda (Cluster-Flowered) Roses

These are the natural successors in line from the 'Polyantha' roses; many could be used as small shrubs in shrubberies and herbaceous borders, and some make attractive hedges. I do not intend, tempting though it is, to go into great detail on these, and have therefore confined the list to those which I consider important enough to be placed in the context of shrub roses generally, or those old and beautiful enough to warrant inclusion as Old-Fashioned roses. I have taken licence and included roses which, in some older books, are described as 'Polypompons' and 'Hybrid Polyanthas', some even as 'Polyanthas'.

'Centenaire de Lourdes', 'Mrs Jones'
Delbard-Chabert FRANCE 1958
('Frau Karl Druschki' × seedling) × unnamed seedling
This is a very good rose which should be more widely grown. Shapely buds open to large, semi-double flowers of soft pink suffused with deeper pink and coral. Petals are waved, particularly at the edges. Very free-flowering. Foliage dark green and glossy, and growth bushy. A good bed of these can be seen at Castle Howard, Yorkshire.
[P ▽ (C)]   3′ × 2′   90 × 60 cm

'Chinatown'   [PB]

'Chanelle'
McGredy UK 1959
'Ma Perkins' × ('Fashion' × 'Mrs William Sprott')
An interesting and beautiful combination of cream, buff and pink. Semi-double flowers open cup-shaped, and are produced very freely on a bushy plant with ample, dark green foliage.
[P ▽ (C)]   3′ × 2′   90 × 60 cm

'Chinatown', 'Ville de Chine'
Poulsen DENMARK 1963
'Columbine' × 'Cläre Grammerstorf'
Very double, clear yellow flowers with pink and sometimes red shadings. An upright, tall rose with fine, crisp, light green foliage. Also makes a very good specimen shrub.
[P H ◐ ▽ (C)]   5′ × 3′   1.5 m × 90 cm

'Dainty Maid'
LeGrice UK 1940
'D. T. Poulsen' × unknown
An upright-growing, vigorous rose with large trusses of single, pink flowers with deeper reverses and pronounced golden brown stamens. Large, dark foliage and strong stems.
[P H ▽ (C)]   3′ × 2′   90 × 60 cm

Above: 'Escapade'
Below: 'Lady Romsey' (see text p. 302)

'Escapade'

Harkness UK 1967

'Pink Parfait' × 'Baby Faurax'

Vigorous and upright in growth with profuse, mid to light green foliage. Semi-double, lavender to lilac-pink flowers, discreetly perfumed, and produced abundantly in large clusters.

[N P ◍ ▽ (C)] 4′×3′ 1.2 m×90 cm

'Everest Double Fragrance'

Beales UK 1979

('Elizabeth of Glamis' × 'Dearest') × 'Sarah Van Fleet'

A special feature of this rose is the very strong perfume. Flowers large, almost fully-double, often opening in rather quartered fashion from well-shaped buds. Colour a pleasing combination of coral-pink, cream and blush-white. Foliage plentiful, large and leathery. Shoots thick and thorny. Recently I have noticed a slight proneness to rust on this rose.

[P H ▽ (C)] 4′×3′ 1.2 m×90 cm

'Frensham'

Norman UK 1946

Floribunda seedling × 'Crimson Glory'

A vigorous, angular shrub with strong, thorny stems and abundant, dark green foliage. Rather prone to mildew, but this can be controlled. Flowers shapely in bud, opening to semi-double, clear red, produced in small clusters.

[H (C)] 5′×4′ 1.5×1.2 m

'Greensleeves'

Harkness UK 1980

('Rudolph Timm' × 'Arthur Bell') × [('Pascali' × 'Elizabeth of Glamis') × ('Sabine' × 'Violette Dot')]

The flowers are a unique combination of greens, with shades of purple and buff, produced in large clusters. The foliage, oddly enough, is also green, and the plant is vigorous. Good for cutting and conversation.

[P ◍ ▽ (C)] 3′×2′ 90×60 cm

'Gruss an Aachen'

Geduldig GERMANY 1909

'Frau Karl Druschki' × 'Frans Deegen'

A superb little rose. I am constantly baffled as to why it has not been more widely grown since its introduction seventy-odd years ago. The flowers are shapely, double, creamy-white and borne in clusters throughout the season. The plant is short and bushy with plenty of dark green foliage.

[▽ (C)] 2′×2′ 60×60 cm

'Horstmann's Rosenresli'

Kordes GERMANY 1955

'Rudolph Timm' × 'Lavender Pinocchio'

Trusses of double flowers opening rather muddled but adding to the charm of this very useful rose. Creamy-white flowers combine with crisp, light green foliage to give an excellent display for most of the summer.

[P H ◍ ▽ (C)] 3′×2′ 90×60 cm

'Gruss an Aachen'   [VP]

'Iceberg', 'Schneewittchen'

Kordes GERMANY 1958

'Robin Hood' × 'Virgo'

This superb white rose is deservedly well known. Small, shapely buds open to semi-double flowers produced in profusion throughout the summer. Left unpruned, it makes a good-sized shrub. Foliage light green and glossy.

[H P ◍ ▽ (C)] 5′×3′ 1.5 m×90 cm

'Horstmann's Rosenresli' (see text p. 301)   [PB]

'Jenny Wren'

Ratcliffe UK 1957

'Cécile Brunner' × 'Fashion'

A pleasing yellow rose akin to the Chinas. Shapely buds open to semi-double flowers of soft lemon. Foliage dark green and abundant. In many ways like 'Perle d'Or', but more yellow.

[P ⊕ ▽ (C)]   3′ × 2′   90 × 60 cm

'Lady Romsey'

Beales UK 1985

('Ivory Fashion' × 'Dearest') × seedling

A charming, soft creamy-white with hints of soft pink. Shapely buds open to semi-double flowers displaying golden anthers to advantage. Scented. Growth vigorous and tidy. Foliage dark green, crisp with a muted gloss. Very healthy.

[P ▽ (C)]   2′ × 2′   60 × 60 cm

'Léonie Lamesch'

P. Lambert GERMANY 1899

'Aglaia' × 'Kleiner Alfred'

One of the first polyanthas placed here though as it was ahead of its time when introduced. A short variety with rather stubby growth but ample, leathery, dark green foliage. Flowers are small, fully double, borne in clusters and an odd mixture of yellow, orange and red.

[P ▽ (C)]   2′ × 2′   60 × 60 cm

'Lilac Charm'

LeGrice UK 1962

Parentage unknown

A real charmer. This short-growing, bushy rose with good, matt, dark green foliage has beautiful single, or almost single flowers of rich lilac with pronounced amber stamens. Free-flowering and scented.

[▽ (C)]   2′ × 2′   60 × 60 cm

'Margaret Merril'

Harkness UK 1977

'Rudolph Timm' × ('Dedication' × 'Pascali')

Shapely buds, satin-pink to almost white, open to large, slightly less than double, scented flowers, displaying anthers to good effect. Growth bushy and upright with plentiful, dark green foliage.

[P H ▽ (C)]   4′ × 3′   1.2 m × 90 cm

'Marie-Jeanne'

Turbat FRANCE 1913

Parentage unknown

Clusters of fully double, rosette shaped flowers of soft pink to almost white with deeper coloured centres. Slightly scented. Foliage glossy light

'Margaret Merril'   [VP]

'Mountbatten' and *right:* 'Norwich Castle' (see text p. 304) [VP/JB]

green tinted bronze, especially when young. Vigorous. Can be left unpruned to produce an excellent, shortish shrub.

[H P ▽ ◍ (C)]   3′ × 3′   90 × 90 cm

'Marie Parvie'

Alégatière FRANCE 1888
Parentage unknown
Clusters of small, white to blush-pink flowers on an upright but bushy plant. Slightly short on foliage but free-flowering enough to compensate for this shortcoming.

[▽ (C)]   3′ × 2′   90 × 60 cm

'Mountbatten'

Harkness UK 1982
('Anne Cocker' × 'Arthur Bell') × 'Southampton'
Huge clusters of clear yellow, fully double flowers on an upright but thorny plant with good, clean, light green foliage. Probably better grown as shrub or specimen rose than as bedder. Also makes an excellent hedging rose.

[H P ◍ ▽ (C)]   5′ × 3′   1.5 m × 90 cm

'Nathalie Nypels', 'Mevrouw Nathalie Nypels'

Leenders HOLLAND 1919
'Orléans Rose' × ('Comtesse du Cayla' × *R. foetida bicolor*)
An exquisite older Floribunda bearing well-spaced clusters of semi-double, silky-textured, deep pink to salmon flowers on a bushy, slightly spreading, well-foliated plant.

[P H ▽ (C)]   3′ × 3′   90 × 90 cm

'Pink Parfait' and *below*: 'Plentiful'   [JB/JB]

'Norwich Castle'

Beales UK 1979
('Whisky Mac' × 'Arthur Bell') × 'Bettina'
Shapely buds opening to rich copper-orange and
changing to soft apricot with age. Flowers almost
fully double, subtly scented. Foliage dark green,
plant upright in habit.
[P H ▽ (C)]   4′ × 3′   1.2 m × 90 cm

'Pink Parfait'

Swim USA 1960
'First Love' × 'Pinocchio'
Very lovely with shapely buds opening to semi-
double blooms combining many shades of pink
and produced in large clusters. Foliage dark
green and abundant. Stems also dark green with
few thorns.
[P H ▽ (C)]   3′ × 3′   90 × 90 cm

'Plentiful'

LeGrice UK 1961
Parentage unknown
An unusual rose. Large trusses of very double,
sometimes quartered flowers on a rather spread-
ing, thorny plant. Foliage crisp and dark green.
Charming in the old-fashioned style.
[▽ (C)]   3′ × 3′   90 × 90 cm

'Queen Elizabeth', 'The Queen Elizabeth Rose'

Lammerts USA 1954
'Charlotte Armstrong' × 'Floradora'
Most people know this rose. Tall and upright with dark, almost purply-brown wood and large, dark green leaves. Pointed buds held on long stems; flower, when open, semi-double and rich clear silvery-pink. Very healthy. When first introduced it was classified as a 'Grandiflora', a term that aptly describes this type of rose, viz. large flowers in large clusters on vigorous shoots, etc. Although this designation is, I believe, still commonly used in the USA and France, it has now been dropped in the UK. Such roses are grouped collectively with the Floribundas which, in turn, are now grouped in the garden group of Cluster-Flowered Roses.
[P H (C)]   6' × 3'   1.8   × 90 cm

'Rosemary Rose'

de Ruiter HOLLAND 1954
'Gruss an Teplitz' × a Floribunda seedling
Charming, fully double flower which opens flat in the old-fashioned style. Rich, cerise-red flowers are produced in huge, tightly packed clusters. Stems dark green, as are the large, leathery leaves. Rather sprawly in growth with a slight tendency to mildew, but most rewarding if these bad habits can be kept in check.
[▽ (C)]   3' × 3'   90 × 90 cm

'Rosenelfe'

Kordes GERMANY 1939
'Else Poulsen' × 'Sir Basil McFarland'
Medium-sized buds opening to high-centred, double flowers of silvery-pink, well scented and produced in great abundance. Foliage light green, leathery and glossy. Growth vigorous and bushy. I am grateful to Mrs Campion of Norwich for giving me this rose.
[P H ◍ ▽ (C)]   5' × 3'   1.5 m × 90 cm

'Southampton'

Harkness UK 1972
('Anne Elizabeth' × 'Allgold') × 'Yellow Cushion'
Tall and upright with thorny stems and glossy, dark, bronzy-green foliage. The double flowers, which are produced in medium-sized clusters, are bright, yellowish-orange with darker tints.
[P H (C)]   4' × 3'   1.2 m × 90 cm

'Southampton'　　　　　　　　　　　　　[VP]

'White Pet', 'Little White Pet'

P. Henderson USA 1879
'Félicité et Perpétue' sport
Large clusters of small, white, fully-double, rosette flowers on a bushy plant which is abundantly clothed in dark green foliage. A useful and superb little rose for any garden. Should strictly be under forms of R. sempervirens, but as the only dwarf in that section is better placed here.
[P G ◍ ▽ (C)]   2' × 2'   60 × 60 cm

'Little White Pet'　　　　　　　　　　　[JB]

'Yvonne Rabier'

Turbat FRANCE 1910
R. wichuraiana × a Polyantha rose
Often listed amongst Polyanthas but its flowers are larger and the plant taller. Its true place would be among Wichuraiana hybrids, but in garden terms it is too short for this. Semi-double, pure white blooms in clusters on a healthy, well-foliated plant. Leaves light rich green; the stems, which are also light green, are almost free of thorns.
[P G ◍ ▽ (C)]   3' × 2'   90 × 60 cm

Cluster-Flowered Roses
as Climbers

Just as with the Large-Flowered Roses, Cluster-Flowered Roses occasionally produce climbing sports. For some reason, these are not nearly as numerous as climbing Hybrid Teas, but since Floribunda numbers are fewer, I suspect they occur in roughly the same ratio. I describe six, again not necessarily as my favourites, but as a representative selection of those which should be available commercially. They should not be ignored since they provide a profusion of flowers on a very vigorous plant, and therefore have a wider application than some of the more modern, long-flowering climbers, that often lack climbing ability.

'Allgold' Climber
Bush form LeGrice UK 1958
'Goldilocks' × 'Ellinor LeGrice'
This form Gandy UK 1961
An excellent climber and, since good yellow climbers are scarce, well worth consideration where such a colour is needed. Clear yellow, almost unfading flowers open to semi-double blooms produced in upright clusters on strong stems. Leaves small but numerous, rich dark green. Flowers slightly scented.
[P (S)]   15′ × 10′   4.5 × 3 m

'Fashion' Climber
Bush form Boerner USA 1949
'Pinocchio' × 'Crimson Glory'
This form Boerner USA 1951
Another identical climbing form introduced by Mattock UK in 1955
This rose has fallen from favour as a bush because of its proneness to rust, but this does not seem to be a problem for the climbing form, probably because of its extra vigour. Clusters of double, bright coral-salmon flowers in profusion on a fairly thornless plant with coppery-green shoots and foliage.
[P ⁙ (S)]   15′ × 10′   4.5 × 3 m

'Iceberg' Climber, 'Schneewittchen'
Bush form Kordes GERMANY 1958
'Robin Hood' × 'Virgo'
This form Cant UK 1968
A shortage of good white climbers justifies the inclusion of this rose, which retains all the good qualities of the bush with the added dimensions of a climber. Freely produced, large trusses of almost double, pure white flowers. Climbing shoots almost thornless with crisp, shiny, pale green leaves.
[P N ◍ (S)]   18′ × 10′   5.5 × 3 m

'Korona' Climber
Bush form Kordes GERMANY 1955
'Obergärtner Wiebicke' × 'Independence'
This form Kordes GERMANY 1957
Clusters of semi-double, bright orange-scarlet flowers on a vigorous, fairly thorny plant with dark green foliage. Rather bright for my taste but included for its remarkable resistance to rain and bad weather.
[P N ◍ (S)]   15′ × 10′   4.5 × 3 m

'Masquerade' Climber
Bush form Boerner USA 1949
'Goldilocks' × 'Holiday'
This form Gregory UK 1958
Clusters of semi-double flowers opening soft yellow, changing to soft pink and then to almost crimson as they age. Vigorous, moderately thorny stems. Dark green foliage.
[P (S)]   18′ × 10′   5.5 × 3 m

'Queen Elizabeth' Climber
Bush form Lammerts USA 1954
'Charlotte Armstrong' × 'Floradora'
This form Wheatcroft UK 1960
A very vigorous climber, almost too vigorous since its flowers are often borne too high up in the branches to be enjoyed. Flowers rich, clear silvery-pink, produced in large clusters. Foliage large, healthy and dark green.
[P (S)]   20′ × 10′   6 × 3 m

Procumbent and Semi-procumbent Roses

Over recent years several varieties of roses have been developed with tendencies to grow more broad than tall. These have diverse uses, from creeping along the ground to cascading down banks and drooping from tubs and urns. They also make useful subjects for under-planting amongst other taller roses. I have already said that the term 'ground cover' is misleading, and I have tried to avoid its use, at least in the literal sense. Scattered throughout the book are other Procumbent roses that are placed in their rightful position among the families to which they belong. The following are those which, through hybridity, are of mixed parentage and difficult to classify. It seems right, therefore, to group these together under this heading.

'Candy Rose'
Meilland FRANCE 1983
Parentage not recorded
Small clusters of medium-sized, semi-double flowers of salmon-pink with paler centres. A most pleasing variety with mid-green, glossy foliage.
[H P G ◍ (C)]   4′ × 6′   1.2 × 1.8 m

'Fairy Changeling'
Harkness UK 1979
'The Fairy' × 'Yesterday'
Variable shades of pink, appearing together, give this rose a charm of its own. Foliage burnished green. Growth twiggy and dense.
[P G ▽ (R)]   1½′ × 2′   45 × 60 cm

'Fairy Damsel'
Harkness UK 1981
'The Fairy' × 'Yesterday'
Deep red flowers amid well-foliated shoots that spread quite densely over the ground.
[P G ▽ (R)]   2′ × 5′   60 m × 1.5 m

'Fairyland'
Harkness UK 1980
'The Fairy' × 'Yesterday'
Cupped, double, rose-pink flowers with a strong fragrance. A good, spreading variety with dense, glossy foliage.
[P G ▽ (R)]   2′ × 5′   60 cm × 1.5 m

'Ferdy'
Keitoli JAPAN 1985
Parentage not recorded
Large, cascading clusters of double, salmon to fuchsia-pink flowers on a vigorous, spreading, healthy plant with numerous light green leaves and dark, thorny shoots. Best in early summer.
[P G ◍ (R)]   3′ × 6′   90 cm × 1.8 m

'Nozomi' and 'American Pillar' at the Botanic Gardens, Dublin   [RCB]
Below: 'Grouse'   [RCB]

'Fiona'

Meilland FRANCE 1983
Parentage not recorded
A tallish shrub but pendulous enough for use as semi-procumbent rose. Flowers deep blood red, semi-double, produced freely throughout summer. Foliage dark green and glossy.

[P G H ◍ (C)]   4′×6′   1.2×1.8 m

'Grouse'

Kordes GERMANY 1984
'The Fairy' × *R. wichuraiana* seedling
A vigorous, sprawling shrub with glossy, mid-green foliage bearing large clusters of small, semi-double, pale pink flowers. Growth seldom exceeds 2′ (60 cm) high but the plant spreads over a considerable area, making this and its companion 'Partridge' fairly efficient ground covering roses.

[P G ◍ (R)]   2′×10′   60 cm×3 m

'Nozomi'

Onodera JAPAN 1968
'Fairy Princess' × 'Sweet Fairy'
A spreading, dense plant with small, burnished green leaves and numerous hooked thorns. Ideal for cascading and quite good as a dense, weeping standard. Small, single, pearly-pink flowers, freely produced in midsummer.

[P G ◍ ▽ (S)]   2′×6′   60 cm×1.8 m

'Partridge'

Kordes GERMANY 1984
'The Fairy' × *R. wichuraiana* seedling
In all respects similar to 'Grouse' except that its flowers are white.

[P G ◍ (R)]   2′×10′   60 cm×3 m

'Pearl Drift'

LeGrice UK 1983
'Mermaid' × 'New Dawn'
Semi-double, white shaded pearl-pink blooms
massed amid attractive, glossy foliage. A very
pleasing rose.

[P G ⦿ ▽ (R)]   3′ × 2′   90 cm × 1.2 m

'Pink Bells', 'Red Bells', 'White Bells'

Poulsen DENMARK 1980
'Mini Poul' × 'Temple Bells'
Admirable little shrub roses with dense shoots
and glossy, dark green foliage. Flowers small and
rather bell-shaped, as their names suggest, are
borne in profusion throughout the summer.

[G ▽ (C)]   2′ × 4′   60 cm × 1.2 m

'Pink Wave'

Mattock UK 1983
'Moon Maiden' × 'Eye Paint'
A profusion of double, soft pink flowers on a
spreading plant with abundant, glossy foliage.

[P G ⦿ ▽ (C)]   3′ × 4′   90 cm × 1.2 m

'Rosy Cushion' (see text p. 310)   [VP]

'Swany' (see text p. 310)   [VP]

'Snow Carpet' (see text p. 310)   [VP]

'Red Blanket'
Ilsink UK 1979
'Yesterday' × unknown seedling
Medium-sized, single, reddish-pink flowers, produced in profusion on a vigorous, rather sprawly plant with good, dark green, glossy foliage.

[P G ⦾ ▽ (R)]   3′ × 4′   90 cm × 1.2 m

'Rosy Cushion'
Ilsink UK 1979
'Yesterday' × unknown seedling
Large, almost single, reddish-pink flowers, produced in great numbers on an arching, spreading plant with dark green foliage.

[P G ⦾ ▽ (C)]   3′ × 4′   90 cm × 1.2 m

'Smarty'
Ilsink UK 1979
'Yesterday' × unknown seedling
Medium-sized, single, reddish-pink flowers, produced in abundance. Foliage dark green and glossy.

[P G ⦾ ▽ (R)]   3′ × 4′   90 cm × 1.2 m

'Snow Carpet'
McGredy NEW ZEALAND 1980
'New Penny' × 'Temple Bells'
Really a miniature rose, but its spreading, ground-hugging ability qualifies it for this section. Glossy foliage and very double, pure white flowers. A most effective and useful little rose.

[P G ⦾ ▽ (C)]   1′ × 3′   90 × 90 cm

'Swany'
Meilland FRANCE 1978
R. sempervirens × 'Mlle Marthe Carron'
An excellent rose. The very double, cupped, pure white flowers open flat and are produced in abundance amid glossy, bronzy-green foliage.

[P G ⦾ ▽ (C)]   3′ × 5′   90 cm × 1.5 m

'Temple Bells'
McGredy NEW ZEALAND 1971
R. wichuraiana × 'Blushing Jewel'
Small, almost single white flowers in great profusion amid small, glossy leaves. Very effective.

[G ⦾ ▽ (C)]   2′ × 4′   60 cm × 1.2 m

'Swany'

R. phoenicia

MIDDLE EAST 1885

A very vigorous, slender growing climber with few thorns. Ample greyish-green leaves. White flowers in large corymbs. Hips small, round and dark red. Not easy to grow but interesting enough to warrant the effort. Has a particular liking for dry, sandy soils. An important if seldom seen species that is now recognized as part of the complex genealogy of *R.* × *centifolia.*

[(S)] 20′×10′ 6×3 m

R. × *polliniana*

CENTRAL EUROPE c. 1880

Single, blush-pink flowers on a sprawly plant with dark green stems and foliage. The stems are moderately thorny, not a contender for space in today's gardens, but could be useful in woodland.

[W P ◍ (S)] 15′×10′ 4.5×3 m

R. rubus, 'Blackberry Rose'

MIDDLE EAST 1907

A vigorous climber with numerous thorns, greenish-purple stems and glossy, dark green foliage. Young shoots are a clear purplish-red. Fragrant white flowers in large clusters, similar to those of the wild blackberry from which it gets its name. Small, round, red hips in profusion in autumn.

[P F T ⁖ (S)] 20′×15′ 6×4.5 m

R. sempervirens

These were known as evergreen roses in Victorian days and, indeed, they do retain their lush foliage in most winters. I suspect, like *R. arvensis*, this species has had more influence on our modern climbers than has ever been acknowledged. Most of the hybrids described here have been with us for many years; few, in fact, have been introduced since early Victorian times.

R. sempervirens

S. EUROPE 17th century

White, fragrant, single flowers produced in small clusters on a semi-vigorous plant. Foliage mid to dark green, as near evergreen as a rose can be. Small, orange-red fruit in late autumn.

[P W F T ◍ ≋ (C)] 15′×8′ 4.5×2.5 m

FORMS AND HYBRIDS OF *R. sempervirens*

'Adélaide d'Orléans'

Jacques FRANCE 1826

R. sempervirens hybrid

Clusters of small, shapely, semi-double, powder-pink to white flowers cascading in profusion from a well foliated, evergreen climber. Vigorous in a rather refined way.

[P T H ◍ (S)] 15′×10′ 4.5×3 m

'Félicité et Perpétue'

Jacques FRANCE 1827

Parentage unknown

Vigorous climber bearing clusters of small, creamy-white fully double, cupped, rosette-shaped flowers often with a hint of pink. Well scented. Makes an admirable climber, with dark green, glossy leaves offsetting the flowers to good

'Félicité et Perpétue' (see text p. 311)   [RCB]

effect. Relatively thornless. Often thought of, mistakenly, as the 'Seven Sisters Rose'. The dwarf form of this rose, 'White Pet' is described among the Cluster-Flowered roses, on page 305.

[P T N ◍ ≋ (S)]   15′ × 10′   4.5 × 3 m

'Flora'

Jacques FRANCE 1829
Parentage unknown
Good, medium-sized climber with dark green foliage and growth. The flowers, produced in clusters, are cupped, open flat and are full of small, folded petals. Colour lilac and soft whitish-pink. Has a refined perfume.

[P T N ◍ (S)]   12′ × 8′   3.5 × 2.5 m

'Princesse Louise'

Jacques FRANCE 1829
Parentage unknown
Double, cupped flowers of creamy-white with lilac-pink shadings. A beautiful rose produced in cascading clusters on a healthy, almost evergreen plant.

[P T N ◍ (S)]   12′ × 8′   3.5 × 2.5 m

'Princesse Marie'

Jacques FRANCE 1929
Parentage unknown
Large cascading clusters of cupped flowers filled with numerous shortish petals which open flattish but fully double and charmingly ragged. Colour bright pinkish lilac on an off-white ground. Foliage dark green on long pliable stems with few thorns.

[P T N ◍ (S)]   15′ × 10′   4.5 × 3 m

'Spectabilis'

c. 1850
Origin and parentage unknown
A useful, shorter growing, climbing rose with small, cupped, double flowers, creamy-lilac to white, produced in clusters, sometimes giving a surprise repeat performance later in the summer. Dark, almost evergreen foliage.

[P N ◍ (R)]   8′ × 6′   2.5 × 1.8 m

R. setigera

R. setigera, 'The Prairie Rose'

N. AMERICA 1810

A trailing but shrubby species with lightish green foliage and long, arching branches. The flowers, which are produced in clusters, are single, deep pink paling to soft pinkish-white, followed by small, globular, red hips.

[W F P G A ◍ ≋ (S)]   5′ × 6′   1.5 × 1.8 m

FORMS AND HYBRIDS OF
R. setigera

'Baltimore Belle'

Feast USA 1843

R. setigera × *R. gallica* hybrid

A healthy, climbing rose bearing smallish clusters of very double pale pink flowers in profusion. Foliage mid-green. Flowering somewhat later than most climbers and remains in flower for rather longer.

[P T N ◍ (S)]   15′ × 8′   4.5 × 2l m

R. setigera, 'Baltimore Belle'   [KM]

'Doubloons'

Howard USA 1934

R. setigera hybrid × *R. foetida bicolor* hybrid

Double, cupped flowers of deep rich yellow borne in clusters on strong, stout stems. Fragrant. Foliage plentiful and glossy mid-green. Sometimes repeats its flowers in the autumn.

[P T N ◍ (R)]   15′ × 8′   4.5 × 2.5 m

'Erinnerung an Brod', 'Souvenir de Brod'

Geschwind HUNGARY 1886

R. setigera hybrid

Only recently acquired, I have not, so far, met this variety as a mature plant. I include it because it crops up from time to time as a parent to other roses. Flowers double, deep pink to magenta-purple.

[P T N ◍ (S)]   12′ × 8′   3.5 × 2.5 m

'Jean Lafitte'

Horvath USA 1934

R. setigera seedling × 'Willowmere'

Rich green leathery foliage and strong stems among which are produced many rich pink, cupped, double flowers each with a good perfume.

[P T N ◍ (R)]   12′ × 8′   3.5 × 2.5 m

'Long John Silver'

Horvath USA 1934

R. setigera seedling × 'Sunburst'

This rose deserves more attention, being seldom seen, at least in Britain. Flowers large, double, and cupped rather like a small, silky-white water-lily, produced freely on strong stems amid large, leathery leaves. Very vigorous and scented.

[P T N ◍ ≋ (S)]   18′ × 10′   5.5 × 3 m

R. sinowilsonii

CHINA 1904

A large, climbing rose with superb, glossy, heavily veined foliage. Flowers white, large, single and produced in flat trusses followed by small, red fruit. Said not to be hardy but seems to survive our Norfolk winters.

[A F ◍ ≋ (S)]   12′ × 8′   3.5 × 2.5 m

HYBRID OF *R. sinowilsonii*

'Wedding Day' Climber

Stern UK 1950

R. sinowilsonii × unknown

An outstanding rose with bright green, glossy foliage and clear green, relatively thornless wood. Flowers large, compared with other such roses. These are single with prominent yellow stamens and are produced in large trusses. Growth is rampant, capable of considerable climbing when festooning trees, seeming not to mind the shade.

[P N T ◍ ≋ (S)]   30′ × 15′   9 × 4.5 m

R. soulieana

CHINA 1896

A vigorous, dense shrub with thin, arching branches bearing grey-green, rather fluffy foliage and numerous small spines. Single white flowers, produced in trusses, followed by bunches of oval, orange-red hips.

[P F W ◍ ≋ (S)]   10′ × 6′   3 × 1.8 m

FORMS AND HYBRIDS OF *R. soulieana*

'Kew Rambler'

Royal Botanic Gardens Kew UK 1912

R. soulieana × 'Hiawatha'

An interesting, vigorous rambler showing the influence of its seed parent *R. soulieana* in the small, plentiful, greyish-green foliage, and the influence of its pollen parent 'Hiawatha' in its shape and colour of its flowers, which are individually single, small, pink in colour with a central white eye, and produced in packed clusters. Stems thorny and stiffish but still pliable. Good orange hips in the autumn.

[W F T N ◍ ≋ (S)]   18′ × 12′   5.5 × 3.5 m

'Ohio'

Shepherd USA 1949

R. soulieana × 'Gruss an Teplitz' seedling

Interesting, recurrent rose, bushy but vigorous with semi-double, bright red flowers. Very hardy.

[H P ▽ (R)]   4′ × 3′   1.2 m × 90 cm

'Wickwar'

Steadman UK c. 1960

Seedling of *R. soulieana*

An unusual and pleasing rose which should perhaps have been given more attention in the 25 or so years since its introduction. Short to medium, dense-growing climber with small, greyish-green foliage. Medium-sized, single, clear pink flowers. Very fragrant.

[P N ◍ ≋ (S)]   8′ × 5′   2.5 × 1.5 m

R. wichuraiana

R. wichuraiana

CHINA 1860

An almost evergreen species, making a dense, procumbent shrub or climber. Foliage dark and glossy. Shoots dark and pliable. Flowers single, white, profusely if briefly produced, somewhat late, usually mid-July in this country. The small oval dark red hips are much enjoyed by birds.

[P G W ◍ ≋ (S)]   6′ × 20′   1.8 × 6 m

FORMS AND HYBRIDS OF
R. wichuraiana

R. wichuraiana has contributed much to modern roses, being directly or indirectly responsible for many ramblers and climbers, especially those with glossy foliage.* A number of breeders used them with much success around the turn of the century, and many a rusty iron arch remains standing, supported by such a rose planted fifty or more years ago. Apart from. a proneness to mildew in a few varieties, these are among our healthiest roses.

'Albéric Barbier'

Barbier FRANCE 1900

R. wichuraiana × 'Shirley Hibbard'

Superb glossy foliage produced on long, pliable stems. Flowers shapely, slightly scrolled in bud, opening to semi-double, creamy-white flushed lemon-yellow. Healthy. One of the best ramblers.

[P T N ◍ (S)]   15′ × 10′   4.5 × 3 m

'Albertine'

Barbier FRANCE 1921

R. wichuraiana × 'Mrs Arthur Robert Waddell'

A famous old rambler with glossy green leaves, heavily burnished with coppery-red, especially when young. Shoots vigorous, equipped with large, spiteful, hooked thorns. Very floriferous in full flush. Flowers open from shapely buds to rather muddled, full blooms of lobster pink each with a golden base, and paling to blush-pink with age. Highly scented. Rather prone to mildew, but usually after flowering.

[P T (S)]   15′ × 10′   4.5 × 3 m

'Alexander Girault'

Barbier FRANCE 1909

R. wichuraiana × 'Papa Gontier'

Vigorous with dark green, glossy foliage on pliable shoots. Very prostrate if not trained as a rambler. Flowers are double, opening flat with muddled centres. These are borne in clusters, and are a mixture of deep rose-pink and copper with hints of yellow. Has a strong, fruity scent.

[G P ◍ (S)]   12′ × 12′   3.5 × 3.5 m

* Having said this, Graham Thomas now believ that Rosa *luciae* was the parent of some of these hybrids and he puts forward some good and interesting reasons for this being so.

It could be that both R. *wichuraiana* and R. *luciae* were involved, with breeders in America and Europe using separately these two very similar species.

'Albertine' and *right:* 'Alexander Girault' [RCB/RCB]
(see text p. 315)

'Alida Lovett'

Van Fleet USA 1905

'Souvenir de Président Carnot' × *R. wichuraiana*

Fragrant, large, double flowers of soft shell-pink with yellow base; opening flat, and borne in clusters on a vigorous, relatively thornless plant with dark green, glossy foliage.

[P T (S)] 12′ × 10′ 3.5 × 3 m

'Améthyste'

Nonin FRANCE 1911

'Non Plus Ultra' sport

Trusses of tightly packed, double, violet to crimson flowers, produced on long, firm but arching shoots. Foliage glossy.

[P T N ◍ (S)] 12′ × 10′ 3.5 × 3 m

'American Pillar'

Van Fleet USA 1909

(*R. wichuraiana* × *R. setigera*) × 'Red Letter Day'

A vigorous, almost coarse rose with strong, thorny, green stems and large, glossy leaves.

Single flowers, at first reddish-pink, paling to deep pink with off-white centres, usually in large trusses.

[P T ◍ (S)]   15′ × 10′   4.5 × 3 m

'Auguste Gervais'

Barbier FRANCE 1918
R. wichuraiana × 'Le Progrès'
Very vigorous, with smallish but plentiful shiny dark green leaves. Flowers large by the standards of its type, semi-double, coppery-yellow suffused salmon, paling quickly with age to creamy-white. Very fragrant.

[N P T (S)]   12′ × 8′   3.5 × 2.5 m

'Aviateur Blériot'

Fauque FRANCE 1910
R. wichuraiana × 'William Allen Richardson'
Vigorous but more upright than most of its kind and rather less thorny. Large trusses of scented, double, orange-yellow flowers, fading to creamy-yellow with age. Foliage dark green, burnished bronze, healthy.

[P (S)]   12′ × 6′   3.5 × 1.8 m

'Breeze Hill'

Van Fleet USA 1926
R. wichuraiana × 'Beauté de Lyon'
Very double, cupped flowers, clear pink flushed tawny-orange, produced in clusters on a vigorous plant with glossy, dark green foliage. Not too well known but worth growing especially as a tree climber. An excellent specimen festoons an apple tree at Sheldon Manor, near Chippenham, Wiltshire, home of Major and Mrs Gibbs.

[P N T S ◍ ≋ (S)]   20′ × 12′   6 × 3.5 m

'Chaplin's Pink', 'Chaplin's Pink Climber'

Chaplin Bros UK 1928
'Paul's Scarlet' × 'American Pillar'
This rose of mixed pedigree might have been better placed among the Multiflora climbers but its main characteristics are derived from *R. wichuraiana*. Glossy, mid-green foliage and pliable growth. Flowers semi-double, bright, startling pink, accentuated by yellow stamens. Very free-flowering; not for those who like a quiet life.

[P N T ◍ (S)]   15′ × 10′   4.5 × 3 m

'Aviateur Blériot'   [VP]
'Chaplin's Pink Companion' (see text p. 318)   [JB]

'Chaplin's Pink Companion'

Chaplin & Sons UK 1961
'Chaplin's Pink' × 'Opera'
Semi-double flowers of bright silvery-pink. Less 'noisy' than 'Chaplin's Pink' but still brightly coloured. Foliage glossy dark green. Vigorous growth.

[P N T ◍ (S)]   15′ × 10′   4.5 × 3 m

'Crimson Showers'

Norman UK 1951
'Excelsa' seedling
Crimson, pompon-like blooms, slightly scented, in large, pendulous clusters on a wiry, vigorous plant. Foliage mid green and glossy.

[P T G ◍ (S)]   12′ × 8′   3.5 × 2.5 m

'Debutante'

Walsh USA 1902
R. wichuraiana × 'Baroness Rothschild'
Clusters of small, fragrant, fully-double blooms of soft rose-pink, borne amid dark green, glossy foliage to good effect. Vigorous, healthy and of slightly spreading habit.

[P G T ◍ (S)]   12′ × 10′   3.5 × 3 m

'Dorothy Perkins'

Jackson & Perkins USA 1902
R. wichuraiana × 'Gabriel Luizet'
A very famous rose known, by name at least, to most gardeners. Colourful cascades of clear pink flowers with the occasional almost white bloom among the cluster. Foliage, when free of mildew early in the season is bright, glossy dark green. Growth is pliable and semi-vigorous. Well scented.

[P G (S)]   10′ × 8′   3 × 2.5 m

'Dr W. Van Fleet'

Van Fleet USA 1910
R. wichuraiana × 'Safrano'
A vigorous, well-foliated plant with rather thorny stems and dark green glossy leaves. Flowers, are shapely in bud and open to semi-double, soft blush-pink. Perfumed.

[P T N ◍ (S)]   15′ × 10′   4.5 × 3 m

'Easlea's Golden Rambler'

Easlea UK 1932
Parentage unknown
Placed here because of its rich glossy foliage. Could well be among climbing Hybrid Teas. An aristocrat of yellow climbers, with shapely, rich golden-yellow flowers on long, strong stems. Growth vigorous and extremely healthy, with plenty of reddish thorns.

[P T ◍ (S)]   20′ × 15′   6 × 4.5 m

'Elegance'

Brownell USA 1937
'Glenn Dale' × ('Mary Wallace' × 'Miss Lolita Armour')
Large, shapely, fully double, clear yellow flowers, losing none of their charm as they pale with age to lemon. Good, healthy, dark green foliage. Sometimes gives a subdued repeat performance in autumn.

[P (R)]   10′ × 8′   3 × 2.5 m

'Emily Gray'   [PB]

'Emily Gray'

A. H. Williams UK 1918
'Jersey Beauty' × 'Comtesse du Cayla'
An outstanding rose with shapely buds opening to almost double yellow flowers, which pale with age to lemon. Fragrant. Very floriferous on a vigorous plant with rich green, highly polished foliage.

[P T N ◍ (S)]   15′ × 10′   4.5 × 3 m

'Ethel'

Turner UK 1912
'Dorothy Perkins' seedling
Large, cascading clusters of mauve-pink, double flowers on a vigorous, scrambling-type plant with glossy foliage and ample thorns. A most useful rose, much healthier than its parent.
[P T N ◍ (S)]   20′×15′   6×4.5 m

'Evangeline'

Walsh USA 1906
R. wichuraiana × 'Crimson Rambler'
Healthy, leathery foliage providing an ideal foil for the clusters of single, soft pinkish-white flowers. These are produced advantageously rather later in the season than most others of its type.
[P T N ◍ (S)]   15′×12′   4.5×3.5 m

'Excelsa', 'Red Dorothy Perkins'

Walsh USA 1909
Parentage unknown
Large trusses of small, crimson flowers, densely

'François Juranville'   [PB]

produced on strong, pliable shoots. Foliage exceptionally dark green. Rather inclined to mildew after flowering, especially around the soft, immature thorns. A most useful rambler or prostrate rose, flowering well into August.
[T P G N ◍ ≈ (S)]   15′×12′   4.5×3.5 m

'François Juranville'

Barbier FRANCE 1906
R. wichuraiana × 'Mme Laurette Messimy'
A tangle of petals create an unusual individual bloom. Spectacular in full flush, this rose, clear pink with deeper shadings, is a rather refined 'Albertine', with which it is sometimes confused. Foliage dark green, burnished bronze. Growth pliable and dense, with few thorns of consequence.
[T P G N ◍ (S)]   15′×10′   4.5×3 m

'Fräulein Octavia Hesse'

Hesse GERMANY 1909
R. wichuraiana × 'Kaiserin Auguste Viktoria'
Creamy-white, semi-double flowers with a fruity scent, produced in small clusters on vigorous, wiry growth with dark green foliage.
[P G (S)]   12′×10′   3.5×3 m

'Gardenia'

Manda USA 1899
R. wichuraiana × 'Perle des Jardins'
Shapely, fully double flowers of creamy-white. These open from pointed buds to give a lovely, muddled effect with deeper-creamy-yellow centre petals. They are produced in small clusters on short, lateral stems along strong but pliable branches of the previous year's growth. Pleasing fragrance reminiscent of apples. Foliage dark green and glossy, growth very vigorous. Quite rare these days.
[P T ◍ ≈ (S)]   20′×15′   6×4.5 m

'Gerbe Rose'

Fauque FRANCE 1904
R. wichuraiana × 'Baroness Rothschild'
A vigorous, healthy climber with abundant, green foliage. The large, double flowers, opening flat, are soft rosy-pink with a faint but sweet fragrance.
[T N ◍ (S)]   10′×8′   3×2.5 m

'Golden Glow'

Brownell USA 1937
'Glenn Dale' × ('Mary Wallace' × a Hybrid Tea)
Shapely, cupped, almost double flowers of golden-yellow, retaining their colour fairly well as they age. Foliage crisp, dark green and plentiful. Growth strong with an average number of thorns.

[P N ⦾ (S)]   10′×8′   3×2.5 m

'Jersey Beauty'

Manda USA 1899
R. wichuraiana × 'Perle des Jardins'
Clusters of good-sized, single, whitish to creamy yellow, sweetly scented flowers with deep golden stamens. Flowers show up well against lush, dark green, glossy foliage. Interesting single with the same parents as 'Gardenia' which is fully double.

[P T N ⦾ ≋ (S)]   15′×10′   4.5×3 m

'Léontine Gervais'

Barbier FRANCE 1903
R. wichuraiana × 'Souvenir de Claudius Denoyel'
Clusters of medium-sized, fully-double, flat flowers opening rather muddled, deep salmon with yellow, red and orange highlights. A semi-vigorous, pliable plant with ample, dark green, glossy foliage.

'Mary Wallace'

Van Fleet USA 1924
R. wichuraiana × a pink Hybrid Tea
Warm pink almost double flowers, with a good perfume, produced freely on a vigorous, relatively upright plant amid dark, shiny but not glossy foliage. Leaves spaced rather wider apart than others of this family.

[P N ⦾ (S)]   10′×8′   3×2.5 m

'May Queen'

Manda USA 1898
R. wichuraiana × 'Champion of the World'
Free-flowering. The semi-double, lilac-pink flowers are well scented. They appear in clusters on a vigorous, densely growing climber with darkish thorns and dark green foliage.

[G N T ⦾ (S)]   15′×8′   4.5×2.5 m

'Paul Transon'   [TW]

'Minnehaha'

Walsh USA 1905
R. wichuraiana × 'Paul Neyron'
Large clusters of cascading, pink flowers which pale to almost white with age. The plant is well endowed with small, dark green, glossy leaves.

[P N T G ⦾ ≋ (S)]   15′×8′   4.5×2.5 m

'Mme Alice Garnier'

Fauque FRANCE 1906
R. wichuraiana × 'Mme Charles Small'
Slender branches carrying small but numerous, glossy, dark green leaves. Medium-sized clusters of scented, double flowers, bright orange-pink with yellow centres. Vigorous and, when required, procumbent.

[P N G ⦾ (S)]   10′×8′   4.5×2.5 m

'New Dawn'

Somerset Rose Company USA 1930
'Dr Van Fleet' sport
An outstanding rose, one of the most useful sports ever discovered. Well scented flowers identical to those of 'Dr Van Fleet' with slightly tubby buds opening to semi-double flowers of soft blush-pink. Foliage dark green and glossy. Its greatest advantage over all others of this group is its remontancy. Flowers freely from June to October. In fact, the ideal, smaller rambling rose.

[P N ⦾ (C)]   10′×8′   4.5×2.5 m

'Paul Transon'

Barbier FRANCE 1900
R. wichuraiana × 'l'Idéal'
Medium-sized, fully-double flowers opening flat,
rich salmon with coppery overtones and a
creamy-yellow base to each petal. Foliage shiny,
coppery tinted, light green, combining beautifully with the flowers to give a pleasing overall
effect. Sometimes repeats in autumn, especially
if placed in a warm position.
[☼ P ◉ (R)]   10′×8′   3×2.5 m

'Purity'

Hoopes Bros & Thomas USA 1917
Unnamed seedling × 'Mme Caroline Testout'
Large, pure white, shapely flowers opening semi-
double and perfumed. Foliage light green and
glossy on a vigorous, somewhat thorny plant.
[P ◉ (S)]   12′×8′   3.5×2.5 m

'René André'

Barbier FRANCE 1901
R. wichuraiana × 'l'Idéal'
The semi-double flowers, which open flat, are a
mixture of coppery-pink and yellow, changing
with age to carmine and soft pink. Growth is very
vigorous with ample, dark green, slightly glossy
leaves. Occasionally repeats.
[G N ◉ (R)]   15′×8′   4.5×2.5 m

'Sanders White', 'Sanders White Rambler'

Sanders & Sons UK 1912
Parentage unknown
One of the best white ramblers. Abundant,
almost rosette-shaped, pure white flowers in
cascading clusters, sometimes singly. Foliage is
dark green and growth pliable with ample,
stubby thorns.
[P T G N ◉ ≋ (S)]   12′×8′   3.5×2.5 m

'Thelma'

Easlea UK 1927
R. wichuraiana × 'Paul's Scarlet'
A pleasing mixture of coral-pink and deeper pink
with a hint of lemon faintly visible in the centre.
Semi-double and quite large when open. Foliage
rather coarse but deep green and glossy. Growth
robust with large but few thorns.
[P T ◉ (S)]   12′×8′   3.5×2.5 m

'Sanders White'   [JB]

ROSA Subgenus II Rosa (Eurosa)
SECTION VII *Chinensis*

Growth very variable, usually upright from 3 ft–10 ft, 1 m–7 m.
Thorns sparse or relatively so, usually hooked.
Leaves 5 to 7 leaflets.
Flowers in small clusters.
Hips mostly roundish.
Sepals dropping when ripe.

SPECIES

R. *chinensis* (R. *indica*, R. *sinica*)
R. × *borboniana*
R. × *odorata*
R. *gigantea*

GARDEN GROUPS
Chinas
Teas
Noisettes
Bourbons
Hybrid Perpetuals
Hybrid Teas (Large Flowered roses)
Climbing Hybrid Teas (Large Flowered Climbers)

ORIGIN AND DISTRIBUTION

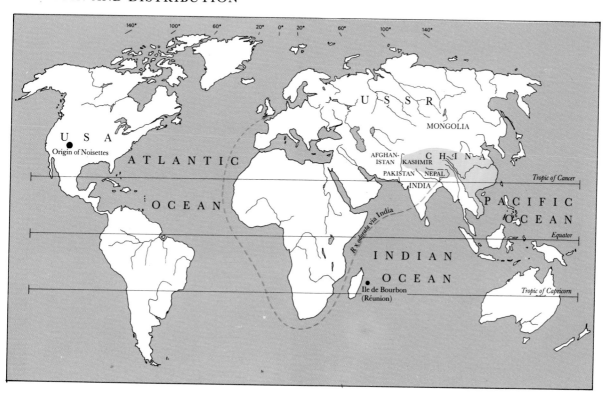

China Rose 'Hermosa' (see text p. 328)

R. chinensis

R. chinensis, 'China Rose', 'Bengal Rose',
R. indica, R. sinica, R. nankiniensis
It is not known whether the originally discovered species still exists, but this is the name given to the species thought to have been the parent of wide and varied Chinese hybrids which reached us, by way of India, in the early 18th century. The last recorded sighting in China itself is reported to have been made around 1885, but this remains speculative. Recent political conditions have im-

peded its rediscovery, but China has of late become less introspective and this gives hope of finding it again. This rose is described as single, red to white, of variable height from 4′ to 20′ (1.2 to 6 m). Hardly the description of a true species, although such erratic heights and colour variations are characteristic of several China hybrids; so possibly the species does have chameleon-like qualities.

FORMS AND HYBRIDS OF R. chinensis

'Anna-Maria de Montravel'

Rambaud FRANCE 1880
A Polyantha × 'Mme de Tartas'
A short-growing, rather sprawly China but nevertheless dense in growth. Pure white flowers, fully double, globular and produced in great profusion. Probably more correctly a Tea Rose.
[Gh ▽ (C)] 2′×3′ 60×90 cm

'Arethusa'

W. Paul UK 1903
Parentage unknown
The double flowers, which are a mixture of sulphur yellow, lemon and apricot, are made up of a host of rather ragged petals and are produced in clusters. Foliage shiny but somewhat sparse.
[P ▽ (C)] 3′×3′ 90×90 cm

'Bloomfield Abundance'

Thomas USA 1920
Said to be 'Sylvia' × 'Dorothy Page-Roberts'
One of the tallest bush Chinas, deserving attention. The small, compact blooms of shell-pink are exquisite, produced freely throughout summer in huge, well-spaced clusters, each on a lengthy stalk – ideal for buttonholes. Wood smooth, brownish-purple, sometimes spindly, with few thorns. Foliage dark green and also smooth. Very similar to and sometimes confused with 'Cécile Brunner', which is much shorter. The most marked difference, however, is seen in the sepals – on 'Bloomfield Abundance' long and extending well beyond the petals, and visible, even when the flower is fully open; on 'Cécile Brunner' shorter, sometimes but not always folding back towards the receptable. Nurserymen have for many years added to the confusion between these two roses. 'Bloomfield Abundance' is unquestionably easier to produce, yet 'Cécile Brunner' sells better, leading one to wonder sadly, how many mistakes have been deliberate.

'Brennus'   [VP]

Whether 'Bloomfield Abundance' is really a sport of 'Cécile Brunner' I do not know, yet in the last ten years not one of the tens of thousands of both varieties we have produced has reverted.

[H P ▽ (C)]   6′×4′   1.8×1.2 m

'Beauty of Rosemawr'

Van Fleet USA 1904
Parentage unknown
A twiggy but dense, upright-growing variety producing loosely formed, sweetly scented flowers of soft carmine with softer veining. Rather short of foliage for my taste.

[Gh P ▽ ☼ (C)]   4′×2′   1.2 m×60 cm

'Brennus'

1830
Origin and parentage unknown, probably a China Gallica cross.
Bears little resemblance at first sight to a typical China, being more upright and less branchy, with larger, more plentiful and less shiny foliage. Flowers cupped, full, rich reddish-carmine.

[P (R)]   5′×4′   1.5×1.2 m

'Cécile Brunner', 'The Sweetheart Rose', 'Mignon', 'Maltese Rose'

Pernet-Ducher FRANCE 1881
A Polyantha Rose × 'Mme de Tartas'
Without doubt, one of the most charming of roses, sometimes temperamental, but capable of giving a lifetime of pleasure. Colour and shape of flowers already discussed under 'Bloomfield Abundance'. Although the plant is short, spindly and rather lacking in foliage, this is fairly typical

Above: 'Cécile Brunner Climber' at Alby Hall, Norfolk. *Right:* Flower shown actual size.   [PB/TW]
Far right: 'Fabvier'   [PB]

of the Chinas and should not put you off this superb little rose. Flowers faintly but distinctively scented.

[Gh ▽ (C)]   4′×2′   1.2 m × 60 cm

'Cécile Brunner' Climber

Hosp USA 1904
'Cécile Brunner' sport
Contradicts its parent by growing into a very vigorous climber indeed. Well endowed with dark green foliage and tolerant of most soils.

Flowers, identical to those of bush form, are freely produced but sometimes hidden by dense foliage. Ideal for growing into trees or over unsightly buildings.

[P N T ◍ (S)]   25′×20′   7.5×6 m

'Cécile Brunner' White

Fauque FRANCE 1909
'Cécile Brunner' sport
A sport with the same attributes and faults as its parent. White with hint of yellow and peach. Quite rare nowadays.

[Gh ▽]   4′×2′   1.2 m × 60 cm

'Comtesse du Cayla'

Guillot FRANCE 1902
Parentage unknown
A most useful, brightly coloured variety. Almost single flowers of orange and pink with red highlights. Angular growth and vigorous, its lack of foliage amply compensated by its free flowering habit. One of the most highly scented China roses.

[Gh P ▽ (C)]   3′×3′   90×90 cm

'Cramoisi Supérieur'

Coquereau FRANCE 1832
Parentage unknown
An outstanding China rose forming a compact, tidy bush. The flowers, which are produced in large clusters, are semi-double and cupped, especially when in bud. Their colour is clear, unfading red with paler centres and with the odd petal sometimes faintly streaked with white. Has little or no perfume.

[P ▽ (C)]   3′×2′   90×60 cm

'Cramoisi Supérieur' Climber

Couturier FRANCE 1885
'Cramoisi Supérieur' sport
This sport from the bush form makes an extremely good, healthy climber and is well worth a prominent position since few red climbers retain their colour so well, even in hot sun.

[P ▽ (S)]   12′×8′   3.5×2.5 m

'Duke of York'

1894
Origin and parentage unknown
The double flowers are variably mixed rosy-pink and white and produced freely on a bushy, branching shrub, with dark shiny foliage.

[Gh ▽ (C)]   3′×2′   90×60 cm

'Fabvier'

Laffay FRANCE 1832
Parentage unknown
A very showy rose, tidy in habit and ideal for massed bedding where an old variety has to be used. Bright crimson flowers, semi-double, and

produced in large clusters. Foliage is very dark, glossy and tinted purple.

[P ▽ (C)]   3' × 2"   90 × 60 cm

'Fellemberg', 'La Belle Marseillaise'

Fellemberg GERMANY 1857
Parentage unknown
Cupped, fully double, cerise to crimson flowers, borne in trusses on a vigorous plant. Attractive, cascading habit if grown free. Makes a useful pillar rose. Foliage mid-green and generously produced. Stems more thorny than most other Chinas.

[P (C)]   7' × 4'   2 × 1.2 m

'Gloire des Rosomanes', 'Ragged Robin', 'Red Robin'

Vibert FRANCE 1825
Parentage unknown
A vigorous hybrid China, semi-double flowers of bright crimson-cerise, very floriferous. Once used extensively as an understock, especially in the USA. Was important in the early breeding of the Bourbons.

[P N ▽ ◍ (C)]   4' × 4'   1.2 × 1.2 m

'Gruss an Teplitz'

Geschwind HUNGARY 1897
('Sir Joseph Paxton' × 'Fellemberg') × ('Papa Gontier' × 'Gloire de Rosomanes')
Rather difficult to classify but has enough China characteristics to be placed here. Shapely, crimson flowers deepening with age, borne in loose clusters but sometimes individually. Good light green foliage but rather inclined to mildew if not in good soil. Sometimes used successfully as a small climber. Also makes a good hedge.

[H (C)]   6' × 4'   1.8 × 1.2 m

'Hermosa', 'Armosa', 'Mélanie Lemaire', 'Mme Neumann'

Marcheseau FRANCE 1840
Parentage unknown
Definitely a good rose for the front of a border or for the smaller garden, where it is best grown in groups of three. Full, globular buds opening to cup-shaped flowers of delicate mid-pink. Leaves greyish-green, rather small but numerous.

[◍ ▽ (C)]   3' × 2'   90 × 60 cm

'Irène Watts'   [PB]

'Irène Watts'

Guillot FRANCE 1896
Parentage unknown
I grow to like this little rose more and more. Very free-flowering and at times, rather un-China-like, its flowers are peachy-pink with hints of salmon. Buds at first rather pointed, opening loosely flat. Dark green foliage margined with purple. It makes an ideal bedding rose.

[▽ (C)]   2' × 2'   60 × 60 cm

'Le Vésuve'

Laffay FRANCE 1825
Parentage unknown
Very free-flowering, this rose has shapely, pointed buds which open to loosely formed, sometimes quartered flowers of silvery-pink with carmine highlights. Needs mollycoddling to give of its best. Rather good under glass.

[✦ Gh ▽ (C)]   3' × 3'   90 × 90 cm

'L'Ouche'

Buatois FRANCE 1901
Parentage unknown
Large, full, pointed buds open to fully double, cupped blooms of flesh pink lightly flecked with buff-yellow. Scented. Not entirely typical of a China, being rather upright in growth with fairly dark, thick foliage.

[(C)]   4' × 3'   1.2 m × 90 cm

'Louis Philippe'

Guérin FRANCE 1834
Another rose of this name was introduced by Hardy (France) in 1824.
Parentage unknown
Deep crimson to purple with some petals white

'Louis XIV'   [TW]

at the margins, as though the dye has been re-moved. Flowers loosely semi-double, retaining their cupped shape throughout. An interesting rose, but prefers good soil. Foliage moderately sparse, growth angular and twiggy.

[☼ Gh ▽ (C)]   2′ × 2′   60 × 60 cm

'Louis XIV'

Guillot Fils FRANCE 1859
Parentage unknown
Well scented, rich deep crimson, semi-double flowers displaying golden stamens when fully open, and produced on a rather angular plant amid glossy but somewhat sparse foliage. Relatively thornless.

[☼ Gh ▽ (C)]   2′ × 2′   60 × 60 cm

'Minima', *R. chinensis minima*, 'Miss Lawrance's Rose', 'Fairy Rose'

CHINA 1815
Not so important a garden rose as for its role in the lineage of modern miniature roses. Single flowers, soft creamy-pink with rather pointed,

well-spaced petals, tips slightly deeper coloured. Dwarf spreading habit with ample small leaves and few thorns.

[☼ Gh ▽]   1′ × 2′   30 × 61 cm

'Miss Lowe's Rose', 'Sanguinea'

Probably originated in CHINA Discovered in 1887
Said to be of 'Slater's Crimson'
Single titian-red, colour deepening with age. Angular growth. Interesting more for its historic and genetic associations that for its garden value.

[☼ ▽ (C)]   3′ × 2′   90 × 60 cm

'Mme Laurette Messimy'

Guillot FRANCE 1887
'Rival de Paestum' × 'Mme Falcot'
One of the best hybrid Chinas. A healthy rose with multitudes of semi-double flowers of bright pink bordering on salmon, each petal suffused yellow at its base. The shrub, fairly tall for a China, is bushy but upright in growth with ample glossy leaves of greyish-green. Good for bedding.

[Gh ▽ ◍ (C)]   2′ × 2′   60 × 60 cm

'Papillon' [PB]

'Mutabilis', 'Tipo Ideale', *R. turkistanica*

CHINA 1932

Although thought by some to be a species, this rose is probably an old Chinese garden hybrid with characteristically mysterious origins. An interesting and useful garden shrub which, I am convinced, has a well developed sense of humour. Capable of reaching a height of 6′ (1.8 m) but more likely to stay relatively dwarf, continuously producing single flowers of honey-yellow, orange and red. Sometimes when fully open, the petal

Above: 'Mutabilis' [RCB/PB]
Below: 'Perle d'Or' at Lime Kiln, Claydon, Suffolk

formation is rather like a butterfly. Extremely healthy and very much older than the given date.

[P H ▽ N ◍ (C)] 3′ × 2′ 90 × 60 cm

'Old Blush', 'Parson's Pink', 'Monthly Rose', 'Pallida'

Parson DISCOVERED IN CHINA
Introduced to Europe 1789
An important rose. This is one of the most garden-worthy of the old Chinas, silvery-pink with a deeper flush. Highly scented. The bush is practically thornless, upright in stature and, if grown as a small climber, will attain 6′–8′ (1.8–2.5 m) in height. Has probably been cultivated in China for many centuries.

[P N ◍ (C)] 6′ × 4′ 1.8 × 1.2 m

'Papa Hémeray'

Hémeray-Aubert FRANCE 1912
A very good China rose. Clusters of small ('Ballerina' size) bright pink to rosy-red flowers, single, with a pronounced white central eye. Growth bushy but upright, foliage dark green. Stems have few thorns.

[P ▽ ☼ (C)] 2′ × 2′ 60 × 60 cm

'Papillon'

Probably FRANCE 1900
Parentage unknown
A vigorous, angular shrub. This rose is well named. The roughly triangular petals which form the semi-double flowers often stand up charmingly like butterfly wings. Colour predominantly shrimp-pink with copper and yellow reflections from a deeper base. Foliage deep green and coppery.

[☼ Gh ▽ (C)] 4′ × 3′ 1.2 m × 90 cm

'Perle d'Or'

Dubreuil FRANCE 1884
R. multiflora seedling × 'Mme Falcot'
Clusters of spaced, small, exquisitely shaped, creamy-buff yellow flowers with hints of pink. Slightly perfumed. Ample rich dark green foliage with twiggy, almost thornless stems. Quite vigorous and dense in growth. Can be temperamental. In good situations will attain a height of over 6′ (1.8 m) but normally only 4′ (1.2 m). Remarkably similar to 'Cécile Brunner' save in colour,

casting doubt on its recorded parentage and suggesting it may be a sport, or perhaps from the same seed pod. I have grown them side by side in nursery rows and until they flower it is difficult to tell the difference between them.

[Gh] 4′ × 2′ 1.2 m × 6′ cm

'Pompon de Paris' Climber

Date of climbing form not known
Bush form 1839
Origin and parentage unknown
A fascinating climber, dainty in growth but vigorous with small, greyish-green foliage and twiggy growth. Flowers small and button-like, produced profusely in small clusters. An excellent plant can be seen at the Royal Horticultural Society's Gardens, Wisley, Surrey. Also good when grown as prostrate shrub rose.

[G Gh ▽ (S)] 12′ × 6′ 3.5 × 1.8 m

'Pompon de Paris' Dwarf form

1839
Origin and parentage unknown
A fashionable mid-19th century pot plant variety in Paris. I have recently acquired this from Mr Frank Buckley of Lancaster and this charming little miniature should, thanks to him, be available in a few years. Said to be synonymous with 'Rouletii' but I find it fairly distinctive.

[☼ Gh ▽ (C)] 1′ × 1′ 30 × 30 cm

'Pumila', 'Bengale Pompon'

Colville UK c. 1806
Parentage unknown
Small, double, almost star-like flowers usually borne singly on a short, slightly spreading, miniature plant with long (for size of plant) thin mid-green leaves.

[☼ Gh ▽ (R)] 1′ × 1′ 30 × 30 cm

'Rouletii'

Correvon SWITZERLAND 1922
Discovered in Switzerland and, after a chequered history, including almost total extinction, eventually became a parent to a race of miniature roses. Almost evergreen, the tiny shrub is bushy and well endowed with small thorns. Fully double, clear pink flowers, borne in upright clusters.

[☼ Gh ▽ (C)] 6′ × 6′ 1.8 × 1.8 m

'Sophie's Perpetual' [PB]

'Viridiflora' [VP]

'Sophie's Perpetual'

UK An old variety reintroduced 1960
Discovery by Humphrey Brooke
A superb shrub or small climber. Globular
flowers, pale whitish-pink heavily overlaid with
deep pink and cerise red. Ample, healthy, dark
green foliage and almost thornless stems.

[P (C)] 8′×4′ 2.5×1.2 m

'Tipo Ideale'. *See* 'Mutabilis'

'Slater's Crimson China', 'Semperflorens', 'Old Crimson China'

Slater UK 1792 Discovered in CHINA
A medium to short, branching bush with darkish
green foliage and sparse, broad, flattish thorns.
Semi-double flowers of crimson to red with the
centre petals sometimes slightly streaked with
white. Good as a small wall plant.

[☼ ▽ (C)] 3′×3′ 90×90 cm

'Viridiflora', 'The Green Rose', *R. viridiflora*

c. 1833
Origin and parentage unknown
A strange and novel rose, very easy to grow and
without any disease problems. Flowers formed
by a multitude of green and brown bracts with
no petals in the accepted sense. These are produced quite freely, making this rose useful for the
flower arranger's collection, especially as they
change to purplish-brown with age.

[P ▽ ◐ (C)] 3′×3′ 90×90 cm

I have by no means described all the many China roses; some, in
fact, more by instinct than actual knowledge, have been placed
elsewhere in the book.

All the Chinas and hybrid Chinas, as stated elsewhere, have
played a major part in the evolution of modern roses, so the next
step to take towards the Hybrid Teas is to the Bourbons, which are
direct descendants of the Chinas.

R. × borboniana
Bourbon Roses

R. × borboniana, 'Bourbon Rose'
FRANCE 1817
Thought to be 'Old Blush' × 'Quatre Saisons'
This, the first of the Bourbons race, is probably now extinct. The original plant was of medium to vigorous growth with large, semi-double to double flowers of deep red, repeating in autumn. probably synonymous with 'Rose Edward'.

[(R)]   4′ × 3′   1.2 m × 90 cm

No-one is completely sure how the prodigious race of Bourbons came about. This is discussed in an earlier chapter. What is fairly certain is that the first Bourbons arose from a cross between Rosa *chinensis* or one of its hybrids and Rosa × *damascena bifera* 'The Autumn Damask' on the Isle de Bourbon in 1817. The Bourbons reigned supreme during the mid-nineteenth Century and these make excellent shrubs and climbers, many are still with us today.

FORMS AND HYBRIDS OF
R. × borboniana

'Adam Messerich'
P. Lambert GERMANY 1920
('Frau Oberhofgärtner Singer' × ('Louise Odier' seedling) × 'Louis Philippe')
Semi-double, bright rosy-red flowers produced in clusters abundantly throughout the season. The shrub is upright and well foliated. Flowers fade to a soft but still pleasing pink in very hot weather and have a good scent.

[P (C)]   5′ × 4′   1.5 × 1.2 m

'Boule de Neige'
Lacharme FRANCE 1867
'Blanche Lafitte' × 'Sappho'
A fine shrub, upright in growth with dark green almost glossy foliage and few thorns. Flowers fully double, globular, sometimes tinged reddish-purple on the petal edges while in bud, but opening to pure white with a strong fragrance.

[H ▽ (R)]   4′ × 3′   1.2 m × 90 cm

'Bourbon Queen', 'Queen of Bourbons', 'Reine des Iles Bourbon', 'Souvenir de la Princess de Lamballe'
Mauget FRANCE 1834
Parentage unknown
A sturdy shrub with thick branches and copious foliage. Semi-double, rose-pink flowers large and cupped when fully open. Highly scented but, sadly, seldom repeats in the autumn. I recall finding a very old plant of this growing wild on the south-east side of the mound of Pembroke Castle where it was competing admirably with brambles and had been doing so for many years, proving a very strong constitution.

[P H ◑ (S)]   6′ × 4′   1.8 × 1.2 m

'Adam Messerich' at Castle Howard, Yorkshire [PB]
(see text p. 333)

Above: 'Boule de Neige' (see text p. 333)   [PB]
Below: 'Commandant Beaurepaire'   [VP]

'Charles Lawson'

Lawson UK 1853
Parentage unknown
Not often seen today, probably because of its relatively short flowering season and rather ungainly habit. With support, however, this rose, soft pink with deeper shadings, is a useful shrub.
[⦾ (S)] 6′ × 4′ 1.8 × 1.2 m

'Commandant Beaurepaire'

Moreau-Robert FRANCE 1874
Parentage unknown
  A strong, dense bush with plentiful, fresh green leaves. Large, double, crimson flowers streaked pink and purple and marbled white. An interesting rose worthy of a place in any shrubbery.
[P H ⦾ (R)] 5′ × 5′ 1.5 × 1.5 m

'Coupe d'Hébé'

Laffay FRANCE 1840
Bourbon hybrid × China hybrid
Tall shrub bearing attractive, light green foliage, marred later in the season by mildew if precautions are not taken in time. Very free-flowering, especially in first flush. The globular, pale pink, fully double flowers have a good scent.
[P (R)] 7′ × 5′ 2 × 1.5 m

Above: 'Coupe d'Hébé'   [PB]
Below: 'Gipsy Boy' (see text p. 336)   [PB]

'Fulgens', 'Malton'

Guérin FRANCE 1830

Parentage unknown

This rose is thought to have been one parent in the early development of the Hybrid Perpetuals. Bright cerise-crimson, semi-double flowers. Although the plant is somewhat sprawly, it nevertheless makes a useful shrub.

[(R)] 5′×4′ 1.5×1.2 m

'Gipsy Boy' hips   ..... [PB]

'Gros Choux d'Hollande'   [RCB]

'Gipsy Boy', 'Zigeunerknabe'

P. Lambert GERMANY 1909

'Russelliana' seedling

Where space permits this rose is probably best grown as a shrub but it can also be happy as small climber. Coarse, rather Centifolia-like foliage should not put you off this lovely rose. Double flowers of deep crimson to almost purple-black with primrose yellow anthers.

[P ◍ (S)] 6′×4′ 1.8×1.2 m

'Great Western'

Laffay FRANCE 1838

Parentage unknown

Once flowering, this rose has large, full, quartered flowers of maroon-purple. Its foliage is dark green and its shoots well endowed with thorns.

[P ◍ (S)] 5′×4′ 1.5×1.2 m

'Gros Choux d'Hollande'

Origin, date and parentage unknown

Obviously an old variety with full, cupped, very double, soft pink blooms. Very fragrant and very vigorous.

[P (R)] 7′×5′ 2×1.5 m

'Honorine de Brabant'

Origin, date and parentage unknown

One of the most acceptable striped roses. Delicate shades of lilac with purple markings on a large, cupped flower, which is sometimes hidden by large, lush foliage. Vigorous, with few thorns. I have also seen this grown successfully as a climber.

[P ◍ (C)] 6′×5′ 1.8×1.5 m

'Kronprinzessin Viktoria'

1888

Origin unknown

'Souvenir de la Malmaison' sport

Has the beautiful petal formation of its parent, together with its superb perfume and grace. Creamy-white with lemon shadings. Very free-flowering and ideal for small gardens, but dislikes wet weather.

[▽ (C)] 4′×3′ 1.2 m×90 cm

'La Reine Victoria'

Schwartz FRANCE 1872

Parentage unknown

A slender, erect bush bearing soft green leaves

'Honorine de Brabant'   [VP]

'Louise Odier'   [VP]

'La Reine Victoria'   [RCB]

and beautiful, rich lilac-pink, cupped blooms with silky textured petals. The overall picture is sometimes spoilt by a proneness to black spot and a dislike of all but the best soils.

[▽ (C)]   4′×3′   1.2 m×90 cm

'Lewison Gower', 'Malmaison Rouge'
Béluze FRANCE 1846
'Souvenir de la Malmaison' sport
A bright pink to red variety with all the virtues and faults of its parent, though with its harder

colouring it loses some of Malmaison's sophistication. One of Mr Arthur Wyatt's rediscoveries.

[▽ (C)]   4′×3′   1.2 m×90 cm

Note: Mr Wyatt did much to rekindle interest in the old roses in the 1950s and 1960s and led a successful search for many old varieties that were then in danger of extinction.

'Louise Odier'
Margottin FRANCE 1851
Parentage unknown
Very double, almost camellia-like, bright rose-pink flowers on a vigorous bush. Flowers are produced in dense clusters which sometimes weigh down the slender branches to give an arching effect. Superbly perfumed.

[H ⊕ (C)]   5′×4′   1.5×1.2 m

'Mme Ernst Calvat'
Schwartz FRANCE 1888
'Mme Isaac Pereire' sport
Large, shaggy, pale rose-pink blooms with a strong perfume. Slightly less vigorous than its

Above: 'Mme Isaac Pereire'
Below: 'Mme Lauriol de Barny'

[VP]
[PB]

'Mme Pierre Oger' [JB]

famous parent, otherwise the same in all but colour.

[P ⦿ (C)] 5′ × 4′ 1.5 × 1.2 m

'Mme Isaac Pereire'

Garçon FRANCE 1881
Parentage unknown
Huge, shaggy, purplish deep-pink blooms exuding a heady perfume and carried on a large, strong bush. Has its critics, but few other Bourbons can rival its bold character. Early blooms can sometimes suffer from malformation but this should not put you off. Equally good as a small climber.

[P ⦿ (C)] 7′ × 5′ 2 × 1.5 m

'Mme Lauriol de Barny'

Trouillard FRANCE 1868
Parentage unknown
The flat, quartered, fully-double blooms of deep silver-pink are blessed with an unusual but pleasant, fruity perfume. The plant is vigorous and healthy. A very worthwhile variety, especially good if 'pegged-down' in the old style.

[P ⦿ (R)] 5′ × 4′ 1.5 × 1.2 m

'Mme Pierre Oger'

Verdier FRANCE 1878
'La Reine Victoria' sport
Very pale silvery-pink, translucent, cupped flowers with the form of small water-lilies, sweetly scented. The flowers are borne on a bush of medium vigour, sadly marred by the same

disease problems that affect its parent, 'La Reine Victoria', but what are a few 'black spots' between friends?

[▽ (C)] 4′ × 4′ 1.2 × 1.2 m

'Mrs Paul'

W. Paul UK 1891
Parentage unknown
Large, soft pale pink to white, fully double though somewhat blowsy flowers borne amid plentiful if rather coarse foliage. Vigorous.

[(R)] 5′ × 3′ 1.5 m × 90 cm

'Parkzierde'

P. Lambert GERMANY 1909
Parentage unknown
Very floriferous for a short period in early summer. Scarlet-crimson flowers on long stems, useful for cutting. Foliage dark green.

[⦿ P (S)] 5′ × 4′ 1.5 × 1.2 m

'Paul Verdier'

Verdier FRANCE 1866
Parentage unknown
A very good rose which deserves more attention,

'Prince Charles' [PB]

useful as shrub or climber. Fully double, slightly frilly flowers, opening flat from globular bud, produced along the length of arching, rather thorny canes amid dark green foliage.

[P (R)] 5′ × 4′ 1.5 × 1.2 m

'Prince Charles'

Pre-1918
Origin and parentage unknown
A medium-tall if somewhat lax bush bearing

heavily veined crimson to maroon flowers of considerable size when fully open, tending to fade slightly but enhanced by golden yellow anthers. The bush has large, thick leaves with a heavy texture. Its origin is a mystery and exact date unknown to me.

[H P ⓦ (S)]   5′×4′   1.5×1.2 m

'Queen of Bedders'
Noble UK 1871
Seedling from 'Sir Joseph Paxton'
A compact growing Bourbon. Out of date now for bedding but very useful as a shorter growing variety for the front of shrubberies, and herbaceous borders or for growing in pots. Shapely, double flowers of deep carmine softening to deep pink with age.

[▽ (R)]   3′×2′   90×60 cm

'Reverend H. d'Ombrain'
Origin, date and parentage unknown
Not well known, this rose has flattish, double flowers of clear rose pink with a quiet, refined perfume. Matt green foliage rather prone to mildew but the bush is of quite tidy habit.

[(R)]   5′×4′   1.5×1.2 m

'Rivers George IV', 'George IV'
Rivers UK 1820
R. × damascena × a China Rose
Loose, double, cuppled flowers of deep red to maroon-crimson. Foliage and growth rather China-like. Not the most distinguished Bourbon but one of the very first introductions.

[▽ (S)]   4′×4′   1.2×1.2 m

'Rose Edward', 'Rose Édouard'
Bréon FRANCE, ILE DE RÉUNION c. 1818
'Old Blush' × 'Quatre Saisons'?
I have yet to see this rose in flower but include it here because it is important in the Bourbon lineage, apparently being one of the first, although two roses of this name existed in the early days of the Bourbons. It could well be much older than the date attributed. Richly perfumed, it forms a lax bush and the flowers are reddish-scarlet. Trevor Griffiths* of New Zealand has sent me budwood of this rose, having received it himself from his compatriot Nancy Steen, who, in turn, had received it from India.

[P ⓦ (R)]   6′×4′   1.8×1.2 m

* See p. 32.

'Souvenir de la Malmaison'   [JB]

'Souvenir de la Malmaison', 'Queen of Beauty' and Fragrance
Beluze FRANCE 1843
'Mme Desprez' × 'a Tea Rose
This rose, at its best, is the most beautiful of all Bourbons, but at its worst can be horrid. It hates wet weather and in such conditions seldom opens properly without help. Flowers blush-white with face-powder-pink shadings, each bloom beautifully proportioned and opening to flat, quartered shape. The finest example I know is at Lime

'Variegata di Bologna'   [VP]

'Prince Charles' at Castle Howard, Yorkshire   [PB]

Kiln, Claydon, Suffolk, where Mr Humphrey Brooke has a plant of huge proportions, an unforgettable sight in full flush. This plant, however, is not typical and no others I know have reached this size.

[▽ (C)]   6′ × 6′   1.8 × 1.8 m

'Souvenir de St Anne's'

Hilling UK 1950

Sport of 'Souvenir de la Malmaison'

A semi-double form of 'Souvenir de la Malmaison'. Its fewer petals enable it to open better in wet weather. Like its parent, very free-flowering and although not quite as refined is none the less attractive. Scented.

[▽ (C)]   5′ × 4′   1.5 × 1.2 m

'Variegata di Bologna'

Bonfiglioli ITALY 1909

Parentage unknown

Double, cupped flowers with pronounced, irregular stripes of purple on a creamy-white background, reminding me of the semolina and blackcurrant jam of school dinner days. A tall, rather lax bush with somewhat sparse and rather coarse foliage.

[P (R)]   6′ × 5′   1.8 × 1.5 m

'Vivid'

Paul UK 1853

Parentage unknown

A very brightly coloured rose of vivid magenta-pink to red. Vigorous, upright and rather prickly. Occasionally repeating.

[P (R)]   5′ × 4′   1.5 × 1.2 m

Bourbons as Climbers

'Blairi No. 1'

Blair UK c. 1845
Parentage unknown
Similar in most respects to the better known and more widely grown 'Blairi No. 2' but more clearly and consistently soft pink. Has a few more petals and is quite beautiful at its best, but rather shy.

[(R)]   12′×6′   3.5×1.8 m

'Blairi No. 2'

Blair UK 1845
Parentage unknown
This rose can be excused a slight proneness to mildew late in the season for it is very beautiful. Large, flattish blooms pale pink with deeper shadings towards centre. Growth and foliage is somewhat coarse but this is not a problem. The overall effect of an established climber in full flush is staggering. Particularly good when grown on a tripod or similar structure.

[(R)]   12′×6′   3.5×1.8 m

'Kathleen Harrop'

Dickson UK 1919
'Zéphirine Drouhin' sport
Oblivious to weather, this rose flowers on from mid-June well into winter. Flowers semi-double, shell-pink and fragrant. Can be grown in children's play areas or by the front door since, like its parent 'Zéphirine Drouhin', it is completely thornless.

[N P ◍ (C)]   10′×6′   3×1.8 m

'Martha'

Zeiner FRANCE 1912
'Zéphirine Drouhin' sport
Thornless and very long-flowering. The colour is slightly a paler pink than 'Zéphirine', with a creamy touch to the centre of each flower.

[N P ◍ (C)]   9′×6′   2.8×1.8 m

'Blairi No. 2'   [PB]

'Souvenir de la Malmaison' Climbing form

Bush form Beluze 1843
This form Bennett UK 1893
Unlike the bush form, this rose repeats only in good years, but flowers generously in late June, so is well worth growing where space permits. Best on a south wall where it is less likely to encounter too much rain, which, like its parent the bush form, it hates.

[(R)]   12′×8′   3.5×2.5 m

'Zéphirine Drouhin'

Bizot FRANCE 1868
Parentage unknown
Lovely though the flowers are, this legendary rose would hardly have gained such popularity had it not been for its long flowering season and its thornless shoots. Flowers semi-double, cerise-pink and distinctly fragrant. Young shoots and leaves are bronzy-red in the first stages of growth, changing to dull greyish-green when mature. In spite of my earlier comments, a fine rose.

[N P ◍ (C)]   9′×6′   2.7×1.8 m

Above: 'Kathleen Harrop'
Below: 'Zéphirine Drouhin'

[PB]
[RCB]

The Noisettes

The story of the Noisettes is told elsewhere in the book, but their development and popularity ran roughly parallel to that of the Bourbons and Teas. Most significantly, they added a new range of colour, especially yellow, to the rather dull climbing and rambler roses of those days. Many are still with us, and deservedly so, adding much charm to the modern garden.

It is worth remembering that the Noisettes have a certain reputation for tenderness. My experience of growing them in chilly Norfolk leads me to believe that they can stand more frost than they are ever given credit for. In the winter of 1981 – our worst for years – one or two were killed, but most came through with no more than a little frostbite, from which they quickly recovered.

'Aimée Vibert', 'Bouquet de la Mariée', 'Nivea'

Vibert FRANCE 1828

'Champney's Pink Cluster' × *R. sempervirens* hybrid

Small clusters of scented, double, pure white flowers on a vigorous, almost thornless plant with lush healthy, dark green leaves. As with several Noisettes, this rose comes into flower a week or two later than, say, the Bourbon climbers, and repeats in a good season.

[P ⊕ (R)] 12′ × 10′ 3.5 × 3 m

'Alister Stella Gray', 'Golden Rambler'

A. H. Gray UK 1894

Parentage unknown

Clusters of double, shapely flowers in cascading clusters. Yellow with 'eggy' centres paling to cream and, eventually, white at the edges. Highly perfumed – of tea, it is said. Shrub vigorous, producing long, slightly spindly branches ideal for arches and trellises. Fairly free of thorns with ample, dark green foliage. Repeats intermittently.

[☼ T ⊕ (R)] 15′ × 10′ 4.5 × 3 m

'Blush Noisette'

Noisette USA c. 1825

Seedling from 'Champneys Pink Cluster'

An attractive rose of gentle growth producing large clusters of semi-double flowers of blush-lilac-pink with pronounced stamens. Can, given time, make a useful short climber or pillar rose but also makes a good, free-standing shrub. Few thorns and dark green foliage. One of first Noisettes introduced.

[P N ⊕ (C)] 7′ × 4′ 2 × 1.2 m

'Bouquet d'Or'

Ducher FRANCE 1872

'Gloire de Dijon' × unknown seedling

A vigorous rose with fully double, quartered or muddled, coppery salmon and yellow flowers, slightly scented. Growth vigorous, foliage dark green and glossy.

[☼ Gh (R)] 10′ × 6′ 3 × 1.8 m

Noisette Rose 'Alister Stella Gray'

[JB]

'Céline Forestier'

Trouillard FRANCE 1842

Parentage unknown

Large flowers opening most attractively to flat blooms with muddled centre petals, primrose yellow with deeper shadings, sometimes tinged pink, scented. Makes an excellent free-flowering small climber. Seldom without a flower throughout the season. Growth vigorous, not in any way coarse, with profuse, light green, healthy foliage and darkish stems.

[P Gh ▽ (C)]   6′×4′   1.8×1.2 m

'Céline Forestier'   [PB]

'Champney's Pink Cluster'

Champney USA c. 1802

R. chinensis × *R. moschata*

If not the first, then one of the first Noisettes. Long clusters of semi-double to double flowers of blush-pink, flushed deep pink, highly scented. Growth vigorous, extremely healthy with mid-to-dark green foliage.

[P T (S)]   15′×8′   4.5×2.5 m

'Claire Jacquier'

Bernaix FRANCE 1888

Possibly *R. multiflora* × a Tea Rose

A very useful rose with considerable prowess as a climber. Flowers shapely, double, not large, rich egg yolk yellow, paling to cream with age and produced in large clusters, pleasingly perfumed. Foliage rich, lightish green. Repeats in most seasons.

[N T ◍ (R)]   15′×8′   4.5×2.5 m

'Cloth of Gold', 'Chromatella'

Coquereau FRANCE 1843

'Lamarque' seedling

Fully double flowers, of soft sulphur-yellow with

'Crépuscule'   [PB]

'Desprez à Fleurs Jaunes'

[PB]

deeper centres, fragrant, borne on long stems. Copious light green foliage. Quite vigorous, needs coddling in cold districts. Excellent under glass.

[∴ Gh ▽ (R)]   12′×8′   3.5×2.5 m

'Crépuscule'

Dubreuil FRANCE 1904
Parentage unknown
Double if rather muddled flowers of rich apricot. An excellent variety but somewhat tender especially in the north. Foliage light green with darker shoots which have but few thorns.

[∴ Gh (R)]   12′×5′   3.5×1.5 m

'Deschamps'

Deschamps FRANCE 1877
Parentage unknown
Cupped flowers, of bright cerise to cherry red, opening full almost blowsy. Very free-flowering. Foliage large and darkish mid-green. Vigorous with few thorns.

[P Gh ◑ (R)]   15′×10′   4.5×3 m

'Desprez à Fleurs Jaunes', 'Jaune Desprez'

Desprez FRANCE 1835
'Blush Noisette' × 'Park's Yellow China'
A beautiful, double, quartered rose in the style of the Tea Rose 'Gloire de Dijon'. Flowers are a mixture of yellow, orange and buff, with a fruity scent, borne in clusters, often at the end of long shoots. Growth is vigorous and the foliage light green. A particular feature of this variety is a dark mottling on the stems, which is particularly prominent in winter.

[P Gh T ◑ (R)]   20′×10′   6×3 m

'Duchesse d'Auerstädt'

A. Bernaix FRANCE 1888
'Rêve d'Or' sport
A little known variety which deserves more attention. The scented flowers are fully double, opening quartered but rather muddled, with an intense colouring of buff, apricot and gold. Growth is vigorous and foliage dark green.

[Gh ∴ (R)]   10′×8′   3×2.5 m

'L'Abundance'

Moreau-Robert FRANCE 1887
Parentage unknown
A small climber of distinction, although little known. Flowers are flesh-pink and double in well-spaced clusters. Growth moderately vigorous and foliage mid-green. Repeats only in the best seasons.

[P (S)]   10′×6′   3×1.8 m

'Lamarque'

Maréchal FRANCE 1830

'Blush Noisette' × 'Park's Yellow China'

This very beautiful rose will thrive if given a warm, sheltered position but needs cold green-house protection in colder areas. Fragrant, pure white blooms borne on long stems amid copious, light green foliage. Stems have few thorns.

[Gh ☼ (R)]   15′×8′   4.5×2.5 m

'Manettii'

Botanic Gardens, Milan ITALY 1837

Not an important garden rose. Once used exten-sively as rootstock, especially in USA. A dense shrub with pale pink semi-double flowers. Wood reddish when young streaked or mottled when older. Well endowed with dark thorns.

[P H W ◍ ▽ (S)]   6′×4′   1.8×1.2 m

'Maréchal Niel'

Pradel FRANCE 1864

Seedling from 'Cloth of Gold'

Fragrant, golden-yellow, double flowers emerg-ing from shapely, pointed buds. Very fragrant. Needs a warm, sheltered position or greenhouse to survive in colder climates. Growth vigorous with dark, coppery-green foliage.

[☼ Gh ▽ (R)]   15′×8′   4.5×2.5 m

'Mme Alfred Carrière'

J. Schwartz FRANCE 1879

Parentage unknown

A superior rose. The lovely, rather loosely formed flowers are large and white with occasional hints of soft pink, highly scented. Growth is vigorous with sparse thorns. Leaves large, plentiful and light green. This rose flowers almost continuously throughout the season and is quite tolerant of a north wall situation.

[Gh P ◍ N T (C)]   12′×10′   3.5×3 m

'Rêve d'Or'

Ducher FRANCE 1869

'Mme Schultz' seedling

This is a very good rose. Shapely, fully double blooms in the mould of 'Gloire de Dijon'. Buff to yellow with sometimes a hint of pink. Fragrant. Growth is strong and the foliage dark green. Rather tender.

[☼ Gh ▽ (R)]   12′×8′   3.5×2.5 m

'William Allen Richardson'

Ducher FRANCE 1878

'Rêve d'Or' sport

Medium-sized, fully double buff to apricot flowers, very free-flowering. This climber needs a warm, sheltered spot to really flourish. Stems are dark with dark green, copper-tinted foliage.

[Gh ▽ ☼ (R)]   15′×8′   4.5×2.5 m

Above: 'Mme Alfred Carrière'   [PB]

Tea Roses

Although some are of doubtful hardiness, the Teas were very popular garden roses during the latter half of the 19th century. Many popular varieties have now become extinct, but some of the best have survived and a few still have sufficient stamina – with our help – to go on for a long time yet. The beauty of roses is, of course, in the eye of the beholder, especially in the case of the high-centred Tea Rose. Gardeners concerned with overall effect should avoid at least the bush forms of these roses, which are definitely for those who enjoy the individual bloom. They do, however, make excellent subjects under glass and for growing in tubs and urns. They are best lightly pruned, reacting against hard pruning with a reduced yield of flowers. The climbing forms are, unless absolutely necessary, best left unpruned.

'Adam', 'The President'

Adam UK 1833

Parentage unknown

A large, fully double rose of buff, amber and apricot, with tints of pink deep in the centre. The fully open flowers are often quartered. Said to be the first of the Tea Roses. Probably a vigorous bush but better as a climber on a short wall, where it can enjoy protection from the severest weather of winter. Well foliated with large dark green leaves.

[✷ Gh ▽ (R)] 7′×5′ 2×1.5 m

'Anna Oliver'

Ducher FRANCE 1872

Parentage unknown

A mixture of flesh pink and deep rose. Fragrant. Shapely, high-centred blooms on a vigorous, branching bush with good mid-green foliage.

[✷ Gh ▽ (C)] 3′×3′ 90×90 cm

'Archiduc Joseph'

G. Nabonnand FRANCE 1872

Seedling from 'Mme Lombard'

One of the outstanding Tea Roses. Flowers, opening flat, and made up of many petals, the whole a pleasing mixture of pink, purple, orange and russet with tints of gold and yellow in the centre. The foliage is dark, glossy and abundant. The stems have few thorns. Apparently quite hardy. Can be used both as a shrub and small climber.

[P Gh ▽ ✷ (C)] 5′×3′ 1.5 m×90 cm

'Baronne Henriette de Snoy'

A. Bernaix FRANCE 1897

'Gloire de Dijon' × 'Mme Lombard'

The scented flowers are flesh pink with a deeper reverse, and open double from fairly high-centred buds. The bush is somewhat angular and the leaves large and mid-green.

[✷ Gh ▽ (C)] 4′×3′ 1.2 m×90 cm

'Belle Lyonnaise'

Levet FRANCE 1870

Parentage unknown

A climbing Tea Rose which is not often seen but worthy of any warm, sheltered garden or cold greenhouse. Not over vigorous but quite generous with its flowers which are large, scented, full, flat, quartered and soft yellow fading to creamy-white with age.

[✷ Gh ▽ (R)] 10′×6′ 3×1.8 m

'Archiduc Joseph' (see text p. 349)   [PB]

'Bon Silène'

Hardy FRANCE 1839
Parentage unknown
Fragrant, fully double, deep rosy-red flowers pro-
duced in profusion on compact,vigorous plant.
Foliage mid-green and stems moderately thorny.

[☼ Gh ▽ (C)]   4′ × 3′   1.2 m × 90 cm

'Catherine Mermet'

Guillot Fils FRANCE 1869
Parentage unknown
Shapely, high-centred buds opening to semi-
double, lilac-pink flowers, held on longish stems.
Well-foliated and bushy with healthy, mid-green,
coppery tinged leaves. An excellent greenhouse
variety but equally at home in an open, sunny,
warm position.

[☼ Gh ▽ (C)]   4′ × 3′   1.2 m × 90 cm

'Catherine Mermet'   [PB]

'Clementina Carbonieri'

Bonfiglioli ITALY 1913
Parentage unknown
An outstanding Tea Rose. Fully double flowers
opening flat and quartered, their colour is a

'Clementina Carbonieri'   [PB]

'Dr Grill'   [PB]

grand mixture of orange, pink and salmon, all on a bright mustard-yellow background. They are freely produced and scented. Foliage dark green on an angular but dense plant with an average number of thorns.

[☼ Gh ▽ (C)]   3′ × 2′   90 × 60 cm

'Dean Hole'
A. Dickson UK 1904
Parentage unknown
Large by Tea Rose standards. The flowers are an interesting combination of silvery-pink, flushed apricot and gold. Growth is vigorous and thorny with darkish green foliage.

[☼ Gh ▽ (S)]   3′ × 2′   90 × 60 cm

'Devoniensis', 'Magnolia Rose'
Foster UK 1838
Parentage unknown
Very large flowers, creamy-white with the occasional blush of pink. A refined rose which needs planting in a warm, sheltered position or under glass to be appreciated. Ample, light green foliage and few thorns.

[☼ Gh ▽ (R)]   12′ × 7′   3.5 × 2 m

'Dr Grill'
Bonnaire FRANCE 1886
'Ophirie' × 'Souvenir de Victor Hugo'
A branching, angular plant which would be better with more foliage. Flowers exquisite, pink overlaid with copper. High-centred in bud but opening flat and full, sometimes quartered. Fragrant.

[☼ Gh ▽ (C)]   3′ × 2′   90 × 60 cm

'Duchesse de Brabant', 'Comtesse de Labarthe', 'Comtesse Ouwaroff'
Bernède FRANCE 1857
Parentage unknown
Very double flowers, clear pink to rose, shapely, cupped and free-flowering. The bush has a spreading habit and is well-foliated for a Tea.

[☼ Gh ▽ (C)]   3′ × 3′   90 × 90 cm

'Étoile de Lyon'
Guillot FRANCE 1881
Parentage unknown
Rich golden-yellow flowers held on flimsy flower stalks on a twiggy, angular bush with sparse foliage. Its main attributes are a strong colour and a strong scent.

[Gh ☼ ▽ (R)]   2′ × 2′   60 × 60 cm

'Fortune's Double Yellow', 'Beauty of Glazenwood', 'San Rafael Rose'

Fortune DISCOVERED IN CHINA 1845

An old Chinese garden rose brought back to Europe by Robert Fortune. Slightly tender. The plant is best grown with support. Loosely formed, double flowers of buff-yellow with faint tints of orange. Scented. Foliage dark green and glossy, few thorns.

[☼ Gh (R)] 8′ × 4′ 2.5 × 1.2 m

'Francis Dubreuil'

Dubreuil FRANCE 1894

Parentage unknown

Long, pointed buds opening to large high-centred flowers, blowsy when fully open, dark crimson red paling slightly with age. Foliage somewhat sparse, glossy, dark green. Stems moderately thorny.

[☼ Gh ▽ (R)] 3′ × 2′ 90 × 60 cm

'Freiherr von Marschall'

P. Lambert GERMANY 1903

'Princesse Alice de Monaco' × 'Rose d'Evian'

Pointed buds opening to flattish flowers of rich carmine and red. Foliage particularly good, being plentiful, dark green and heavily tinted with red.

[☼ Gh ▽ (C)] 3′ × 2′ 90 × 60 cm

'Général Galliéni'

G. Nabonnand FRANCE 1899

'Souvenir de Thérèse Levet' × 'Reine Emma des Pays-Bas'

One of the most popular roses of its day. Main colour buff, but heavily overlaid with red and pink with hints of yellow in the base. Vigorous and relatively free of thorns, with good, mid-green foliage.

[☼ Gh ▽ (R)] 4′ × 3′ 1.2 m × 90 cm

'Général Schablikine'

G. Nabonnand FRANCE 1878

Parentage unknown

A useful rose. Very double flowers opening flat, combining copper-red and cherry to good effect. A compact and well-foliated plant.

[☼ Gh ▽ (C)] 3′ × 2′ 90 × 60 cm

'Gloire de Dijon'

Jacotot FRANCE 1853

Unknown Tea Rose × 'Souvenir de la Malmaison'

This is a deservedly well-loved, old variety, made more famous by the writings of the Rev. Deans Hole, first president of The National Rose Society. This gentleman seems to have persuaded almost each new encumbent that the thing to do was plant one in the garden of every rectory in the late Victorian era. Large, perfumed flowers, full, opening flat and quartered, of buff-apricot to orange, often giving a second flush in the autumn. Foliage dark green but slightly prone to black spot, especially after the first flush. Flowers dislike wet weather. With all her faults, well worth living with.

[☼ Gh (R)] 12′ × 8′ 3.5 × 2.5 m

'Homère'

Robert and Moreau FRANCE 1858

Parentage unknown

If some of the other Teas are not fully hardy, 'Homère' definitely is. Shapely, cupped-flowers are a pleasing mixture of soft blush-pink and pure white, sometimes with the margins of petals blushed-red. A relatively thornless bush with a twiggy growth habit and dark foliage.

[Gh ▽ (C)] 3′ × 2′ 90 × 60 cm

'Hume's Blush Tea-scented China'
R. × odorata

Fa Tee Nurseries, Canton CHINA 1810

Thought to be R. chinensis × R. gigantea

Found cultivated in China, this, the first Tea Rose from that country, is probably the result of a spontaneous cross but could have been deliberate hybridisation by an early Chinese gardener. Flowers vary from off-white – sometimes with hint of lemon – to blush-pink, sometimes almost brownish-pink, semi-double to almost single. Growth vigorous but erratic. Foliage slightly glossy, mid-green. My stock arrived by a circuitous route from Sangerhausen, East Germany, and I believe it to be correct.

[☼ Gh (R)] variable from 4′ × 4′ to 15′ × 10′ 1.2 × 1.2 m to 4.5 × 3 m

'Lady Hillingdon'

Lowe and Shawyer UK 1910

'Papa Gontier' × 'Mme Hoste'

An outstandingly good rose, deservedly popular since its introduction. The long, pointed buds are rich yoky-yellow, opening to large, blowsy, semi-double flowers with a lovely perfume. Leaves glossy, dark purplish-green, combining superbly with relatively thornless, plum-coloured shoots.

[Gh ▽ (C)]   3′ × 2′   90 × 60 cm

'Lady Hillingdon' Climbing form

Hicks UK 1917

Undoubtedly outstanding as a climber. Its plum-coloured wood and dark foliage are great assets. Needs careful placing but its reputation for tenderness is somewhat exaggerated; although sometimes forcibly pruned by frost, it will survive most winters.

[☼ P (R)]   15′ × 8′   4.5 × 2.5 m

Above: 'Gloire de Dijon'   [PB]
Below: 'Lady Hillingdon'   [RCB]

'Lady Plymouth'

A. Dickson UK 1914

Parentage unknown

A lovely, old variety in typical Tea Rose vein. Flowers ivory-white to flushed cream and blush-pink, well formed and evenly spaced. Slightly scented. Bush, dense and thorny although it would be better with more of its darkish green foliage.

[☼ Gh ▽ (C)]   3′ × 3′   90 × 90 cm

'Maman Cochet'

Cochet FRANCE 1893
'Marie Van Houtte' × 'Mme Lombard'
A very free-flowering rose, initially globular, opening blowsy, pale pink flushed deeper pink with lemon centre. The bush is vigorous with few thorns, carrying dark green foliage of a leathery texture.
[☼ Gh ▽ (C)] 3′ × 2′ 90 × 60 cm

'Marie van Houtte'

Ducher FRANCE 1871
'Mme de Tartas' × 'Mme Falcot'
Bright pink tinged with orange and suffused cream. Fragrant and very free-flowering. Rich green foliage on a vigorous but sprawly plant.
[☼ Gh ▽ (C)] 3′ × 2′ 90 × 60 cm

'Mme Antoine Mari'

Mari FRANCE 1901
Parentage unknown
Fragrant with shapely flowers, especially in the late bud stage. Pink in bud opening to soft flesh pink with lavender-lilac highlights. Foliage light to mid-green on an angular but tidy plant.
[☼ Gh ▽ (R)] 3′ × 3′ 90 × 90 cm

'Mme Berkeley'

Bernaix FRANCE 1899
Parentage unknown
A mixture of salmon, pink, cerise and gold. Flowers initially high-centred, opening somewhat muddled, but attractively so. Extremely free-flowering on a vigorous plant.
[☼ Gh ▽ (C)] 3′ × 2′ 90 × 60 cm

'Mme Bravy', 'Adèle Pradel', 'Mme de Sertot'

Guillot Père FRANCE 1846
Parentage unknown
One of the early Teas. Large, double, creamy-white flowers with pink shadings. Very free-flowering and with a strong, supposedly 'tea' fragrance. Bush dense and bushy.
[☼ Gh ▽ (C)] 3′ × 2′ 90 × 60 cm

'Mme de Tartas'

Bernède FRANCE 1859
Parentage unknown
An important rose, used extensively in Victorian times for breeding. Flowers large, full and cupped, blush-pink, scented. Bush vigorous, rather sprawly in habit but none the less charming. Foliage dark green and leathery. Quite hardy, probably one of few Teas better outdoors than in.
[☼ P ▽ (C)] 3′ × 3′ 90 × 90 cm

'Mme de Watteville'

Guillot Fils FRANCE 1883
Parentage unknown
A dense medium-growing plant with small but plentiful dark green foliage and several thorns. Flowers shapely, fully double, soft yellow with pinkish tinges to the petal edges, scented.
[☼ ▽ (C)] 3′ × 3′ 90 × 90 cm

'Mme Jules Gravereaux'

Soupert and Notting LUXEMBOURG 1901
'Rêve d'Or' × 'Viscountess Folkstone'
I am very fond of this accommodating climbing rose and can only assume that its suspect hardiness has prevented more widespread distribution.

'Mme Jules Gravereaux'   [PB]

'Mons Tillier'   [PB]

Shapely, fully double, sometimes quartered blooms of yellowish-buff, shaded peach with hints of pink as undertones. It is scented. Foliage lush, dark green and the wood, dark. The best plant I know is at Mottisfont Abbey, Hants.

[☼ Gh (R)]   8' × 6'   2.5 × 1.8 m

'Mme Lombard'

Lacharme FRANCE 1878
'Mme de Tartas' seedling
Flowers full, very double, salmon with deeper centres, scented. Bush vigorous with dark green foliage. Similar, save in colour, to Mme de Tartas.

[☼ ▽ (C)]   3' × 3'   90 × 90 cm

'Mme Wagram', 'Comtesse de Turin'

Bernaix FRANCE 1895
Parentage unknown
Large, rosy-red petals with yellow bases make up fully double, globular flowers, borne freely on a healthy bush with dark green foliage.

[Gh ▽ (C)]   3' × 3'   90 × 90 cm

'Mons Tillier'

Bernaix FRANCE 1891
Parentage unknown
A good but little known rose better endowed than most Teas with foliage. Large loosely double flowers, blood red with violet smudges, freely produced on a vigorous bush. Growth quite tall and lax.

[Gh ▽ (C)]   4' × 3'   1.2 m × 90 cm

'Mrs Campbell Hall'

Hall – introduced by Dickson UK 1914
Parentage unknown
Creamy-white edged salmon flowers with deeper salmon centres, quite large and high-centred in bud, opening full and somewhat blowsy. Dark, leathery foliage on a vigorous bush.

[☼ Gh ▽ (C)]   4' × 3'   1.2 m × 90 cm

'Niphetos'

Keynes, Williams & Co. UK
Bush form Bougère FRANCE 1843
Parentage unknown
Climbing form Keynes, Williams and Co. UK 1889
Used extensively as florist's rose during late Vic-

torian and Edwardian times. Lovely, creamy buds opens to pure white, with pointed petals creating a muddled, star-like shape. Foliage light green. Makes a vigorous climber but needs placing under glass for the best blooms.

[∴ Gh ▽ (R)]
Bush form   4′×3′   1.2 m × 90 cm
Climbing form   10′×6′   3 × 1.8 m

'Noella Nabonnand' Climber

Nabonnand FRANCE 1901
'Reine Marie Henriette' × 'Bardou Job'
Not often seen, perhaps because it seldom repeats or due to its reputation for tenderness. Nevertheless, a fine variety. Globular yet pointed buds open to a blowsy, large, rose of velvety crimson. Foliage mid-green and quite healthy.

[Gh P (S)]   10′×6′   3 × 1.8 m

'Papa Gontier'

G. Nabonnand FRANCE 1883
Parentage unknown
Used extensively as a forcing rose in its early career. Flowers rich-pink, almost red, sometimes slightly mottled and with a deeper reverse, semi-double and slightly scented. Growth habit rather twiggy; I would prefer to see more of its dark green glossy foliage.

[∴ Gh ▽ (C)]   3′×2′   90 × 60 cm

'Parks' Yellow Tea-scented China'

R. × odorata ochroleuca

CHINA 1824
Said to be the original Tea Rose. I believe I have this rose, but sadly have no recollection or record of whence or from whom it came. Perhaps a reader will remember and remind me to acknowledge. It is an angular-growing climber with fairly large, double, cupped flowers of soft, sulphur-yellow, unusually perfumed, although I fail to detect any resemblance to tea. The foliage, although large, is none the less typical of a China or Tea. It has but few thorns.

[∴ Gh ▽ (R)]   6′×4′   1.8 × 1.2 m

'Perle des Jardins'

F. Levet FRANCE 1874
'Mme Falcot' seedling
A fragrant, many-petalled rose often opening quartered. Sulphur-yellow to buff on a sturdy

'Papa Gontier'   [PB]

compact plant. Apparently quite hardy out of doors but probably better under glass in cold or wet districts, since it fails to open properly in those conditions.

[Gh ▽ ∴ (C)]   3′×2′   90 × 60 cm

'Rival de Paestum'

Paul UK 1848
Parentage unknown
Fully double flowers, ivory-white tinged pink, more so in the bud stage. Scented. Bush well foliated with dark green leaves.

[Gh ▽ (C)]   3′×2′   90 × 60 cm

'Rosette Delizy'

P. Nabonnand FRANCE 1922
'Général Galliéni' × 'Comtesse Bardi'
Pleasing combination of rose-pink, buff and apricot with deeper colouring on the outside of each petal. Bush branchy but still refined in habit with good foliage.

[∴ Gh ▽ (C)]   3′×2′   90 × 60 cm

[TW/PB]

Above: 'Perle des Jardins'
Below: 'Sombreuil'

'Safrano'

Beauregard FRANCE 1839
Parentage unknown
This rose, one of the oldest of the Teas, is still
worthy of consideration, especially if planted in
groups or in pots. Will not enjoy an exposed
position. Very floriferous, each flower fully-
double, opening flat from a high-centred bud,
buff and pinkish-apricot with a sulphur-yellow
base. Foliage mid-green and plentiful.

[☼ Gh ▽ (C)] 3′×2′ 90×60 cm

'Solfaterre', 'Solfatare'

Boyau FRANCE 1843
Seedling from 'Lamarque'
A beautiful, large, double, pale sulphur yellow
rose, which needs extra loving care and a warm,
sheltered site or greenhouse to flourish, when it
can be most rewarding.

[☼ ▽ (R)] 10′×8′ 3×2.5 m

'Sombreuil' Climber

Robert FRANCE 1850
A fully double, flattish flower, pure white with
hints of cream in the base, sweetly scented. A

'Souvenir de Mme Léonie Viennot'   [PB]

vigorous, slightly prone to mildew. Although a very good climbing rose, it is seldom seen these days. My stock came to me via Keith Money, whose mother sent it by ordinary post from New Zealand, wrapped in polythene, in a pencil case.

[☼ Gh ⦿ (R)]   12′×8′   3.5×2.5 m

'Souvenir d'un Ami'

Bélot-Defougère FRANCE 1846
Parentage unknown
Cupped, fully double flowers of rose-pink tinted deeper pink to salmon. Highly scented. Foliage rich green on a vigorous and branchy plant.

[P Gh (R)]   8′×4′   2.5×1.2 m

'The Bride'

May USA 1885
'Catherine Mermet' sport
An interesting rose well named, in that its colour is pure white with a mere hint of pink on each petal edge. William Paul said of it "in all respects a first class rose". Quite vigorous for a Tea, with good foliage.

[Gh ▽ (C)]   4′×3′   1.2 m×90 cm

beautiful rose which, with loving care, is most rewarding. With its ample, lush green foliage it makes a dense shrub with support or a small climber.

[Gh (R)]   8′×5′   2.5×1.5 m

'Souvenir d'Elise Vardon'

Marest FRANCE 1855
Parentage unknown
A shapely, fragrant rose of cream overlaid with coppery-yellow. Foliage leathery and glossy, but rather tender.

[☼ Gh ▽ (C)]   3′×2′   90×60 cm

'Souvenir de Mme Léonie Viennot'

Bernaix FRANCE 1897
Parentage unknown
Strongly fragrant, shapely, almost fully double flowers borne sometimes in clusters, sometimes singly. The colour is a mixture of primrose yellow with variable coppery-orange overtones, sometimes veined pink. Quite free-flowering and

'Triomphe de Luxembourg'

Hardy FRANCE 1840
Parentage unknown
Fully double flowers produced in clusters; salmon-pink, changing to pinkish-buff with age. Foliage dark green. I dated this rose from an old general gardening catalogue of 1839, when it was a new variety and priced at 7/6d. (37½ pence) each – probably a week's wages for a gardener in those days.

[Gh ▽ (C)]   3′×2′   90×60 cm

'William R. Smith', 'Charles Dingee', 'Blush Maman Cochet', 'President William Smith', 'Jeanette Heller'

Bagg USA 1909
Parentage unknown
A rose known by many and varied names over the years. Flowers creamy-white flushed pink with buff and gold at the base, rather blowsy when fully open but produced on a compact, tidy plant.

[Gh ▽ (C)]   3′×2′   90×60 cm

Above: 'The Bride'   [PB]
Below: 'William R. Smith'   [PB]

Note: Although it might appear that the Hybrid Teas should follow the Teas in line, their genealogy has become so complicated that they are better suited to follow the Hybrid Perpetuals.

Hybrid Perpetual Roses

The Hybrid Perpetuals emerged in the 1830s and were born from a varied and complex union, in which the Portlands, Bourbons, Noisettes and, later, the Teas all played their part.

Few were completely perpetual, but most were remontant to some degree. After a few years of uncertain popularity, they became one of the major groups of roses.

Throughout Queen Victoria's reign they led the field as exhibition roses, and as flower shows became fashionable, breeders were impelled to seek ever larger, more shapely blooms. Despite this quest for size of flower, many very useful garden shrubs emerged and, as such, have come down to us today.

'Alfred Colomb' [PB]

'Alfred Colomb'
Lacharme FRANCE 1865
'Général Jacqueminot' × unknown
A large, full rose, rounded in late bud and high-centred, brickish-red with flecks of deep pink and carmine. Slightly vulgar but nevertheless appealing. Growth tidy and foliage abundant.
[P (R)] 4′ × 3′ 1.2 m × 90 cm

'American Beauty', 'Mme Ferdinand Jamin'
Lédéchaux FRANCE 1875
Parentage unknown
First introduced as a forcing variety, its longish, strong stems making it ideal for bouquets. Also a useful garden plant. Crimson, high-centred flowers rather modern in appearance. The bush was perhaps rather ahead of its time in being very Hybrid Tea-like in stature.
[Gh ▽ (R)] 3′ × 3′ 90 × 90 cm

'Anna de Diesbach', 'Gloire de Paris'
Lacharme FRANCE 1858
'La Reine' × seedling
A tall rose with many fragrant flowers of rich, deep rose-pink with deeper shadings, initially quite large and cupped, later opening rather flat. Bush tall, a little ungainly, but well foliated.
[▽ (R)] 4′ × 3′ 1.2 m × 90 cm

'Archiduchesse Elizabeth d'Autriche'
Moreau-Robert FRANCE 1881
Parentage unknown
Soft rose-pink flowers, fully double, opening flat. I find the plant rather inclined to sprawl, but effective if pruned hard each season. Obviously enjoys full sun.
[☼ (R)] 5′ × 4′ 1.5 × 1.2 m

Top: 'Mme Gabriel Luizet' (see text p. 372)   *Bottom:* 'Gloire Lyonnaise' (see text p. 370)   [RCB/PB]

'Ardoisée de Lyon'

Damaizin FRANCE 1858

Parentage unknown

Superb, fully double, quartered flower of rich cerise with violet and purple shadings, held on strong neck and exuding a rich perfume. Ample greyish-green foliage on a compact, tidy plant with numerous thorns. Little known but a splendid rose.

[P ▽ (R)]   4′ × 3′   1.2 m × 90 cm

'Ards Rover'

Dickson UK 1898

Parentage unknown

Excellent old pillar rose. Shapely, crimson flowers opening blowsily, with a strong scent. Definitely has a place in the modern garden, especially since good, deep red climbers are so few. Of medium stature, it fulfils the role of both a wall climber and pillar rose with considerable effect, especially as it is sometimes, in good seasons, recurrent. Foliage quite lush and dark green. Needs attention for mildew early each season for it to give of its very best.

[(R)]   10′ × 6′   3 × 1.8 m

'Roger Lambelin' (see text p. 376)   [PB]

'Baron Girod de l'Ain'   [JB]

'Baron de Bonstetten'

Liabaud FRANCE 1871

'Général Jacqueminot' × 'Géant des Batailles'

Very double, very dark red and very fragrant. Upright and vigorous in growth and rather thorny with mid to dark green foliage.

[▽ (R)]   4′ × 3′   1.2 m × 90 cm

'Baron Girod de l'Ain'

Reverchon FRANCE 1897

'Eugène Fürst' sport

A popular novelty since its introduction, this unusual rose is well worth garden space. Its very double flowers are bright crimson, they open cup-shaped, with the petal edges rather ragged-looking, an illusion enhanced by the fringe of white edging the margins. As a shrub it is rather straggly but quite dense with firm, stout thorns and leathery dark green leaves.

[P (R)]   4′ × 3′   1.2 m × 90 cm

'Baroness Rothschild', 'Baronne Adolphe de Rothschild'

Pernet Père FRANCE 1868
'Souvenir de la Reine d'Angleterre' sport
A superior member of its group. Large, full flowers remain slightly cupped when fully open, held erect on strong, stout stems. Petals are of a soft to clear rose-pink colour and have a soft silky texture. Highly scented. Bush well covered with large grey-green foliage.

[P H ▽ (R)]   4′ × 3′   1.2 m × 90 cm

'Baronne Prévost'

Desprez FRANCE 1842
Parentage unknown
Deep rose pink scented flowers opening flat and double from globular buds. A reliable rose of considerable longevity, with many bushes still growing in cottage gardens, having survived from its heyday. Somewhat coarse in growth and rather thorny, it still makes a most useful shrub.

[P (R)]   5′ × 4′   1.5 × 1.2 m

'Baronne Prévost'   [VP]

'Captain Hayward' (see text p. 364)   [JB]

'Black Prince'

W. Paul UK 1866
Parentage unknown
Vigorous variety with good foliage, if rather prone to mildew. Flowers large and cupped, opening from shapely buds to rich dark crimson to almost black. Scented.

[(R)]   5′×3′   1.5 m×90 cm

'Captain Hayward' Climber

Bennett UK
Bush form 1893
'Triomphe de l'Expedition' seedling
This form W. Paul 1906
A tall rose, needing support as a shrub. Ideal as pillar rose when its healthy disposition can be fully appreciated. Pinkish-crimson flowers large and cupped until fully open, when they become rather blowsy. Does not always repeat. Hips large and rather attractive so dead-heading best avoided.

[P (R)]   8′×4′   2.5×1.2 m

'Champion of the World', 'Mrs de Graw'

Woodhouse UK 1894
'Hermosa' × 'Magna Charta'
A presumptuous name, probably describing the size of its deep rosy-pink flowers. A bush of medium stature, rather sprawly, leaves dark green.

[P ▽ (R)]   4′×3′   1.2 m×90 cm

'Charles Gater'

W. Paul UK 1893
Parentage unknown
An upright-growing plant which can be slotted into the smallest space. Flowers clear bright red and globular throughout their life. Scented. Good strong foliage, rather thorny. Inclined to mildew after first flush.

[▽ (R)]   4′×2′   1.2 m×60 cm

'Charles Lefèbvre'

Lacharme FRANCE 1861
'Général Jacqueminot' × 'Victor Verdier'
Very large, many-petalled, flowers of rich crimson shaded maroon, high-centred, opening cupped, held on a strong, firm neck. Foliage dark green and sufficient.

[▽ (R)]   4′×3′   1.2 m×90 cm

'Clio'

W. Paul UK 1894
Parentage unknown
Clusters of fully double, initially cupped, fragrant, soft silvery-pink flowers on strong, almost arching stems. Rich leathery foliage on a vigorous, if somewhat sprawly plant, with ample thorns.

[(R)]   4′×4′   1.2×1.2 m

'Comtesse Cécile de Chabrillant'

Marest FRANCE 1858
Parentage unknown
The clear mid-pink flowers are shapely, full and globular, and strongly perfumed. They are supported on strong flower stalks. Growth is upright, and the rose is very free-flowering which qualifies this excellent variety for general garden use.

[▽ (R)]   4′×4′   1.2×1.2 m

'Countess of Oxford', 'Comtesse d'Oxford'

Guillot Père FRANCE 1869
Parentage unknown
William Paul spoke highly of this rose. Double globular flowers opening cupped, of rich carmine-red and scented. A vigorous, tidy plant with ample healthy foliage.

[P ▽ (R)]   4′×3′   1.2 m×90 cm

'Charles Lefèbvre'   [PB]

'Crown Prince'

W. Paul UK 1880
Parentage unknown
A free-flowering fully double rose of purple and red. Tidy and compact in growth with dark green foliage.

[▽ (R)]   3′×3′   90×90 cm

'Duke of Wellington' [PB]

'Dembrowski'
Vibert FRANCE 1849
Parentage unknown
Very shapely, fully double, reddish-purple flowers on a strong but medium-growing plant with mid-green foliage.
[(C)] 4' × 3' 1.2 m × 90 cm

'Dr Andry'
E. Verdier FRANCE 1864
Parentage unknown
Very bright red with deeper shadings towards the centre of each fully double flower. Vigorous growth with dark green foliage, only a slight scent.
[▽ (R)] 4' × 3' 1.2 m × 90 cm

'Duke of Edinburgh'
Paul UK 1868
'Général Jacqueminot' × unknown
Not easy to grow except in the very best soils where it can be rewarding. Shortish in stature and slightly spreading in habit, it produces semi-double flowers of bright scarlet to crimson, sweetly scented.
[▽ (R)] 2' × 2' 60 × 60 cm

'Duke of Wellington'
Granger FRANCE 1864
Parentage unknown
A surprising name for a French rose? Large, shapely, high-centred flowers of deep crimson, these tend to dislike hot sun which turns their outer petals somewhat blackish. Upright in growth, the blooms are produced on thick, stout, thorny stems with dark foliage.
[▽ (R)] 4' × 3' 1.2 m × 90 cm

'Dupuy Jamain'
Jamain FRANCE 1868
Parentage unknown
I place this rose high on my list of favourite Hybrid Perpetuals. Large, full, cerise-red flowers held on strong necks, with a good, strong perfume. The shrub is healthy with an abundance of lush, grey-green leaves. Relatively free of thorns, upright growth.
[P ▽ (R)] 4' × 3' 1.2 m × 90 cm

'Eliza Boelle'
Guillot Père FRANCE 1869
Parentage unknown
A vigorous rose having shapely, cupped, whitish-pink, scented flowers, with incurving centre petals. Ample foliage on a tidy, well-groomed plant.
[▽ (R)]   4′ × 3′   1.2 m × 90 cm

Left: 'Eclair' and *below:* 'Comtesse Cécile de Chabrillant' (see p. 364)   [PB/PB]

'Eclair'
Lacharme FRANCE 1833
'Général Jacqueminot' × unknown
Well scented, very dark red, almost black flowers, opening flat in rosette shape. Not the easiest of roses to grow but well worth some extra loving care. Upright in growth. Can perhaps be faulted by its rather sparse foliage. Almost fits the Portlands in type. Sent to me by Margaret Wray of Langport, near Taunton.
[▽ (R)]   4′ × 3′   1.2 m × 90 cm

'Empereur du Maroc', 'Emperor of Morocco'
Guinoisseau FRANCE 1858
'Géant des Batailles' seedling
Very double flowers, opening flat; deep crimson tinged maroon. A superb rose when weather permits. Flowers borne in large clusters which are sometimes too heavy for the thorny branches to support. Hard pruning helps prevent this over the years. Needs precautions against black spot and mildew.
[(R)]   4′ × 3′   1.2 m × 90 cm

'Enfant de France'

Lartay FRANCE 1860
Parentage unknown
For a number of years I have grown a rose under this name. I am not sure if it is correct, but it fits the descriptions I have read in old books and catalogues. Whatever its name, such a good rose should not be omitted. The fully double flowers, which are sometimes quartered, are silky pink and beautifully perfumed. Growth is upright and foliage plentiful. Rather of the Portland mould.
[Gh P ▽ (R)]   3′ × 2′   90 × 60 cm

'Eugène Fürst'

Soupert and Notting LUXEMBOURG 1875
'Baron de Bonstetten' × unknown
Ragged edged, crimson-purple, cupped flowers of considerable size, highly scented. The bush is upright in growth and the flowers are borne on strong necks amid good, dark green foliage.
[▽ (R)]   4′ × 3′   1.2 m × 90 cm

'Ferdinand de Lesseps'

Verdier FRANCE 1869
Parentage unknown
An interesting rose bearing shapely flowers of

Above: 'Eugène Fürst' [JB]
Below: 'Ferdinand Pichard' (see text p. 368) [JB]

lavender, shaded purple and magenta, opening
flat, with many petals in the Centifolia form. Bush
shrubby and vigorous.

[(R)]   4′ × 3′   1.2 m × 90 cm

'Ferdinand Pichard'

Tanne FRANCE 1921
Parentage unknown
Flowers of rich, carmine red, heavily laced and
striped with white, opening large and cup-
shaped with a distinct scent; these combine well
with rich green foliage and are produced on a
vigorous, healthy shrub. One of the best of the
striped roses available today.

[P H (R)]   5′ × 4′   1.5 × 1.2 m

'Fisher Holmes', 'Fisher and Holmes'

Verdier FRANCE 1865
'Maurice Bernardin' seedling
Well-formed, double flowers from shapely,
pointed buds. Shades of scarlet and crimson.
Scented. Bush of medium height and moderately
vigorous with good foliage. Rather prone to
disease, the result perhaps of over propagation,
for it was very popular in Victorian times.

[▽ (C)]   3′ × 3′   90 × 90 cm

'Frau Karl Druschki', 'Snow Queen', 'Reine des Neiges', 'White American Beauty.

P. Lambert GERMANY 1901
'Merveille de Lyon' × 'Mme Caroline Testout'
For many years the most popular white rose, and
deservedly so, its only significant faults being a

'Frau Karl Druschki'   [KM]

'Général Jacqueminot'   [PB]

lack of scent and a dislike of wet weather. Pure
white blooms large and globular, with high centres in bud. Shrub vigorous and strong with
plenty of leathery, lightish green leaves.

[P (R)]   5′ × 3′   1.5 m × 90 cm

'Frau Karl Druschki' Climbing form

Lawrenson UK 1906
Parentage unknown
As bush form, except that it makes a vigorous and
useful climber.

[P (S)]   15′ × 8′   4.5 × 2.5 m

'Général Jacqueminot', 'General Jack', 'Jack Rose'

Roussel FRANCE 1853
'Gloire des Rosomanes' seedling
Clear red, shapely, pointed buds opening to well-
formed, perfumed flowers, produced on fairly
long stems. A vigorous shrub with rich-green
foliage. Rather prone to rust from mid-summer
onwards.

[(R)]   5′ × 4′   1.5 × 1.2 m

'Georg Arends', 'Fortuné Besson'

W. Hinner GERMANY 1910
'Frau Karl Druschki' × 'La France'
A first-class rose. Large, initially high-centred but
blowsy blooms of clear rose-pink paling to soft
pink. Free-flowering, fragrant and, as a shrub,
vigorous with plenty of large, grey-green leaves.

[H P (C)]   5′ × 4′   1.5 × 1.2 m

'Georg Arends' [PB]

'Gloire de Bruxelles', 'Gloire de l'Exposition'
Soupert and Notting LUXEMBOURG 1889
'Souvenir de William Wood' × 'Lord Macaulay'
Sixty or more velvety petals make up a flower
which opens flat in large rosette form, dark red to
crimson-purple and scented. The shrub is loose
and untidy despite small stature but well worth
the effort of support.
[(R)] 4′×4′ 1.2 × 1.2 m

'Gloire de Chédane-Guinoisseau'
Chédane-Pajotin FRANCE 1907
'Gloire de Ducher' × unknown
Shapely cupped flowers produced in consider-
able numbers, bright rich pinkish red, scented.
Foliage dark green and abundant on a vigorous
quite healthy plant.
[P ▽ (R)] 4′×3′ 1.2 m × 90 cm

'Gloire de Ducher'
Ducher FRANCE 1865
Parentage unknown
More credit is due to this rose than it has ever
received. Huge, fully double blooms of deep
pinkish-red, somewhat blowsy in structure, produced freely along long, arching branches amid
dark grey-green leaves. Well scented.
[P (R)] 6′×4′ 1.8 × 1.2 m

'Gloire de l'Exposition.
See 'Gloire de Bruxelles'

'Gloire de Paris'. *See* 'Anna de Diesbach'

'Gloire de Ducher' [PB]

'Gloire d'un Enfant d'Hiram'
Vilin FRANCE 1899
Parentage unknown
Large, bright pink, scented, cupped flowers on a strong, sturdy, upright growing plant with few thorns and good, greyish-green leathery foliage.
[P ▽ (R)] 4′×3′ 1.2 m×90 cm

'Gloire Lyonnaise'
Guillot Fils FRANCE 1885
'Baroness Rothschild' × 'Mme Falcot'
A favourite of mine, this creamy-white rose has semi-double flowers that open flat with a good perfume. The shrub is upright in growth with strong stems supporting the flowers without arching. Few thorns, foliage is dark green and healthy. Should be more widely grown.
[P H ▽ (C)] 4′×2′ 1.2 m×60 cm

'Hans Mackart'
E. Verdier Fils FRANCE 1885
Parentage unknown
Double flowers of bright but deep pink opening flat from cupped buds, inclined to sprawl. Ample lightish-green foliage with but few thorns.
[P (R)] 5′×3′ 1.5 m×90 cm

Above: 'Heinrich Schultheis' [PB]

'Heinrich Schultheis'
Bennett UK 1882
'Mabel Morrison' × 'E.Y. Teas'
A Victorian exhibition rose which probably won many prizes for size alone. Flowers high-centred until fully open, then cupped, flat-topped and slightly ragged, rich pink with hints of a deeper shade in the base, scented. Vigorous, well-foliated and upright. Worth growing.
[▽ (C)] 4′×3′ 1.2 m×90 cm

'Henry Nevard'
Cants UK 1924
Parentage unknown
Fragrant, bright crimson, cupped flowers of considerable size. Bushy growth with dark green, leathery leaves.
[(R)] 4′×3′ 1.2 m×90 cm

'Her Majesty'
Bennett UK 1885
'Mabel Morrison' × 'Canary'
Huge, fully double blooms of clear pink. Another Victorian exhibition rose well worth growing today. Foliage large and grey, but inclined to

'John Hopper' and *right:* 'Mabel Morrison' [PB/TW]
(see text p. 372)

mildew. Shrub vigorous but less tall than most
of its type.

[▽ (R)]   3′ × 2′   90 × 60 cm

'Horace Vernet'

Guillot Fils FRANCE 1866
'Général Jacqueminot' × unknown
A high-centred rose of rich crimson, retaining
its shape well into maturity, fragrant. The shrub
is upright and tidy in habit with abundant dark
foliage.

[▽ (R)]   4′ × 3′   1.2 m × 90 cm

'Hugh Dickson'

Dickson UK 1905
'Lord Bacon' × 'Gruss an Teplitz'
A tall, lanky rose from the latter end of the Hybrid
Perpetual cycle. Rich dark red, powerfully perfumed flowers borne on long, arching stems,
making it an ideal rose for 'pegging-down' or for
pillars. Can be grown as a shrub but needs support. Foliage rich, dark green with hints of
maroon.

[P (R)]   8′ × 5′   2.5 × 1.5 m

'Jean Rosenkrantz'

Portemer FRANCE 1864
Parentage unknown
Big flowers of neatly formed, deep pinkish-red
petals with perfume. The shrub is well foliated,
vigorous and upright.

[▽ (R)]   4′ × 3′   1.2 m × 90 cm

'John Hopper'

Ward UK 1862
'Jules Margottin' × 'Mme Vidot'
The large, fragrant flowers are a pleasing combination of bright pink and lilac, with deeper
centres produced on an upright vigorous plant
which remains tidy and seems to enjoy most soils.
A first-class rose.

[H P ▽ (R)]   4′ × 3′   1.2 m × 90 cm

'Jules Margottin'

Margottin FRANCE 1853
'La Reine' seedling
This rose has lots of thick, dark green foliage on
strong, thorny stems. From these emerge equally
strong, pointed buds opening into large, flattish
flowers of deep carmine each with a strong scent.

[(R)]   4′ × 3′   1.2 m × 90 cm

'La Reine', 'Reine des Francais'

Laffay FRANCE 1842
Parentage unknown
Large, globular almost portly blooms, high-
centred as buds but opening to cupped blooms
with flattish tops, the numerous petals giving an
almost serrated effect. Colour silvery rose-pink
with an undertone of lilac. The shrub is upright,
well foliated but not too tall. One of the first
Hybrid Perpetuals, its influence can still be seen
in roses to this day.

[▽ (C)]   3′ × 2′   90 × 60 cm

'Le Havre'

Eudes FRANCE 1871
Parentage unknown
Scented, very double, almost vermilion-red
flowers on a healthy, strong plant with dark
green, leathery foliage.

[▽ (R)]   4′ × 3′   1.2 m × 90 cm

'Mabel Morrison'

Broughton UK 1878
'Baroness Rothschild' sport
A white sport of the excellent 'Baroness Roth-schild', inheriting most of her attributes except height, as this rose – for me at least – is somewhat shorter. Flowers pure white with flecks of pink in hot weather.

[P H ▽ (R)]   4′ × 3′   1.2 m × 90 cm

'Marguerite Guillard'

Chambard FRANCE 1915
'Frau Karl Druschki' sport
Has fewer petals than its parent, enabling it to open better in wet weather. Otherwise similar in both colour and habit.

[(R)]   5′ × 3′   1.5 m × 90 cm

'Mme Ferdinand Jamin'

See 'American Beauty'

'Mme Gabriel Luizet'

Liabaud FRANCE 1877
Parentage unknown
Large, often quartered, fully double flowers of deep glowing pink with paler petal edges when fully open. Very vigorous with good foliage and stout strong stems. Seldom repeats although the occasional autumn bloom can be rewarding.

[P (S)]   6′ × 4′   1.8 × 1.2 m

'Mme Scipion Cochet'

S. Cochet FRANCE 1873
Parentage unknown
Attractively wrinkled, cup-shaped flowers, deep purplish-pink paling to softer shades at the edges. Good, dark green foliage and vigorous, bushy growth.

[(R)]   4′ × 3′   1.2 m × 90 cm

'Mme Victor Verdier'

E. Verdier FRANCE 1863
'Sénateur Vaisse' × unknown
Huge buds open to shaggy, but attractive, double, light crimson to carmine flowers with slightly weak necks. Plenty of good, dark-green foliage. Shrub vigorous and healthy.

[P H (R)]   5′ × 4′   1.5 × 1.2 m

'Mrs John Laing'   [TW]

'Mrs John Laing'

Bennett UK 1887
'François Michelon' seedling
Undoubtedly one of the superior Hybrid Per-petuals and one of the best from Henry Bennett's stable in late Victorian times. Upright in growth with large, grey-green leaves. A healthy plant producing an abundance of scented, shapely, silver-pink flowers, which would have been used extensively for exhibition by Victorian and Ed-wardian gardeners. Today it makes an excellent bushy shrub.

[Gh P H ▽ (R)]   4′ × 3′   1.2 m × 90 cm

'Paul Ricault' (see text p. 374)   [VP]

Above: 'La Reine' (see text p. 371) [PB]
Below: 'Paul Neyron' (see text p. 374) [PB]

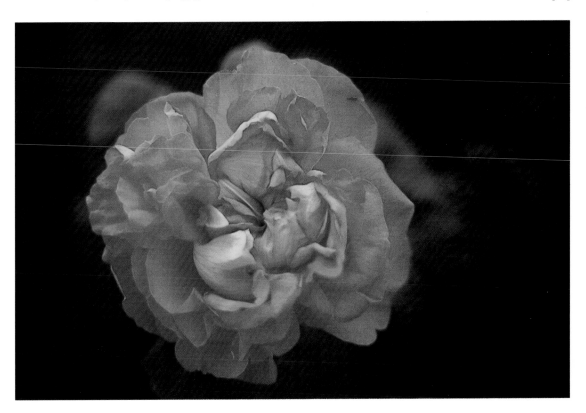

'Paul Neyron'

Levet FRANCE 1869

'Victor Verdier' × 'Anna de Diesbach'

This sturdy, healthy variety should be grown more extensively. Very large unfading, rich, warm pink flowers with a pleasing, muddled appearance when fully open. Scented. Growth strong and upright, with large, matt, dark-green leaves.

[Gh P H ▽ (R)]   3′ × 2′   90 × 60 cm

'Paul's Early Blush'   [TW]

'Prince Camille de Rohan'   [PB]

'Paul Ricault'

Portemer FRANCE 1845

Parentage unknown

A rose with large, almost Centifolia-like, fully double flowers opening flat and quartered, borne along long, arching stems on a vigorous, thorny, well-foliated shrub.

[P (R)]   5′ × 4′   1.5 × 1.2 m

'Paul's Early Blush', 'Mrs Harkness'

W. Paul UK 1893

'Heinrich Schultheis' sport

Blush-pink flowers, which as the name suggests, appear a few days earlier than most, large, very double and scented, produced on a strong, thorny bush, with thickish branches. Foliage dark green.

[P ▽ (R)]   4′ × 3′   1.2 m × 90 cm

'Pierre Notting'

Portemer FRANCE 1863

'Alfred Colomb' seedling

An upright grower with deep crimson, globular flowers. Highly scented. One of many such types from the middle of the 19th century, presumably owing their survival to a strong constitution, which this rose certainly has.

[P (R)]   4′ × 3′   1.2 m × 92 cm

'Prince Camille de Rohan', 'La Rosière'

E. Verdier FRANCE 1861

'Général Jacqueminot' × 'Géant des Batailles'

Can be faulted by its very weak neck, otherwise a fascinating rose. Deep blackish-red blooms of colossal size, opening flat and deepening with age. The shrub is rather sprawly and until mature has difficulty in carrying the weight of the blooms on its thinnish stems. Foliage dark green.

[▽ (R)]   4′ × 3′   1.2 m × 90 cm

'Reine des Violettes', 'Queen of the Violets'

Millet-Malet FRANCE 1860

'Pius IX' seedling

If I had to choose just one Hybrid Perpetual, it would have to be this one. An upright-growing and almost thornless shrub with stout, erect branches. Foliage grey-green and soft to touch. Flowers, sometimes charmingly hidden among the foliage, with which they blend so well, are

'Baroness Rothschild' (see text p. 365)

[VP]

soft, velvety violet, opening flat and quartered. To cap all this, it has a lovely perfume. Flowers shatter very quickly after reaching perfection, but this small fault helps us appreciate it even more.

[P H (C)]   5′ × 3′   1.5 m × 90 cm

'Roger Lambelin'

Schwartz FRANCE 1890
'Fisher Holmes' sport
A strange rose, whose addiction to mildew and

'Ruhm von Steinfurth'   [VP]

other diseases renders it no more than a novelty. Flowers double and crimson-maroon with white streaks and stripes, especially on the edges of the petals.

[▽ (R)]   4′ × 3′   1.2 m × 90 cm

'Ruhm von Steinfurth', 'Red Druschki'

Weigand GERMANY 1920
'Frau Karl Druschki' × 'Ulrich Brunner Fils'
An old exhibition variety. Plump, double, high-centred flowers of ruby red fading to cerise, cupped when open. Scented. Bush upright and sturdy with leathery, dark green foliage. A Hybrid Tea in all but pedigree.

[P ▽ (R)]   3′ × 2′   90 × 60 cm

'Sidonie'

Vibert FRANCE 1847
Parentage unknown
Almost a Portland. Scented, slightly fimbriated, fully double flowers of medium size, of clear glowing pink, usually in well-spaced clusters. Has a short tidy habit but is vigorous with good if somewhat coarse foliage and an unfortunate addiction to black spot.

[P ▽ (C)]   3′ × 2′   90 × 60 cm

'Snow Queen'. *See* 'Frau Karl Druschki'

'Souvenir de Jeanne Balandreau'   [PB]

'Souvenir d'Alphonse Lavallée'

Verdier FRANCE 1884
Parentage unknown
For years there has been some confusion between this rose and another Hybrid Perpetual, 'Souvenir du Docteur Jamain'. 'Lavallée' is a lovely full, scented rose, combining several shades of crimson and purple. Inclined to wander if grown as a shrub unless tethered to a stake or a tripod. Best grown as a small climber. More thorny than 'Jamain'.

[P (R)]   8′ × 6′   2.5 × 1.8 m

'Souvenir du Dr Jamain'   [JB]

'Souvenir de Jeanne Balandreau'

Robichon FRANCE 1899
Parentage unknown
The large, double, cupped flowers, of deep cerise with pink stripes and vermilion highlights, are shapely and held erect on strong necks amid good, dark grey-green foliage on an upright, tidy shrub.

[P H ▽ (R)]   4′ × 3′   1.2 m × 90 cm

'Souvenir du Docteur Jamain'

Lacharme FRANCE 1865
'Charles Lefèbvre' seedling
A superb rose if kept away from scorching sun, which it hates. Flowers are rich ruby-red and, although semi-double, open to a cupped shape, sometimes showing off their anthers to good effect. Foliage is dark green and the stems relatively thornless. Scented. At best it is of rare beauty and even at its worst can still be enjoyed.
[N P ◑ (R)]   10′ × 7′   3 × 2 m

'Spencer'

W. Paul UK 1892
'Merveille de Lyon' sport
Fully double flowers opening flat from globular buds, soft satin-pink, with paler, almost white reverse. Growth vigorous but tidy, with good dark foliage.
[▽ (R)]   4′ × 3′   1.2 m × 90 cm

'Surpassing Beauty', 'Woolverstone Church Rose'

Rediscovery by Mr Humphrey Brooke
Date unknown. Reintroduced Beales 1980
An old variety of climbing rose discovered growing at Woolverstone Church, Suffolk. Flowers deep red to crimson, blowsy when open and very strongly fragrant, appearing particularly early each season. Well worth its reintroduction. Growth relaxed and vigorous.
[P (R)]   8′ × 6′   2.5 × 1.8 m

Above: 'Surpassing Beauty'   [PB]

'Ulrich Brunner Fils', 'Ulrich Brunner'

A. Levet FRANCE 1882
Confused parentage – probably 'Paul Neyron' sport
Large, plump, initially high centred blooms opening rather loosely but attractively; rosy-carmine fading to pink with age. Sweetly scented. The bush is upright and well endowed with dark green foliage. Stems have few thorns.
[H P ▽ (R)]   4′ × 3′   1.2 m × 90 cm

'Vick's Caprice'

Vick USA 1891
'Archiduchesse Elizabeth d'Autriche' sport
Large, double, cupped flowers with high centres. An unusual colour combination of pale pink and lilac with white, flecked and striped deeper pink. Foliage large, attractively light green, taking an upright stance on relatively thornless shoots.
[H ▽ P (C)]   4′ × 3′   1.2 m × 90 cm

'Victor Verdier'

Lacharme FRANCE 1859
'Jules Margottin' × 'Safrano'
Large, fully double, clear bright rose, pink flowers held on a strong neck, with a good perfume. Stems strong and thorny with good strong dark green foliage. Upright in growth. An important stud rose. I have not seen this rose in the UK but plants are growing at the Roseraie de l'Hay, Paris.
[P ▽ (R)]   4′ × 3′   1.2 m × 90 cm

'Xavier Olibo'

Lacharme FRANCE 1865
'Général Jacqueminot' sport
This rose has all the attributes and faults of 'Général Jacqueminot', but its colour is a much darker red.
[(R)]   5′ × 4′   1.5 × 1.2 m

'Yolande d'Aragon'

Vibert FRANCE 1843
Parentage unknown
Flat, fully double flowers of considerable size, bright purplish to rich pink, scented. A good, healthy shrub with strong upright growth and light green foliage.
[P ▽ (R)]   4′ × 3′   1.2 m × 90 cm

Above: 'Vick's Caprice' (see text p. 377)
Below: 'Victor Verdier' (see text p. 377)

Hybrid Teas
Large-Flowered Roses

We now progress from the Hybrid Perpetuals to the group now known collectively as 'Large Flowered Roses', the Hybrid Teas. The early Hybrid Teas, although of complicated origin, are more accurately described by their designated collective name than are their modern equivalents. The latter, whilst still possessing the genes of the Teas as their principal behavioural components, are now more complex as a result of having been mated frequently with, for example, the Floribundas.

Although a number of the 'pioneer' varieties are now extinct, many are still with us; but sadly some have lost their initial vigour – continuous vegetative propagation having proved incompatible with their hybridity. There are now many hundreds of these so I have decided to confine this section to a mere twenty-one, selected as being the most historically interesting; of most value in today's gardens; or simply impossible to omit, on grounds of favouritism.

'Angèle Pernet'
Pernet-Ducher FRANCE 1924
'Bénédicte Seguin' × a Hybrid Tea
Beautifully formed orange and yellow flowers with a heady fragrance, augmented by rich dark green, bronzy foliage.
[▽ (C)]   2′ × 2′   60 × 60 cm

'Anna Pavlova'
Beales UK 1981
Parentage unknown
A lapse in records has unfortunately rendered this rose an orphan. It is very beautiful; soft blush-pink laced with deeper shadings in the base, and has the strongest perfume of any rose I know. The flowers, very double and cupped, with slightly frilled edges to each petal, can get quite large in good soil and are borne on stiff, strong necks. The foliage is dark green, large and

'Angèle Pernet'   [PB]

slightly rounded. As a plant I find it better left to grow without pruning when it will make a good, upright shrub.

[☼ ▽ (C)]   4′ × 3′   1.2 m × 90 cm

'Dainty Bess'

Archer UK 1925
'Ophelia' × 'Kitchener of Khartoum'
A lovely variety from the 1920s evoking much of the vitality of that period. The shapely single flowers are made up of fine, slightly ragged-edged petals, and produced in clusters. They are soft pink with deeper shadings, combining superbly with golden-brown stamens when fully open. Foliage dark green and growth upright.

[(C)]   3′ × 2′   90 × 60 cm

'Dame Edith Helen'

Dickson UK 1926
Parentage unknown
Huge, very double, glowing pink flowers each held on a strong neck, with an exquisite perfume. Foliage large and dark green, stems well armed with thorns.

[P (C)]   3′ × 2′   90 × 60 cm

'Diamond Jubilee'

Boerner USA 1947
'Maréchal Niel' × 'Feu Pernet-Ducher'
Large flowers of deep creamy-buff with hints of pinkish-orange and lemon. Scented. Very free flowering on an upright, well-foliated bush. Leaves large, glossy and dark green.

[▽ H (C)]   4′ × 2′   1.2 m × 60 cm

'Ellen Willmott'

Archer UK 1936
'Dainty Bess' × 'Lady Hillingdon'
A charming, single variety. Pronounced golden anthers framed by wavy petals of cream and pink. Growth vigorous and bushy with dark green foliage.

[▽ (C)]   4′ × 3′   1.2 m × 90 cm

'Golden Melody', 'Irene Churruca'

La Florida USA 1934
'Mme Butterfly' × ('Lady Hillingdon' × 'Souvenir de Claudius Pernet')
Large, long, pointed buds of perfect, classical,

'Dainty Bess'   [PB]

high-centred shape. Golden-yellow heavily overlaid with light buff and slightly stained pink. Petals thick in texture and heavily veined, produced on long, strong necks, scented. Foliage dark green burnished purple. Growth vigorous and slightly angular.

[(C)]   3′ × 2′   90 × 60 cm

'Grace Darling'

Bennett UK 1884
Parentage unknown
A very useful, older Hybrid Tea; indeed, one of the first to be introduced. Globular flowers of creamy-white with petal edges touched pink, scented and produced freely on rather angular but sturdy plants with dark, neat, grey-green foliage.

[☼ ▽ (R)]   3′ × 2′   90 × 60 cm

'Grandpa Dickson', 'Irish Gold'

Dickson UK 1966
('Kordes Perfecta' × 'Governador Braga da Cruz') × 'Piccadilly'
Large, shapely, high-centred flower of clear, mid yellow with tints of pink especially on the outer petals, sweetly scented and very free flowering. Foliage plentiful, mid-green and glossy. Stems also mid-green, with even lighter-coloured thorns.

[(C)]   3′ × 2′   90 × 60 cm

'Helen Traubel'

Swim USA 1951
'Charlotte Armstrong' × 'Glowing Sunset'
A vigorous, tallish, upright-growing variety with

Above: 'Diamond Jubilee'   [PB]
Below: 'Mrs Oakley Fisher' (see text p. 382)   [PB]

dense, glossy, dark green foliage. Flowers large opening from shapely, high-centred buds to blowsy, full blooms of rich tawny-apricot suffused pink, scented and free-flowering. Criticized for a rather weak neck, but this, in my opinion, should not detract from this very lovely variety.

[H (C)]　4′ × 2′　1.2 m × 60 cm

'La France'

Guillot Fils FRANCE 1865
Probably 'Mme Falcot' seedling
Said to be the first Hybrid Tea ever introduced. High-centred flowers of silvery-pink borne in small clusters and scented, opening to show rather muddled centres. Bush upright and foliage mid-green. A beautiful if somewhat inconspicuous rose to carry the mantle of being the first of its race.

[Gh ▽ (R)]　4′ × 3′　1.2 m × 90 cm

'Mme Louis Laperrière'

Laperrière FRANCE 1951
'Crimson Glory' × seedling
A very floriferous rose producing clusters of highly scented, deep crimson, shapely flowers on a compact, bushy plant with deep green, plentiful foliage. A most useful rose which never deserves to disappear.

[▽ (C)]　2′ × 2′　60 × 60 cm

'Mrs Oakley Fisher'

B. R. Cant UK 1921
Parentage unknown
One of the many single Hybrid Teas from the 1920s which are well worth growing today. A group of these in a mixed border can be quite effective. Flowers, borne in clusters, combining orange and yellow without the harshness of some double roses of a similar shade. Highly scented. Foliage dark green; growth upright but bushy.

[▽ (C)]　3′ × 3′　90 × 90 cm

'Ophelia'

W. Paul UK 1912
Parentage unknown
Superbly shaped, soft pink almost white flowers with lemon centres, richly fragrant, usually produced in spaced clusters on a medium, vigorous

'Peace'　　　　　　　　　　　　　　　　　　　　[VP]

plant with dark, matt, greyish-green leaves. Used extensively for forcing earlier this century. Over the years it has produced directly or indirectly, a number of equally valuable sports, most notably 'Mme Butterfly', 1914, soft pink, and 'Lady Sylvia', 1926, a slightly deeper pink.

[∴ Gh ▽ (C)]　3′ × 2′　90 × 60 cm

'Peace', 'Gloria Dei', 'Mme A. Meilland', 'Gioia'

F. Meilland FRANCE 1945
('George Dickson' × 'Souvenir de Claudius Pernet') × ('Joanna Hill' × 'Chas. P. Kilham') × 'Margaret McGredy'
Perhaps the best known and one of the best loved roses of all time. Large, high-centred, opening cupped, sometimes delightfully ragged. Subtly perfumed, it tends to vary in colour from soil to soil and even from day to day in the same garden. Most often creamy-yellow (sometimes almost golden-yellow in cooler weather), with a pinkish edging to each petal, intensifying almost to red as the flower ages. Can be rather shy at times. Beautiful deep green, glossy foliage plus a strong constitution makes this a superb rose for any garden. Unpruned in good soil much taller than the height stated.

[P H (C)]　4′ × 3′　1.2 m × 90 cm

'Shot Silk'

Dickson UK 1924
'High Dickson' seedling × 'Sunstar'
Large, double, silky-textured flowers of soft cherry-cerise with golden yellow and lemon deep in the centre. Foliage plentiful, dark green and slightly crinkled. Growth vigorous and bushy.

[▽ (C)]　3′ × 3′　90 × 90 cm

'Silver Jubilee'

Cocker UK 1978

('Highlight' × 'Colour Wonder') × ('Parkdirektor Riggers' × 'Piccadilly') × 'Mischief'

This very disease-resistant rose is one of the most outstanding of recent introductions. Foliage plentiful and glossy dark green. The high-centred, scented flowers are a colourful mixture of peachy-cream and salmon-pink, shapely even when fully open. Growth bushy and vigorous, very free-flowering throughout the summer.

[Gh P H ▽ (C)] 3′ × 2′ 90 × 60 cm

'Sir Frederick Ashton'

Beales UK 1985

'Anna Pavlova' sport

Quite by chance while walking through my rose fields last year, I came upon this beautiful white sport of 'Anna Pavlova'. Since it was Sir Frederick's 80th birthday year, the name seemed appropriate. Almost pure white with a hint of lemon at the base of each petal, it has all the attributes of its parent, including its superb perfume.

[☼ ▽ (C)] 4′ × 3′ 1.2 m × 90 cm

Above: 'Silver Jubilee' [VP]
Below: 'Sir Frederick Ashton' [PB]

'Shot Silk' (see text p. 382)   [VP]

'Whisky Mac'   [VP]

'Soleil d'Or'

Pernet-Ducher FRANCE 1900

'Antoine Ducher' × *R. foetida persiana*

An important rose, being with 'Rayon d'Or' one of the 'Pernettiana' roses, significant as the source of most of the yellow and bright colours in today's roses. This classification has since been dropped and such roses are now included in Hybrid Teas. 'Soleil d'Or' is very large and double, opening to a cupped, flattish flower with a muddled centre, fragrant, deep orange-yellow to tawny-gold shaded red. Foliage rich green on a thorny plant.

[P ▽ (R)]   3′ × 3′   90 × 90 cm

'White Wings'   [PB]

'Whisky Mac'

Tantau GERMANY 1967

Seedling × 'Golden Wings'

Globular buds open through the high-centred stage to cupped blooms of rich golden-amber to yellowish-orange. Highly scented. Foliage dark green burnished copper, stems dark with numerous thorns. Growth habit rather sprawly. Can be tender in severe winters but usually survives if planted deeply.

[▽ (C)]   3′ × 2′   90 × 60 cm

'White Wings'

Krebs USA 1947

'Dainty Bess' × unnamed seedling

A lovely single rose having large, papery flowers of pure white with pronounced, chocolate-coloured stamens. Foliage leathery and dark green on an upright plant. A group of these in a mixed border can be very beautiful.

[(R)]   4′ × 3′   1.2 m × 90 cm

Climbing Hybrid Teas

From time to time in their history some bush Hybrid Teas have changed spontaneously into Climbers by suddenly throwing a climbing shoot from an otherwise non-climbing plant. The reason is genetic and the survival of the new form depends upon reproduction, by budding or grafting, of this first climbing shoot and its subsequent climbing shoots. Many Climbing Hybrid Teas are very worthy subjects and, although some are fairly modern, they are quite relevant to this book.

'Allen Chandler'
Chandler USA 1923
'Hugh Dickson' × unnamed seedling
A sturdy, healthy rose of brilliant red. Large, semi-double flowers displaying golden stamens to advantage. A good, repeat-flowering variety with dark green foliage.
[P (R)]   12′ × 8′   3.5 × 2.5 m

'Bettina' Climber
Bush form Meilland FRANCE 1953
'Peace' × ('Mme Joseph Perraud' × 'Demain')
This form Meilland FRANCE 1958
Shapely, cupped flowers opening flat; orange suffused with salmon. Foliage very dark green on relatively thornless stems. Needs a sheltered, warm situation to thrive.
[⁙ (S)]   15′ × 8′   4.5 × 2.5 m

'Captain Christy' Climber
Bush form Lacharme FRANCE 1873
'Victor Verdier' × 'Safrano'
This form Ducher FRANCE 1881
Semi-double soft pink with deeper pink centres, cupped until fully open. Flowers are generously produced and fragrant, occasionally repeated in the autumn. Growth is upright and vigorous with mid-green foliage.
[P (R)]   12′ × 8′   3.5 × 2.5 m

'Château de Clos Vougeot' Climber
Bush form Pernet-Ducher FRANCE 1908
Parentage unknown
This form Morse UK 1920
Flowers of a superb, deep velvety red, highly scented. An awkward rose, however, with angular growth and sprawly habit. Shoots relatively thornless, foliage dark green but rather sparse.
[(S)]   15′ × 8′   4.5 × 2.5 m

'Christine' Climber
Bush form McGredy UK 1918
Parentage unknown
This form Willink IRELAND 1936
Shapely flowers of rich golden yellow, semi-double and unusually well scented for a yellow. Growth upright and foliage medium-sized, mid to light green.
[P (S)]   12′ × 8′   3.5 × 2.5 m

'Comtesse Vandal' Climber
Bush form Leenders HOLLAND 1932
('Ophelia' × 'Mrs Aaron Ward') × 'Souvenir de Claudius Pernet'
This form Jackson & Perkins USA 1936
A very beautiful, rather elegant rose with long pointed buds opening to loosely formed flowers of silvery-buff pink with orange shadings and

Above: Climbing 'Crimson Glory' and *right:* 'Crimson Conquest'   [RCB/VP]
Below: Climbing 'Eden Rose'   [RCP]

deeper reverse. Slightly scented. Growth vigorous and upright. Foliage large and dark green.
[P (S)]   12′×8′   3.5×2.5 m

'Crimson Conquest'
Chaplin Bros UK 1931
'Red Letter Day' sport
Medium-sized, semi-double, rich crimson flowers on a healthy plant with dark green, glossy foliage. An excellent, underrated climbing rose, duplicating a famous old bush Hybrid Tea now extinct.
[N P ① (S)]   15′×8′   4.5×2.5 m

'Crimson Glory' Climber
Bush form Kordes GERMANY 1935
'Cathrine Kordes' seedling × 'W. E. Chaplin'
This form Jackson & Perkins USA 1946
The climbing form of this famous Hybrid Tea makes an excellent specimen. The colour speaks for itself. Blooms velvety and very full of petals. Its notoriously weak neck is an advantage since, as a climber, the flowers can hang down to effect. Has a strong, heady perfume. Wood reddish-brown and foliage dark green.
[P (S)]   15′×8′   4.5×2.5 m

Above: 'Lady Waterlow' (see text p. 390)

'Cupid'
B. R. Cant UK 1915
Parentage unknown
A lovely single variety. Superbly formed, large, peachy-pink flowers with a yellow base and pronounced golden anthers. Sometimes rather shy but worth growing even for one perfect bloom each year; however, it occasionally repeats in autumn.
[P N ① (S)]   12′×6′   3.5×1.8 m

'Eden Rose' Climber
Bush form F. Meilland FRANCE 1953
'Peace'× 'Signora'
This form A. Meilland FRANCE 1962
The shapely, large, high-centred bud opens to a blowsy, fully double bloom of bright pink with silvery highlights. Very fragrant. Foliage large, crisp and glossy, produced on thick, strong stems. Very vigorous.
[P N ① (S)]   15′×10′   4.5×3 m

'Etoile de Hollande'   [PB]

'Ena Harkness' Climber

Murrell UK
Bush form Norman 1946
'Crimson Glory' × 'Southport'
This form Murrell UK 1954
Flowers shapely in the Hybrid Tea style, with pointed buds of rich velvety crimson, highly scented. The weak neck inherited from its parent 'Crimson Glory' can be an advantage in the climber. Wood dark and thorny with plentiful dark, matt-green foliage.

[P (S)]   15′×8′   4.5×2.5 m

'Etoile de Hollande' Climber

Bush form Verschuren HOLLAND 1919
'General MacArthur' × 'Hadley'
This form Leenders HOLLAND 1931
A very famous and popular red rose between the wars. Superbly fragrant. Rich velvety red with shapely flowers – turning purple with age – its only fault. Shoots plum-coloured and foliage dull, dark green.

[(S)]   12′×8′   3.5×2.5 m

'General MacArthur' Climber

Bush form E. G. Hill & Co. USA 1905
Parentage unknown
This form Dickson UK 1923
Large, deep, rosy-red, highly scented, loosely formed blooms emerge from pointed buds. Free-flowering and very vigorous. Wood maroon with large dark green leaves.

[P (S)]   18′×10′   5.5×3 m

'Golden Dawn' Climber

Bush form Grant AUSTRALIA 1929
'Elegante' × 'Ethel Somerset'
This form LeGrice UK 1947
Its name is rather misleading in that its colour is yellow with hints of pink. Flowers large and globular, with a strong, sweet perfume. Foliage quite striking, dark green overlaid with copper. Vigorous and healthy.

[N P ◑ (S)]   12′×8′   3.5×2.5 m

'Grandmère Jenny'

Bush form Meilland FRANCE 1950
'Peace' × ('Julien Potin' × 'Sensation')
This form Meilland FRANCE 1958
The long pointed buds produce flowers of considerable size. Their colour is primrose overlaid with copper and pink. Sounds vulgar but the effect is quite refined. Growth is vigorous, foliage large and very dark green.

[P (S)]   18′×10′   5.5×3 m

'Guinée'

Mallerin FRANCE 1938
'Souvenir de Claudius Denoyel' × 'Ami Quinard'
Very dark crimson, the double flowers emerge from rather tubby buds to open flat and display golden-brown anthers, surrounded by velvety-textured petals. Fragrant. A superb variety with dark wood and dark green foliage. Sometimes produces a second flush in the autumn.

[P (R)]   15′×8′   4.5×2.5 m

'Home Sweet Home'

Bush form Wood & Ingram UK
Parentage unknown
This form, date and raiser unknown
Large, globular flowers of pure rose-pink with a large number of velvety-textured petals and considerable scent. Thick, very vigorous stems. Well endowed with large, dark foliage.

[P (S)]   15′×8′   4.5×2.5 m

'Irish Fireflame' Climber

Bush form Dickson UK 1914
Parentage unknown
This form Dickson UK 1916
Large, single flowers with pronounced anthers,

'Guinée' [PB]

a mixture of quiet orange, yellow and peach, the name belying its refinement. A healthy shrub, which is not too tall. Ideal for pillar work, especially as it often repeats in the autumn. Foliage dark green.

[(R)] 10′×6′ 3×1.8 m

'Josephine Bruce' Climber
Bush form Bees UK 1949
'Crimson Glory' × 'Madge Whipp'
This form BEES UK 1954
Fully double flowers of deep velvety red, at times quite blackish. Highly scented. As a climber, it is superior to the bush form. Foliage is plentiful, dull, dark green, and borne on vigorous thorny stems.

[P (S)] 15′×10′ 4.5×3 m

'Josephine Bruce' [VP]

'Lady Sylvia' Climber
Bush form Stevens UK 1926
'Mme Butterfly' sport
This form Stevens UK 1933
One of the most popular roses of the 1930s. Shapely buds, opening to full flowers of flesh-

Above: 'Lady Sylvia' (see text p. 389)   [RCB]
Below: 'Lady Waterlow'   [PB]

pink with deeper undertones, and a fine perfume. Makes an outstanding climber with an upright habit and grey-green foliage. Good for cutting.

[Gh P (S)]   15' × 10'   3.5 × 3 m

'Lady Waterlow'

G. Nabonnand FRANCE 1903
'La France de '89' × 'Mme Marie Lavalley'
Semi-double flowers of soft pink with deeper undertones and veining, particularly at the edges of the petals. A healthy, robust climber, amply foliated and upright in growth. Scented.

[P N ⓜ (S)]   12' × 8'   3.5 × 2.5 m

'Meg'

Gosset UK 1954
Thought to be 'Paul's Lemon Pillar' × 'Mme Butterfly'
An outstandingly beautiful climber. The large, almost single flowers, are scented, and have pronounced russet-red stamens and petals of buff-yellow, flushed apricot and peach. The foliage is dark green, glossy and healthy.

[P (R)]   8' × 4'   2.5 × 1.2 m

'Mme Abel Chatenay' Climber

Bush form Pernet-Ducher FRANCE 1895
'Dr Grill' × 'Victor Verdier'
This form Page UK 1917
One of the early climbing Hybrid Teas and still worth garden space even at the exclusion of others. Flowers globular but pointed, scented, soft silky-pink with a deeper centre when open. I suspect that over the years, this rose may have lost

Above: 'Meg' [RCB]
Below: 'Mme Butterfly' (see text p. 392) [VP]

'Mme Abel Chatenay' (see text p. 390) [JB]

'Mme Grégoire Staechelin' and *below:* [RCB]
'Mrs Aaron Ward' [RCB]

some vigour. Foliage small but dense and dark green. Growth rather angular and thorny.

[(R)] 10′×8′ 3×2.5 m

'Mme Butterfly' Climber

Bush form Hill & Co. USA 1918
'Ophelia' sport
This form E. P. Smith UK 1926
Shapely scrolled buds open to full, pale soft pink flowers with a fine perfume, strong-necked, good for cutting. Grey-green foliage on an upright vigorous plant.

[Gh P (S)] 15′×10′ 4.5×3 m

'Mme Edouard Herriot' [VP]

'Mme Caroline Testout' Climber

Bush form Pernet-Ducher FRANCE 1890
'Mme de Tartas' × 'Lady Mary Fitzwilliam'
This form Chauvry FRANCE 1901
A very vigorous climber with lush grey-green foliage and thick, upright, thorny shoots. Flowers large, cabbage-like, deep silvery-pink, with a strong perfume. Sometimes repeats in the autumn.

[P N ◍ (R)] 15′×8′ 4.5×2.5 m

'Mme Edouard Herriot', 'Daily Mail Rose' Climber

Bush form Pernet-Ducher FRANCE 1913
'Mme Caroline Testout' × a Hybrid Tea
This form Ketten Bros LUXEMBOURG 1921
A vigorous climbing rose, coral with a faint yellow base. Pointed buds open loosely to semi-double, flattish flowers. Growth upright and thorny with brownish flecks on the bark. Foliage light green.

[(S)] 12′×8′ 3.5×2.5 m

'Mme Grégoire Staechelin', 'Spanish Beauty'

P. Dot SPAIN 1927
'Frau Karl Druschki' × 'Château de Clos Vougeot'
A climbing rose of exceptional vigour. The large pale-pink flowers have a deeper pink reverse and are heavily veined at the edges. Early-flowering and very free-blooming. Growth vigorous and foliage dark green. If it is not dead-headed it produces superb, large, orange-red hips in the autumn. A superb variety.

[F P N ◍ (R)] 15′×10′ 4.5×3 m

'Mme Henri Guillot' Climber
Bush form Mallerin FRANCE 1938
'Rochefort' × *R. foetida bicolor* seedling
This form Meilland FRANCE 1942
Large, rather loose semi-double flowers of deep, burnt orange. Not much scent. A vigorous grower with plentiful dark green leaves.
[P N ◍ (S)]   15′ × 10′   4.5 × 3 m

'Mrs Aaron Ward'
Bush form Pernet-Ducher FRANCE 1907
Parentage unknown
Bush form Dickson UK 1922
High-centred buds opening to shapely flowers of creamy yellow flushed pink, occasionally deeper in dull weather, free-flowering, scented. Strong growth with plenty of dark green foliage.
[P (S)]   15′ × 8′   4.5 × 2.5 m

'Mrs G. A. van Rossem' Climber
Bush form Van Rossem HOLLAND 1929
'Souvenir de Claudius Pernet' × 'Gorgeous'
This form Gaujard FRANCE 1937
Large globular buds opening to flowers of orange and apricot on a yellow backcloth with an even deeper reverse. Growth strong and upright. Foliage highly glossed, rich dark green with only a few thorns.
[P (S)]   12′ × 10′   3.5 × 3 m

'Mrs Herbert Stevens' Climber
Bush form McGredy UK 1910
'Frau Karl Druschki' × 'Niphetos'
This form Pernet-Ducher FRANCE 1922
One of the best white climbers. Shapely flowers produced in quantity, superbly scented. Foliage dark, on vigorous shoots. An old favourite, frequently found in older gardens and often sent to me for identification. Quite happy in difficult situations.
[P N ◍ (R)]   12′ × 8′   3.5 × 2.5 m

'Mrs Sam McGredy' Climber
Bush form McGredy IRELAND 1929
('Donald Macdonald' × 'Golden Emblem') × (seedling × 'The Queen Alexander Rose')
This form Buisman HOLLAND 1937
Very vigorous rose with coppery-red foliage and orange-red young shoots. Flowers shaggy when

fully open, fiery copper-orange and scented. Needs plenty of space to develop fully.
[P N ◍ (R)]   20′ × 15′   6 × 4.5 m

'Ophelia' Climber
Bush form W. Paul UK 1912
Parentage unknown
This form Dickson IRELAND 1920
Shapely buds opening soft flesh-pink with deeper

'Paul Lédé'   [PB]

shadings and light yellow tints in the centre. Has a strong fragrance. Upright in growth with plenty of foliage.
[P (R)]   15′ × 10′   4.5 × 3 m

'Paul Lédé', 'Mons. Paul Lédé' Climber
Bush form Pernet-Ducher FRANCE 1902
Parentage unknown
This form Lowe UK 1913
Large, shapely flowers of soft pink with peachy shadings in the base, sweetly scented and free-flowering. Foliage plentiful and mid-green. Seldom seen but a sight to remember in full flush.
[P (R)]   12′ × 8′   3.5 × 2.5 m

'Picture' and *right:* 'Réveil Dijonnais'   [PB/VP]

'Paul's Lemon Pillar'

Paul UK 1915
'Frau Karl Druschki' × 'Maréchal Niel'
Massive blooms of creamy-white suffused with lemon; of unusually high quality in most weathers. Scented. A vigorous climber with very thick branches and large, dark green leaves. A deservedly popular old variety.

[P N ◍ (S)]   15′ × 10′   4.5 × 3 m

'Picture' Climber

Bush form McGredy UK 1932
Parentage unknown
This form Swim USA 1942
Flowers not large but shapely, rich clear pink, suffused with many other shades of pink. Scented. An upright grower with plenty of prickles and ample, if somewhat small foliage.

[P (S)]   12′ × 8′   3.5 × 2.5 m

'Reine Marie Henriette'

F. Levet FRANCE 1878
'Mme Bérard' × 'Général Jacqueminot'
Large, loosely-double flowers, deep cherry-red,

very free-flowering and scented. Vigorous. Foliage large, leathery and dark green. Stems maroon, with few thorns.

[(R)]   12′ × 8′   3.5 × 2.5 m

'Réveil Dijonnais'

Buatois FRANCE 1931
'Eugène Fürst' × 'Constance'
A striking rose. Loosely formed, semi-double flowers of vivid orange, red and yellow, slightly fragrant. Prolific light green leaves and very thorny stems.

[P N ◍ (R)]   10′ × 6′   3 × 1.8 m

'Richmond' Climber
Bush form E. G. Hill & Co. USA 1905
'Lady Battersea' × 'Liberty'
This form Dickson UK 1912
Variable, from light carmine to scarlet, semi-double, scented blooms cupped initially, opening flattish, freely produced. Foliage dark green with upright growth.

[N P (S)]   10′ × 6′   3 × 1.8 m

'Shot Silk' Climber
Bush form Dickson UK 1924
'Hugh Dickson' seedling × 'Sunstar'
This form C. Knight AUSTRALIA 1931
A popular variety, one of the nicest and most reliable. Fully double, cupped flowers, soft cherry-cerise with golden-yellow and lemon base, fragrant, freely produced. Petal texture silky, but stands up to weather very well. Foliage lush dark green and plentiful.

[P N ◐ (R)]   18′ × 10′   5.5 × 3 m

'Souvenir de Claudius Denoyel'
Chambard FRANCE 1920
'Château de Clos Vougeot' × 'Commandeur Jules Gravereaux'
Shapely, double, cupped flowers of rich red to scarlet, produced in loose clusters. Fragrant. Foliage large and darkish green. Growth vigorous and rather angular. Not the easiest to grow.

[(R)]   12′ × 8′   3.5 × 2.5 m

'Spek's Yellow' Climber, 'Golden Sceptre'
Bush form Verschuren-Pechtold HOLLAND 1950
'Golden Rapture' × unnamed seedling
This form Walters 1956
Double, rich golden-yellow flowers from pointed, shapely buds with long stems, ideal for cutting. Foliage particularly good, light green and glossy. Growth upright and vigorous.

[N P Gh ◐ (S)]   15′ × 10′   4.5 × 3 m

'Souvenir de Claudius Denoyel'   [RCB]

'Talisman' Climber
Bush form Montgomery & Co. USA 1929
'Ophelia' × 'Souvenir de Claudius Pernet'
This form Western Rose Co. USA 1930
Fully-double flowers, golden-yellow with orange and copper highlights. Foliage tough and leathery on vigorous, upright, thorny shoots.

[P (S)]   12′ × 8′   3.5 × 2.5 m

'Vicomtesse Pierre du Fou'
Sauvageot FRANCE 1923
'L'Idéal' × 'Joseph Hill'
The luxuriant, glossy foliage of copper-dark green makes an ideal foil for the fragrant, double, loosely-quartered flowers, which are coppery-pink when fully open. Vigorous and branching in habit.

[P N ◐ (R)]   15′ × 10′   4.5 × 3 m

R. gigantea

R. gigantea

HIMALAYAS 1889

In specific form this rose has little garden value, although it is very important as a parent to the Tea Roses. Flowers large, white and single, produced very reluctantly on a vigorous, thorny, climbing shrub with crisp, dark foliage. Not totally hardy in northern Europe.

[P T ◑ (S)]   40′ × 10′   12 × 3 m

FORMS AND HYBRIDS OF R. gigantea

'Belle Portugaise', 'Belle of Portugal'

Cayeux PORTUGAL C. 1900
R. gigantea × 'Reine Marie Henriette'?
Flowers semi-double, loosely arranged petals of pale pink with deeper shadings. Makes a good climbing rose, flowering profusely and growing vigorously. Needs a warm, sheltered position to give of its best. Foliage dark green and slightly crumpled.

[T ◑ (S)]   15′ × 10′   4.5 × 3 m

'La Follette'

Busby FRANCE C. 1900
R. gigantea × unknown
A very attractive rose, sadly not hardy enough for British gardens. Makes a good climber for growing under glass or in warmer climates, with large, fragrant, deep pink flowers and dark, abundant foliage.

[Gh (R)]   20′ × 15′   6 × 4.5 m

'Lorraine Lee'

Clarke AUSTRALIA 1924
'Jessie Clarke' × 'Capitaine Millet'
Falls into this group as a second-generation hybrid, 'Jessie Clarke' being a R. gigantea seedling which is now seemingly extinct in Europe. Double, fragrant rich pinkish apricot, with lush green, very glossy foliage. Not hardy enough for northern Europe.

[Gh (S)]   10′ × 6′   3 × 1.8 m

'Sénateur Amic'   [PB]

'Sénateur Amic'

P. Nabonnand FRANCE 1924
R. gigantea × 'General MacArthur'
Much hardier than given credit for. I know an old, established plant growing as a dense, pillar rose in south Norfolk, which must have survived many a biting north-easterly. Quite beautiful, the flowers are semi-double, large, loosely formed when open, rich pink with hints of yellow at the base and prominent stamens. Superb scent. Growth not as thorny as one would expect. Foliage dark with a dull gloss.

[(R)]   12′ × 8′   3.5 × 2.5 m

ROSA Subgenus II Rosa (Eurosa)
SECTION VIII *Banksianae*

Growth vigorous, climbing to 20 ft, 7 m.
Thorns few or none.
Foliage smooth – 5 to 7 leaflets.
Flowers in clusters or singly.
Hips small.
Sepals drop before ripening.

SPECIES

R. banksiae normalis
R. banksiae alba plena

R. banksiae lutea
R. banksiae lutescens
R. × fortuniana

ORIGIN AND DISTRIBUTION

R. banksiae lutescens. Flower enlarged $1\frac{1}{2}$ times actual size   [VP]

R. banksiae

R. banksiae normalis

CHINA 1877

Although coming to Europe rather later than its offspring, this climber is probably the true species. Flowers white and single, foliage light green and plentiful, stems free of thorns. Not fully hardy.

[☼ (S)]   15′ × 8′   4.5 × 2.5 m

FORMS AND HYBRIDS OF
R. banksiae

R. banksiae lutescens

CHINA 1870

Flower diameter rather larger than that of *R. banksiae lutea*, but single and more sweetly scented. Foliage and growth habit also similar

but young shoots and leaves sometimes copper-tinted. A good example can be seen on the south wall of Mannington Hall, Norfolk, home of Robin and Laurel Walpole.

[☼ (S)]   20′ × 10′   6 × 3 m

R. banksiae alba plena, R. banksia banksiae

CHINA 1807

Small, rosette-like, double white flowers. Otherwise as *normalis*.

[☼ (S)]   15′ × 8′   4.5 × 2.5 m

R. banksiae lutea, 'Yellow Banksia'

CHINA c. 1825

Needs a sheltered, sunny spot to flower but hardier than given credit for. Profuse foliage and

R. banksiae alba plena   [RCB]

R. ×*fortuniana*   [PB]

growth produces large cascading trusses of small, pale yellow, double flowers in late spring. Slightly scented.

[☼ (S)]   20′ × 10′   6 × 3 m

R. ×*fortuniana*

CHINA 1850

Thought to be cross between *R. banksiae* and *R. laevigata* Not known in the wild

Large, scented, double, white flowers, almost thornless, resembling *R. banksiae*, with slightly darker green leaves and stems. A most interesting rose but needs protection or a sheltered, warm position to flourish. From a nurseryman's viewpoint, much easier to propagate than *R. banksiae* and its other relatives. In fact in some parts of the world it is used as an understock for such varieties as *R. banksiae lutea*.

[☼ (S)]   12′ × 8′   3.5 × 2.5 m

ROSA Subgenus II Rosa (Eurosa)
SECTION IX *Laevigatae*

Growth sprawling or climbing with hooked, irregular thorns.
Leaves large, mostly of 3, rarely 5, leaflets.
Almost evergreen.
Flowers produced singly.
Hips when formed have persistent sepals.

SPECIES

R. laevigata

ORIGIN AND DISTRIBUTION

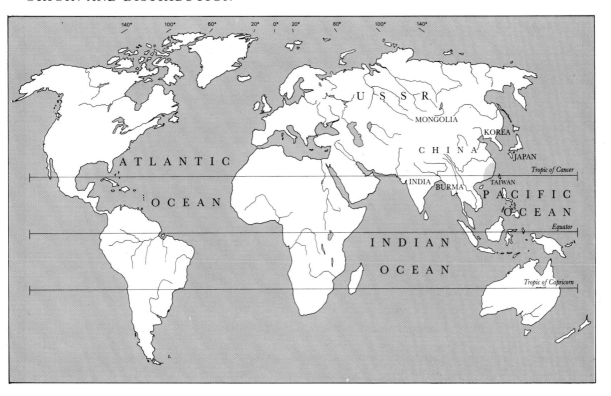

'Cooper's Burmese'

[RCB]

R. laevigata

R. laevigata, 'Cherokee Rose'

CHINA C. 1759 LATER NATURALIZED N. AMERICA
Not hardy enough for colder climes. In southern USA, however, it grows wild, having become naturalized since arriving there from China, at the end of the 18th century. Flowers single, very large, white with superb, golden-yellow stamens.

Leaves crisp, polished and dark, as is the wood, which is armed with large hooked thorns. Fruit oval, with sparse bristles. I have an interesting and rare pale pink form kindly sent to me by Mr Trevor Griffiths of New Zealand.

[F ☼ (SP)]   20'×15'   6×4.5 m

FORMS AND HYBRIDS OF
R. laevigata

'Anemone Rose', '*R. × anemonoides*'

J. C. Schmidt GERMANY 1895
R. laevigata × a Tea Rose
Large, single, papery, pink flowers with a touch of mauve, giving this rose a vaguely oriental look. A vigorous climber with angular, branching shoots of darkish brown, liberally armed with hooked thorns. The foliage is dark green, glossy and healthy. Although it prefers a sunny position, it will tolerate sheltered shade.

[P N ☼ ◐ (R)]   10'×8'   3×2.5 m

'Cooper's Burmese', '*R. cooperi*'

1927
R. laevigata seedling?
An excellent, creamy-white rose which, if carefully placed in a warm, sheltered position, can be

very rewarding. The dark, glossy foliage makes a superb foil for the large, single, scented flowers. The shoots are quite thorny, fawn-brown in colour, and produced in angular fashion. Until recently, this rose was thought to be a hybrid of *R. gigantea*.

[☼ P (R)]   20'×15'   6×4.5 m

'Ramona', 'Red Cherokee'

Dietrich and Turner USA 1913
'Anemone Rose' sport
This beautiful rose is of much deeper pink than

Above: 'Anemone Rose' and *right:* 'Ramona'

[VP/RCB]

'Silver Moon'   [VP]

its parent, almost red in fact. In other ways it is identical.

[P N ∴ ⓦ (R)]   10′ × 8′   3 × 2.5 m

'Silver Moon'

Van Fleet USA 1910

R. laevigata hybrid

An interesting rose. Large pure white, single flowers on a vigorous, well-foliated plant. Well scented. Inclined to be rather shy at times but well worth space, even for just a few of its very lovely flowers. Good in small trees or on trellis. Good examples can be seen in the Queen Mary Rose Garden, Regents Park, London.

[T N ⓦ (R)]   15′ × 8′   4.5 × 2.5 m

ROSA Subgenus II Rosa (Eurosa)
SECTION X *Bracteata*

Growth climbing or angularly sprawling.
Thorns numerous, hooked and in pairs, smaller thorns scattered.
Leaves – 7 to 9 leaflets.
Hips with reflexed sepals which drop off when ripe.

SPECIES

R. bracteata

ORIGIN AND DISTRIBUTION

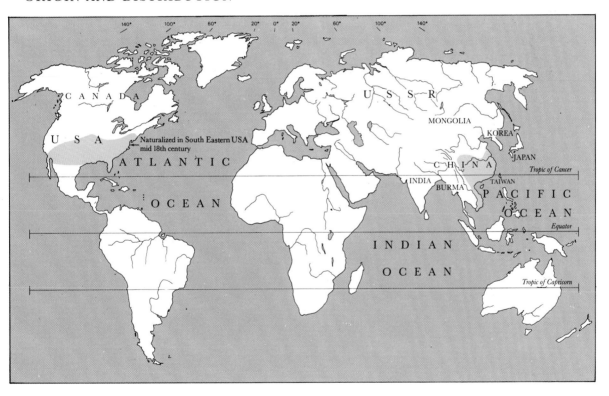

'Mermaid' [PB]

R. bracteata

R. bracteata, 'The Macartney Rose'

CHINA Introduced 1793

A rose of Chinese origin which is rather tender but, somewhat paradoxically, flowers happily on a north wall. Lord Macartney brought it back from a diplomatic visit to China in the late 18th century. When introduced to America in the early 19th century, it found the climate in the south and east much to its liking and established itself in the wild. Despite its reputation for tenderness, I would like to see this species used more nowadays, even if only as an occasional change from 'Mermaid'. Single, pure white with pronounced golden stamens, the rose has much to offer, especially as it flowers intermittently from June until the November frosts. Well armed with vicious thorns, the stems are fawny-brown and the leaves dark green and slightly downy to touch. Best grown as a climber.

[N ◍ (C)]   8′ × 8′   2.5 × 2.5 m

produced throughout the summer, often improving in quality as the season progresses. Slightly more hardy than its parent, *R. bracteata*, from which it inherits tolerance of shade. Quite at home on most walls, including those facing north. In very severe winters it will die back badly from frost damage. During the winters of 1981 and 1985 many well-established plants were killed in the UK.

[N ◍ (C)]   30′ × 20′   9 × 6 m

HYBRID OF *R. bracteata*

'Mermaid'

W. Paul UK 1917

R. bracteata × Double Yellow Tea Rose

Undoubtedly, a most useful and beautiful climber. Almost evergreen, the foliage alone has much to commend it, being large and a rich dark green. It is vigorous and the dark brownish maroon wood is armed with cruel thorns. The rewards from the flowers, however, give ample compensation for scratches received whilst pruning, which should be done sparingly. Each flower is single, 3″–4″ (8 cm–10 cm) across, lemon yellow with pronounced golden brown stamens. It is also fragrant. Furthermore, the flowers are

ROSA Subgenus III
Platyrhodon

Flaky bark and prickly hips.
Small leaves.

SPECIES

R. roxburghii
R. roxburghii normalis
R. roxburghii plena

ORIGIN AND DISTRIBUTION

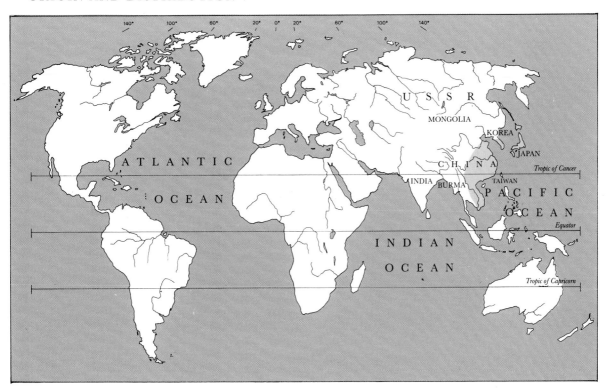

R. roxburghii   [JB]

R. roxburghii, 'Burr Rose', 'Chestnut Rose'
CHINA 1814
Quite distinct. This medium to tall shrub has leaves composed of up to 15 small, firmly textured, light green leaflets. Stems tawny-brown and slightly angular, both in structure and direction. Bark is flaky on the older wood. Thorns stout and quite long, often arranged in pairs. Flowers single, clear shell-pink. Fruit spherical, orange-yellow and covered in pronounced, stiff stubble.
[W P F A ⦾ (S)]　8′×8′　2.5×2.5 m

R. roxburghii normalis
CHINA 1908
A taller form of *roxburghii* with pure white, sometimes blush-white single flowers.
[W P F A ⦾ (S)]　10′×8′　3×2.5 m

R. roxburghii plena
1824
Less vigorous than either of other forms. Fully double flowers, not produced very freely in my experience.
[W P F A ⦾ (S)]　6′×5′　1.8×1.5 m

ROSA Subgenus IV
Hesperhodos

Very prickly with small leaves.

SPECIES

R. stellata
R. stellata mirifica

ORIGIN AND DISTRIBUTION

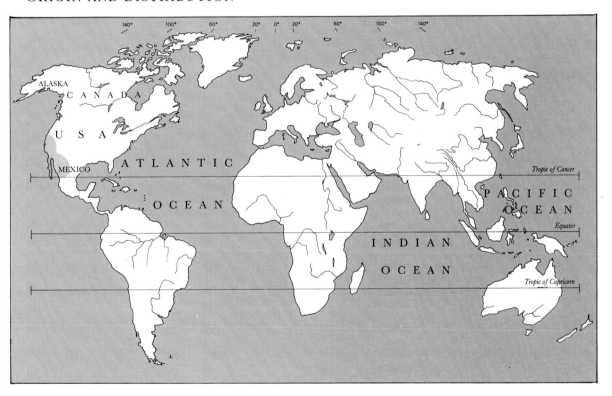

R. stellata mirifica

R. stellata

S. USA 1902

An interesting species with dense, spiney wood and gooseberry-like, light green foliage. Not an easy rose to grow. Flowers rich pinkish-purple, produced solitarily among dense foliage.

[W ◍ ▽ (S)] 3' × 3'   90 × 90 cm

R. stellata mirifica, 'The Sacramento Rose'

Greene S. USA 1916

Compact plant, slightly more vigorous than the other form, with many long spines and gooseberry-like foliage. Flowers single, lilac-pink, with prominent stamens. Bush dense and reasonably compact. Easier to grow in the garden than *stellata* but quite difficult for the nurseryman to produce.

[W (S)] 4' × 4'   1.2 × 1.2 m

The gardens at La Roseraie de l'Hay les Roses, Paris [RCB]

Appendix A

ROSE GARDENS OF GREAT BRITAIN

The following gardens are open to the public during the rose season and are well worth visiting to see Old Fashioned and Shrub Roses in bloom.

BONE HILL, Chiswell Green, St Albans, Herts. Rose gardens of The Royal National Rose Society. A fine collection of roses, both old and new. A Rose Festival is held annually, in early July.

CASTLE HOWARD, near York, N. Yorkshire Central to extensive acres of beautiful gardens is a large well laid out walled area which is devoted entirely to a fine collection of the older roses.

CHARLESTON MANOR, West Dean, W. Sussex A private collection of old roses, displayed in the French style.

CLIVEDEN, near Maidenhead, Bucks. National Trust. A well tended collection with emphasis on older roses, and an especially good range of climbers festooning trees.

CRATHES CASTLE, near Banchory, Aberdeenshire. The National Trust for Scotland. A formal rose garden with floribunda and shrub roses.

DIXON PARK, Belfast, N. Ireland. Impressive collection of roses, old and new.

HARLOW CARR, Harrogate, N. Yorks. Gardens of the Northern Horticultural Society. A good, representative collection of older roses and species.

HIDCOTE MANOR, Gloucestershire. National Trust. A good representative collection of old roses in extensive grounds and gardens.

HILLIER'S ARBORETUM, Ampfield, near Winchester, Hants. A good collection of well established plants, particularly of species.

1 Bone Hill
2 Castle Howard
3 Charleston Manor
4 Cliveden
5 Crathes Castle
6 Dixon Park
7 Harlow Carr
8 Hidcote Manor
9 Hillier's Arboretum
10 Kiftsgate Court
11 Lime Kiln
12 Malleny House
13 Mannington Hall
14 Mottisfont Abbey
15 Nymans
16 Queen Mary's Rose Gardens
17 Rosemoor
18 Rowallane
19 Sheldon Manor
20 Sissinghurst Castle
21 Tyninghame
22 Wisley
23 Cambridge Botanic Gardens
24 Kew Gardens
25 David Austin Roses, Albrighton
26 Peter Beales Roses, Attleborough
27 Harkness Roses, Hitchin
28 Scotts Nurseries, Merriott
29 Le Grice Roses, North Walsham
30 Mattocks Roses, Nuneham Courtney
31 Notcutts Nurseries, Woodbridge

KIFTSGATE COURT, Gloucestershire.
Many species and older roses including a huge specimen of *R. filipes* 'Kiftsgate'.

LIME KILN, Claydon, Ipswich, Suffolk.
An unique private rosarium with special emphasis on hybrid perpetuals, by courtesy of Mr Humphrey Brooke.

MALLENY HOUSE, Balerno, near Edinburgh.
The National Trust for Scotland.
A large collection mainly of shrub roses.

MANNINGTON HALL, near Saxthorpe, Norfolk.
A fine collection displayed in historical order, by courtesy of the Hon. Robin and Mrs. Laurel Walpole. A rose festival is held annually in early July.

MOTTISFONT ABBEY, near Romsey, Hants.
The National Trust collection of old roses with many rare and unusual varieties.

NYMANS, Handcross, W. Sussex.
National Trust. A very good collection, especially of climbers and ramblers.

QUEEN MARY'S ROSE GARDENS, Regent's Park, London.
A large collection of modern roses, augmented by many old shrub roses, ramblers and climbers.

ROSEMOOR GARDEN CHARITABLE TRUST, Torrington, Devon.
A collection of species and other older varieties.

ROWALLANE GARDEN, Saintfield, Co. Down, N. Ireland.
National Trust. Walled garden of old roses, shrub roses, ramblers and climbers.

SHELDON MANOR, near Chippenham, Wilts.
Home of Major and Mrs Gibbs. A good collection in a well maintained setting.

SISSINGHURST CASTLE, Kent. National Trust.
Beautiful, representative collection, in a superb setting. Noted particularly for its beautiful white garden.

TYNINGHAME, East Lothian. The Earl and Countess of Haddington.
A formal yellow and white rose garden, and a secret garden containing old-fashioned roses with other plants.

WISLEY GARDENS, Ripley, Surrey.
Gardens of The Royal Horticultural Society.
Interesting roses throughout the gardens.

THE ROYAL NATIONAL ROSE SOCIETY

Situated at Bone Hill, Chiswell Green, St Albans, Herts, the Society offers a quarterly journal and holds spring, summer and autumn rose shows. Its extensive gardens may be visited (see p. 417).

NATIONAL TRUST GARDENS

Many of these have interesting collections of old roses, both as special features and as part of the overall gardens. They are too numerous to list, but details can be obtained from The National Trust, 36 Queen Anne's Gate, London SW1 and The National Trust for Scotland, 5 Charlotte Square, Edinburgh 2.

PRIVATE GARDENS

Many private gardens with very good collections of old roses are open to the public, usually for charity, on specific days in the summer. A useful guide, published annually, *Gardens of England and Wales Open to the Public*, can be obtained from good bookshops and libraries, or from The National Gardens Scheme, 57 Lower Belgrave Street, London SW1. An equivalent publication is available for Scotland from Scotland's Gardens Scheme, 31 Castle Terrace, Edinburgh.

BOTANIC GARDENS

Most botanic gardens have very good collections of roses; Cambridge and Kew possess special representative collections.

NURSERY DISPLAY GARDENS

The following are always worth a visit to see old roses in flower.
Albrighton, Staffs. David Austin Roses.
Attleborough, Norfolk. Peter Beales Roses.
Hitchin, Herts. Harkness Roses.
Merriott, Somerset. Scotts Nurseries.
North Walsham, Norfolk. LeGrice Roses.
Nuneham Courtney, Oxford. Mattocks Roses.
Woodbridge, Suffolk. Notcutts Nurseries.

Appendix B

AMERICAN ROSE GARDENS

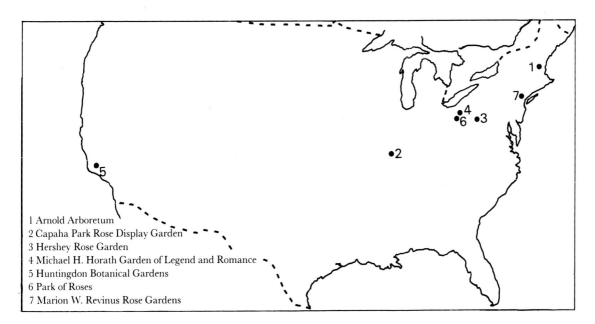

1 Arnold Arboretum
2 Capaha Park Rose Display Garden
3 Hershey Rose Garden
4 Michael H. Horath Garden of Legend and Romance
5 Huntingdon Botanical Gardens
6 Park of Roses
7 Marion W. Revinus Rose Gardens

ARNOLD ARBORETUM, Jamaica Plain, Massachusetts
The rose garden has an extensive collection of species and many good examples of older varieties.

CAPAHA PARK ROSE DISPLAY GARDEN, Cape Girardeau, Missouri
Good collection of old roses.

HERSHEY ROSE GARDEN, Pennsylvania
This garden has a vast collection of roses including hundreds of varieties of older roses and climbers.

MICHAEL H. HOVATH GARDEN OF LEGEND AND ROMANCE, Wooster, Ohio
Rose garden with special emphasis on heritage roses.

HUNTINGDON BOTANICAL GARDENS, San Marino, California
Large collection of older roses, some recently planted. Especially famous for large collection of tea roses.

PARK OF ROSES, Columbus, Ohio
Large, well laid out garden with many varieties of older roses.

MARION W. REVINUS ROSE GARDEN, Morris Arboretum, Philadelphia, Pennsylvania
Many species and old roses in a supporting role to more modern varieties.

Information for American Rose Growers:
The Combined Rose List by
Dobson, Beverly
215 Harriman Road
Irvington, NY 10533
(914/591-6736)
This valuable book, updated frequently, offers a rating system as to colour, fragrance, hardiness, resistance to disease, etc. It also offers reliable information on sources of supply for each of more than 1000 species, both domestic and foreign nurseries.

Handbook for Selecting Roses
American Rose Society
Department HB
P.O. Box 30,000
Shreveport, LA 71130
This booklet rates roses by type, but doesn't offer sources of supply. Especially helpful are the lists organised by colour, hardiness and type of plant: climbers, shrubs, etc.

Appendix C

ROSE GARDENS WORLD WIDE

FRANCE

CHÂLON-SUR-SAÔNE
Parc Saint-Nicholas, Châlon-sur-Saône.
An important collection of old roses started in
1977.

ROSERAIE DU PARC DE BAGATELLE, Paris
A Beautifully laid out garden of roses with a
good representative collection of older varieties
especially hybrids of *R. wichuraiana*.

ROSERAIE DE L'HAY LES ROSES near Paris
Rosarium devoted to a display of the history
of the rose, by the roses themselves.

ROSERAIE DU PARC DE LA SOURCE, Orléans
A fine rose garden in a historically important
area for the rose. Older climbers and ramblers
are particularly well displayed.

GERMAN DEMOCRATIC REPUBLIC

SANGERHAUSEN ROSARIUM
One of the oldest rose gardens in the world. Its
vast collection is said to comprise some 6500
species and hybrids.

GERMAN FEDERAL REPUBLIC

WESTFALENPARK, Dortmund
The German National Rosarium; many old
and modern roses are displayed in superbly laid
out grounds.

ZWEIBRÜCKEN ROSARIUM, near Saarbrücken
Magnificent rose gardens in a woodland park
setting, with many good features; among
thousands of modern roses are lots of species
and old roses.

HOLLAND

WESTBROEK PARK, The Hague
Large rose garden, mainly modern roses but
several older species displayed to advantage.

ITALY

MUNICIPAL ROSE GARDEN, Rome
This garden is in a superb setting on the slopes
of the Aventine Hill. Fine collection of climbers
and many historical roses.

CABRIGLIA D'AREZZO
A superb private collection by courtesy of
Professor Fineschi. Appointment only.

LA MORTOLA
A good collection of species and old roses on the
Mediterranean coast near the French border.

SPAIN

PARQUE DE OESTE, Madrid
A most impressive garden displaying many
thousands of roses in beautifully landscaped
grounds. Climbers and pillar roses are displayed
in many original ways.

SWITZERLAND

PARC DE LA GRANGE, Geneva
Beautifully designed rose gardens with terraces
of various roses, including many older varieties.

AUSTRALIA

ROYAL BOTANIC GARDENS, South Yarra,
Victoria.

ROYAL BOTANIC GARDENS, Melbourne.

Both these gardens have good collections of
heritage roses, among many others.

Good collections of old varieties and species
can also be seen at Zephyr Brook Heritage
Rose Garden, Penjana, W.A. Ross Roses, St
Andrew's Terrace, Willunga, W.A.; Alister
Clark Rose Garden, St Kilda Public Gardens,
Dickens St, St Kilda, Victoria; and Hobart
Botanical Gardens, Tasmanian Rose Society
Gardens, Hobart. The Flower Garden,
PO Box 18, Watervale, S.A.

NEW ZEALAND

CHRISTCHURCH BOTANIC GARDENS, Christchurch
Long-established collection of heritage roses, beautifully displayed in a lovely setting.

TREVOR GRIFFITHS' DISPLAY GARDEN, Timaru, S. Island
An extensive collection.

THE NANCY STEEN GARDEN
Work is in hand developing a collection of old roses adjacent to another garden in the city of Auckland. This is to be known as The Nancy Steen Garden.

ISRAEL

WOHL ROSE PARK, Jerusalem
Twenty-five acre park and gardens devoted to roses. Centrally situated opposite the Knesset.

JAPAN

YATSU-YUEN ROSE GARDEN, near Tokyo
Mostly modern roses with quite a good range of older ones.

SOUTH AFRICA

THE DROSTDY MUSEUM, Swellendam, Western Cape Province
A good collection of old roses.

South Africa, like Australia and New Zealand, is rich in old varieties taken there by 19th century settlers.

CANADA

CENTENNIAL ROSE GARDEN, Burlington, Ontario
A good collection of older roses and species arranged in their family groups, with a large number of climbers and ramblers among many modern varieties.

Other Canadian Rose Gardens

BUTCHARTS GARDENS, Victoria, British Columbia

CONNAUGHT PARK ROSE GARDENS, Montreal

DOMINION ARBORETUM AND BOTANIC GARDENS, Ottawa

ROYAL HORTICULTURAL GARDENS, Niagara Falls

Bibliography

Before embarking upon this book, I resolved to write as much as possible without reference to other books, a resolution that was broken on the very first page and on many pages thereafter. I succeeded, however, in containing my references only to books in my own collection. Many of these long out of print and, I suspect, the source of much information to other authors on the subject of Old Roses.

Anderson, F. J. *An Illustrated Treasury of Redouté Roses* Crown, USA 1979

Beales, P. and Money, K. *Georgian and Regency Roses* Jarrolds 1978

Beales, P. and Money, K. *Early Victorian Roses* Jarrolds 1978

Beales, P. and Money, K. *Late Victorian Roses* Jarrolds 1980

Beales, P. and Money, K. *Edwardian Roses* Jarrolds 1980

Bean, W. J. *Trees and Shrubs Hardy in the British Isles* 8th edition revised. John Murray 1980

Blunt, W. and Russell, J. *Old Garden Roses. Part II* George Rainbird 1957

Bunyard, A. E. *Old Garden Roses* Collingridge 1936

Dobson, B. R. Combined Rose List. *Hard to Find Roses and Where to Find Them* Beverly R. Dobson Irvington N.Y. 10533 1985

Dodds, F. W. *Practical Rose Growing in all Forms* Publisher not known c. 1908

Foster, Mellier A. *The Book of the Rose* Macmillan 1864

Gault, S. M. and Synge, P. M. *The Dictionary of Roses in Colour* Michael Joseph and Ebury Press 1970

Genders, R. *The Rose. A Complete Handbook* Robert Hale 1965

Gibson, M. *Shrub Roses for Every Garden* Collins 1973

Gibson, M. *The Book of the Rose* Macdonald General Books 1980

Goor, A. *The History of the Rose in Holy Lands Throughout the Ages* Agricultural Publications Division, State of Israel 1969 English edition 1981

Gore, C. F. *The Book of Roses or The Rose Fancier's Manual* Original publication 1838. Latest publication Heyden 1978

Griffiths, T. *My World of Old Roses* English edition Michael Joseph 1984

Harkness, J. *Roses* Dent 1978

Hellyer, A. G. L. *Simple Rose Growing* W. H. & L. Collingridge Ltd. c. 1930

Henslow, T. G. W. *The Rose Encyclopaedia* Pearson 1922

Hillier's *Manual of Trees and Shrubs* 4th Edition 1974

Hole, S. Reynolds *A Book about Roses* William Blackwood 1869

Jekyll, G. and Mawley, E. *Roses for English Gardens* Country Life 1902

Keble Martin, W. *The Concise British Flora* Ebury Press and Michael Joseph 1965

Kingsley, R. G. *Roses and Rose Growing* P.T.Y. Ltd. Whittaker & Co. (USA) 1908

Kordes, W. *Roses* Studio Vista 1964

Krüssman, G. *Roses* English edition Batsford B.T. Ltd 1982

LeGrice, E. B. *Rose Growing Complete* Faber & Faber 1965

Macself, A. J. *The Rose Grower's Treasury* Collingridge 1934

Mansfield, T. C. *Roses in Colour and Cultivation* Collins 1947

Mayhew, A. & Pollard, M. *The Rose, Myth, Folklore and Legend* New English
     Library 1979

McFarland, J. H. *Modern Roses 8* The McFarland Co. (USA) 1980

McFarland, J. H. *Roses of the World in Colour* Cassell & Co. 1936

Nottle, T. *Growing Old Fashioned Roses in Australia and New Zealand* Kangaroo
     Press 1983

Park, B. *Collins Guide to Roses* Collins 1965

Parsons, S. B. *Parsons on the Rose* Orange Judd Co. New York 1888

Paul, W. *A Shilling Book of Roses* Simpkin, Marshall, Hamilton, Kent & Co.
     c. 1880

Paul, W. *The Rose Garden* 10th Edition. Simpkin, Marshall, Hamilton, Kent &
     Co. 1903

Poulsen, S. *Poulsen on the Rose* MacGibbon & Kee 1955

Redouté, P. J. *Roses, Books One and Two* (facsimile) Ariel Press 1954 & 1956

Ridge, A. *For the Love of a Rose* Faber & Faber 1965

Rigg, C. H. *Roses of Quality* Ernest Benn Ltd 1933

Rivers, T. *The Rose Amateur's Guide* Longman Green 1837

Rose Annuals The National Rose Society from 1911 onwards

Rose Annuals American Rose Society 1917 and others

Ross, D. *Shrub Roses in Australia* Deane Ross 1981

Rossi, B. V. *Modern Roses in Australia* Mitchell & Casey 1930

Royal Horticultural Society Journals Numerous and various

Sanders, T. W. *Roses and their Cultivation* c. 1932

Shepherd, R. *History of the Rose* Macmillan, New York 1954

Sitwell, S. and Russell, J. *Old Garden Roses Part I* George Rainbird 1955

Steen, N. *The Charm of Old Roses* Herbert Jenkins 1966

Testu, C. *Les Roses Anciennes* Flammarion 1984

'The Rose' Magazine Various copies 1950s, and 1960s

Thomas, A. S. *Growing Roses in Australia* Nelson 1983

Thomas, G. S. *Climbing Roses Old and New* Phoenix House 1965

Thomas, G. S. *The Old Shrub Roses* Phoenix House 1955

Thomas, G. S. *Shrub Roses of Today* Phoenix House 1962

Thomas, G. C. *The Practical Book of Outdoor Rose Growing* J. B. Lippincott
     (USA) 1920

Thomas, H. H. *The Rose Book* Cassell 1913

Weathers, J. *Beautiful Roses* Simpkin, Marshall, Hamilton, Kent & Co. 1903

Wright, W. P. *Roses and Rose Gardens* Headley 1911

Rose catalogues were a valuable source of reference, in particular those of
David Austin, Bowling Green Lane, Albrighton, Wolverhampton;
Peter Beales, London Road, Attleborough, Norfolk;
Harkness Roses, Hitchin, Herts;
LeGrice Roses, North Walsham, Norfolk;
Mattocks Roses, Nuneham Courtney, Oxfordshire;
Notcutts Nurseries, Woodbridge, Suffolk;
Scotts Nurseries, Merriott, Somerset.

Index

Notes on the Indexes

INDEX OF ROSES

This index lists in one alphabetical sequence, names of roses, species and hybrids. It would be confusing to list here the subgeneric section headings under which the roses are listed in the Dictionary: for these the reader is referred to the Contents pages and the explanation given on page 125.

GENERAL INDEX

In this index will be found entries referring to the first three parts of the book, together with a few names of persons mentioned in the Dictionary. Garden Groups are also listed here: the first reference is to the pages in the Dictionary where descriptions are given, followed by historical and cultivation references in the first three parts.

Page numbers in **bold type** refer to illustrations. Where the only page number given is in bold type and that number is for pages 129–415 a description of the rose illustrated will be found on the same page.

Entries are arranged alphabetically 'letter-by-letter', except occasionally where alternative names would come together, when the one chosen as the first name is the one by which the rose is usually known.

INDEX OF ROSES

GENERAL INDEX